The
Criminal Records Manual

The Complete National Reference for the Legal Access and Use of Criminal Records

by
Derek Hinton

Edited by Michael L. Sankey and Peter J. Weber

©2004 By Facts on Demand Press
Post Office Box 27869
Tempe, AZ 85285
(800) 929-3811
www.brbpub.com

The Criminal Records Manual
The Complete National Reference for the Legal Access and Use of Criminal Records

©2004 by Facts on Demand Press
PO Box 27869
Tempe, AZ 85285
(800) 929-3811

ISBN: 1-889150-43-6

Cover Design by Robin Fox & Associates; Derek Hinton Photo by Mark Moore

Derek Hinton; Edited by Michael L. Sankey, Peter J. Weber.

Second Edition, First Printing, 2004

Cataloging-in-Publication Data

> Hinton, Derek.
>   The criminal records manual : the complete national
> reference for the legal access and use of criminal
> records / [Derek Hinton]. 2nd ed., enhanced.
>   p. cm.
>   Includes index.
>   ISBN: 1-889150-43-6
>
>   1. Criminal registers–United States. 2. Criminal
> registers--Access control--United States. 3. Police--
> Records and correspondence--United States. I. Title.
>
>   KF9751.Z9H56 2004   345.73'052
>   QBI04-200181

Acknowledgements

This book is dedicated to my family and friends.
I especially thank my wife and children for their
tolerance of the time this book took away from them.
I would also like to thank my parents and brother
who, complete and honest truth be told,
probably suspected that I might someday
become familiar with criminal records.

My friends know who they are.
If there is any doubt, the fault is mine.

To the people who bought the first edition of this
book, I thank you too. The comments I received
were mostly kind, and besides, you kept my Mother
from buying at least of few of the copies.

Finally, while technically covered under
the category of a friend above, I want to thank
Larry Henry for his legal research contributions.
Lawyer jokes just aren't as funny any more.

And once more, Mike, Mark, Carl, and Peter.
You are a pleasure to work with. It's been fun.

Derek Hinton

It ain't no sin if you crack a few laws now and then, just so long as you don't break any.

—Mae West

Contents

Introduction **9**

Section 1: An Essential Starting Point — What Do You Really Know About Criminal Records?

Chapter 1: **Why All This Attention to Criminal Records?** **13**

Crminal Records are Public, 14;   The Most Prominent Criminal Records Users, 15;
Test Your Criminal Record Quotent, 16;   A Criminal Record Quiz, 19

Chapter 2: **Why Employers Should Use Criminal Records** **23**

The Negligent Hiring Doctrine, 23;   Workplace Violence, 26;   Workplace Theft, 26;
When it is Required by Law, 27;   About State Mandated Regulations, 32

Chapter 3: **Privacy Issues With Criminal Records** **33**

The Debate Over the Use of Criminal Records, 34;   Using Personal Identifers to Find
Criminal Records, 34;   Victimless and Non-Violent Crime, 37

Section 2: Criminal Records Sources

Chapter 4: **Essential Criminal Record Terminology** 41

Felonies and Misdemeanors, 42; With or Without a Disposition, 42; Distinction Between *Public* and *Non-Public* Criminal records, 43; Significant Criminal Record Phrases, 45

Chapter 5: **Criminal Records at the County Level**........................47

Statewide Courts Structure Begins at the County, 47; How Courts Maintain Records, 48; Court Computerization, 49; Searching State Courts Online, 50; Court Record Search Tips, 51

Chapter 6: **Criminal Records at the State Level** 53

The State Central Repository, 53; Non-Uniformity of State Systems, 54; State Statutory Provisions for Access to FBI Records, 56; State and Interstate Dissemination Policies, 58

Chapter 7: **Criminal Records at the Federal Level** 59

Federal Criminal Records and the U.S. District Courts, 59; How U.S. District Courts Maintain Records, 60; Recent Restrictions Imposed to Electronically Accessed Criminal Documents, 61; Other Federal Criminal Record Trends, 62; The FBI NCIC Database, 63; National Crime Prevention and Privacy Compact, 64; Access to NCIC for Non-Criminal Justice Purposes, 66; When Non-Criminal Justice Agencies are Granted Access to FBI Records – The Fingerprint Dilemma, 67

Chapter 8: **Other Important Criminal Offender Records**..............69

Incarceration Records, 69; Parole Records, 71; Probation Records, 71; State Sexual Offender Records, 72; Federal Fugitives, 74; Military Criminal Records, 74

Section 3: Employer & Vendor Guidelines to Accessing and Using Criminal Records

Chapter 9: Advice When Obtaining Criminal Records Yourself.....77

Know Thy Repositories, 78; State Versus County Searching, 80; The Myth of Public Records and the Internet, 81; Using the Freedom of Information Act and Other Acts, 82

Chapter 10: Advice When Using a Criminal Record Vendor.......83

The Advent of Criminal Record Vendors, 83; Types of Vendor Services Offered, 84; Benefits of Service Vendors, 85; Ancillary Tools that Criminal Record Vendors Provide, 87; Where to Find a Vendor, 91; How to Choose the Best Vendor for You, 91

Chapter 11: Evaluate Your Record Request Process..................95

Identification Issues, 95; Asking for the Date of Birth, 97; The Importance of Proper Documentation, 98; Sample Criminal Record Release Form, 99; Pros and Cons of Using Misdemeanor Records, 100

Chapter 12: Compliance With The Fair Credit Reporting Act.....101

FCRA and Employers, 101; Overview of The Fair Credit Reporting Act, 102; The Sword and the Shield, 103; Primary Effects of the FCRA on Employers Using a Vendor to Obtain Criminal Records, 104; FCRA Restrictions on Reporting Arrest Information, 108; Using Aged Public Records for Employment Purposes, 109

Chapter 13: Federal FCRA Interrelation with State FCRAs.........111

What Do Federal and State Interrelations Have To Do with Ordering Criminal Records? 112; When in Conflict, Which Law - Federal or State - Pre-empts the Other? 113; Summary of FCRA and State Law Interrelations—Good News for Users, 114

Chapter 14: Title VII and Using Criminal Records.......................115

Criminal Records and Bias Employment Practices, 115; What Are The EEOC's Guidelines? 117; Four Important EEOC Notices, 119

Chapter 15: State Restrictions on Record Use by Employers....121

States that Prohibit the Use of Arrest Records (i.e., non-conviction records), 121; States that Prohibit the Use of Misdemeanor Convictions, 123; States that Prohibit the Use of Expunged or Sealed Records, 124; States that Limit the Use of First Offense Records, 125; States that Restrict the Use of Arrest Records Based on Time Periods, 125; States that Limit Record Access to Employers Within Certain Industries, 126; Legal Concerns Versus Gut Reactions, 126; If You Get Into Trouble, 127

Section 4: Government Agency Profiles

Chapter 16: State Profiles 133

This chapter consists of detail pages for each state. The following information is included: access requirements, restrictions, fees, online modes, policies and procedures for state criminal record agencies; analysis of county courts; statewide court systems; profiles for obtaining records from state prisons; state sexual offender registries and how to access them.

Chapter 17: U.S. District Courts 313

How to Access Federal Records by Mail or Phone, 313;   Online Access to Records, 313; PACER Access, 314;   U.S. Party/Case Index, 314;   CM/ECF-Case Management/Electronic Case Files, 314;   Federal Record Centers and the National Archives, 315; Locations of the U.S. District Courts, listed in order by state, 315

Section 5: Appendix

Appendix 1: State Charts 339

Compact Memberships, 339;   State Criminal Records Required Data to be Submitted to State Criminal Record Agencies, 340

Appendix 2: Fair Credit Reporting Act Summaries 343

Prescribed Summary of Consumer Rights, 343;   Prescribed Notice of Furnisher Responsibilities, 346;   Prescribed Notice of User Responsibilities, 348

Appendix 3: Title VII EEOC Notices 353

Job advertising and pre-employment inquires, 353;   Evaluation of employer's policy of refusing to hire individuals with conviction records, 361;   Commission's procedure for determining whether arrest records may be considered in employment decisions, 370; A business justifying the exclusion of an individual from employment on the basis of a conviction record, 372

Appendix 4: Common Criminal Record Terms 375

Criminal Records Offense Glossary

Appendix 5: Common Criminal Record Abbreviations 392

Common Criminal Record Offense Abbreviations

▼ Quick-Find Index 414

Introduction

All serious conversations gravitate towards philosophy.
—Ernest Dimnet

This book is written to benefit the public, employers, pre-employment screening companies, and criminal record vendors.

I especially hope this book helps the small employer who cannot change the world, but is tending his own garden, who is using criminal records in the hiring process because he believes in his gut that it is the right thing to do; who is ordering criminal records in an effort to insure that other employees and the general public are not exposed to someone that would do them harm.

At the same time, most of us believe a criminal record should not inevitably disqualify an individual from all future employment. I hope this book gives guidance to the employer that knowingly hires the individual with a criminal record, who does not automatically reject anyone with any past transgression, regardless of severity and age.

For the individual who has committed a crime in which there was no victim and is trying to find a job? Keep looking. Employers are out there who will hire you. Regarding those employers who will not, consider this: do you really want to devote whatever you have to offer to them anyway?

Finally, to the felon who committed a crime — who hurt, stole or defrauded another — I will work up all the sympathy I can for you with what sympathy is left over for your victims.

The purpose of this book is to help all of the above parties understand the various justice systems in the United States; the information stored, the circumstances under which it can be released and finally, how the information may be legally used by the recipients.

—Derek Hinton

Section 1

An Essential Starting Point — What Do You Know About Criminal Records?

This section examines--

-- who uses criminal records, if and when they are public

-- explores why employers use criminal records in hiring decisions

-- examines the differences between records ordered by criminal justice agencies and the private sector

-- touches on the privacy concerns regarding the use of criminal records and purposes for which they are used.

Chapter 1

Why All This Attention to Criminal Records?

You can get much farther with a kind word
and a gun than you can with a kind word alone.

—Al Capone

I hate to admit it, but I think Chicago gangleader Al Capone was right.

I wish all individuals were created to at least behave in a responsible manner, and that given the same stimuli, individuals would exhibit enlightened behavior.

The problem is that there are some people who, to quote a Southern friend of mine, "just ain't right." All the wishing in the world will not change that fact. The vast majority of us behave as responsible members of society — but lock our doors at night. We avoid going to certain areas at certain times. We spend a lot of money on everything from police protection, jails, prisons, court systems and security systems to airport metal detectors, department store surveillance equipment and gated communities. We also order criminal records before hiring individuals who will spend half their waking life among us.

Comedian W. C. Fields once said there is not an adult alive who, at one time or another, has not wanted to boot a child in the ass. There is probably not a working adult who at one time or another has not wanted to wring a co-worker's neck. Of course we don't do it. Frustration goes hand-in-hand with work. 98.7% of us never go past daydreams in which we have a co-worker in a headlock and are giving them a good and true Dutch rub.

Yet, there are those who "ain't right." They have a history. So, the need to check criminal records exists.

Criminal Records Are Public

Criminal records are a matter of public record. The accusation, trial and sentencing are public record. The Supreme Court, in a 1976 decision (Paul v. Davis, 424 U.S. 693), effectively ended debate on whether the records were public or private. Interestingly, this case revolved around a criminal charge that was dismissed. In the Paul v. Davis case, a flyer identifying "active shoplifters" was distributed to local merchants. The flyer included a photograph of Edward C. Davis III, who had been arrested on a shoplifting charge. When the charge was dismissed, Davis brought an action against Edgar Paul, the local chief of police. Davis alleged that the distribution of the flyer had stigmatized him and deprived him of his constitutional rights.

In a 5-to-3 decision, the Court held that Davis had not been deprived of any constitutional rights under the Due Process Clause. The Court also emphasized that constitutional privacy interests did not cover Davis's claims. The Court stated that the constitutional right to privacy was limited to matters relating to "marriage, procreation, contraception, family relationships, and child rearing and education." The publication of records of official acts, such as arrests, did not fall under the rubric of privacy rights.

So criminal records are, as a rule, accessible. Some may find this lack of privacy disturbing, almost "Orwellian." After all, government agencies have collected all this sensitive information and it is available to the general public. I believe the public debate on this aspect of privacy has become somewhat convoluted.

Originally, the information was public to protect citizens. The thought was that the government could not secretly charge a person, convict them, and put them away. The charges, court decision, and penalties were public.

Consider the former Soviet Union. Now there was a society with a lot of privacy. A person could be accused, sentenced, shipped to refrigerator country and be worked to death in privacy. The crime of which the person was accused? Private information. The verdict? The sentence? Private.

The point is, privacy is not an automatic good. If you are considering in-home care for an elderly parent, a business venture with a neighbor or thinking about hiring a nanny for your child, you may well appreciate the fact that these records are public rather than private.

This does not mean you can use the records for any purpose once you obtain them. If you use them or attempt to use them for an illegal purpose such as blackmail, you may join the ranks of potential blackmailees. Generally speaking, criminal records are accessible by private citizens on other private citizens. These records may be used for any legal purpose.

There are Accessibility and Use Issues Involved

Although criminal records are public, the reality of how they can be used and the manner of access are extremely complicated. Later in this book we will look at these issues:

- Accessibility restrictions
- Information reporting restrictions
- Use restrictions
- Non-Public Databases

The Most Prominent Criminal Records Users

Many different entities order and use criminal records. These general users can be subdivided into the three primary categories described below. These are not idle category distinctions. The records obtained by the first two groups are more national in scope than the last group. The first two broad groupings are criminal justice agencies or groups that have been granted statutory authority to use non-public criminal records.

1. Criminal Justice Agencies

Among the more prominent criminal justice agency users of criminal records are:

- Court systems, e.g., judges, prosecutors
- Government agencies involved in the justice system

These users have unfettered access to all criminal record databases including *public* and *non-public*. (See page 43 for definitions.)

2. Non-Criminal Justice Agencies As Required by Law

Three types of prominent private agencies use criminal records due to statutory requirements.

- Government Regulatory Agencies, e.g., FAA
- Occupational Licensing Bodies, e.g., teaching, nursing, casino or racetrack workers, liquor sales
- Financial and Commerce Agencies, e.g., financial institutions, insurance and securities related institutions

There is a perhaps confusing but important point to be made here. Criminal justice agency records are maintained for criminal justice purposes and are part of the FBI system. See

Chapter 7. As mentioned above, criminal justice agency criminal records can be either public or non-public. Whether or not they are open — or partially open — to the public is dependent upon the inherent restrictions of that criminal justice agency.

3. The General Public

This group includes entities that order and use criminal records on their own accord. Typically, this group includes:

- Leasing institutions — both residential and commercial

- Businesses, for "relationship" purposes, e.g., mergers and acquisitions, evaluating business partners

- Personal users, e.g., checking out daughter's new boyfriend, father's new girlfriend, great-grandpa's new young girlfriend

- Miscellaneous uses such as genealogy (no, not the study of automatic garage door openers) and skip tracing

- Employers

Use of Criminal Records by Employers

By far and away, the **largest group** of non-criminal justice users of criminal records is **employers.** Not only are they the biggest group, they are the fastest growing group.

According to members of the National Association of Professional Background Screeners (www.napbs.com), pre-employment screening is a five billion dollar industry today. Arguably, the most important piece of information supplied by this industry to employers is the criminal record check. Chapter 2 takes a deeper look at the use of criminal record information by employers.

Test Your Criminal Record Quotient

The following story is based upon true events. The names and a few of the circumstances have been changed to protect the parties involved. The story illustrates why it is important to order criminal records, the questions that can arise and the consequences of not ordering. At the end are questions to see how much you know about conducting criminal record checks.

Jean and Harvey's Dream

Jean and Harvey dream of running their own California-based business had worked out quite well. The business was becoming a true asset and would help fund their retirement. A leisurely life of family, hobbies and travel was within sight.

As the business grew, adding new employees, management of the staff, dealing with suppliers, and addressing the "small business infrastructure crisis of the day" began to lay claim to their days. The solution was not difficult to see: hire an office manager.

One applicant for their new office manager position swept them off their feet. Marilou was conversant about basic accounting, payroll software, human resource issues and customer service. Her college degree was confirmed, the references listed on her employment application checked out, and she reported no past criminal convictions. She had recently moved into the area from Tennessee and was available immediately.

Marilou was hired at a significant salary. She was a fast learner, intelligent, and worked well with the office personnel. Employees showed up for work on time, smoke breaks did not last all morning, and morale was good. By year end, revenues were the highest they had ever been.

The first cloud on the horizon was the next year's mid-year numbers. Gross revenue was higher, but the net was disappointing. At year end, they were surprised to find themselves with higher gross revenues, but the business was just breaking even.

With Marilou's help, Jean and Harvey made strategic plans to cut costs. Marilou tactfully negotiated significant discounts for goods from suppliers that the owners would not have imagined practical.

Revitalized, Jean and Harvey promptly landed several huge accounts. Net revenue leaped and the mid-year net figures were a little higher than break-even.

Late one night, Harvey picked up in incoming fax from company "XYZ" concerning some goods that had been ordered. The tone of the fax was not rude, but there was a hint of testiness that prompted the husband to log on to the computer to check on the order's status. He could not find the client, which was not unusual. Many of their clients had several operating divisions, sister companies, or operated under various d/b/a's. Tired, he left the fax with a short note on Marilou's desk, then went home.

The next day, Harvey checked in with Marilou if she had seen the fax and taken care of company "XYZ." Overhearing the conversation, Jean remarked that she would sure like to get "XYZ's" business. Harvey informed her they apparently had it. Jean was surprised, explaining that she had called on XYZ only two weeks previously and could not meet their price. Harvey and Jean decided to dig a little deeper.

That is when the nightmare started. Jean and Harvey's next few days were filled with first open — and then surreptitious — inquiries of employees, clients, and suppliers. Records and accounts were checked. Then, one morning, Marilou did not show up. A voice mail from her said there had been a sudden parental sickness and she was resigning — effective yesterday. The next day her telephone was disconnected.

As the facts became known, Jean and Harvey determined that Marilou had set up her own thriving business within their business. Here is how it worked: Marilou would offer a client the same goods offered by Jean and Harvey's business, but at a lower price. Marilou would obtain the goods herself for free through the business, but she would bill the clients herself. As a result, she had netted well over $100,000 using Jean and Harvey's business to supply the product, at a 100% loss to the business.

Jean and Harvey went to an attorney but concluded that there would probably be no money left to recover. Plus, the recovery process would be extremely expensive in legal fees. Next, they talked to a detective about criminal charges. The detective was sympathetic but honest about how long the process might take, how much of the owners' time would be involved, and all the interviews that would have to be made with hesitant clients.

Jean and Harvey realized that the numbers that had shown the business breaking even had been skillfully manipulated. They faced bankruptcy. They had a hard decision to make. They could spend their time and money pursuing the office manager, or they could attempt to salvage their business. They obtained a second mortgage and went back to doing what they did best: work the business.

Something like this is hard to forget. One day they decided to make an inquiry. It was an easy inquiry to make, as it was their business. During Marilou's tenure as office manager, the company had branched out into criminal records—and it was criminal records that the office manager had been obtaining and selling at the owners' expense. So, they ordered a criminal record check on Marilou. The record check showed that she had previously been arrested for felony embezzlement and she had pled it down to a misdemeanor. With that blemish on her record, she had decided that a change in venue was in order. Thus she moved across country, and later managed to land the office manager position with Jean and Harvey.

* * *

I got a call from Jean within the past year. She asked if I had read a certain newspaper story about a successful business in a small town. The article gushed on the prospects of the business and had a photograph of the top managers. One was a sharp, professional-looking lady. It was Marilou.

You can not help but feel sorry for Jean and Harvey. They got taken to the cleaners. On the positive side, they did save their business. Think of the emotions running through their heads when they saw Marilou being touted in print!

This story breezes over several issues that will be discussed in this book. For starters, consider the following questions —

A Criminal Record Quiz

Using the Jean and Harvey story as a starting point, let us test your knowledge of criminal records. The good news is that this is an open-book quiz. For some of the questions, an assumption is made and an answer is given. In others, there is no answer until more questions are answered. The chapter that discusses the pertinent questions is referenced.

1. Would it have been legal for Jean and Harvey (the employers) to order a criminal record before they employed the office manager?

    It would have been legal to order a criminal record provided, of course, that they obtained the information from a legal source. On the other hand, if they happened to have had a friend in law enforcement and this friend had inquired surreptitiously into the FBI's files or into the local law enforcement network, it would have been illegal. (See Chapter 2 for which records are public and which are not.)

2. Would they have had to have the office manager's permission (Marilou) to order a criminal record?

    While certainly not a bad idea, the legal question depends on 1) whether they obtained the information themselves or through the use of a third-party service, and 2) in what state the person was to be employed. In the case of our story the place of employment was California, a state which has additional requirements over what is required by federal law when vendors are used. If the criminal record was obtained from a service — and there are excellent reasons to do so — then they would have needed express permission from Marilou. In the example above, a vendor was not used, so the various regulations would not have been applicable.[1] (See Chapter 12 and Chapter 15 for details.)

3. Would it have been legal to use the information received to deny the office manager a job?

    Jean and Harvey would have had to make several determinations regarding the information. See Chapter 14 for what some of those determinations are. Given the

---

[1] There is current legislation in California that would impose regulations on users of criminal information even when a vendor is not used.

circumstances, Jean and Harvey almost certainly could have used the information to deny the manager a position.

4. Was it legal for the owners to order a criminal record on
    the office manager after she had already left their employ?

    Criminal records obtained from counties and most states are public records. Jean and Harvey obtained the information from a public source. It was legal. However, in some states a signed release or fingerprints may be required. See the Chapter 16 State Profiles to learn each state's nuances.

5. What are the legal ramifications of the felony arrest for
    embezzlement evolving into a misdemeanor conviction?

    This is a tricky question in that it mingles two different considerations, that of an arrest versus a conviction, and a felony versus a misdemeanor. The first step is to understand the differences. These terms are defined in Chapter 4.

    The legal ramifications are myriad. It is best to separate the question into two parts:

    - *To what degree may arrest records be used
      as compared with conviction records?*

      In general, more care must be used when using arrest records. The EEOC's guidelines are more stringent (see Chapter 14), and on the state level, the use of arrest records may be restricted. (See Chapter 15)

    - *Felonies versus misdemeanors: are felonies more important?*

      Not necessarily. There are several reasons why. There is the job-relatedness of the misdemeanor crime. There is also the possibility that a plea bargain was struck that reduced the crime from a felony to a misdemeanor. See the "Pros and Cons of Using Misdemeanor Records" discussion at the end of Chapter 11. Find out which states forbid or restrict the use of misdemeanor records in Chapter 15.

6. Would the fact that the office manager was a female
    have affected the owners' use of the criminal record?

    Probably not in this case. However, if Jean and Harvey were to learn a false lesson from their experience and institute a policy of only ordering a criminal record on female applicants, this disparate practice might cause them future peril.

7. If Marilou were African-American,
    would it have affected the use of the record?

It may have. The issue of race has affected policy regarding employers' use of criminal records. See Chapter 14 for the EEOC guidelines.

8. Would it have made any difference if the previous act had been committed twenty years ago instead of recently?

It could have in several ways. First, the court or repository may simply not have made the record available to find because of the record's age. Many records repositories purge or archive their records after ten years. If so, then Jean and Harvey would not have found the record.

The second consideration before *using* a record for employment purposes is the length of time that has elapsed since the act was committed.

9. The office manager later went into business providing background checks. That is an odd twist of fate, but it does happen. What are some steps employers can take to choose reputable vendors?

Employment screening, in general, and criminal record usage in particular, can be dauntingly complex. Federal Equal Employment Opportunity and Fair Credit Reporting law bump into state Equal Employment and Fair Credit Reporting law. A Texas company may order a criminal record from the state of Arizona to employ a person to work in California. This raises the question of which state's law should be followed.

About the time an employer wonders if it is worthwhile, they look at the negligent hiring statistics or encounter a Marilou.

A knowledgeable vendor can save an employer considerable expense and headache over a "data gathering and warehousing" vendor. In Chapter 10, choosing a vendor is discussed in more detail.

10. Do you think the owners wish they had ordered the criminal record before they hired the office manager, then dealt with any legal ramifications later?

The answer, of course, is that if the owners had known what was about to transpire, they most certainly would have ordered a criminal record and rejected the applicant.

However, they did not have the requisite knowledge to acquire, evaluate, and legally use the criminal record information that would have averted their ordeal.

That is the goal of this book: to impart the knowledge on how to acquire, evaluate, and use criminal record information.

Author Tip

Be sure that your employment application asks the applicant if they have ever been convicted of a crime. Do not limit the question to felonies or "serious crimes" -- whatever *serious* means.

Be double sure that the question has been answered and the application signed. In many of the cases where a company is being sued for the actions of one of its employees, the application question regarding criminal convictions had been left blank. I have an attorney friend who calls this the "honest criminal" syndrome. The applicant does not want to lie, but also does not want to disclose damaging information.

Upon review of an employment application, if you discover the criminal record question has not been answered, then you should pay particular attention to your criminal record screening process. As a matter of fact, I would recommend you speak with the applicant and say something like the following:

"Mr. Doe, I noticed that you did not answer the question regarding criminal record convictions on our application. You should know that a criminal record conviction will not automatically disqualify you from employment with us, but we will be checking your criminal history. Is there anything we will find that you would like to explain before we review the record?"

Chapter 2

Why Employers Should Use Criminal Records

Somebody once said that in looking for people to hire, you look for three qualities: integrity, intelligence, and energy. And if they don't have the first, the other two will kill you. Think about it; it is true. If you hire somebody without the first, you really want them to be dumb and lazy.

—Warren Buffet

Employers order criminal records on applicants because the law requires it. Others order criminal records because they fear the harm that may come to them, their business or other employees if they hire someone they shouldn't. A growing reason why businesses order criminal records is the fear of being sued for negligent hiring.

Watching an employer who does a lot of hiring but neglects to order criminal records is like watching a train wreck unfold. You can see the disaster coming from a long way away and the wreck is inevitable, but you can't do anything to stop it.

In this chapter are the main reasons why the larger and progressive employers decide to order criminal records – and why you should too. While criminal records are legal to use, there are issues to watch. How you obtain them has risks, and costs, which are discussed here and in Chapter 3.

The Negligent Hiring Doctrine

Created through case law, negligent hiring is a legal doctrine that imposes a duty upon employers to "assess the nature of the employment, its degree of risk to third parties and then perform a reasonable background investigation to insure that the applicant is competent and fit for duty." A closely associated theory is negligent retention. Negligent retention is when the employee, already hired, is retained when the employer knows, or should have known, that the employee was unfit to be retained.

The primary difference between the two is timing. Negligent hiring is a matter of "should have known" before hiring. Negligent retention is a matter of "should have become aware of" after hiring. Employers are most often faulted for failing to order a criminal record check before someone is hired.

There is no consistent, de facto requirement that an employer check applicants for a criminal record although as discussed earlier, there may be state and federal industry-specific requirements that say a criminal record be obtained. Different courts have come to different conclusions, but the trend is clearly moving in the direction that employers have more obligations to perform checks, depending on the nature of the job.

The "Nature of the Position"

There is a difference in the degree and nature of care that must be used between hiring a daycare worker and a construction worker. Clearly, a daycare worker working unsupervised in close proximity to young children probably presents more of a risk than does someone stomping on a shovel. On the issue of "job relatedness," courts have been extremely liberal in their opinions, a trend that says it is the employer's responsibility not to put the wrong person on the job.

Protections Afforded

It is important to note that ordering criminal records can offer protection to the employer, even if no information is found. In many cases, the employer is portrayed as an uncaring entity that was too tight to spend even a nominal amount to insure that someone was not injured — and it is time to punish the employer for their greediness.

What if the employer does order a criminal record and, through no fault of his own, the crime committed in Tupelo, Mississippi by the applicant does not appear in the Dallas County, Texas search performed by the employer? The point is the employer tried. The employer assessed the nature of the job, its degree of risk and then conducted a background investigation perhaps above that required by law. The fact that this search effort did not reveal information is another matter.

Florida House Bill H0775 — An Example of a Law Creating a Presumption *Against* Negligent Hiring

A statute, approved by Florida Governor J. Bush on May 26, 1999, which became effective on October 1, 1999, created a presumption against negligent hiring when employers take certain pre-employment screening steps. Employers who follow the steps will be presumed not to have been negligent if the background investigation fails to reveal any information that reasonably demonstrates the unsuitability of the applicant for the particular work to be performed, or for employment in general. One of these steps is ordering a criminal record.

Among the prescribed steps are:

- Ordering a Florida state criminal record check.

- Taking reasonable efforts to contact the applicant's past employers.

- Having the applicant complete an employment application that elicits the following information:

  - Convictions of crimes including type, date, and penalty imposed;

  - Whether the applicant was a defendant in a civil action for an intentional tort, including the nature and disposition of the action.

- A driving record must be ordered if it is relevant to the work to be performed.

- The employer must interview the applicant.

Notice that the law does not require that employers find criminal record information if there is any to be obtained. The law only requires that employers make a state inquiry.

Nothing in this legislation requires employers to adopt new procedures. It does afford some protection to those employers who attempt to hire safe, responsible employees.

...And for Non-Florida Denizens?

Do you have a similar law in your state? Even if not, the steps prescribed by this Florida law make good sense. While your state may not have codified the protection, a plaintiff would have a tough time proving hiring negligence against you if you had taken the "Florida steps."

In other words, even if you are not in Florida, following the Florida guidelines may provide your company *de facto* protection, if not codified protection.

Workplace Violence

Workplace violence can be related to negligent hiring in that employers have been sued for hiring someone with a propensity for violence, and that employee subsequently harms another employee. A negligent hiring suit does not always follow an act of workplace violence, but when a lawsuit results, courts have increasingly found that employers have at least some duty to provide a safe workplace.

Reports from Ronet Bachman, a statistician with the Bureau of Justice Statistics, say "each year, nearly 1 million individuals become victims of violent crime while working or on duty. The victimizations account for 15% of the over 6½ million acts of violence experienced by U.S. residents age twelve or older."

Unfortunately, these statistics do not show the percentage of these victimizations committed by co-workers, but unempirical surveys have shown that co-workers do commit a significant percentage of these victimizations.

Even if an employer is not sued for an act of workplace violence committed by an employee, workplace violence is, to put it mildly, not conducive to productivity. Among those persons injured by a crime victimization at work, an estimated 876,800 workdays were lost annually, costing employees over $16 million in wages. This does not include the "sick days" and the "annual leave" that the victim might not otherwise take.

The fact is, the hiring process is one of the areas where the employer is most able to control the qualities of who they employ. More and more employers are ordering criminal records as a measure that helps thwart workplace violence.

Workplace Theft

It is tough for a business to make a profit when some of its best customers are employees who are not paying for the goods. John Locke, known as the Philosopher of Freedom, felt men entered into society to preserve their property. Many employers are ordering criminal records for the same reason.

Retailers attribute 42.7 percent of their inventory shrinkage — 12-*billion* dollars lost annually in missing merchandise, cash, fraud — to employee theft. As a rule, retailers spend approximately $3500 to recruit, screen, and hire one employee. The length of time worked by a dishonest employee is 9.4 months. The average cost of hiring and releasing a dishonest employee averages $15,000. In order to thwart the onslaught of shrinkage, large retailers hire ten loss prevention employees per $100 million in annual sales ... with an average of 1.12 employees per store specifically dedicated to loss prevention.

Considering that 42% of their inventory losses come from employees — and that the total recruiting and screening cost is around $3500 — a $20 criminal record makes good sense.

What if Your Employees Must Enter Canada?

Some businesses require their employees go into Canada. Under sections 19(1)(c) and 19(2)(a) of the Canada Immigration Act of 1976, individuals who have been convicted of a "crime or offense" are considered "inadmissible" and precluded from entering in Canada.

Therefore, prior to being permitted to enter into Canada, U.S. workers are subject to random criminal history checks by the Canadian authorities who use information obtained from the NCIC. Using the NCIC database, Canadian authorities are able to determine whether an individual has a "criminal record" and therefore, cannot be admitted without first obtaining a "Minister's Permit." According to the Canadian Consulate General, a "Minister's Permit" can be issued in a limited number of instances to overcome the inadmissibility rules. This decision to issue or deny a permit is entirely discretionary with the Canadian office before whom the request is pending and will be based on such factors as:

o   The seriousness of the past offense.

o   The number of past offenses committed.

o   The perceived likelihood that the individual will commit another offense.

A Minister's Permit can only be obtained from a Canadian Consulate, are expensive to obtain, and are good for only a limited period of time.

As discussed earlier, the vast majority of US employers do not have access to NCIC, and so many employers who require their employees to travel into Canada order a criminal record from public record sources in the U.S. This decreases problems at the border.

When it is Required by Law

There are many smart reasons to order criminal records on employees, a few dumb ones, and several cases in which the Federal or state government has given one of my father's all time favorite reasons: "Because I said so."

A number of industries have Federal or state mandates. These mandates are laws that generally require a criminal record to be performed prior to hiring. The law may include penalties against a firm for hiring someone who does not pass the criminal record check.

Although this book cannot list every state and federal requirement, we have selected several useful examples. The first three are Federally-related.

• Motor Carrier Hazardous Material Regulations

The events surrounding the War on Terrorism in 2001 started a trend toward more criminal record checking requirements on employers. In particular, Section 1012 of the Patriot Act included a requirement that state department of motor vehicles is not be allowed to issue or renew hazardous material endorsements on commercial driver licenses until the individual was approved by the Department of Transportation, who checks for criminal information from the Department of Justice. Implementation of this requirement has not been finalized. While employers will not have access to the actual criminal record, it does involve a check for certain crimes. You would dare not to let a person without DOT endorsement drive for your company. A copy of Section 1012 follows:

SEC. 1012. LIMITATION ON ISSUANCE OF HAZMAT LICENSES.

(a) LIMITATION-

(1) IN GENERAL- Chapter 51 of title 49, United States Code, is amended by inserting after section 5103 the following new section:

Sec. 5103a. Limitation on issuance of hazmat licenses

(a) LIMITATION-

(1) ISSUANCE OF LICENSES- A State may not issue to any individual a license to operate a motor vehicle transporting in commerce a hazardous material unless the Secretary of Transportation has first determined, upon receipt of a notification under subsection (c)(1)(B), that the individual does not pose a security risk warranting denial of the license.

(2) RENEWALS INCLUDED- For the purposes of this section, the term "issue", with respect to a license, includes renewal of the license.

(b) HAZARDOUS MATERIALS DESCRIBED- The limitation in subsection (a) shall apply with respect to--

(1) any material defined as a hazardous material by the Secretary of Transportation; and

(2) any chemical or biological material or agent determined by the Secretary of Health and Human Services or the Attorney General as being a threat to the national security of the United States.

(c) BACKGROUND RECORDS CHECK-

(1) IN GENERAL- Upon the request of a State regarding issuance of a license described in subsection (a)(1) to an individual, the Attorney General--

(A) shall carry out a background records check regarding the individual; and

(B) upon completing the background records check, shall notify the Secretary of Transportation of the completion and results of the background records check.

(2) SCOPE- A background records check regarding an individual under this subsection shall consist of the following:

(A) A check of the relevant criminal history data bases.

(B) In the case of an alien, a check of the relevant data bases to determine the status of the alien under the immigration laws of the United States.

(C) As appropriate, a check of the relevant international data bases through Interpol- U.S. National Central Bureau or other appropriate means.

(d) REPORTING REQUIREMENT- Each State shall submit to the Secretary of Transportation, at such time and in such manner as the Secretary may prescribe, the name, address, and such other information as the Secretary may require, concerning--

(1) each alien to whom the State issues a license described in subsection (a); and

(2) each other individual to whom such a license is issued, as the Secretary may require.

(e) ALIEN DEFINED- In this section, the term "alien" has the meaning given the term in section 101(a)(3) of the Immigration and Nationality Act.

(2) CLERICAL AMENDMENT- The table of sections at the beginning of such chapter is amended by inserting after the item relating to section 5103 the following new item:

5103a. Limitation on issuance of hazmat licenses.

(b) REGULATION OF DRIVER FITNESS- Section 31305(a)(5) of title 49, United States Code, is amended--

(1) by striking "and" at the end of subparagraph (A);

(2) by inserting "and" at the end of subparagraph (B); and

(3) by adding at the end the following new subparagraph:

(C) is licensed by a State to operate the vehicle after having first been determined under section 5103a of this title as not posing a security risk warranting license denia.

(c) AUTHORIZATION OF APPROPRIATIONS- There is authorized to be appropriated for the Department of Transportation and the Department of Justice such amounts as may be necessary to carry out section 5103a of title 49, United States Code, as added by subsection (a).

- ## Federal Aviation Regulations

This example outlines certain Federal Aviation Administration requirements.

TITLE 14--AERONAUTICS AND SPACE

CHAPTER I--FEDERAL AVIATION ADMINISTRATION, DEPARTMENT OF TRANSPORTATION (Continued)

PART 107--AIRPORT SECURITY--Table of Contents

Sec. 107.31 Employment history, verification and criminal history records checks.

(a) Scope. On or after January 31, 1996, this section applies to all airport operators; airport users; individuals currently having unescorted access to a security identification display area (SIDA) that is identified by Sec. 107.25; all individuals seeking authorization for, or seeking the authority to authorize others to have, unescorted access to the SIDA; and each airport user and air carrier making a certification to an airport operator pursuant to paragraph (n) of this section. An airport user, for the purposes of Sec. 107.31 only, is any person making a certification under this section other than an air carrier subject to Sec. 108.33.

(b) Employment history investigations required. Except as provided in paragraph (m) of this section, each airport operator must ensure that no individual is granted authorization for, or is granted authority to authorize others to have, unescorted access to the SIDA unless the following requirements are met:

   (1) The individual has satisfactorily undergone Part 1 of an employment history investigation. Part 1 consists of a review of the previous 10 years of employment history and verification of the 5 employment years preceding the date the appropriate investigation is initiated as provided in paragraph (c) of this section; and

   (2) If required by paragraph (c)(5) of this section, the individual has satisfied Part 2 of the employment history investigation. Part 2 is the process to determine if the individual has a criminal record. To satisfy Part 2 of the investigation the criminal record check must not disclose that the individual has been convicted or found not guilty by reason of insanity, in any jurisdiction, during the 10 years ending on the date of such investigation, of any of the crimes listed below:

   (i) Forgery of certificates, false marking of aircraft, and other aircraft registration violation, 49 U.S.C. 46306;
   (ii) Interference with air navigation, 49 U.S.C. 46308;
   (iii) Improper transportation of a hazardous material, 49 U.S.C. 46312;
   (iv) Aircraft piracy, 49 U.S.C. 46502;
   (v) Interference with flightcrew members or flight attendants, 49 U.S.C. 46504;
   (vi) Commission of certain crimes aboard aircraft in flight, 49 U.S.C. 46506;
   (vii) Carrying a weapon or explosive aboard aircraft, 49 U.S.C. 46505;

(viii) Conveying false information and threats, 49 U.S.C. 46507;

(ix) Aircraft piracy outside the special aircraft jurisdiction of the United States, 49 U.S.C. 46502(b);

(x) Lighting violations involving transporting controlled substances, 49 U.S.C. 46315;

(xi) Unlawful entry into an aircraft or airport area that serves air carriers or foreign air carriers contrary to established security requirements, 49 U.S.C. 46314;

(xii) Destruction of an aircraft or aircraft facility, 18 U.S.C. 32;

(xiii) Murder;

(xiv) Assault with intent to murder;

(xv) Espionage;

(xvi) Sedition;

(xvii) Kidnapping or hostage taking;

(xviii) Treason;

(xix) Rape or aggravated sexual abuse;

(xx) Unlawful possession, use, sale, distribution, or manufacture of an explosive or weapon;

(xxi) Extortion;

(xxii) Armed robbery;

(xxiii) Distribution of, or intent to distribute, a controlled substance;

(xxiv) Felony arson; or

(xxv) Conspiracy or attempt to commit any of the aforementioned criminal acts.

* * *

Do you think they mean it?

• Banking Industry Regulations

Here are excerpts from regulations concerning the banking industry.

Federal Deposit Insurance Act

SEC. 19. PENALTY FOR UNAUTHORIZED PARTICIPATION BY CONVICTED INDIVIDUAL.

 (a) PROHIBITION.--

  (1) IN GENERAL.--Except with the prior written consent of the Corporation--

  (A) any person who has been convicted of any criminal offense involving dishonesty or a breach of trust or money laundering, or has agreed to enter into a pretrial diversion or similar program in connection with a prosecution for such offense, may not--

   (i) become, or continue as, an institution-affiliated party with respect to any insured depository institution;

   (ii) own or control, directly or indirectly, any insured depository institution; or

   (iii) otherwise participate, directly or indirectly, in the conduct of the affairs of any insured depository institution; and

  (B) any insured depository institution may not permit any person referred to in subparagraph (A) to engage in any conduct or continue any relationship prohibited.

(2) Minimum 10-year prohibition period for certain offenses.--

(A) IN GENERAL.--If the offense referred to in paragraph (1)(A) in connection with any person referred to in such paragraph is--

(i) an offense under--

(I) section 215, 656, 657, 1005, 1006, 1007, 1008, 1014, 1032, 1344, 1517, 1956, or 1957 of title 18, United States Code; or

(II) section 1341 or 1343 of such title which affects any financial institution (as defined in section 20 of such title); or

(ii) the offense of conspiring to commit any such offense, the Corporation may not consent to any exception to the application of paragraph (1) to such person during the 10-year period beginning on the date the conviction or the agreement becomes final.

About State Mandated Regulations

Every state has a myriad of laws that mandate criminal record checks for certain occupations. Usually these occupations are regulated by state licensing boards. Examples of typical industries involved include:

- Child Care
- Elderly Care
- Heath Care
- Insurance
- Gaming
- Security and Investigation

Within each broad industry within each state are differing requirements. For example, within the health care category, the requirements for nurse aides might be completely different than radiologists. In the next state, an occupation's requirements may be the same but requirements can vary, or licensing of that profession may be altogether non-existent.

In the Government Agencies Profiles Section of this book you will learn that certain state criminal justice agencies (in California, Louisiana, Mississippi, North Carolina, New York, Tennessee, and Vermont) restrict the general public from access to their criminal record databases. However, ALL state agencies, including the restrictive seven listed above, do permit access by employers who are mandated by state law to do criminal record checks. In those seven restrictive states, the records usually must be requested directly by the employer, meaning that a third-party vendor cannot act as an agent for the employer.

Chapter 3

Privacy Issues with Criminal Records

Memories are the key not to the past, but to the future.

—Corrie ten Boom

I believe that men, at heart, are good.

—Anne Frank

The quotes above are amazing statements considering the sources.

Corrie ten Boom, a Dutch woman, was born in 1892 and put into a concentration camp for sheltering individuals — Jewish individuals who had done nothing wrong — from certain death. In a time and place of profound hunger, betraying the locale of hiding Jews meant sacrificing one's food. Hiding Jews brought hideous reprisals. Yet, Corrie and her family hid Jews on principle. Her most noble, selfless and courageous deeds were rewarded with a stint in Ravensbruck Concentration camp. There she watched her sister die. Her father also died, and Corrie's brother died of a disease contracted at the camp.

The story of Anne Frank is well known. Anne died in a concentration camp, and yet, her amazing statement: "I believe that men, at heart, are good." She was a better person than I.

Yet, we can agree with Anne Frank. The problem is, the quote is not speaking in absolutes, but rather in "averages." The average person is good. The heck of it is, averages are averages. An old mentor of mine was fond of saying "a man can drown in a river that, on average, is an inch deep." While on average, man is good, there are some deep, deep holes out there that will drown you.

The Debate Over the Use of Criminal Records

And so, to paraphrase Corrie ten Boom's quote, are "memories—perhaps court-recorded criminal record memories — the key not to the past, but to the future?" Or, is Anne Frank's sentiment correct, that "men, at heart, are good" — good and perhaps undeserving of having past transgressions interfere with their unfettered pursuit of life?

This is the debate played out in American society and legal systems today: "given that most individuals are good, even those who have previously done bad, should we not let bygones be bygones and suppress previous records of criminal behavior?"

Why shouldn't we? We have a system that is pretty decent at catching wrongdoers. Crime usually does not pay. Thus, wrongdoers are usually caught. They are put before a jury of their peers and guilt or innocence is — correctly or incorrectly — adjudicated. Provided the individual is deemed guilty of the offense with which he has been accused, a penalty — too harsh, just right or too lenient — is rendered. The individual serves whatever penalty is meted out (if any) and is judged to have "paid his debt to society." Justice has been served. The victims have received retribution in relation to the offense. The slate has been wiped clean. While law enforcement, in case of a repeat offense, might need to have record of this information, why in the world should this information be "public information?"

As will be seen in Chapter 16 State Profiles, not all states have come down on the same side of the fence on the issue of public access to criminal records.

Using Personal Identifiers to Find Criminal Records

Some state, county, and federal agencies are not only concerned with making offense data private, they want the identifying information private, too – primarily the date of birth and social security number.

Some agencies have established review boards or committees to look at this problem, namely in Maine, Florida, the federal court system, and in Los Angeles county. The lack of these identifiers on the free Internet sites makes sense; the lack of these identifiers when the government agency is presented with a signed release does not seem to make sense. The main concern appears to be identity theft — which is a growing problem in our society — but identity thieves are typically attempting to find better false identities than can be obtained from criminal records. Add to that, few identity thieves will go to the trouble of completing a release. Without identifiers to distinguish them, "Computer twins" (two people with same first name, middle initial, last name, or with a similar name and the same date of birth) causes problems for employers — how do you match a record to an applicant? There is now a need to be cautious not to disqualify a job applicant simply because the applicant's name matches that on a criminal record.

Employers and Job Applicants

The workplace — this is where the real debate rages. Is it moral, ethical, or just *right* for employers to order criminal records?

Getting down to brass tacks, no one objects to an employer *ordering* a criminal record on a job applicant. The objection is that the employer may *use* the information, i.e., refuse to hire the applicant based on information on the criminal record.

So, why do some people believe employers should never use information obtained on a criminal record to discriminate against an applicant? The reasoning is this: if the person is applying for a job, then that must mean they have completed their punishment. This of course assumes they have not fled prosecution, escaped from incarceration, or are seeking a job they are barred from holding. That person has paid the price for their offense and their debt to society is over. Furthermore, to deny them a job is to nudge them into obtaining the money they need in one of two undesirable alternatives:

- They depend on the state or the kindness of family, friends or charity for the rest of their life.

- They steal or otherwise unlawfully obtain what they need to live.

So, in other words, the argument is that after someone has paid their debt to society, it would be immoral, wrong or, at a minimum, vindictive to continue to punish an individual for something they have already paid for.

And, not only is it wrong from a moral standpoint, it is wrong from a public policy standpoint because the continued punishment for past undesirable behavior will not only fail to deter but may *cause* future undesirable behavior.

It is a compelling, logical argument. Do you buy it? What would your reaction be in the following scenario? Assume you had your children in a daycare that — in a spirit of progressive rehabilitative fervor — hired a convicted pedophile who had done his time. Remember, the pedophile has paid his debt to society. Would your kids be at the daycare come Monday morning? Humph. Societal Neanderthal.

While most states have enacted laws to prevent convicted pedophiles from working with children, the example is instructive. This is not a cut-and-dried issue — and job-relatedness is a key consideration. Job-relatedness is discussed at length in Chapter 14.

Consider another angle to the debate: the nature of the offense.

Ann Frank and Corrie ten Boom were not just ushered off to prison camps. They were arrested, found guilty, and shipped off. Their "crimes" were documented — and their crimes were "on the books." So, the fact that something is on the books and the person has been found guilty is something for the beholder to consider. If you think this is something that could never happen here, think again, maybe about Rosa Parks — or any other person writing a letter from a Birmingham jail after being convicted of sitting in the front part of a city bus — and the "crimes" for which they were "guilty."

Not all of us are fighting for universal justices. Consider this fellow. He was ticketed after he went to help a person who had been knocked down by a police horse. The police use the horses to control crowds, but when the horse rears up, the police start writing fines under the presumption of protecting their officers and the four-legged city property from getting hurt. We might laugh at a criminal record for "failure to yield to a police horse." An employer, however, might not laugh when reading a criminal record of "obstruction of police duty."

In Chapter 14, Federal hiring guidelines will be discussed. These guidelines emphasize that employers have some responsibility to ascertain that the individual actually committed the crime for which they were arrested or convicted.

The point here is that once it has been determined that the individual actually committed the action of which he was accused, the nature of the crime itself should be considered. "Obstruction of police duties" sounds pretty bad, but not determining the facts of the situation could cause an employer to reject the best candidate or deny a promotion to a deserving employee.

This issue is subjective. It is not a matter of law so much as it is judgment, common sense, and fairness. Subjective as it may be, there are several cut-and-dried circumstances relating to the record that can be used as a factor in your decision making process, either as an employer or as an individual thinking about where you stand on the issue.

There are also several other criteria that, perhaps while they are not so clear cut, can be used, again, either to evaluate an applicant if you are an employer or to think out where you stand on the issue the next time this aspect of privacy comes front and center as a political issue. Several schools of thought advocate considering the criteria of whether there was a *victim* of the crime and, if so, were they the victim of a *violent* crime?

The Personal Privacy versus Public Protection Debate Continues

As this book was going to press, an Illinois bill that would hide low-level felony drug and prostitution convictions from most employers was going before the full House. The bill passed the Illinois House Criminal Law Committee on an 11-2 vote — and the Senate has already approved the bill.

Victimless and Non-Violent Crime

Outside of the job relatedness, fairness and the true facts of the record itself — and another way to view the seriousness of the crime — is to consider who or what was injured. Was there a victim? Was the victim injured by violence or "merely" inconvenienced?

Victimless Crime

Some dispute there is such a thing as victimless crime. Others insist that an illegal transaction between two consenting adults is, by definition, victimless.

Drug possession, prostitution and sexual mores offenses are the most common crimes described by some as victimless. Proponents argue that there are no victims of this "crime," arguing that these alleged victims were victimized by bad law, and not by the lawbreaker. Others insist that there are indeed victims such as the Drug Enforcement Agent killed in the line of duty or that society as a whole is damaged through the degradation of morals, whatever the morals might be.

Violent Crime

More and more, a distinction is being made today regarding whether a crime was "violent." For example, some "three strikes and you're in prison" laws take into consideration whether one or all of the strikes were violent.

There is some credence to classifying a crime as violent or non-violent. However, the distinction has its limitations. Consider the following true story.

Violent Crime, Victimless Crime and Damned Crime

I have a co-worker friend who brought her two-year old to daycare before coming to work. She parked her car, ran her daughter into the room right inside the door, and came back to her car within four minutes to find her purse had been stolen. Inside her purse was the typical stuff: drivers license, credit cards, cell phone and checkbook — as well as an undeveloped roll of pictures taken over the course of a month of her daughter and family. Also, on this day, she had a ring that had belonged to her husband's grandmother. The diamond ring was not worth a fortune, but it was the only thing of the grandmother's they had.

Within the hour, the thief was video taped purchasing over $500 of merchandise using one of the stolen credit cards. $4,000 in bad checks followed in the days and weeks to follow.

Everyday at lunch, my co-worker drove across town to her credit union to sign affidavits as the bad checks rolled in. She worked with all her credit card issuers and spent some pleasant time in the State Department of Health making sure her birth certificate was notarized in all the right places so she could move on to the lines and waiting rooms of the friendly, helpful and courteous Department of Motor Vehicles to replace her driving license. She also spent some quality time at the local office of the Social Security Administration getting her social security card replaced. While without identification, she needed lots of cash for purchases — from a bank account soaked by bad checks.

Meanwhile, she visited the businesses that had accepted the bad checks and asked for video and witnesses to identify the thief. The police were bemused by these efforts — it happens all the time and the thief is rarely caught. In this case, thanks to my co-worker's prodding, cajoling — and frankly, investigative work — the thief was arrested and later received a $200 fine and a suspended sentence for writing a bad check. There were no charges filed for the actual theft, and the film, ring, purse and billfold were never found.

I dare you to tell my co-worker that we should really be spending more money on law enforcement to eradicate wild marijuana plants and enforce moral turpitude in desolate areas at 2:00 AM.

I double dare you to tell her that a non-violent, suspended sentence, fraudulent check charge is no big deal.

Section 2

Criminal Records Sources

This Section presents an in-depth analysis of the three primary government levels where criminal records can be accessed: county, state, and federal.

This Section also presents an overview of criminal-related records including prison, parole, probation, sex offender, and military records.

Chapter 4

Essential Criminal Record Terminology

I had always assumed that cliché was a suburb of
Paris, until I discovered it to be a street in Oxford.
—Philip Guedalla

Sometimes you can draw some slightly erroneous conclusions if you do not know how things work. One aspect of understanding how things work is to understand the words used.

A ***Criminal Record*** is a paper or computerized accounting that includes individual identifiers and describes an individual's arrests and subsequent dispositions.

Keep in mind that this "accounting" may be complete or incomplete. Also, not all parts may be available to the public, depending on the administering jurisdiction's rules. Criminal history records do not include intelligence or investigative data or sociological data such as drug use history.

In most states, the available criminal records can include information on juveniles only if they are tried as adults in criminal courts. Even then a juvenile criminal record does not usually include all the data describing that subject's involvement in the juvenile justice system.

Two important record types are associated with, and sometimes even confused as, criminal records:

- *Incarceration Records* are histories of time spent in jail.

- *Sexual Offender Records* indicate if a person is registered on a state sexual offender registry.

Refer to Chapter 8 for more about these two important record categories.

Felonies and Misdemeanors

There are two broad categories of criminal severity — felonies and misdemeanors. In the U.S. the distinction between the two has been blurred. Here are the common definitions:

- A *Felony* is the more serious class of offense and punishment ranges from imprisonment for over one year up to the death penalty.

- A *Misdemeanor* is an offense of a minor degree and is anything less than a felony.

There are degrees of severity within both definitions. For example, "gross misdemeanors" are more serious misdemeanors. Incidentally, the use of misdemeanors records by employers varies by state. See Chapter 15 for details.

Some people believe that misdemeanor records should be ignored, that misdemeanors really do not mean anything, and to base any kind of decision on a misdemeanor is wrong. They have a good point, but nothing a good barber could not disguise.

Seriously, there are several scenarios in which misdemeanor records might prove useful: Do I like the moral character of this job applicant? Is my daughter's boyfriend really okay? Has this potential babysitter committed an offense I should worry about? Having knowledge from a misdemeanor record might help to clear the muddy waters.

Whatever the scenario, there are two cogent reasons why misdemeanors should be considered:

- A misdemeanor record may be as pertinent as a felony, or more. From a human resource viewpoint, this is especially true if the misdemeanor is job-related.

- Many recorded misdemeanors are originally the result of felony crimes.

Even so, it is important — sometimes legally necessary — to understand the difference between felonies and misdemeanors. The distinctions between felonies and misdemeanors, and the reasons that felonies are not necessarily more important or significant than a misdemeanor, are discussed in Chapter 11.

With or Without a Disposition?

The terms "arrest" and "disposition" were used in the definition of a criminal record.

An *Arrest* is the taking of an individual into custody by law enforcement personnel; i.e. the person's behavior is arrested in order to charge the person with an illegal act.

An arrest differs from a conviction. A *Conviction* is a finding of guilt after a judicial trial. In some states, a conviction includes deferred sentences and in other states it does not.

A *Disposition* is the final outcome. This may or may not be a conviction.

It is important to note that many criminal records may not contain a disposition. Some states will purge a record (at least from the public file) if there is no disposition after a specified time frame. About one-half of all state criminal record repositories 1. do not release records without dispositions after a period of time, usually one year; or 2. will not release records without dispositions at all. On the other hand, there are times when a case is dropped but the record without disposition remains on the books because the court fails to notify the record center.

The use and reporting of criminal records without dispositions is regulated by state and federal law. See Chapter 14 for details.

Distinction Between *Public* & *Non-Public* Criminal Records

One of the most significant keys to understanding the U.S. criminal record system is to know the differences between *public record* and *non-public record* criminal records.

Non-Public criminal records are available only to law enforcement or criminal justice agencies, or other groups who have been granted statutory authority to access the records.

Public criminal records are those that can be obtained by a private citizen without some form of government authorization. The vast majority of criminal records found at the county level are public records. Public access to state criminal record depositories is somewhat more complicated.

FBI Records are Non-Public

Perhaps the most prolific of the non-public criminal records are those at the Federal Bureau of Investigation (FBI). The FBI makes its records available to law enforcement agencies nationwide and to certain approved entities. Even so, these entities' access to these records is not carte blanche. For example, gun dealers have access to FBI records in order to screen potential gun purchasers. Over the telephone (via modem going through the FBI state gateway), dealers can usually obtain an answer within minutes. However, they are only allowed to use the system for potential gun purchasers. A gun dealer may not use the system to open up a pre-employment screening business on the side.

A key component of the FBI's records is that they are nationwide. While the FBI does not have record of all crimes — let alone dispositions — they do have records from across the country. A search of the FBI's system — even when it is conducted through a local state repository — is a linked search that encompasses much of the other state and Federal law enforcement records. For more information about the FBI system, turn to Chapter 7.

Non-Public State Repository Criminal Records

While central criminal record repository data is available to the general public in most states, other states have classified their repository criminal records or portions thereof as non-public information.

Tennessee is good example of a state whose central repository considers *criminal records* non-public. Record access from their Nashville repository is limited only to agencies that have specific authorization by law. California, Louisiana, Mississippi, New York, North Carolina, and Vermont have similar restrictions. That does not mean that felony and misdemeanor records are not available in Louisiana, New York, and North Carolina. In these three states the State Court Administration agency offers access to a statewide database of *court records*, which contains the criminal information!

Another factor to consider is that most states cloak or mask certain portions of their records to the public, but do provide full information to those with statutory access.

Public Criminal Records

Nearly all county courts and most state record repositories classify their records as public.

As a counter-example to Tennessee, with their restrictions, Florida is "open." Florida state records are available to search without restriction to anyone by mail, in-person, or by computer. Florida can offer records going back to the 1930's. Their fee is $23.00 each.

Hybrids: States with Release Requirements

Anyone who has conducted nationwide criminal record searches knows that there are states where the repository records are not strictly public or non-public. While these states do not have statutory prohibitions at the state level as Tennessee does, neither do these "hybrid" states follow Florida's example of open records for all.

The most common requirement is a signed release by the subject of the request. As with many aspects of criminal records, there may be no other consistency between the states that require a release. Some states, Indiana for example, require that a release request be on a specific, state-approved form. Ohio has no state-numbered form, but requires the release to be signed and a witness signature. Virginia has a special form that must contain the notarized signature of the subject as well as the notarized signature of the requester. All these searches are at the state's repository; in Virginia, almost all counties' court docket records are available *free* on the internet *without* restriction.

The second most common type of hybrid access requires the subject's fingerprints. A record request *must* include a set of the subject's fingerprints at fourteen state repositories, or merely a thumbprint as they do in West Virginia. Under certain statutory conditions, fingerprints are required in seven more states. In essence, the supplying of fingerprints means that the subject has given approval for the record search. Nearly all states that process fingerprints as part of a record request will also submit the prints to the FBI to determine if the subject may be "wanted" in another state or by the feds. The submission of fingerprints is "an option" in nineteen states. In ten states, fingerprints are not asked for.

To find the individual search requirements and options for each state, turn to *Government Agency Profiles*, starting on page 133.

Significant Criminal Record Phrases

Criminal records often contain a myriad of unfamiliar terms or meanings. Each state has a veritable dictionary of crimes and penalties. While it is true that the definitions of most common crimes and penalties are fairly uniform from state to state, arcane state-unique terms are frequently found. In one state a pyramid scheme is a fraud; in another, that same crime might be known as a Ponzi scheme.

Unfortunately, these and other inconsistencies have led to the development of great gray areas in the use of criminal records. In one state, a family-related court matter may result in a publicly accessible criminal record, but in a neighboring state, a family court record is not public. These gray areas are why individuals, particularly employers, now have a much more difficult time making well-informed decisions from what is, or what is not, available.

Quasi-Dispositions

Adding to the mix, states have developed modified convictions, also known as "quasi-dispositions." These phrases include:

- **"Prayer for Judgment"** A request of the court to give leniency in which no finding of guilt by the court is found.

- **"1st Offender Act"** After fulfilling the terms of probation, and release by the court prior to the termination of the period thereof, upon release from confinement, the defendant is discharged without court adjudication of guilt. The discharge completely exonerates the defendant of any criminal purpose and does not affect any of his civil rights or liberties. The defendant is not considered to have a criminal conviction.

- **"Diversion Programs"** A court direction which calls a defendant, who has been found guilty, to attend a work or educational program as part of probation. Usually, a "diversion" will "set aside" the criminal record.

- **"Deferred Adjudication of Guilt"** The final judgment is delayed for a period of time. This can be likened to probation before a final verdict. If probation is completed without incident, the charges are usually dropped and the case dismissed. During the "probationary period," the disposition is not necessarily considered a conviction, and may or may not wind up on the record of the subject's criminal history.

Other Key Phrases

Listed below are certain words and phrases used frequently in the criminal record process.

Arraignment	A court hearing in a criminal case where a defendant is advised of the charges and asked to plead guilty or not guilty.
Bench Warrant	A process initiated by the court or "from the bench" for the arrest or the attachment of a person.
Class	Within government jurisdictions, the severity of a felony or misdemeanor is ranked by classification, moving from most serious to least serious.
Consecutive Sentence	Two or more sentences which run one after another.
Concurrent Sentence	Two or more sentences which run at the same time.
Docket	A book containing entries of all proceedings in a court. A *Docket Sheet* contains the case history from initial filings to the current status.
General Jurisdiction Courts	These courts hear felony cases. Some also hear misdemeanor cases.
Limited Jurisdiction Courts	These courts are limited in the types of classes of criminal cases they may hear.
Non-Biometric Identifiers	Non-physical (e.g. non-fingerprints, non-photographic) criteria used to determine the correct identity of a person when doing a criminal record check. In addition to name, may include aliases, date of birth, address, Social Security Number, etc.

While there is no overall translation list of every code, term, phrase, or descriptive nuance used by every state and county court, and criminal record agency, we have compiled some of the common terms and abbreviations. Appendices 4 and 5 are two Glossaries:

- Common Criminal Records Offense Terms, starting on page 375.
- Common Criminal Records Offense Abbreviations, starting on page 392.

Chapter 5

Criminal Records at the County Level

We have a criminal jury system which is superior to any in the world; and its efficiency is only marred by the difficulty of finding twelve men every day who don't know anything and can't read.

—Mark Twain

Statewide Court Structure Begins at the County

Before trudging into your local county courthouse and demanding to view a criminal record document, you should first be aware of some basic court procedures. Whether the case is filed in a state court, county court, municipal court, or federal court, each case follows a similar process.

In a **criminal case**, the plaintiff is a government jurisdiction. The Government brings the action against the defendant for violation of one or more of its statutes.

The county courts that oversee felony cases are actually part of the state court systems. Misdemeanor cases are held at local courts that can be either part of the state court system, or a local court many be a municipal or town court.

The secret to determining where a state court case may be located is to understand how the court system is structured in that particular state. There are over 7,000 significant courts in the U.S. that maintain a database of criminal records. Note that these courts generally submit records of major misdemeanors, felony arrest records, and convictions to a central state repository. The states, in turn, submit criminal record activity to the FBI's National Crime Information Center, which is not open to the public. This is examined in more detail in the next chapter.

The general structure of all state court systems has four parts:

- Appellate courts

- Intermediate appellate courts

- General jurisdiction trial courts

- Limited jurisdiction trial courts

The two highest levels — appellate and intermediate appellate courts — only hear cases on appeal from the trial courts. Opinions of these appellate courts are of interest primarily to attorneys seeking legal precedents for new cases.

General jurisdiction trial courts usually handle a full range of civil and criminal litigation. These courts usually handle felonies and larger civil cases.

Limited jurisdiction trial courts come in two varieties. First, many limited jurisdiction courts handle smaller civil claims (usually $10,000 or less, but the maximums do rise as courts systems adjust to the changing times). They also hear misdemeanors, and pretrial hearings for felonies.

Second, some of these *Limited Jurisdiction* courts — sometimes called special jurisdiction courts — are limited to one type of litigation. For example, the Court of Claims in New York. This court only handles liability cases against the state.

Some states, Iowa for instance, have consolidated their general and limited jurisdiction court structure into one combined court system. In other states there may be a further distinction between state-supported courts and municipal courts. In New York, for example, nearly 1,300 Justice Courts handle local ordinance and traffic violations, including DWI.

Generalizations should not be made about where specific types of cases are handled in the various states. Depending on the state, misdemeanors, probate, landlord/tenant (eviction), domestic relations (family), and juvenile cases may be handled in either or both the general and limited jurisdiction courts.

How Courts Maintain Records

Case Numbering

When a case is filed or a warrant is issued, it is assigned a case number. This is the primary indexing method in every court. In searching for case records, you will need to know — or find — the applicable case number. If you have the number in good form already, your search for records connected to this case should be fast and reasonably inexpensive.

You should be aware that case numbering procedures are not consistent throughout a state court system. One district may assign numbers by district while another may assign numbers by location (division) within the district, or by judge. Keep in mind, case numbers appearing in legal text citations may not be adequate for searching unless they appear in the proper form for the particular court where you are searching.

Docket Sheet

All basic case information is entered onto docket sheets.

Information from cover sheets and from documents filed as a case goes forward is recorded on the docket sheet. Thus, the docket sheet contains an outline of the case history from initial filing to its current status.

While docket sheets differ somewhat in format, the basic information contained on a docket sheet is consistent from court to court. All docket sheets contain:

- Name of court, including location (division) and the judge assigned;
- Case number and case name;
- Names of all plaintiffs and defendants/debtors;
- Names and addresses of attorneys for the plaintiff or debtor;
- Nature and cause (e.g., statute) of action.

Court Computerization

Most courts are computerized, which means that docket sheet data is entered into a computer system. Within a state or judicial district, the courts *may* be linked together via a single computer system. Access to this system may or may not be open to the public, depending on the state.

Docket sheets from cases closed before the advent of computerization may not be in the computer system. For pre-computer era cases, most courts keep summary case information on microfilm, microfiche, or index cards.

At present, images of actual case documents are not generally available on computer. Courts are still experimenting with electronic filing and imaging of court documents. Generally, documents are only available to be photocopied. You may inquire about where you must go for photocopies by contacting the court where the case records are located.

Certain Court Records are Reported to the State

Each state has its own rules regarding what records a court must report to that state's central records repository, and when.

It would seem logical that searching the state central repository would be the easy solution when searching for criminal records. However, there are access restrictions and pitfalls, as you will learn in Chapter 6 - Criminal Records at the State Level. For quick reference on what data is to housed at the repository, turn to pages 340-341 where you can read the State Required Data to be Submitted to State Criminal Record Agencies chart.

Searching State Courts Online

Online searching is generally limited to a copy of the courts' docket sheets, as explained above. Most courts are computerized in-house, which means that the docket sheet data is entered into a computer system of the courthouse itself. Checking a courthouse's computer index is the quickest way to find if case records exist online.

A growing number of state courts provide electronic access to their records, and you will find them in the *Government Agency Profiles* Section. For example, in Alabama, Maryland, Minnesota, New Mexico, Oregon, Washington, and Wisconsin where "statewide" online systems are available, you still need to understand (1) the court structure in that state, (2) which particular courts are included in their online system, and (3) what types of cases are included.

Without proper consideration of these variables, these online systems are subject to misuse, which can lead to disastrous consequences like failing to discover that an applicant for a security guard position is a convicted burglar.

If Records Are Not Available Online

If you need copies of a specific case record and you know the case number, court personnel generally will honor mail, fax, and sometimes phone requests to make copies for you. Also, court personnel may certify the document for you for a fee.

If you are conducting a name search – that is, you do not supply a specific case number, just a name – then you may find that many courts that previously conducted searches of court records on behalf of the public are no longer making that service available. Typically, these courts do one of two things. In some states, such as Kentucky, the courts only refer the searcher to a state agency that maintains a database combining individual court records, which may not be current. In other states, Nebraska for instance, the court has public access terminals or microfilm/fiche readers available for public use.

If you cannot come to the courthouse yourself, and the court personnel will not perform the search for you, then you must hire a local retrieval firm or other individual to conduct the search. An excellent source of local court record searchers is the Public Record Retriever Network found at www.brbpub.com/prrn.

Court Record Searching Tips

Learn the Index and Record Systems

During the past decade, thousands of courts have installed computerized indexing systems. Computerized systems are considerably faster and easier to search, allowing for more indexing capability than the microfilm and card indexes that preceded them.

There is a strong tendency for courts to overstate their search requirements beyond the full name. For criminal cases, the court may require the date of birth (DOB), to ascertain the correct individual. Other information "required" by courts — such as Social Security Number (SSN) — is often just "helpful" information with can be used to narrow the search on a common name, and verify the identity.

Be Aware of Restricted Records

Most courts have a number of types of case records, such as sealed, mental, or juvenile, which are not released without a court order.

Other Court Search Tips

- Watch for name variations from state to state. Do not assume that the structure of the court system in another state is anything like your own. In one state, the Circuit Court may be the highest trial court whereas in another it is a limited jurisdiction court. Examples are: (1) New York, where the Supreme Court is not very "supreme," and the downstate court structure varies from upstate; and (2) Tennessee, where circuit courts are in districts.

- In many instances the two types of courts within a county, e.g., a circuit court and a district court, are combined. When phoning or writing these courts, we recommend that your specifically state in your request that you want *both* courts included in the search.

- When searching for case records, keep in mind that many of the higher level courts also handle appeals from lower courts.

- If you send requests by mail, include a self-addressed, stamped envelope (SASE). This may very well insure quicker service.

Author Tip

Each state's court system is profiled within the *Government Agency Profiles* Section. The state court's profile will tell where and what records can be found at the local level. Also, we note which courts offer online access to their records.

Chapter 6

Criminal Records at the State Level

Facts do not cease to exist because they are ignored.

—Aldous Huxley

The State Central Repository

All states have a central repository of criminal records. Most states make this repository available to the public. The state repository maintains criminal history records of those individuals who have been subject to that state's criminal justice system. A state's record repository will not include records of crimes its citizens committed in other states. The information at the state repository is obtained from local county, parish, and municipal courts as well as from law enforcement.

A *Central Repository* is defined as the database, or the agency housing the database, that maintains criminal history records on all offenders in the state. Records include fingerprint files and files containing identification segments, and notations of arrests and dispositions. Although usually housed in the Department of Public Safety, often it is the State Police or other state agency that maintains the central repository.

The central repository is generally responsible for state-level identification of arrestees, and the repository commonly serves as the central control terminal for contact with FBI record systems. Inquiries from local agencies for a national record check — usually for criminal justice purposes or firearm checks — are routed to the FBI via the state central repository. It should be noted here that not all states conduct a national FBI check.

In summary, the source of the vast majority of any state's records is from county courts and law enforcement. The crime trail begins when a criminal action is first processed at the local or county level, then it is gradually forwarded to the state repository. What information is reported, when it is reported, and how it is reported will all affect the quality and completeness of state data. The charts in the Appendix give information on what is required.

Also, since states are dependent on counties for case information, the state repository may not have the latest information available, e.g., they may have the arrest information, but be lacking the disposition.

Unified Courts

Several states have unified court searches. In these states, the administrative office of the courts for the state have joined all the county courts into one searchable system. Unlike the typical state repository, this is not a law enforcement system.

A unified court search can be a particularly useful tool in those states that do not permit a state repository search. However, be aware that the value of a unified court search varies by state. In some states, a few counties may not be included. In other states, there is no uniformity with respect to the length of time criminal activity is archived. For example, one county may have cases dating back for seven years, while another county may have only two years of history.

Examples of some of the states that offer a form of a unified search are:

- Alabama
- Colorado
- North Carolina
- Utah (all district courts)
- Washington (all higher courts)
- Wisconsin

Other states are working on unified records systems. It should be noted that some criminal record vendors, through proprietary processes, are able to offer "all county" searches in additional states.

Non-Uniformity of State Systems

As you might expect, state statutes governing dissemination of public criminal history records are as varied as those statutes dealing with non-public information. A few states have no statutory provisions setting statewide policies on access by non-criminal justice agencies; in these states, the Federal Department of Justice regulations control access and use. In a few other states, the statute simply delegates to a designated official the authority to issue rules and regulations on dissemination. In states that do have laws dealing with the subject, the statutory approaches vary. In Florida and other "open record" states, anyone can obtain access to criminal history records for any purpose. In Tennessee, which prohibits access and use except for limited purposes specifically authorized by statute, it is a criminal offense to release criminal history records for unauthorized purposes. The other states fall somewhere in between, and as pointed out earlier, those states with release requirements are hard to categorize.

States that release criminal records to the general public:

Colorado	Connecticut
Florida	Hawaii (but some restrictions on employers)
Idaho	Iowa
Kansas	Maine
Massachusetts	Michigan
Minnesota (release needed for full records)	Missouri
Montana	Nebraska
Oklahoma	Oregon
Pennsylvania	South Carolina
Texas (for a Conviction Only report)	Washington
Wisconsin	

States that release criminal records to the general public with some form of a release from the subject:

Alaska (for limited records only)	Alabama
Arkansas	Delaware
District of Columbia	Illinois
Maryland (fingerprints show consent)	Minnesota (for full record information)
Nevada	New Hampshire
New Mexico	New York[1]
North Dakota	Ohio
Rhode Island[2]	South Dakota
Texas (for full record information)	Utah (fingerprints also required)
West Virginia	Wyoming

---

[1] New York imposes severe restrictions on a request with a singed release. The release must be date limited and a reason for the request given by the subject, personally. The release must be topic specific, and directed to the agency only.

[2] Rhode Island imposes severe restrictions on a request with a signed release. The subjects's signature must be notarized, and a reason for the request given by the subject, personally. The release must be topic specific, and directed to the agency specifically.

States that require statutory authority to access their records:

Alaska (for full record access)	Arizona
California	Georgia[3]
Indiana	Kansas (statutorily required requests get a reduced fee)
Kentucky	Louisiana
Mississippi	New Jersey
New York	North Carolina
Rhode Island	Tennessee
Vermont	Virginia

State Statutory Provisions for Access to FBI Records

Unlike the disparity between state repositories, there are some patterns and similarities among state provisions pertaining to access to FBI records under Department of Justice regulations. To begin with, the Federal regulations do not place restrictions on the dissemination of conviction records or open arrest records (arrest records with no recorded disposition) less than one year old. Non-conviction records may be disseminated for any purpose authorized by statute, ordinance, executive order, or court ruling. This includes favorable dispositions, including decisions not to refer or prosecute charges, indefinite postponements, and open arrest records over a year old and not actively pending. Most of the states have followed this approach of treating conviction records differently from non-conviction records.

Commonly, the states place few or no restrictions on the dissemination of conviction records. Also, a number of states do not restrict the dissemination of open arrest records less than one year old. Non-conviction records are restricted to a greater degree, and in some states non-conviction records may not be disseminated for non-criminal justice purposes, or they may be disseminated *only* for particular purposes, under specified circumstances.

Statutory Provisions by Category of Need

Another similarity among many states is that the statutory provisions do not specifically identify which non-criminal justice agencies or organizations may obtain criminal history records. Instead, these states define classes or types of agencies or organizations that may obtain certain records, or the state may define a specified purpose. So, some states may

---

[3] Although the state criminal record agency in Georgia will not release records to the public, anyone may make a record request at any local law enforcement office and the statewide record will be provided. Fees for this may vary; the maximum fee is $20.00.

authorize the use of criminal history records for any occupational licensing or employment purpose, while others authorize such use only for screening applicants for high-risk occupations, such as those involving the public safety, supervision of children, or custody of cash, valuable property, or sensitive personal information. A state's statutes may define permitted purposes in specific terms, or more general terms. Out-of-state or federal agencies may also fall under a state's special rules, having to conform just as in-state, private, and governmental agencies do. Many state-specific rules are explained in that state's profile, found in the Chapter 16 - State Profiles.

Need to Know Standards

Many of the laws require that certain agencies or organizations must be able to show specific legal authority under other statutory provisions to obtain criminal records. This helps to prevent those who are not authorized from gaining access to restricted records. Often, the need for the record must be approved by a designated board, council, or official. These statutory provisions that require separate legal authority for certain types of agencies vary considerably from state to state. The requirement may simply provide that the requestor must be "authorized by law" or must have "legal authority," or that the records must be necessary for a "lawful purpose." Such provisions are interpreted in some states as authorizing the dissemination of criminal records for employment and occupational licensing purposes where the employing or licensing agencies are required by law to screen for applicants who are not of "good moral character." Other state criminal record statutes, however, authorize the release of records for non-criminal justice purposes only if the requesting agency is "expressly authorized by some other provision of state or federal law to obtain criminal records for use in the course of official duties." This is a much stricter standard. Still stricter provisions authorize the release of criminal records only pursuant to statutory provisions that expressly refer to criminal conduct or to criminal records. These may contain requirements, exclusions, or limitations based upon such conduct or records.

Where prior approval by a council, board, or designated official is required for the release of criminal records for non-criminal justice purposes, the designated standard for approval varies among the states. For example, to determine who may have access, criminal record laws in New Hampshire and South Dakota delegate general discretion to the director of the criminal history record repository. Massachusetts' law provides that the Criminal History Systems Board must find that the public interest in releasing criminal records to particular non-criminal justice requesters outweighs the security and privacy interests of the record subject.

Several states require that the record subject must consent in writing to any release of his or her criminal history record for non-criminal justice purposes.

State and Interstate Dissemination Policies

On close examination, the criminal history record laws in many states provide only the framework for the state's policies on dissemination of law enforcement records. Specific legal authority for particular agencies or organizations to obtain criminal records may be set out in widely separate statutory provisions, executive orders, or even local ordinances. In addition, the actual policies and practices of particular states may be set out in regulations or may be based upon written or unwritten repository policies. These policies and practices often provide for more restrictive dissemination approaches than the criminal record laws require them to be.

Additionally, concerning interstate dissemination, the fact that most states' dissemination laws are more restrictive than the Federal standard makes it possible for authorized Federal and state non-criminal justice agencies to legally obtain state-contributed records from the FBI for purposes for which they could not, in some cases, obtain the records directly from the states in which the records originated. Georgia's state record repository recently closed a loophole in their system that had allowed access to the national Wants and Warrants lists. For $3.00, requesters received what could be perceived as "criminal information"—often before an arrest, and before a disposition. In most state systems this information is prohibited from the public eye.

Suffice it to say, state statutory provisions for access to FBI records and their dissemination — interstate and otherwise — are complex and filled with nuance.

Author Tip

For more information, an excellent source for statistics and inter-relationships is the *Compendium of State Privacy and Security Legislation* published by the U.S. Department of Justice Office of Justice Programs, Bureau of Justice Statistics. This compendium, as well as other statistical analyses can be found at www.ojp.usdoj.gov/bjs/.

Chapter 7

Criminal Records at the Federal Level

For a nation which has an almost evil reputation for bustle, bustle, bustle, and rush, rush, rush, we spend an enormous amount of time standing around in line in front of windows, just waiting.

—Robert Benchley

This chapter examines two primary and distinctly different locations of federally maintained criminal records — the U.S. District Court System and the FBI.

The *Federal Criminal Records* found at the U.S. District Courts are open to the public, for now. The records maintained by the FBI are primarily non-public records. They are only available to government law enforcement agencies and to those other groups who have been granted statutory authority to access the records.

Federal Criminal Records and The U.S. District Courts

Federal criminal records are a result of an individual committing a federal crime. An example of a federal crime would be kidnapping, hijacking a plane, and increasingly, many crimes involving illegal drugs and the activities facilitating drug trafficking.

Federal criminal records in the United States result from federal district courts and federal appellate courts. There are ninety-four federal judicial districts. A district never crosses state lines, although a state may contain several districts. Likewise, a district may be subdivided into divisions. In fact, there are 296 divisional federal criminal courts within the Federal Court System.

Moving up the hierarchy, the ninety-four federal judicial districts are clustered in twelve regional circuits, each of which has a court of appeals that hears criminal appeals from cases in their respective circuits.

How the U.S. District Courts Maintain Records

Case Numbering

When a case is filed with a federal court, a case number is assigned. This is the primary indexing method. Therefore, when searching for case records, you will need to know or find the applicable case number. If you have the number in good form already, your search should be fast and reasonably inexpensive.

You should be aware that case numbering procedures are not consistent throughout the Federal Court System: one judicial district may assign numbers by district while another may assign numbers by location, i.e. the division, within the judicial district, or by judge. Remember that case numbers appearing in legal text citations may not be adequate for searching unless they appear in the proper form for the particular court.

Assignment of Cases

Traditionally, cases were assigned within a district or division by county. Although this is still true in most states, the introduction of computer systems to track dockets has led to a more flexible approach to case assignment, as is the case in Minnesota and Connecticut. Rather than blindly assigning all cases from a county to one judge, their districts are using random numbers and other logical methods to balance caseloads among their judges.

This trend may appear to confuse the case search process. Actually, the only problem that the searcher may face is to figure out where the case records themselves are located. Finding cases has become significantly easier with the wide availability of PACER from remote access and on-site terminals in each court location with the same district-wide information. Note that Chapter 17, U.S. District Courts lists all the Federal District Courts, their Divisional Courts, and the counties each court serves.

Computerized Indexes are Available

Computerized courts generally index each case record by the names of some or all the parties to the case — the plaintiffs and defendants (defendants are debtors in Bankruptcy Court) — as well as by case number. Therefore, when you search by name you will first receive a listing of all cases in which the name appears, both as plaintiff and defendant.

All the basic case information is entered onto docket sheets and into computerized systems like **PACER**. PACER, the acronym for **P**ublic **A**ccess to **E**lectronic **C**ourt **R**ecords, provides docket information online for open cases at most U.S. District courts and all U.S. Bankruptcy courts. Access is via either a commercial dial-up system (user fee of $.60 a minute) or through the Internet (user fee is $.07 per page). Cases for the U.S. Court of Federal Claims are also available.

Five districts offer free but limited Internet access to their court records. They are 1. Idaho District, 2. New Mexico District (basic info only; registration required), 3. Indiana Southern District, and 4. Pennsylvania Eastern District (basic info only). 5. Arkansas Western District offers only Pending Case information for free.

As each court controls its own computer system and case information database; there are variations among jurisdictions as to how the information is offered.

Author Tip

For more information about how to search individual federal courts, including information on the electronic access systems including PACER, RACER, and The National U.S. Party Index, turn to Chapter 17, U.S. District Courts.

Recent Restrictions Imposed to Electronically Accessed Criminal Documents

Established in 1939, the Administrative Office of the U.S. Courts provides service to the federal courts in three essential areas: administrative support, program management, and policy development. It is charged with implementing the policies of the Judicial Conference of the United States and supporting the network of Conference committees.

In September 2001, the Judicial Conference took action regarding Internet and online dial-up systems used to access criminal records. The Conference mandated that **images of documents** filed in a criminal case could no longer be viewed online by the public. However, criminal case documents could still be viewed in-person or ordered by mail. Further, the mandate **did not restrict access to docket sheets.** Docket information is still available in all courts, except the U.S. District Court of South Dakota who has removed all criminal record information from PACER.

The reality is that few PACER courts permit viewing document images — PACER courts primarily offer access to docket sheets. Most of the document images of criminal record filings that are available online appear on the Case Management-Electronic Case Files system — CM/ECF system. This new electronic case management system gives each federal court the option of permitting case documents — pleadings, motions, petitions — to be filed with the court over the Internet. CM/ECF allows courts to maintain case documents in electronic form. Also, CM/ECF allows courts to decide who can view the document, and typically permit attorneys and others involved with cases to do so. Therefore, the Judicial Conference ruling affects the ability of the general public to view the documents. CM/ECF implementation in the bankruptcy courts and district courts has already started; appellate court implementation began in 2003.

Other Federal Criminal Record Trends

Federal criminal records have long been considered a distant third in value to state and county criminal records. This perception continues, partially due to the inexact matching, partially because of the limited scope and number of records present. The number of records is, however, growing extremely rapidly. Looking at the rate of growth for federal prisoners is instructive.

Under President Reagan, the number of federal prisoners grew from 24,363 to 49,928. Under the elder President Bush, the number increased to 80,259 by 1992. That nearly doubled to 147,126 under President Clinton and continues upward. This increase is largely a result of new drug laws, many passed during Clinton's administration and new anti-terrorism laws under the President George Walker Bush. Laws setting mandatory prison sentences, coupled with increased spending for new prisons and law enforcement officials, are blamed by most for the increase. While still small compared to the approximately two million Americans incarcerated, federal incarceration is increasing.

About 58 percent of federal prisoners are there for drug offenses. Whether you are for or against the "war on drugs," that is an eye-opening number.

The FBI NCIC Database

The FBI database's formal name is the *National Crime Information Center (NCIC)* and is an automated database of criminal justice and justice-related records maintained by the FBI. The database includes the "hot files" of wanted and missing persons, stolen vehicles and identifiable stolen property, including firearms. Two important points about the NCIC are:

The NCIC is not nearly as complete as portrayed in the movies. Because of the chain of events that must happen in multiple jurisdictions in order for a crime to appear in NCIC, many records of crime do not make it.

The information the NCIC does have is predominantly solely arrest-related. The disposition of most crimes in NCIC must be obtained by going to the adjudicating jurisdiction. This can be an important issue to employers as will be detailed later in the federal and state legal chapters.

This national database is currently evolving due to the National Crime Prevention and Privacy Compact, which are discussed on the following pages.

Author Tip

Lack of good identifiers — and the time, expense and legal liabilities this lack may cause — as well as the limited number of records present keep federal criminal records from being used by the vast majority of U.S. employers. As a federal court's jurisdiction can include a population of millions, the chance of a name error on a federal record is greater than at the county level. More care must be taken when connecting a name to a federal record.

Source of the NCIC Data

The sources of the FBI's information are the counties and states that contribute information as well as the federal justice agencies. Public criminal records are found at federal court repositories (for federal crimes), state repositories, and county courthouses. As discussed earlier, private citizens and businesses — non-criminal justice agencies — cannot, as a general rule, obtain access to the national FBI database. However, because the FBI database is perhaps the most well known repository of criminal records, some discussion is in order.

Access to NCIC files is through central control terminal operators in each state. The operators are connected to NCIC via dedicated telecommunications lines maintained by the FBI. Local agencies and officers on-the-beat can access the state control terminal via the state law enforcement network. Inquiries are based on name and other non-fingerprint identification. Also, most criminal history inquiries of the Interstate Identification Index (usually referred to as "III" or the "Triple I") system are made via the NCIC telecommunications system.

Interstate Identification System

In the discussion of the NCIC above, the term Interstate Identification System (III or "Triple I") was used. The *Interstate Identification Index (III)* is an "index-pointer" system for the interstate exchange of criminal history records. Under III, the FBI maintains an identification index to persons arrested for felonies or serious misdemeanors under state or federal law. The index includes identification information such as name, date of birth, race, and sex, FBI Numbers and State Identification Numbers (SID) from each state holding information about an individual. Search inquiries from criminal justice agencies nationwide are transmitted automatically via state telecommunications networks and the FBI's National Crime Information Center (NCIC) telecommunications lines.

Searches are made on the basis of name and other identifiers. The process is entirely automated and takes approximately five seconds to complete. If a hit is made against the Index, record requests are made using the SID or FBI Number, and data are automatically retrieved from each repository holding records on the individual and forwarded to the requesting agency.

> **NCIC data may be provided only for criminal justice and other specifically authorized purposes. For criminal history searches, this includes criminal justice employment, employment by federally chartered or insured banking institutions or securities firms, and use by state and local governments for purposes of employment and licensing pursuant to a state statute approved by the U.S. Attorney General. Inquiries regarding presale firearm checks are included as a criminal justice use.**

The bold section in the NCIC definition above is significant. Occasionally, an employer happens upon a "good deal." This good deal usually consists of a friend in law enforcement who obtains criminal records from NCIC and provides them free or sells them to the employer. The problem is that this is illegal, and the Feds have been targeting and prosecuting violators. If you want to check criminal records and have a friend in law enforcement — and want to keep the friend — you should not use the friend as a source of criminal records.

National Crime Prevention and Privacy Compact

The entire FBI record system and infrastructure is currently in a state of transition due to the National Crime Prevention and Privacy Compact. The compact became law when passed by Congress and signed by President Clinton in October 1998. It became effective in April 1999, when ratified by the second state. The compact's purpose is to authorize and require participating state criminal history repositories and the FBI to make all unsealed criminal history records available in response to *authorized* non-criminal justice requests.

This compact is changing the functions and relationship between the FBI and state systems. To understand how, it is helpful to look at past system performance and the new, evolving system.

Before the Compact

Before the compact, arrest fingerprint cards were submitted to the FBI by federal, state and local agencies on a voluntary basis. Law enforcement agencies, primarily local police and sheriff's offices, maintained a system of records specific to their state or locality and submitted duplicate prints of arrested and charged persons to the FBI. In exchange, local authorities received information on the individual's prior nationwide criminal history.

The FBI would report its findings back to the state and maintain the new fingerprint and accompanying data in its criminal history files. The FBI began maintaining this duplicate criminal history file in 1924, and by the late 1990's had over 200 million fingerprint cards on file.

After the Compact

The compact provides a decentralized national records system and is intended to facilitate efficient and effective exchange of criminal records. States must ratify their participation in the compact. Once a state has ratified the compact, they are required to forward criminal record information to the FBI. The FBI, rather than actually storing duplicate information, will instead store the "pointer" information. This information will point the inquiring party to the state holding the information. Therefore, there will be far less duplication of information.

When the system is fully operational nationwide, the III index maintained at the national level will contain personal identification data on individuals whose criminal records are maintained in state criminal record repositories (state offenders) and in the criminal files of the FBI (federal offenders), but it will not contain any charge or disposition information. The index will serve as a "pointer" to refer inquiring criminal justice agencies to the state or federal files where the requested criminal history records are maintained. The records will be exchanged directly between the states and between state and federal criminal justice agencies by means of telecommunications lines linking federal, state, and local criminal justice agencies throughout the country. The laws and policies of the receiving jurisdictions will govern dissemination and use of the records obtained by means of the system. Each state will enforce its own laws and policies within its borders; federal law will govern record dissemination and use by federal agencies.

An excellent review of National Crime Prevention and Privacy Compact can be found at www.ojp.usdoj.gov/bjs/abstract/ncppcrm.htm.

Access to NCIC for Non-Criminal Justice Purposes

Background

Certain industries or groups have been granted state or federal authority to access NCIC data. It is suspected that more industries will be granted access as a result of the continuing War on Terrorism. The industries granted access usually obtain the information through their state system, and usually as a result of state law. A majority of the states now permit access to some criminal history records by some types of non-criminal justice agencies and private entities.

For example, special access rights are increasingly accorded to governmental agencies with national security missions, and to licensing boards and some governmental and private employers screening applicants for sensitive positions, such as those involving public safety, supervision of children or the elderly, or custody of valuable property. There is one commonality: this access usually requires the use of fingerprint cards rather than the standard non-biometric identifiers such as name, date of birth, address, social security number, race, etc.

In the 1970s, Congress attempted to enact federal legislation setting nationwide dissemination standards for state criminal history record systems. These efforts failed. This has resulted in the states having a hodge-podge of statutory schemes. It also resulted in a steadily increasing volume of authorized non-criminal justice use. A national survey conducted in 1998 determined that roughly 35 percent of the fingerprint cards submitted by states to the FBI and processed in Fiscal Year 1997 were for non-criminal justice purposes. The survey found that nine "state" jurisdictions — Delaware, the District of Columbia, Florida, Idaho, Massachusetts, Nevada, New Jersey, Oregon, and Washington — submitted more fingerprint cards during that period for non-criminal justice than for criminal justice purposes.

In most states, nearly every session of the legislature now results in new statutory authority for some new non-criminal justice agency or organization to obtain criminal record checks. These new statutes specifically permit record access for such purposes as public and private employment, occupational licensing, and the issuance of various permits, certifications, and clearances. One area of intense activity is health care.

When Non-Criminal Justice Agencies are Granted Access to FBI Records – The Fingerprint Dilemma

As explained previously, the FBI's cache of criminal records is extensive, nationwide, but not easily accessible by non-law-enforcement entities. Employers who have been granted access to FBI records have not been granted the silver bullet it might seem. The reason is that in most instances, the search must include "positive identification." This means fingerprints. Fingerprints are messy in the figurative as well as literal sense. To begin with, they are physically messy if the standard ink and paper method is used. There is also an art to getting good prints. The transfer and verification process is messy. There is the problem of obtaining an acceptable set of prints. Next, there is getting those prints into the proper hands at the FBI. Then, there is the waiting for the response. All this is time consuming and expensive.

Automated Fingerprint Identification Systems

If you do not meet the fingerprint requirements, don't bet that the FBI will give you the records. Hope appears on the horizon for non-criminal justice agencies, though. **Automated Fingerprint Identification Systems (AFIS)** are coming and the War on Terrorism has helped speed their development. At its heart, an AFIS is an automated system for searching fingerprint files and transmitting fingerprint images. AFIS's computerized equipment can scan fingerprint impressions and automatically extract and digitize ridge details and other identifying characteristics in sufficient detail. This enables the AFIS computer's searching and matching components to distinguish a single fingerprint from innumerable fingerprints previously scanned and digitally stored. Digital fingerprint images generated by AFIS equipment can be transmitted electronically to remote sites, eliminating the necessity of mailing fingerprint cards. Remote access to AFIS will make fingerprint files accessible to more users. So, this new system reduces the need for manually searching fingerprint files, while the new scanning capability increases the speed and accuracy of ten-print processing, the old standard which includes arrest fingerprint cards and non-criminal justice applicant fingerprint cards.

There are three types of AFIS finger scan capture devices. Current AFIS systems only use optical scanners while the other simple identification systems are developing. The three scanning methods are:

1. Optical

The finger is placed against a platen (usually made of glass, often with a soft coating), and a picture of the finger is captured. These devices have become much smaller and less expensive over the past few years. There are multiple vendors of optical scanners.

2. Ultrasound

While ultrasound technologies have been around for many years, their use in fingerprinting is not widespread. When a finger is placed on the glass platen, a buzzing is heard and a vibration felt as the ultrasonic scan is taken. Since sound is used, direct contact with the platen is not needed. The scanning will work through a thin latex glove or on very dirty fingers.

3. Chip-Based

Users place their fingers directly on silicon chip-based sensor. The sensor has the surface area of a postage stamp.

Until these AFIS and other new technologies become less costly, many employers in industries with mandatory criminal record fingerprint checks will, initially, obtain the much faster and cheaper state or county criminal record using non-biometric identifiers — name, date of birth, address, etc. Then, once the hiring decision has been made, there is a follow up fingerprint check to remain in compliance with the law. So, an employer might hire an individual after obtaining the faster criminal information and ask the applicant to affirm that they had no disqualifying offenses. In the rare instance in which the subsequent fingerprint search discloses a disqualifying offense, the employer would terminate the employee for falsification of the employment application.

In any event, if you are an employer in a specialized or regulated industry, you will probably wish to order a cheaper and timelier criminal record. If so, look for a service provider with expertise in your industry. See Chapter 10, Advice When Using a Criminal Record Vendor.

Chapter 8

Other Important Criminal Offender Records

What's in a name? That which we call a rose
By any other name would smell as sweet.

—William Shakespeare

There are several other types of public records that, while not strictly "criminal records," will disclose past criminal activity. While the information may not be particularly germane or useful for employment screening in all cases, the careful researcher may choose to search these various sources to complement their criminal record check.

Following is a short overview of some "non-criminal criminal records." Please note that additional information on sex offenders and incarcerations records is provided in the *Government Agency Profiles, Section 4.*

Incarceration Records

Federal Incarceration Records

These are records of offenders who have been incarcerated in a federal facility after commission of a federal offense. The information is public record, and the value of this search is that you do not have to know the particular federal court that convicted the individual. The federal incarceration search is nationwide in scope.

The downside of this search is that it will not disclose minor offenses or, at least, those that did not result in incarceration.

The Federal Bureau of Prisons offers an inmate locator on its website, www.bop.gov. At this website, click "Inmate Info" at left. This Inmate Locator database also contains information about former inmates, dating back to 1982.

The following article, written by Mr. Lawrence C. Lopez, is an interesting overview of this website. Thank you to Mr. Lopez for allowing us to include the article in this book.

About the Federal Bureau of Prisons Website

by Lawrence C. Lopez

While this can be a very useful tool, a few words of warning are in order: it is not search-friendly.

I tested it on a couple of names and found the following:

While it provides name, race and age to the nearest year, it does not have middle initials, Jrs., exact DOBs or other details that can help you determine if the inmate Joe Blow is the same Joe Blow that you are researching.

There does not appear to be any standardized data input provisions. For example, I searched for an inmate whose first name is Natel but could not find him that way -- he was only listed as "N." And testing for the last name "Johnson" I found 66 "Joseph Johnson" entries, and 12 "Joe Johnson" entries as well as three "J. Johnson" entries on inmates whose first names may or may not have been Joe.

Do not use "Senior" or "Jr." or the like when you search. In my tests, the database located two "Charles Keating" entries of ages that seem to correspond to the former Arizona S&L chief and his son. But when I searched for "Charles Keating Junior" or "Jr." or "III", the database told me there were no entries.

Overall, this is a great database, but it takes a fair amount of patience to search properly. For those who have serious searching needs, I would recommend cross-searching the names in PACER, which should show the conviction that put the subject into prison in the first place. Of course, many PACER courts do not go back to 1982. PACER is *so* good and cheap that you might as well run it too, unless all you are looking for is where a current inmate is presently imprisoned.

===================

Lawrence C. Lopez is the chairman of Strategic Research and head of its Northeast operations. Strategic Research specializes in complex civil litigation, due diligence and criminal cases, along with research for news organizations. Mr. Lopez has worked previously with the Associated Press as an investigative reporter and has spent four years as a senior investigator at the Investigative Group International. Mr. Lopez can be reached at www.srresearch.com.

State Incarceration Records

Most states allow access to incarceration records. As with Federal incarceration records, state incarceration records may offer current and past information regarding an individual's incarceration history. In most states, inmates on probation are considered as current inmates. Twenty-seven states permit access to current inmate records via their website. Of these, 10-12 state websites also provide past inmate records.

You will read how to access incarceration records from every state as you read Chapter 16, State Profiles. These profiles may indicate free access to limited records is available via the Internet.

Here are recommended websites that have multiple links to state inmate locators:

- http://www.corrections.com/links/viewlinks.asp?Cat=20
- http://www.crimetime.com/bbostate.htm — select state and search for "inmates"
- http://www.brbpub.com/pubrecsites.asp

Parole Records

Federal Records

After serving all or part of their sentence, most federal offenders are paroled. These records are a matter of public record and may prove useful in detecting a previous offense.

State Records

There is usually a central state repository for verification of historical parole information. To track or verify current parolees, you must contact the appropriate State Parole Board.

Probation Records

Federal Probation Records

Some federal offenders are not sentenced to prison, but instead are fined and sentenced to probation. Probation means that all or part of the sentence has been reduced in return for a promise of proper conduct. These records are public, but must be obtained by contacting the Federal Chief Probation Officer in the judicial district where the individual was sentenced.

State Probation Records

Most states do not have a central state repository for the records of individuals currently serving probation. However, these records do not have the utility of other records. You will learn in the *State Profiles* in Chapter 16, a number of the incarceration agency websites permit searches of inmates online and also have limited searching for former inmates on probation.

State Sexual Offender Records

In 1994, the Jacob Wetterling Crimes Against Children and Sexually Violent Offender Registration Act was enacted. The Jacob Wetterling Act required all states to establish stringent registration programs for sex offenders by September 1997, including the identification and lifetime registration of "sexual predators." The Jacob Wetterling Act is a National law that is designed to protect children and was named after Jacob Wetterling, an eleven year old boy who was kidnapped in October 1989. Jacob is still missing.

Megan's Law, the first amendment to the Jacob Wetterling Crimes Against Children and Sexually Violent Offenders Act, was passed in 1996. Megan's Law goals include:

Sex Offender Registration - Each state and the federal government are compelled to register individuals who have been convicted of sex crimes against children.

Community Notification - Each state and the federal government are compelled to make private and personal information on convicted sex offenders available to the public. Community notification is based on the presumption that it will:

- Assist law enforcement in investigations;

- Establish legal grounds to hold known offenders;

- Deter sex offenders from committing new offenses, and;

- Offer citizens information they can use to protect children from victimization.

The criteria for implementing Megan's Law are left up to the states, with the understanding that the state is to follow certain specific guidelines. Despite the guidelines, what has resulted is disparities among the states' rules, and access. For instance, many states make information on registered offenders available on the Internet or by mail, some only the severe offenders either one or by access methods, and some states barely make the information available at all.

Approximately forty-one state agencies plus the District of Columbia post their sex offender registry via the Internet. In some cases a state agency may not post the information, although a local law enforcement agency may post for offenders within their jurisdiction only. In some cases, the state agency posts the registry and the local agencies post as well.

Here are three recommended websites that maintain multiple links to state sex offender databases:

- http://www.sexoffender.com
- http://www.parentsformeganslaw.com/html/links.lasso
- http://www.publicrecordsources.com

For more information on a particular state, see Chapter 16, State Profiles.

More About Megan's Law—

Megan's Law is named for 7-year-old Megan Kanka who was brutally raped and murdered in Monmouth County, NJ.

Megan's Law, which went into effect on October 31, 1994, requires law enforcement agencies to provide information about convicted sex offenders to community organizations and the public. The law provides that sex offenders are required to register with the police, including offenders who were on parole or probation as of October 31, 1994. Also, repeat offenders, regardless of date, are required to register.

Under Megan's Law, sex offenders are classified in one of three levels or "tiers" based on the severity of their crime as follows: high (Tier 3); moderate (Tier 2); or low (Tier 1).

When a registered sex offender moves into a community, there is a notification process. Neighbors are notified of Tier 3 offenders. Registered community organizations involved with children such as schools, day care centers, and camps are notified of Tier 3 and Tier 2 offenders. Local law enforcement agencies are notified of the presence of all sex offenders.

Residents may visit local law enforcement and review all registered sexual offenders in the community or county. The information provided includes the offender's name, description of offense, personal description, photograph, address, place of employment or school, and a description of the offender's vehicle and license plate number.

Typical offenses include aggravated sexual assault, sexual assault, aggravated criminal sexual contact, endangering the welfare of a child by engaging in sexual conduct, kidnapping, and false imprisonment.

Federal Fugitives

Through the U.S. Marshal's Service the Federal government maintains files on individuals who are wanted fugitives. These wanted individuals — assuming their guilt — have not yet "paid their debt to society" and, needless to say, are probably not a good bet as an employee, business partner, or as a prospect for a position requiring responsibility.

There is not a readily available database of federal fugitives open to the private sector. However, as you will see in Chapter 16, State Profiles, some state agencies will check with the FBI for outstanding federal warrants, and perhaps out-of-state warrants.

Military Criminal Records

Some individuals are naughty in uniform. Court Marshal information as well as military incarceration information is available and may prove useful if the individual in question was in the armed forces.

There are a number of great Internet sites that provide valuable information on obtaining military and military personnel records:

www.nara.gov/regional/mpr.html   The National Personnel Records Center (NPRC), maintained by the National Archives and Records Administration. This site is full of useful information and links.

www.army.mil	The official site of the U.S. Army
www.af.mil	The official site of the U.S. Air Force
www.navy.mil	The official site of the U.S. Navy
www.usmc.mil	The official site of the U.S. Marine Corps
www.ngb.army.mil	The official site of the National Guard
www.uscg.mil	The official site of the U.S. Coast Guard

Section 3

Employer and Vendor Guidelines to Access and Use of Criminal Records

This Section includes--

-- advice to employers for accessing criminal records

-- explains what services a criminal record vendor may offer

-- how to tell the difference between a good vendor and a not-so-good one.

-- legal compliance when using criminal records. It is essential that both the employer and the vendor are aware of and adhere to the criteria mandated by the Fair Credit Reporting Act and Title VII of the Civil Rights Act.

-- the trident to these federal mandates is compliance with state laws and state restrictions. The ability to obtain criminal records is of minimal value unless you are legally compliant in their use.

Chapter 9

Advice When Obtaining Criminal Records Yourself

I am only one; but still I am one.
I cannot do everything, but still I can do something;
I will not refuse to do something I can do.

—Helen Keller

There are several ways you can obtain a criminal record on an individual. First you have to choose between doing it yourself or hiring someone to do it for you.

If you plan to do it yourself, and you will be requesting criminal records from various locales, you will need source materials to tell you where to look and what procedures are there. What county courts will you need to search? What records will the state repository be able to supply you?

If you need criminal records from multiple locales, or have more than an occasional need for criminal records, you will probably decide to hire someone else with expertise in the field — a criminal record vendor. These record retrieval experts offer advantages — they know the territory and have knowledge about such things as costs, turnaround times, and what doors to open. Some have specialized search tools that you are not likely to have. When using a vendor, however, you are getting into an area where there are laws and provisions of which you should be aware. Chapter 10 evaluates the use of criminal record vendors.

You may not need a vendor. If you are in need of only a single record, or if you have a low *volume* of requests — and the *nature* of the request is simple — it will be easy enough to do it yourself.

Your decision to do it yourself or hire a retriever will, in large part, depend on whether you are doing local searches, i.e., searches in your immediate vicinity, or remote searches, i.e., searches from those locales too distant to conveniently do yourself. Let us look at some of the things you will need to know. Note that Chapter 11 looks at the record request process whether you access criminal records yourself or if you use a vendor.

Know Thy Repositories

The first step in searching criminal records is to know where to look. If you have read Chapters 5 through 8, you are now aware of the possible record locations — the county, the state repository, online, perhaps even the U.S. District Courts. Deciding which locations to search requires a basic understanding of the differences.

Local Searches

If you are a casual, infrequent user of criminal records and you want to order a criminal record on an individual from your local county, you may elect to go down to the courthouse in person and search the courthouse files.

With over 3,000 local courthouses in the US, the procedures will (literally) vary all over the map. In some locales, a computer terminal in the lobby lets you can do an initial search using name, SSN, DOB or other identifying information. From this computer, you will only be able to determine if that jurisdiction has criminal files of some type on the individual— or an individual with the same or similar name. The attending clerk should be able to tell you if the records from other courts, or other jurisdictions, are also on that computer database. That is helpful. If your search finds there are no files — no hits — that match the subject's name, you can be on your way. However, if you do find a match or potential match, the computer terminal will point you to the actual files, which are usually on paper. From here, turn to the clerk who may allow you to search the actual files, but most likely, the clerk will locate and search the files for you. There may be a fee, there may be a wait. In other jurisdictions, the clerk may have control of the computer and will do all the searching while you wait.

If you are in a state that allows it and you live nearby, you may also choose to search at state repository. Remember: how the state agency operates is quite different from the local courthouse. First, the turnaround time will probably be much longer. Even if the state agency permits you to order the record in person, most likely the report will be returned by mail three to ten days later. Second, state agencies do not permit free name searches using a public access computer terminal, as described above. Third, there are likely to be some sort of restrictions, and state people are pretty firm about following the rules.

Searching Several Record Locations

Obtaining a criminal record from your own county or obtaining a state criminal record from your state repository is one thing. You can become familiar with the methods and procedures in your own backyard and perhaps cobble together an efficient process. Obtaining a criminal record from a distant, out-of-state county is often a horse of a different feather. Just because your local county clerk or state agency does things a certain way does not mean you can expect the same process and courtesies elsewhere.

Often, the first obstacle is simply determining what counties should be searched. There are, after all, over 3,200 U.S. counties to choose from. Let us say that you are checking for a criminal record for someone who lists a ZIP Code in Crittenden County, Arkansas. You may not know that directly across the river is a rather large place called Memphis, Tennessee. To complicate matters, a few miles south of Memphis, just past Graceland, is Mississippi. Should you check these areas that border on Crittenden County?

Once the scope of your search is determined, next is the matter of determining the address of the county courts, the identifying information needed, the prices, who to make out the check to (if the search is being conducted through the mail), and the turnaround times that can be expected.

Do-It-Yourself Search Quandary

Here is a typical example: assume an individual applies for a position at an office in Chicago, Illinois. This individual had previously lived and worked in Mannford, Oklahoma. If the Chicago employer decides to order a county criminal record, he must first determine the county where Mannford is located. Through the use of a map, city/county cross directory or other method, the employer determines Mannford is located in Creek County. A good cross-directory is *The County Locator*[1] book.

Now, the employer must find out where the county seat or courthouse is located. Assuming the employer eventually determines that the Creek County courthouse is located in Sapulpa, Oklahoma, the employer must now determine how to get access to the records there.

Area code and telephone number to call, address, cost and procedures are all questions that must be answered. At the district court in Sapulpa, the clerk will *not* do a records search for you, so our employer in Chicago will have to hire a public record retriever to go in for him, as this employer obviously cannot do it personally.

Other courts may make the records available over the phone, although this is becoming rare and is not as dependable as an in-person search or even a mailed-in request. Further, most requesters like a written record of the results of their search; a phone search is not particularly reliable. Most jurisdictions, whether they are county or state level, charge a fee for a criminal record. This fee may be a set fee, or it may be based on whether a criminal record exists. The fee may depend on how extensive the record is. Many jurisdictions charge a set fee plus the cost for any copies they make. For mailed-in requests, the court may require a self addressed, stamped envelope. The vast majority of jurisdictions do not take credit cards. They may take checks — business, cashiers, and money order checks over personal checks — and many will wait for the check to clear before mailing your search results. This results in a considerable turnaround time.

---

[1] *The County Locator, The Guide to Locating Places and Finding the Right County for Public Record Searching*, ©1998 BRB Publications, Tempe, AZ, USA.

The complexity of obtaining records from distant sources, again whether county or state, coupled with the fact that there is usually a cost in time as well as money, is what prompts many employers to use a record retrieval service.

State Versus County Searching

The decision on whether to order a state or a county criminal record requires an understanding of the differences between the two. This is not necessarily an "either/or" decision. At its most basic, the question can be phrased: "Would you like that search to be a mile wide and an inch deep, or a mile deep and an inch wide?"

A Mile Wide and an Inch Deep

A state search is a wide search, encompassing all counties within the state. As discussed earlier however, state searches are dependant on the counties reporting the information. A state search, while broad, may not have the latest information, or the detail information that might be contained in a county search.

A Mile Deep and an Inch Wide

A county search is a deep search, often containing the latest and most complete information available *from that particular county*. The drawback inherent in a county search is the limited scope of the search. Many U.S. cities have spilled over into several counties. A search in one county — while revealing a great level of detail in that county — may literally miss criminal information that occurred across the street. Consider places like the City of Texarkana, where the state boundary line is a main street.

What is an upstanding, conscientious, resourceful criminal record searcher to do? Well, it depends. In those states in which a state repository search is not available, your decision will be fairly easy. You take what you can get.

A strategy that many searchers use is to first order a state record, if access is available. If something comes up that is conclusive, then the process may well end there. A pharmacy that discovers multiple convictions for drug trafficking on a subject's state search probably will not go much farther in the process.

Often, a state search may prove inconclusive, i.e., not contain the disposition. In a case such as this, the results of the state search would point to the county where the latest information could be obtained. The state search might also serve to validate a locale where the searcher had intended to search.

Conversely, if you start with a county search in a locale where there are close, adjoining counties and find something inconclusive — minor arrests or minor convictions — it may be cause for concern. It may behoove you to order a statewide search to see if anything else pops up.

The Myth of Public Records and the Internet

Up to this point, readers have probably noted there has been very little mention of accessing criminal records via the Internet. The truth is, very few criminal records are available on the net. To date, there are few counties that offer access to their criminal records via the Internet, and few who offer them for free. Nevertheless, the growing number of court records online shows promise for vendors and the casual searcher. Several states offer online access, but most of these systems are private dial-up commercial systems. Several states that do have Internet access are indicated in the *Government Agency Profiles Section 4*. Also, your will learn more about accessing criminal records at the local, county level in Chapter 5. See the Court Record Searching Tips section.

For now, the reality is that obtaining criminal records without hiring a retriever will most likely be a manual, non-online process. It may be a viable alternative if you only need local criminal record searches, but if you will be ordering records from various, distant locales, you should look into outsourcing the job.

It is worth mentioning that the Internet is a good place to find general information about government agencies. Many websites enable one to download, read and/or print current forms, policies and regulations. A growing number of state departments of corrections websites are offering access to inmate, parolee, and sex offender registries. See the *Government Agency Profiles Section 4*.

About the Internet and Access to Public Records

Overall, the availability of online public records is not as widespread as one might think. According to studies conducted by the BRB Publications, only 25% of public records can be found online.

Keep in mind that the Internet may be a free means to certain agency records, or it may be the conduit to a subscription or commercial site. The commercial online access method to public records is much more prevalent at the state level compared to the county level. Many agencies, such as DMVs, make the information available to pre-approved, high-volume, ongoing accounts. Typically, this access involves fees and a specified, minimum amount of usage. Frequency of usage is a key consideration when purchasing public records online direct from a government agency. Many agencies require a minimum amount of requests per month or per session. Certainly, it does not make economic sense to spend a lot of money for programming and set-up fees if you will be ordering fewer than five records a month. You would be better off to do the search by more conventional methods — in-person, via mail, fax, or by hiring a vendor. Going online direct to the source is not always the least expensive way to go!

However, the trend of agencies posting public record data on the Internet for free is upward. Two examples are: 1. Secretary of State offices whose records include corporation, UCC and tax liens, and 2. county/city tax assessor offices whose records reveal property ownership. Usually this information is limited to name indexes and summary data, rather than document images. In addition, a growing number of state licensing boards are posting their membership lists on the net, although addresses and phone numbers of the licensed individuals typically are not listed, making identification uncertain. When address information is available, such as real estate records, it can point to locales to search for criminal records.

Author Tip

There are several premier resources for obtaining the information you need to order criminal records on your own.

The Sourcebook to Public Record Information,[2] is printed annually in October. A CD-rom version of the product is updated every six months. This same information is available by online subscription via the Internet, with weekly updates. Go to www.publicrecordsources.com and look for the *Public Record Research System.*

All products contain a city/county cross reference that references cities to counties. Therefore, if you know the city or ZIP Code where your subject lived, worked, or perhaps ran into trouble, these resources will point you to the county where you need to search. These products list the addresses, availability, identification requirements, prices, and turnaround times for state and local searches. For more on these sources, visit www.brbpub.com

Using the Freedom of Information Act and Other Acts

The Federal Freedom of Information Act (FOIA) has no bearing on state, county or local government agencies because these agencies are subject to that state's individual act. Further, the government agencies that handle criminal records generally have systems in place to release information, so the FOIA is not needed. However, if you are trying to obtain non-criminal records from agencies, there are many useful Internet sites that give the information you need to complete such a request. We recommend these sites:

www.epic.org/open_gov/rights.html   http://spj.org/foia.asp

---

[2] *The Sourcebook to Public Record Information,* ©2004, BRB Publications, Tempe, AZ, 800-929-3811; www.brb.pub.com

Chapter 10

Advice When Using a Criminal Record Vendor

The greatest improvement in the productive powers of labour, and the greater part of the skill, dexterity, and judgment with which it is any where directed, or applied, seem to have been the effects of the division of labour.

—Adam Smith

If you plan on ordering any type of volume from a variety of county or state sources, your best bet will probably be to hire a vendor to perform the searches for you. The service will be faster and more convenient. Many vendors provide in-depth customer services such as interpreting obscure provincial charges that court personnel are not equipped to do.

Businesses that provide criminal records may be court retrievers, private detectives, or pre-employment screening companies. For purposes of discussion here, they will be referred to as "criminal record vendors."

The Advent of Criminal Record Vendors

The criminal record retrieval business exploded in the 1990s. Sophisticated companies that had a nationwide customer base and provided other types of computerized pre-employment screening information (such as driving records or employment history reports) began setting up nationwide criminal record retrieval networks. As they grew, these national companies hired employees and contracted with multiple local companies that had courthouse retrieval services. Some purchased and absorbed local retrieval firms. Small retrievers, who heretofore serviced one or two local employers, began to branch out into new counties and market to new industries.

Part of the reason for this explosion has been the increase in negligent hiring lawsuits. In the 1970s and even early 1980s, the negligent hiring suit was still a gleam in most plaintiff attorneys' eyes. The idea that an employer would be held responsible for an act of their employee — even when the employee was acting outside the scope of his employment — was farfetched for the times.

For whatever reasons, workplace violence also became a bigger issue. Historical statistics regarding workplace violence were not tracked as they are today. Our tolerance of violence is less. One theory is that women entering the workplace in greater numbers have caused greater awareness. If a couple of assembly line workers working on Ford "Model Ts" or a couple of roustabouts drilling an oil well went to fisticuffs, often the attitude was "well, boys will be boys." On the other hand, a couple of men going at it in a mixed gender office is somewhat different.

In any event, businesses have increasingly felt compelled to order criminal records on employee applicants. In doing so they have encountered the morass that is the present state of our criminal record repositories available to employers. The employer's solution is to outsource the criminal record research work, which has led to the proliferation of criminal record vendors.

Types of Vendor Services Offered

There are two broad categories of services provided by criminal record vendors. One category consists of the hands-on court record retrievers and the general search firms who employ any number of record retrievers to "cover" certain geographical areas. These companies obtain the records for other companies that, in turn, sell that information to employers. The general search firms are, in effect, the "wholesalers" of the records.

The other broad type of vendor is the all-encompassing pre-employment screening company that sells to the end user — employers. Pre-employment screening companies are, in effect, the "retailers" of the information.

It is important to note several variations. Many private investigators offer the above-mentioned "record retrieval" or "pre-employment screening" services. There are a number of vendor companies that specialize in compiling proprietary databases of public records. These companies, sometimes known as public record provider companies, may compile state-specific databases of criminal record activity. However, the caveat is that some of these databases may not be compliant with the Fair Credit Reporting Act (FCRA). This issue is discussed in detail in Chapters 13 and 14.

Retrievers and Search Firms

As "wholesalers," retrievers and search firms are *probably* not "consumer reporting agencies," as defined by the Fair Credit Reporting Act.

"Probably?" There is some debate on this point, but in any event, many wholesalers follow FCRA restrictions because their clients want them to.

Wholesalers frequently use local document retrievers. Local document retrievers use their own personnel to search specific requested categories of public records usually in order to obtain documentation for legal compliance such as incorporations, for lending, and for litigation. They do not usually review or interpret the results or issue reports in the sense that investigators do, but rather return documents — the results of searches. While document retrievers tend to be localized, there are some who offer a national network of retrievers and/or correspondents. The retriever or his/her personnel go directly to the agency to look up the information. A retriever may be relied upon for strong knowledge in a local area, whereas a search generalist has a breadth of knowledge and experience in a wider geographic range.

Companies That Provide Records to Employers

Those companies that provide records to end users, e.g., employers using criminal records as a factor in establishing eligibility for employment, *are* "consumer reporting agencies." They may obtain criminal records directly from the jurisdiction or from a criminal record wholesaler. In turn, they provide these records to employers for a fee. In Chapter 13, the significance of being a Consumer Reporting Agency (CRA) is discussed at length.

Because criminal records are by no means the only type of pre-employment screening information needed by employers, many of these companies also provide other services. These services may include driving records, also known as motor vehicle reports or MVRs. Other services offered are employment histories, educational verifications, social security number verifications, employment credit reports, worker's compensation history reports along with other industry-specific screening tools.

In the criminal record arena, most of these companies offer statewide records. A few only offer county records. Because of their cost, limited scope and lack of positive identifiers, Federal criminal records are a distant third offering.

Benefits of Service Vendors

Professional criminal record service vendors offer (or should offer) several benefits. These benefits are knowledge and expertise, faster turnaround time, quality control, Fair Credit Reporting Act protections, and ancillary tools that may include automated delivery, email ordering and Internet gateways.

The Knowledge Benefit

The first knowledge aspect is simply having the information on hand to obtain a criminal record from any county in the country. A service provider will have the know-how to obtain criminal records from locales nationwide. They have the databases that can quickly cross-reference the city to the county. They then should be able to immediately ask for the information required by the jurisdiction along with any necessary forms. Earlier in this section, some of the problems inherent in cross-country county searches were detailed.

The Turnaround Benefit

The faster, the better — if accurate. Turnaround advantages are usually directly attributable to having someone "on the ground" who can physically go into a jurisdiction, get the information, get it court-certified if need be, and get out. Counties and states are, of course, becoming more computerized, but this does not mean they are allowing outsiders to perform computerized searches of their databases. Any court that is computerized is marginally faster for retrieving records. Those few places that allow online access let the researcher get to the records from afar, so you may expect a speedier turnaround time.

The Expertise and Quality Control Benefit

Many service providers can provide valuable expertise in deciphering reports, knowing what courts will contain what types of offenses. That same service may be able to provide guidance regarding state law. Perhaps more importantly, a service provider worth their salt will "salt" their requests to their field people with known records. "Salting" means that, unknown to the field agent, the provider will occasionally ask the agent to perform a search on an individual that is known to have criminal record in that jurisdiction. If their agent comes back with a "clear" report — a "no record found" — the provider knows they have a problem: the agent is not doing a thorough job. Most service providers let their court record retrievers know they are salting their records, and a retriever doing thousands of requests for a service provider will not want to gamble the entire book of business to save a few pennies once in awhile with a "lazy search." In this manner, service providers can assert some degree of quality control.

Incidentally, phone searches — especially those performed by a court deputy clerk — are among the least reliable searches. If you absolutely, positively need to know, for the record, an individual's criminal history from a jurisdiction, get it in writing some way or another.

Fair Credit Reporting Act Protections

The Fair Credit Reporting Act is discussed at length in Chapters 13 and 14, but it is appropriate to point out here that this law can be to the record requester's advantage if a vendor is used. While an employer may be sued over a wrongful employment practice, when a company uses a criminal record vendor to obtain criminal records, the company is afforded some legal protections.

For example, if an employer orders a criminal record on their own and bungles the search, e.g., they obtain the wrong record and fire an employee, they are going to have their hands full. If they order the record from a "consumer reporting agency" and take the same action due to the vendor's mistake, the employer will be somewhat shielded from liability.

Ancillary Tools That Criminal Record Vendors Provide

Some criminal record vendors offer ancillary tools that can make the difference between a sub-par and excellent search.

Database Assisted Searches

When a vendor says they offer a database search, two of your primary questions should be "how far back do the records go," and "how current are they?" As detailed in Chapters 13 and 14, the Fair Credit Reporting Act requires additional compliance procedures when public record information is used for employment purposes and the public record information is not the latest available. This fact in no way negates the value of database-assisted searches, as explained below.

There are three main factors that hamper the value of public criminal record searches, particularly for employers ordering criminal records on job applicants.

1. Knowing where to look
2. Turnaround time
3. Cost

A database search can address all three. A database search is one in which a vendor has obtained a database of criminal records from, say, a county or state, or, the vendor has warehoused previously-ordered criminal records. Because the records are databased, the turnaround can be instantaneous as opposed to the hours or days a physical search of a jurisdiction can take. Because there are fewer costs per item associated with a database search, the price is usually less.

Perhaps the biggest advantage, however, is that the database search can — with the right system — *dramatically* increase the scope of the search and thereby make the difference between finding or not finding a criminal record.

What is the "right" system? Well, there are variations of database searches, some limited and some global. An example of a limited database search would be one in which a vendor purchases a county's database of criminal records. Say, for example, the vendor purchases the Watadoosie criminal record database. It should be noted that most counties do not make their entire database available, but a few do. When the vendor's client wants to search Watadoosie County, they may be offered the option of searching just the vendor's Watadoosie database.

This limited database search would address two of the three issues: turnaround and cost. Dear friends and good neighbors, remember: when you combine databases from multiple sources, the search value rises dramatically.

A global database search differs from a limited database search in that it searches records from various sources and databases. To illustrate, let us go back to the Watadoosie County example. An employer orders a criminal record from Watadoosie County. The vendor employing a global search would — regardless of whether Watadoosie's county data was in their database — perform a search of all the other data in their database. This might mean searching county databases from across the country or across the street, which might happen to be another county.

The global database might also contain previously ordered criminal records. Our employer requesting a Watadoosie County record might discover a criminal record that had been ordered by a previous employer six months earlier from a different county. Warehousing previously ordered criminal records can be particularly effective if a vendor has a high concentration of clients in a particular industry.

Database Caveats

As you can see, database searches can be a powerful tool in criminal record searches. However, they are supplemental and not a substitute. The main reasons why are detailed below.

Criminal record vendors should also offer you options and inform you of the type of search they are performing. If you want a current, up-to-the-minute search of Watadoosie County, that should be what you get.

Perhaps the main caveat with database searches — if the information is to be used for employment purposes and is not the latest available — a notice must be sent to the subject of the search. This is a Fair Credit Reporting Act requirement, and is discussed at length in Chapter 12.

The following sidebar is an edited excerpt from a recent article written by Lester S. Rosen, author of *The Safe Hiring Manual*. We thank Mr. Rosen for allowing us to edit and reprint.

Shortcomings of Vendor Criminal History Databases

There are a number of public record vendors who advertise they have a "national database of criminal record information." However, a search of a vendor's private or proprietary criminal record database may not contain the latest and most complete data. The fact is, there is no such thing as a truly "national" criminal record database. Perhaps the vendor has purchased some "data" from every state — be it a list of current inmates, or local police records, or unified court records — but no one has all the "data" from all the jurisdictions. Listed below are three major reasons a database search may fail to discover a criminal matter.

Completeness— The various databases that vendors purchase or collect may not be the equivalent of a true all-encompassing multi-statewide database. First, the databases purchased by the vendor for resale (or accessed as a gateway) may not contain complete records from all jurisdictions. For example, not all unified court systems contain all counties. Second, for reporting purposes, the records that are actually reported may be incomplete or lack sufficient detail about the offense or the subject. Third, some databases contain only felonies or contain only offenses where a state corrections unit was involved. Fourth, the database may not carry subsequent information such as a pardon or some other matter that could render an item not reportable under the FCRA.

Name Variations— An electronic search of a vendor's database may not be able to recognize variations in a subject name, which a person would notice if looking at the index. The applicant may have been arrested under a different first name, or some variation of first and middle name. A female applicant may have a record under her maiden name.

Timeliness— There is always the possibility that the records in a vendor database are stale to some extent. The vendor may only enter new data at intervals that may lag behind the timeliness of the available index from the corresponding state or county agency. Generally, this means that the most current offenses are the ones least likely to appear in a search of a vendor database.

Criminal record vendors should make clear what data they are providing when their customers are performing a search of that vendor's database. These searches are ancillary and can be very useful, but proceed with caution. In other words, it cannot be assumed that a search of a proprietary criminal history database solely meets the level of due diligence required to be compliant with the FCRA.

- Lester S Rosen[1]

---

[1] Lester S. Rosen, author of The Safe Hiring Manual, ©2004, BRB Publications, www.brbpub.com

Using Credit Headers as Criminal Record Pointers

The major credit bureaus contain files on hundreds of millions of people and credit header reports can be a powerful tool to address the problem of knowing where to look for criminal records.

Credit headers are, at their most basic, credit reports without any credit information. They only contain the "headings" of credit reports, which is primarily identifying information such as name, and current and past addresses.

Some vendors have a program in which a credit header is ordered and the past addresses are used to order criminal records from the locales in which the person has resided. It can be a slick tool, particularly if the header-to-county criminal record jurisdiction is automated. For example, an employer might decide to order a criminal record from every county where their applicant had resided the past three years. The vendor would order a header report, and their system would determine if there were multiple addresses. If so, the vendor would cross-reference the addresses against their county directory and automatically order the requisite criminal records.

Adjoining County Database

An up-and-coming tool offered by a few vendors is an adjoining county locator. This tool provides employers with adjoining county information, including relative population of adjoining counties. This helps employers make more informed and complete searches.

For example, assume an employer requests a count criminal record from "Podunk county." Vendors offering the adjoining county locater could find adjoining counties and provide to the employer. If one of the counties was high population "Gotham county," the employer might well choose to order a criminal record from both Podunk and Gotham counties and compound the value of their search.

Author Tip

The Ultimate County Locator With Adjoining County Search[2] is a database product that lists adjoining counties of every county in the United States, and lets you cross-reference ZIP Codes or place names to counties. The database also lists those counties that adjoin Canada or Mexico.

---

[2] *The Ultimate County Locator With Adjoining County Search*, ©2004, BRB Publications, Tempe, AZ; 800-929-3811 or visit www.brbpub.com

Where to Find a Vendor

We list several good sources below. When you search for a vendor using a search engine on the Internet, you will find a myriad of screening companies. Some of the more professional websites can indicate their high level of technical expertise and ability to meet fast turnaround times. That is all well and good, but be sure to look, or ask, for their statements on compliance with FCRA. If they respond to your FCRA inquiry with an "of course we have Fine Criminal Record Access," you should suddenly remember you are late for a meeting.

As we have discussed however, many industries have their own specific laws and nuances regarding criminal records. If you are able, talk to others in your industry to determine what vendor they use. What you are looking for is a criminal records vendor who might "specialize" in your industry.

- www.publicrecordsources.com Click on the section called *Screening firms* and you will be able to search among 250+ of the nation's leading screening companies. Also, this site is an excellent source to find specialty vendors. Click on *Sources and Search Firms*.

- *Public Records Online*[3] has an entire section dedicated to finding specialty vendors. This book is available at many bookstores, and can be ordered through most U.S. bookstores.

How to Choose the Best Vendor for You

You will not see the consumer magazines reviewing the different criminal record services and issuing "best buys" any time soon. However, like a consumer magazine, the information here can help to point out a provider's attributes that you should evaluate before making a decision.

The business of criminal record retrieval is more of a service than a product. It probably won't always be so. Someday you may be able to choose a criminal record service by price and turnaround time. All systems will be computerized, right down to the municipal court level. Criminal records will become a commodity. Today they are not. It is a service because there are so many variables. Knowledge — operational, legal and otherwise — affects the quality of the service as much as price and turnaround. The following are some attributes you can use to compare vendors.

---

[3] *Public Records Online*, ©2004, by Facts on Demand Press, Tempe, AZ; 800-929-3811.

Consider Vendor Accuracy

Accuracy can be hard to gauge. You can ask if the vendor "salts" his requests with known criminal records on a random basis. You can do the same to the vendor if you have some known records in a given jurisdiction.

One of the biggest causes of "inaccuracy" in criminal records is actually mis-identification. In fact, the criminal record is accurate, but not accurate for the individual on which it was ordered. This usually happens in instances when a record is ordered on a subject with a common name and the individual's identifying information at the jurisdiction is incomplete. This will be discussed in detail in the next chapter, but for purposes here, look at an example of the vendor's criminal record report. You should be able to readily distinguish between the information you used to request the search and the information that was actually returned from that jurisdiction. Better is a section on the report that highlights discrepancies between the two.

Consider Vendor Knowledge

The most accurate report in the world is of limited value if you do not fully understand what it means. Most vendors will help you decipher unusual reports and some have a glossary with common terms and charges defined. If they do not, you may start with the glossary and common abbreviations section of this book.

A report that includes coding and ambiguous abbreviations may look impressive in your file, but how meaningful is it? For all reports, except those you deal with regularly, interpretation assistance can be very important. Some information vendors offer searches for information they really do not know much about through sources they only use occasionally. Protecting their credibility or their professional pride sometimes prohibits them from disclosing their limitations — until you ask the right questions.

A vendor should also be knowledgeable about laws regarding the use of criminal record information. This includes the FCRA as well as EEOC information discussed later in this book. If you are in an industry with some unique requirements, connecting up with a vendor with knowledge and experience in your industry is an excellent benefit.

Consider the Vendor's Ancillary Services

Database, adjoining county and credit header-assisted searches were discussed earlier. If you believe these services could improve your results, look for a vendor that offers them.

How is their Turnaround Time?

The faster the better as long as it is not traded for accuracy. The vendor should publish an expected turnaround schedule for each state served, and have a standard for most counties.

Consider Price

You get what you pay for? Yeah, this little homily probably has a grain of truth, but on the other hand, there are people who go to different car dealerships and buy identical cars and the price they pay differs by thousands. Buyer beware. One of them made a "best buy," one of them paid more than he should have. The fair price could be somewhere in between.

With that said, there are a lot of hucksters who have opened themselves a little website, bought a phone and gone into the criminal record business. They may be less expensive — until their erroneous report causes you to hire or fire someone you should not, the turnaround is not what they said it would be, or their lack of knowledge catches up to them, or you, in other ways.

Consider the Locale

"I lost my glasses in the alley, but the light is better out here on the street corner."

This is a punch line to an old joke, but instructive when choosing a vendor. With the Internet and other computerized ordering and delivering systems, the locale of your vendor and proximity to you should not be an issue, but it might be. A vendor in the state capital might offer quicker access to state agency records. A vendor might be able to deliver a hard-copy of a document overnight from the local courthouse.

Summary

All of the above factors are useful to compare vendors. Our best advice when choosing a vendor: talk to the vendor's customers. They have first-hand knowledge of that vendor's accuracy, turnaround, and overall knowledge.

If you are a user in a specialized industry, or you have unique requirements, it may also behoove you to determine how many other customers in your industry that vendor has.

Chapter 11

Evaluate Your Record Request Process

I Really Want to Know…Who Are You?

—The Who

Ever wonder if the rock band *The Who* ever ordered criminal records on their roadies? Ah, probably not. In any event, if you have decided to order criminal records on job applicants, you should look at several issues within your criminal record process.

The record request process involves a number of steps. These steps should be followed whether you plan to access the records yourself or if you plan to use a vendor.

Proper identification — and recognition of improper identification before action is taken — is of primary importance. Two other processes you should examine are the use of misdemeanor records and proper documentation.

Identification Issues

A key issue in using criminal records is evaluating whether the information you have received pertains to the person on whom you inquired. It sounds so simple. Yet, more criminal record legal trouble starts here than anywhere else.

There are two categories of methodology used to identify individuals when ordering criminal records.

- Biometric Identifiers
- Demographics

It is important to understand the strengths and limitations of both.

Biometric Systems

Biometric systems measure an individual's unique physical characteristics. The most common biometric identifiers are fingerprints and retina scans. Of these, fingerprints are far more common and the only biometric identifier in use for criminal record matching. The use of other biometrics such as DNA and retina scans are found in the criminal justice field, but their use for matching an individual to past records is novel.

The problem is that existing technology for storing, copying, and matching these great biometric identifiers — fingerprints, photographs and retina scans — makes their use slow and expensive. Nevertheless, the definition of "expensive" has changed since the War on Terrorism began. Fingerprinting applications have been jump-started, and prices for them are expected to decrease. Although rarely used by the general public, fingerprinting will become more common. As mentioned in Chapter 2, fingerprinting drivers who apply for new or renewed hazardous material endorsements has been proposed and the means of implementation is under study. A short discussion on the fingerprinting process is in order.

Fingerprints

Fingerprint identification is based upon the fact that individual fingerprints have unique characteristics. These characteristics are whorls, arches, loops, ridge endings, and ridge bifurcations.

Many fingerprints today are still taken the way they were decades ago: with paper and ink. The fingerprints are taken and put on a "ten-print" card. This card is then scanned and digitized for matching purposes.

Finger scan systems can be broadly categorized into two types—verification systems and identification systems. It is important to understand the distinction, and the cost between the two systems varies several hundredfold.

Verification systems capture the flat image of a finger and perform a one-to-one verification. That is, the original print is compared to the subsequent print to determine if it matches. A verification is performed in a few seconds. Applications of this technology have filtered down to the private sector, including personal computer security.

On the other hand, identification systems are used by law enforcement to match one set of fingerprints against millions of other, current prints. To be accurate, this one-to-many task requires that the original fingerprints be of a higher standard of clarity. Currently, a basic fingerprint identification system used simply to capture, digitize and transmit fingerprints costs over $10,000.

As discussed earlier, few employers have been granted statutory authority to access NCIC with fingerprints. As a result, for criminal record searches, most employers will continue to use non-biometric identifiers—name, date of birth, address, etc. In the business, the term used for this type of matching criteria is "demographics."

Demographic Identifiers

Using demographic identifiers means using items such as name, social security number, address, date of birth or other non-physical characteristics in order to identify a person.

Every person's fingerprint is unique. Every person's name is not, even when combined with a date of birth. The Social Security Number should be a unique identifier, but many criminal records do not have a social security number attached to it, and, imagine this: the criminal speaketh with forked tongue when asked for his correct Social Security Number! So, the number on this record winds up being the wrong one, maybe even yours.

When using non-biometric identifiers, employers and the record retrievers need all the demographics they can get. Unfortunately there is a misconception on the part of some employers that a key demographic — the date of birth — cannot be obtained from job applicants. Because of its importance, it deserves a detailed discussion.

Asking for the Date of Birth

An area that gives many employers pause is asking applicants for their date of birth. A correct DOB is very important when ordering a criminal record. Many jurisdictions ask that a DOB be included in a criminal record request. Some may not perform a name search without a DOB attached. The main reason for asking for a date of birth, as discussed earlier, is to have another identifier. Criminal records do not always contain a Social Security Number, and while using the name and DOB is not always conclusive, it is many times better than a name-only search.

The problem arises when employers are afraid to ask applicants their DOB. The reason for their fear? Since the Equal Employment Opportunity Commission (EEOC) prohibits age discrimination, some employers reason that they are much less likely to be accused of age discrimination if they do not know the age of the applicant to begin with.

The fact of the matter is that the EEOC does not prohibit employers from asking applicants for their DOB as long as it is asked for a legitimate, non-discriminatory reason and not used for an impermissible purpose. In practice, asking for DOB should be done uniformly, not just on select applicants.

In fact, the EEOC has put out an eleven-page guidance document regarding job advertising, and pre-employment inquiries — such as those asked for on printed employment applications — under the Age Discrimination in Employment Act (ADEA). You may be interested to know that the chairman of the EEOC who signed this document into law was U.S. Supreme Court Justice Clarence Thomas. Would it be a safe bet that during his confirmation hearing Justice Thomas may have later wished for a few good hardball age-related inquiries if they would make some other questions go away?

In any event, a copy of the 1989 EEOC guidance document that addresses the subject of asking for the DOB is provided in Chapter 14.

Matching the Date of Birth with the Name

A jurisdiction may be using a name and date of birth from the employer to make a match. Many employers believe that a full first and last name with a date of birth is unique. It is not. As an exercise, pick a first and last name, and date of birth. Assume the chances of there being another person with the same first and last name and a matching DOB are only one in one million. Calculated, there are about 280 of these combinations in the United States. The fact is however, that the chances are much greater than one in one million for most names. There are a lot of common first names — David and John and Debbie and Karen — and a whole lot of Smiths, Jones and other ubiquitous surnames. That's not to mention the possibility of identity theft.

The lesson in all this is:

> Look very carefully at any criminal records for identifying
> information that does **not match** your subject's information.

Do not just assume that the information returned applies to your subject. For example, if you order information on John Doe, 1/1/61 and a record comes back on John Quincy Doe, 1/1/61, be sure to ascertain your subject's middle name. If you order a record on Jane Doe, DOB of 12/12/62, SSN of 123456789 and a record comes back on Jane Doe, 12/12/62, SSN of 12345678, do not automatically assume it is Jane — but do not assume it isn't.

A solution could be as simple as running a check on the social security number, or questioning Jane and speaking with the company or jurisdiction that supplied the record. The solution may come down to this: have your applicant fingerprinted and submit those prints for comparison with those taken at the time of arrest.

Again, simply not reviewing the information they have received is a common area where employers stub their toe when ordering criminal records. They order a report on one person, get back a record on another and, because they have not looked carefully at the record, they mistakenly take some adverse action against their applicant or employee. It is certainly not fair to disqualify an individual for having a name similar to one on a criminal record, or any public record. This mistake should be avoided.

The Importance of Proper Documentation

On the next page is an example of a criminal Background Check Release Form that appears in *25 Essential Lessons for Employee Management* by employment expert Dennis DeMey and published by Facts on Demand Press. You may download copies of employment related forms by going to www.brbpub.com/forms.

This form has fields for commonly used demographic data and also includes a place for the applicant to give his permission for your search. It should be noted that the vast majority of record requests do not require a notary signature and seal.

Sample Criminal Record Release Form

Criminal Background Check – Release Form

NAME_____
          Last   First   Middle   Maiden

ADDRESS_____
          Street   City   State

ALIASES OR OTHER NAMES USED _____

DATE OF BIRTH _____ AGE ____ RACE _____ SEX ____

SOCIAL SECURITY # _____

DRIVER'S LICENSE # _____ STATE _____

* * *

I hereby authorize _____ of _____
              Name   Name of Company

_____
              Company Address/City/State/Zip

to conduct a criminal background check on myself through the

_____ .
              Name of State and Police Agency

X_____
     Applicant Signature

* * *

STATE of:_____   This Instrument was acknowledged before me this ____ day of

COUNTY of:_____   _____, 20 ____, by _____

My commission will expire: _____AS WITNESS.

_____

_____   _____
      Notary Public   No.

Pros and Cons of Using Misdemeanor Records

Perhaps you are thinking you will not hire anyone with a felony conviction, but you will let misdemeanor records slide. Perhaps you will ignore arrest records unless there is more than one in the past year, but a felony conviction — regardless of age — will always disqualify an applicant. Whoops, it is not that easy. Here are some facts to consider before deciding how to evaluate misdemeanor and felony records, as well as convictions and arrests.

Misdemeanor records were defined earlier as "offenses of a minor degree and anything less than a felony." Misdemeanors are often discarded as a factor by some, kind of like "college records" i.e., "if not for the grace of God, there go I" records.

Well, sometimes misdemeanors *are* minor. Let those of you without misdemeanor sin cast the first stone while we duck. Before dismissing them though, consider:

1. A misdemeanor record may be more pertinent than a felony.

How? Imagine you own a construction company and your crew needs some extra hands at an excavation project. One individual who applies for a job looks to be a good prospect, but he has a conviction for felony embezzlement. Should this automatically disqualify the applicant? After all, if while that person is on the job they want to slyly peer around and sneak a dirt clod or two in their pocket to take home, well, no harm is done.

On the other hand, assume you are hiring drivers to haul away the dirt fill that Mr. Sticky Fingers has not spirited away in his pockets. One prospect who applies for this position "just" has one misdemeanor on his record: a "Driving While Intoxicated" (DWI) conviction. If you hire this individual and he has an accident that injures someone while drinking, you might as well buy a mirror and start practice saying, "it was just a misdemeanor" without looking dumb. Good Luck.

The point? Consider the severity of the crime in relation to the *job-relatedness* of the crime.

2. Many recorded misdemeanors are for felony crimes.

Sad to say, but the fact that an offense is recorded as a misdemeanor does not mean that the crime committed was a misdemeanor. Plea Bargains — a plea of guilt to a lesser offense in return for a lighter sentence — are common in the legal system. Overloaded court systems, prosecutors with a challenging case to prove and savvy defense attorneys all contribute to the fact that charges are often downgraded in return for defendant's guilty plea.

~~~~~~

Author Tip

If you have an applicant with a few "minor" convictions, do some digging to determine what happened in the legal proceeding process. Look at an arrest record — if the law allows — and compare it to the applicant's version of the incident. If this is a key position and the record troubles you, you may wish to call the court or prosecutor to find out what you can.

Chapter 12

Compliance With the Fair Credit Reporting Act

Common sense often makes good law.

—William O. Douglas

As discussed earlier in this book, the vast majority of criminal records used outside of law enforcement are for used for employment purposes. If you are obtaining criminal records from a vendor and using these records to make decisions (e.g., you are not merely reselling the records) a law called the Fair Credit Reporting Act (FCRA) will almost certainly regulate the vendor. As discussed earlier, if a vendor does not have a good knowledge of the FCRA, it is a good indicator to choose another vendor.

The FCRA directly affects areas as diverse as what information can be contained on a report, to what notifications to make to the subject prior to the criminal record inquiry.

FCRA and Employers

The first hurdle to understand is that the "Fair Credit Reporting Act" is really misnamed. It should be called the "Fair Credit *and Employment* Reporting Act." The lack of "employment" in the title has contributed to the lack of understanding and knowledge of this law in employment screening. If you are an employer, ordering criminal records on potential employees, you will want to be familiar with this law.

There are three main areas in which the FCRA can affect an employer ordering criminal records—

- **Releases**—What notifications must be made and permissions granted from the subject of the search.

- **Arrest vs. convictions, seven year rule**—What information can appear on the report, and what must be suppressed.

- **Aged public record for employment purposes**—When the vendor databases records, what additional notifications to the subject must be performed.

Before detailing specifics, it is helpful to have a general overview of the act.

Overview of The Fair Credit Reporting Act (FCRA)

In general, the FCRA manages the relationship between the parties who are involved in informational transactions that fall under the Act. Usually, there are at least three affected parties:

- The provider of the information
- The subject of the information
- The user of the information

Before going further, several terms must be defined.

Consumer Reporting Agency

A *Consumer Reporting Agency (CRA)* is "any person which, for monetary fees, dues, or on a cooperative nonprofit basis, regularly engages in whole or in part in the practice of assembling or evaluating consumer credit information or other information on consumers for the purpose of furnishing consumer reports to third parties, and which uses any means or facility of interstate commerce for the purpose of furnishing consumer reports."

Consumer Report

The term consumer report was used in the definition above. A *Consumer Report* is "any written, oral, or other communication of any information by a consumer reporting agency bearing on a consumer's credit worthiness, credit standing, credit capacity, character, general reputation, personal characteristics, or mode of living which is used or expected to be used or collected in whole or in part for the purpose of serving as a factor in establishing the consumer's eligibility for:

- credit or insurance to be used primarily for personal, family, or household purposes;
- employment purposes; or
- any other purpose authorized under section 604 [§ 1681b]."

What are Employment Purposes?

Employment purposes, when used in connection with a consumer report means " a report used for the purpose of evaluating a consumer for employment, promotion, reassignment or retention as an employee."

The purpose of the FCRA is to facilitate the flow of essential information concerning an individual's background, while at the same time protecting that individual's privacy rights. This is accomplished through the imposition of statutory and regulatory safeguards imposed on CRAs and the users and providers of their information. The regulations are designed to ensure the accuracy of the information being provided. A failure to comply with the FCRA's requirements exposes the CRA as well as the CRA customer, to both civil and criminal penalties.

In addition to the federal FCRA, there are state versions of the FCRA. Often, these state versions are more restrictive than the federal FCRA. Their inter-relationship will be detailed in the next chapter.

The Sword and the Shield

The FCRA is both a triple-edged sword *and* a triple-sided shield. The sword imposes obligations on providers, users, and consumers. The shield protects.

The Sword Hanging over CRAs

Criminal record vendors must comply with a host of regulatory guidelines, among the most critical being to "use reasonable procedures to insure maximum possible accuracy" of the information they report. Failure to comply with these requirements can expose the CRA to civil penalties. In addition, CRAs must provide to users a notice of their responsibilities. This is shown in Appendix 2. Incidentally, there is another entity regulated by the FTC. These are the *furnishers* of information. This would include creditors reporting credit transaction histories. A copy of the notice to furnishers is shown in the Appendix.

The Shield Protecting CRAs

On the other hand, the FCRA recognizes the need for the free flow of essential information. It recognizes that mistakes will be made and that some information is subjective, i.e., the "truth" of an event can be viewed differently by the consumer and reporting company. The FCRA therefore offers CRAs a shield against defamation and slander lawsuits if they act without malice and a modicum of care.

The Sword Hanging over Users

The sword hanging over users is not very sharp but is does have a little edge to it. Among the more prominent requirements imposed on users is: 1. the duty to inform job applicants before they order information from a CRA; 2. notify the consumer before they "take adverse action," (e.g., not hire the person based in whole or part upon the information received), and; 3. provide the consumer with the Federal Trade Commission-authored "summary of their rights" notice. A copy of this notice is shown in the Appendix.

The Shield Protecting Users

Most of the shield afforded to users is provided by the CRA. If an employment decision is made based on erroneous information, an employer obtaining the information on his own will be defending his data retrieval practices, but the employer using a CRA is usually able to defer this liability to the CRA, provided they chose their CRA with some due diligence.

The Sword Hanging over Consumers

The consumer's ability to successfully sue CRAs is somewhat constrained by the FCRA. Consumers will not "win the lottery" by suing a CRA even when the CRA has, in fact, reported erroneous information that harmed the individual—provided the CRA has taken reasonable precautions to report accurate information. While the FCRA mandates that CRAs must verify information if disputed by consumers, the FCRA gives them time— about 30 days—to verify and correct the information.

For the most part however, the FCRA does not threaten, but instead protects consumers.

The Shield Protecting Consumers

This is probably the biggest goal of the FCRA. Most of the law deals with consumer protections, from releases that must be provided to the individual, to the information that can be reported, to the procedures in case of disputed accuracy.

Primary Effects of the FCRA on Employers Using a Vendor to Obtain Criminal Records

Criminal records obtained from a vendor and used for employment purposes are "consumer reports" as defined by the FCRA. So are other reports obtained from vendors, such as driving records, credit reports, and employment histories. The following discussion on releases and notifications is not exclusive to criminal records.

There are three primary areas where the FCRA will affect employers who obtain criminal records from criminal record vendors. As discussed above, the FCRA affects the entire relationship, and the three areas discussed below pertain to the major considerations of employers using criminal records obtained from a vendor.

Releases and Notifications

Written Notification Before Ordering

Before ordering a criminal record from a vendor that you intend to use as a factor in establishing an individual's eligibility for employment, the FCRA requires that:

> (i) a clear and conspicuous disclosure has been made in writing to the consumer at any time before the report is procured or caused to be procured, in a document that consists solely of the disclosure, that a consumer report may be obtained for employment purposes; *(Section 604(b)(2)(A))*

So, "a clear and conspicuous disclosure" must be made to the applicant. In the next paragraph, the FCRA requires the consumer to authorize the company to obtain the report.

> (ii) the consumer has authorized in writing (which authorization may be made on the document referred to in clause (i)) the procurement of the report by that person. *(Section 604(b)(2)(B))*

This is a detailed section of the law, in that it goes to the level of mandating what can and cannot be on the written disclosure. CRAs, for their part, must obtain certification from the employer that it has given the required notice and received written authorization from the employee or applicant to obtain the report. So, the FCRA imposes the obligation on the employer to disclose and obtain releases, but it also imposes the obligation on the CRA to obtain certification from the employer that it will be done.

Notices Required Before and After "Adverse Action" is Taken

The FCRA also requires that before taking any "adverse action" based in whole or part on the criminal record, the employer must provide the applicant or employee a copy of the report and a written description of the consumer's rights as written by the Federal Trade Commission. The Federal Trade Commission (FTC) is the primary agency that enforces and interprets FCRA issues. A copy of this notice can be found in the Appendix.

> *Adverse Action* is defined by the FCRA as "a denial of employment or any other decision for employment purposes that adversely affects any current or prospective employee." *{Section 603(k)(1)(B)(ii)}*

Aside from the above requirements *before* taking adverse action, there are other, somewhat redundant, steps that must be taken *after* the adverse action.

> (1) provide oral, written, or electronic notice of the adverse action to the consumer;

> (2) provide to the consumer orally, in writing, or electronically the name, address, and telephone number of the consumer reporting agency (including a toll-free telephone

number established by the agency if the agency compiles and maintains files on consumers on a nationwide basis) that furnished the report to the person; and a statement that the consumer reporting agency did not make the decision to take the adverse action and is unable to provide the consumer the specific reasons why the adverse action was taken; and

(3) provide to the consumer an oral, written, or electronic notice of the consumer's right to obtain, under section 612 [§ 1681j], a free copy of a consumer report on the consumer from the consumer reporting agency referred to in paragraph (2), which notice shall include an indication of the 60-day period under that section for obtaining such a copy; and to dispute, under section 611 [§ 1681i], with a consumer reporting agency the accuracy or completeness of any information in a consumer report furnished by the agency. {615(a)}

A FCRA Notification Exception

The prior written notice and release, as well as the adverse action requirements, have been modified for trucking companies who pre-screen commercial drivers applying for a job remotely. It should be noted here that while the FCRA may waive the prior written notice, there are some states that still require a written release be obtained before ordering certain information that will be used for employment screening. Driving record (MVR) reporting — in some states — is an example of information where written permission prior to ordering is required in all cases involving employment.

No doubt about it, the following information detailing the commercial driver limited exemption is dry-as-a-sawpit stuff. If you are not a trucking company hiring drivers by phone, mail or computer, skip it. If you are a trucking company, find a vendor that knows your business.

The government-speak for the disclosure and release waiver in those instances when a trucking company is pre-screening applicants from a remote location is as follows:

(i) the consumer is applying for a position over which the Secretary of Transportation has the power to establish qualifications and maximum hours of service pursuant to the provisions of section 31502 of title 49, or a position subject to safety regulation by a State transportation agency; and

(ii) as of the time at which the person procures the report or causes the report to be procured the only interaction between the consumer and the person in connection with that employment application has been by mail, telephone, computer, or other similar means. {604(b)(2)(B) and (C)}

In addition, the adverse action requirements have been amended, as follows:

(B) Application by mail, telephone, computer, or other similar means.

(i)   If a consumer described in subparagraph (C) applies for employment by mail, telephone, computer, or other similar means, and if a person who has procured a consumer report on the consumer for employment purposes takes adverse action on the employment application based in whole or in part on the report, then the person must provide to the consumer to whom the report relates, in lieu of the notices required under subparagraph (A) of this section and under section 615(a), within 3 business days of taking such action, an oral, written or electronic notification—

    a.   that adverse action has been taken based in whole or in part on a consumer report received from a consumer reporting agency;

    b.   of the name, address and telephone number of the consumer reporting agency that furnished the consumer report (including a toll-free telephone number established by the agency if the agency compiles and maintains files on consumers on a nationwide basis);

    c.   that the consumer reporting agency did not make the decision to take the adverse action and is unable to provide to the consumer the specific reasons why the adverse action was taken; and

    d.   that the consumer may, upon providing proper identification, request a free copy of a report and may dispute with the consumer reporting agency the accuracy or completeness of any information in a report.

(ii)   If, under clause (B)(i)(IV), the consumer requests a copy of a consumer report from the person who procured the report, then, within 3 business days of receiving the consumer's request, together with proper identification, the person must send or provide to the consumer a copy of a report and a copy of the consumer's rights as prescribed by the Federal Trade Commission under section 609(c)(3)

(C) Scope. Subparagraph (B) shall apply to a person procuring a consumer report on a consumer in connection with the consumer's application for employment only if

(i)   the consumer is applying for a position over which the Secretary of Transportation has the power to establish qualifications and maximum hours of service pursuant to the provisions of section 31502 of title 49, or a position subject to safety regulation by a State transportation agency; and

(ii)   (ii) as of the time at which the person procures the report or causes the report to be procured the only interaction between the consumer and the person in connection with that employment application has been by mail, telephone, computer, or other similar means. *{604(b)(3)(B) and (C)}*

Told you it was dry stuff. Again, this is a narrow exception for trucking companies hiring commercial drivers in certain instances.

FCRA Restrictions on Reporting Arrest Information

The FCRA also affects employers obtaining criminal records from criminal record vendors because it prescribes limits on what data can be provided. Specifically, it limits the amount of time arrest information may be reported. This does not apply to conviction information.

Arrests were defined in Chapter 4 as follows:

> An *Arrest* is the taking of an individual into custody by law enforcement personnel (i.e. the person's behavior is arrested) in order to charge them with an illegal act.

Convictions, in contrast to arrests, were defined in Chapter 4 as follows:

> A *Conviction* is a finding of guilt after a judicial trial. However, some states have expanded this definition to include such dispositions as a "deferred sentence, adjudication withheld." These are proceedings in which the defendant admits guilt, but if they behave themselves for a specified period of time, the charges are dismissed. With recent changes, these dismissals will still be considered convictions.

The FCRA states that a CRA may not report arrest information that is older than 7 years. In the fed's inimitable legal-speak, it is worded as follows:

> (a) *Information excluded from consumer reports*. Except as authorized under subsection (b) of this section, no consumer reporting agency may make any consumer report containing any of the following items of information:
>
>> (2) Civil suits, civil judgments, and records of arrest that from date of entry, antedate the report by more than seven years or until the governing statute of limitations has expired, whichever is the longer period. *{605(a)(2)}*

A clear distinction is made for conviction information. Conviction information may be reported without limitation. The FCRA spells it out it in subsection (5). Continuing from part (b) above, they are saying no CRA can report...

>> (5) Any other adverse item of information, other than records of convictions of crimes which antedates the report by more than seven years. *{605(a)(5)}*

A FCRA Arrest Information Exception

Of course, it would not be Federal law without an exception would it? Above, in part (a) it says "...except as authorized under subsection (b)..."

Subsection (b) allows arrest data older than 7 years to be reported if the report will be used in connection with a job where the annual salary is (or expected to be) $75,000 or more.

> (b) *Exempted cases*. The provisions of subsection (a) of this section are not applicable in the case of any consumer credit report to be used in connection with...
>
>> (3) the employment of any individual at an annual salary which equals, or which may reasonably be expected to equal $75,000, or more. *{605(b)(3)}*

FCRA Caveat

If the Federal FCRA was the only law pertaining to the use of arrest records, we could be on our merry way. Unfortunately, some states also have laws that restrict the reporting of arrest and conviction information. Some states do not want employers to use *any* arrest information. Some state laws still limit conviction information to seven years. In other words, some state laws are in direct conflict with the Federal FCRA. In Chapter 14, the Federal and state law interrelation will be discussed in detail. The point is, while the Federal FCRA guidelines discussed above are the norm, they are not absolute in all states.

Using Aged Public Records for Employment Purposes

Criminal record vendors providing public record information to companies intending to use the information for employment purposes—and the information is likely to have an adverse impact on the individual—must either insure the information they are providing is up-to-date, or, they must notify the subject of the report that a report is being provided along with the name and address of the person to whom it is being reported.

When will this come into play with a criminal record vendor? When a database contains public record data that is not the most complete or up-to-date available from actual public sources, **and** the record contains derogatory information, i.e., an arrest or conviction record.

> **An Example—** A vendor has obtained Watadoosie County's entire database and the database contains less than up-to-date info. ACME Employer requests a criminal record on an individual and that vendor reports a record containing an arrest and conviction. The subject of the search must be notified by the vendor that a report has been provided to ACME, along with ACME's address.
>
> The record vendor warehouses criminal records previously ordered by other clients. ACME requests a criminal record. The vendor searches its database and informs ACME that a criminal record was ordered on the subject by another employer two months previously. ACME elects to obtain the two month-old record instead of ordering a fresh record. If the two-month-old record is clear, i.e., it does not contain a record of arrest or conviction, the notice need not be sent by the vendor, as there is nothing on the report "likely to have an adverse effect upon the consumer."

What about these searches using aged data? A database search can be FCRA-compliant fully, but wholly deficient for employment due dilligence. If an employer searches a database that has not been updated in 60 days, recent information may be missed. For honest business practices and self-protection, the CRA should clearly state that they are accessing a database, and not "retrieving." If the vendor cuts a corner and the employer hires an individual because the retriever did not retrieve the proper record, and if the employer is sued, the retriever also could be sued. So, when a vendor states that its database searches are "FCRA compliant," that is great – but it is not the only consideration.

Using Records from Vendor Databases

In previous chapters, database searches were discussed and it was noted that they could assist users by addressing three aspects of criminal record searching:

- Knowing where to look
- Turnaround time
- Cost

Database searches can be dynamite—but if you avail yourself of a vendor who uses them, insure that they are complying with the following FCRA requirement.

This requirement regarding aged public record for employment purposes is found in section 613 of the FCRA. The FCRA text is as follows:

Public record information for employment purposes

(a) *In general.* A consumer reporting agency which furnishes a consumer report for employment purposes and which for that purpose compiles and reports items of information on consumers which are matters of public record and are likely to have an adverse effect upon a consumer's ability to obtain employment shall

1. at the time such public record information is reported to the user of such consumer report, notify the consumer of the fact that public record information is being reported by the consumer reporting agency, together with the name and address of the person to whom such information is being reported; or

2. maintain strict procedures designed to insure that whenever public record information which is likely to have an adverse effect on a consumer's ability to obtain employment is reported it is complete and up to date. For purposes of this paragraph, items of public record relating to arrests, indictments, convictions, suits, tax liens, and outstanding judgments shall be considered up to date if the current public record status of the item at the time of the report is reported.

Oh, one more thing. The feds do grant themselves an exemption:

(b) *Exemption for national security investigations.* Subsection (a) does not apply in the case of an agency or department of the United States Government that seeks to obtain and use a consumer report for employment purposes, if the head of the agency or department makes a written finding as prescribed under section 604(b)(4)(A).

It is a shame they could not have stopped here, with a federal law that governed all transactions of this type across the country. Unfortunately, there are state laws in direct conflict with the federal FCRA, and you must follow the state law in some instances. The next chapter details these instances.

Chapter 13

The Federal FCRA Interrelation with State FCRAs

Laws are like sausages.
It's better not to see them being made.

—Otto von Bismarck

When the German statesman Otto Von Bismarck said the public should not watch sausage or laws being made, he was making a couple of points.

Explicit in the comment was that watching either of the processes was not a pretty sight. When making "law," unwritten deals are cut between incongruous allies that are interdependent on secret deals later denied.

Implicit was the thought that after the process, the laws and sausages would not look too bad. The finished law would be a blend of the various constituencies and while not perfect, perhaps a pretty good compromise.

The Federal Fair Credit Reporting Act and its relationship with the various state Fair Credit Reporting Acts is different. The laws in and of themselves are kind of pretty, but when you take the finished product, i.e., how the Federal and state FCRAs interrelate, it gets ugly.

By most accounts, the original Federal FCRA was a thoughtful, forward-looking piece of legislation. It certainly stood the test of time well, protecting users, consumers and providers. The original law was enacted in October 1970, and while amended several times over the years, the amendments were, until the late 1990s, minor. The September 30, 1996 "amendment" was really a re-write of the law. It was after this re-write that the inter-relation between the federal and state FCRAs got ugly. The ugliness is seen, in great part, in our efforts to unravel the complexity and figure out — on a state-by-state basis — which law (federal or state) we should be trying to follow.

What Do Federal and State Interrelations Have To Do with Ordering Criminal Records?

As we saw in the previous chapter, Section 605 of the federal Fair Credit Reporting Act (FCRA) allows criminal record *conviction* information to be reported through *a consumer reporting agency* in perpetuity. Non-conviction information must be, ahem, arrested after seven years i.e., suppressed or hidden. So far, so easy. The rub comes when you have a state with their own version of the FCRA in conflict with the federal version. Now you find yourself in a position where an interpretation based on the inter-relation of the state and federal law will dictate what information you can receive from a criminal record provider.

Why is it so darn complicated?

Prior to the 1996 FCRA amendment, federal and state law (when a state law was present) was consistent. Furthermore, when there was a difference, the federal FCRA pre-empted the state law. Prior to the 1996 amendment, there was no distinction made between arrests and convictions. The FCRA simply stated that there were to be no:

> "Records of arrest, indictment, or conviction of crime which, for the date of disposition, release or parole, antedate the report by more than 7 years."

Unless

> The report was to be used in connection with

- "(1) a credit transaction involving, or which may reasonably be expected to involve, a principal amount of **$50,000** or more;

- (2) the underwriting of life insurance involving, or which may reasonably be expected to involve, a face amount of **$50,000** or more; or

- (3) the employment of any individual at an annual salary which equals, or which may reasonably be expected to equal **$20,000** or more."

That was simple enough. The 1996 FCRA Amendment changed the exceptions to:

> "The report was to be used in connection with

- (1) a credit transaction involving, or which may reasonably be expected to involve, a principal amount of **$150,000** or more;

- (2) the underwriting of life insurance involving, or which may reasonably be expected to involve, a face amount of **$150,000** or more; or

- (3) the employment of any individual at an annual salary which equals, or which may reasonably be expected to equal **$75,000** or more."

Okay, no need to call in a rocket scientist yet. One problem is that not all the states changed their state FCRAs to mirror the federal amounts. So, what amount do you use — the federal amount or your state's amount?

Problem two is that exactly one year after the 1996 amendment was implemented there was another amendment titled (you gotta love this) "The Consumer Reporting Employment Clarification Act of 1998." This clarification changed the *type* of information that could be reported to today's federal standard. It also created an FCRA distinction between arrest information and conviction information.

Today, the FCRA allows conviction information to be reported by a CRA regardless of the record's age. Non-conviction records must be suppressed if they did not happen within the past seven years and do not meet the exceptions as outlined above. Again, however, not all states have changed their laws to fit this new national standard. Some states still limit the release of *records with convictions* to seven years, no more.

In summary, there is a stew of federal law and state laws dealing with exceptions to rules for the types of information that may be reported.

When in Conflict, Which Law — Federal or State — Pre-empts the Other?

The Federal FCRA provides the answer ... if you can decipher it.

Thank heaven the federal FCRA clears all this up with section 624, *Relation to State Laws.* It says this:

> Except as provided in subsections (b) and (c), this title does not annul, alter, affect, or exempt any person subject to the provisions of this title from complying with the laws of any State with respect to the collection, distribution, or use of any information on consumers, except to the extent that those laws are inconsistent with any provision of this title, and then only to the extent of the inconsistency. *{§624(a)}*

Okay, this is saying that the federal law does not overrule a state law unless they differ, and if they do, only the differing parts of the state law are overruled. There was that first sentence, though, about "except as provided in subsections (b) and (c)." Section (c) we can skip. However, Subsection (b) says:

> *General exceptions.* No requirement or prohibition may be imposed under the laws of any State
>
> (1) with respect to any subject matter regulated under
>
>> (E) section 605, relating to information in consumer reports, except that this subparagraph shall not apply to any State law in effect on the date of enactment of the Consumer Credit Reporting Reform Act of 1996. *{§624(b)(1)(E)})*

I dunno about you, but my head is starting to hurt. Once this has been read about forty times however, it can easily be determined that this says that the federal law prevails over the state law unless the state law was in effect on or before September 30, 1996. It is bad enough that the *General Exceptions* stopped here, but it tries to get worse. The pertinent parts in Subsection (d) read as follows:

Limitations. Subsections (b) and (c)
(2) do not apply to any provision of State law (including any provision of a State constitution) that

- is enacted after January 1, 2004;
- states explicitly that the provision is intended to supplement this title; and
- gives greater protection to consumers than is provided under this title.

Now I am looking around for Werner Von Braun's pager number. The sum of all this is that federal law does not supercede any state law enacted before September 30, 1996 or, any state law passed after January 1, 2004 if the future law states explicitly that the provision is intended to supplement the federal FCRA, and gives greater protection to the consumer than the federal FCRA. "Greater protection" in our criminal record context means fewer years reported or convictions only, or higher money exceptions.

Examples—

State A has a 7-year restriction in 1992. They have not updated their law to date. State law prevails.

State B had no law in 1996, but its legislature passed one that was more restrictive than the federal law in 1998. The federal law applies.

Summary of FCRA and State Law Interrelations — Good News for Users

It is a devilishly complex task to determine what information should be reported, but if you are a user of criminal records — say, as part of your duties as an employer — *there is good news*. You don't have to understand and monitor the intricacies of compliance because you are not at risk. Why? Because, *in regard to reporting information*, the FCRA and the state equivalents do not apply to you. They apply to the CRAs. CRAs are prohibited from reporting the information. As a recipient or user of the information, you are not prohibited by the FCRA from using the information.

What you do have to concern yourself with is the **use** of criminal record information — both arrest and conviction information. For employers, there are federal guidelines and there are also several states that prohibit employers from using arrest information if the arrest information does not have a resulting conviction, or if the disposition is pending.

The following chapter deals with federal considerations when using criminal records for employment purposes. Following the federal chapter, state guidelines are detailed.

Chapter 14

Title VII and Criminal Records

Injustice anywhere is a threat to justice everywhere.
We are caught in an inescapable network of
mutuality, tied in a single garment of destiny.
Whatever affects one directly, affects all indirectly.

—Martin Luther King Jr.

Determining how you feel about the issue as a moral or political matter is one thing. However, when you are an employer, many issues have already been decided for you. It is your responsibility to be aware of what is legal and what is not. When it is your business, you are considered accountable. When considering minorities, the main Federal law dealing with the legality of criminal records is Title VII of the Civil Rights Act.

Criminal Records and Bias Employment Practices

What is "fair?" Title VII of the Civil Rights Act prohibits apparently neutral or "color blind" employment practices if these practices have a disparate impact against minorities or other protected groups.

Why this prohibition exists requires some explaining. Consider this scenario. Assume you were to receive employment applications by mail and had an independent third party delete any references to race. In addition, names, all addresses and any other clues that someone might use to infer an individual's race were suppressed. Now, assume that criminal records checks were ordered and those found to have a criminal record of any severity were automatically disqualified. You might think that because you did not even know the race of the person being disqualified, you could not possibly be discriminating against minorities. You would be wrong.

The Use of Statistics

The Equal Employment Opportunity Commission (EEOC) enforces Title VII. It is their position that "an employer's policy or practice of excluding individuals from employment on the basis of their conviction records has an adverse impact on Blacks and Hispanics in light of statistics showing that they are convicted at a rate disproportionately greater than their representation in the population." (Policy Statement on the Issue of Conviction Records Under Title VII [February 4,1987]).

The leading Title VII case on the issue of conviction records is Green v. Missouri Pacific Railroad Company. (523 F.2d 1290, 10 EPD ¶ 10, 314 (8th Cir. 1975). In this case, the court held that the defendant's policy of refusing employment to any person convicted of a crime other than a minor traffic offense had an adverse impact on Black applicants and was not justified by business necessity. In a second appeal following remand, the court upheld the district court's injunctive order prohibiting the defendant from using an applicant's conviction record as an absolute bar to employment, but allowed it to consider a prior criminal record as long as it constituted a "business necessity." The EEOC later expanded on "business necessity," and this subject will be addressed later.

The main point here however, is that an employer's policy or practice of excluding individuals from employment on the basis of their conviction records may have an adverse impact on Black and Hispanics in light of statistics showing that they are convicted at a rate disproportionately greater than their representation in the population.

"May have" an adverse impact? Yes, statistics can also be used by the employer for defense. The EEOC has stated that "when the employer can present more narrowly drawn statistics showing either that Blacks and Hispanics are not convicted at a disproportionately greater rate or that there is no adverse impact in its own hiring process resulting from the convictions policy, then a no cause determination would be appropriate." By "more narrowly drawn statistics," the EEOC means that "local, regional or applicant flow data" may be different than the national statistics, and more appropriate. So, if an employer could prove that Whites in their town were evenly convicted in relation to their population with minority groups, the "blind" exclusion policy would probably cause no EEOC problems.

Granted, few employers have a statistician on staff who is monitoring local and national rates of conviction, so it would be a task to turn around the "adverse impact" position with statistics. The key point for an employer to take away from all this is that the EEOC does presume that employers using criminal records as an absolute bar to employment has a disparate impact. So, this aspect of Title VII is something for the employer to be aware of when using criminal records *even though* their employment procedures may seem neutral. A "cookie cutter" or blanket policy of exclusion based on a criminal conviction is not the intelligent way for an employer to operate.

What are the EEOC's Guidelines?

Thus far, the EEOC and *conviction* records have been discussed. The EEOC also differentiates between arrest and conviction records.

EEOC Policy on the Use of Arrest Records

In short, the EEOC summarizes their policy regarding the use of arrest records by saying that:

> "the use of arrest records as an absolute bar to employment has a disparate impact on some protected groups and arrest records cannot be used to routinely exclude persons from employment. However, conduct which indicates unsuitability for a particular position is a basis for exclusion. Where it appears that the applicant or employee engaged in the conduct for which he was arrested and that the conduct is job-related and relatively recent, exclusion is justified."

Obviously, there are some subjective factors here. First, notice that the EEOC notes that Blacks and Hispanics are not only convicted of crimes at a disparate rate than non-protected groups, but that they are also arrested at a disparate rate.

Again, with the use of arrest records, no blanket exclusions—no matter how color blind—should be adopted.

Second (provided that you have not hired a statistician to disprove a disparate impact in your area using local statistics) there must be a "business justification" for using the arrest records as a factor in your decision making.

There must be a "Business Justification" for your use of arrest records.

Business justification revolves around two issues—

1. Job relatedness. Does the conduct for which the person is accused render them unsuitable for the particular position for which they are being considered?

2. Credibility. Did the individual actually commit the action for which he was arrested?

The Job Relatedness Issue

The EEOC has ruled that "an employer may deny employment opportunities to persons based on any prior conduct which indicates that they would be unfit for the position in question, whether that conduct is evidenced by an arrest, conviction or other information provided to the employer. It is the conduct, not the arrest or conviction per se, which the employer may consider in relation to the position sought."

So, if you believe that the individual committed the conduct, even if you know the individual committed the conduct because you watched him do it, there is another consideration: job relatedness.

Sometimes this is easy. A convicted pedophile's prior conduct would make them unfit to work in a Daycare profession. The individual applying for a job digging a ditch should probably not have his past bad check charge exclude him. Sometimes "job-related-ness" is not easy to determine, and, the problem is, you can not just impose a strict standard, i.e., "I will hire anyone with a criminal record unless it directly relates to the position being sought" because the courts, through the negligent hiring doctrine have sometimes been extremely liberal in what they consider "job-related." Consider what an appeals court found "job related."

The Case of Malorney vs. B & L Motor Freight, Inc

In this case a hitchhiker sued the employer of an over-the-road truck driver for sexual assault committed by the truck driver.

Here is the case summary. A man named Edward Harbour applied for a position of over-the-road driver with defendant, B & L. On the employment application, Harbour was questioned as to whether he had any vehicular offenses or other criminal convictions. His response to the vehicular question was verified by B & L, but Harbour's negative reply to the criminal conviction question was not checked by B & L. It turns out that Harbour did have a history of convictions for sex-related crimes. Harbour had been arrested just the previous year for aggravated sodomy of two teenage hitchhikers while driving an over-the-road truck for another employer. Upon being hired by B & L, Harbour was given the company's written instructions, which included a prohibition against picking up hitchhikers in a B & L truck.

Later, Harbour picked up the plaintiff, a 17-year-old hitchhiker. In the sleeping compartment of the truck, he repeatedly raped, assaulted and viciously beat her. After being released, the plaintiff notified police and Harbour was arrested, convicted and sentenced to fifty years with no parole. The plaintiff sued B & L for negligent hiring.

B & L contended that they could not foresee that one of its drivers would rape and assault a hitchhiker, that sexual assault isn't job-related to driving a truck anyway. The Circuit Court denied B & L's motion for summary judgment. B & L appealed. The Appellate Court agreed with the circuit court (did not rule for B & L), and stated:

> "...it is clear that B & L has a duty to entrust its truck to a competent employee fit to driver an over-the-road truck *equipped with a sleeping compartment.* Lack of forethought may exist where one remains in voluntary ignorance of facts concerning the danger in a particular act or instrumentality, where a reasonably prudent person would become advised on the theory that such ignorance is the equivalent of negligence. B & L gave Harbour an over-the-road vehicle *with a sleeping compartment*

and B & L knew, or should have known, that *truckers are prone to give rides to hitchhikers despite rules against such actions* and so the question now becomes one of fact—whether B & L breached its duty to hire a competent driver who was to be entrusted with a B & L over-the-road truck." (*Italics added*).

As talk-show host Johnny Carson would have said, "that's wild, weird, wacky stuff." Virtually all trucks employed in interstate commerce, many in intrastate commerce and some in intra-city commerce, are equipped with a sleeping berth for the driver. How this fact was used as a justification or "business necessity" to order a criminal record is instructive to the careful employer who has to consider job relatedness.

Before you dismiss a criminal offense as unrelated to the job, give this case a quick remembrance if only in your subconscious. The courts have caused many employers grief by making some interesting determinations.

Four Important EEOC Notices

The Appendix contains copies of four important notices written by the EEOC. These notices have set the bar so to speak on what an employer and cannot do with criminal records.

- Evaluation of employer's policy of refusing to hire individuals with conviction records

- Commission's procedure for determining whether arrest records may be considered in employment decisions

- Job advertising and pre-employment inquiries

- A business justifying the exclusion of an individual from employment on the basis of a conviction record

For more information about the EEOC, visit their website at www.eeoc.gov.

Chapter 15

State Restrictions on Criminal Record Use by Employers

Crime wouldn't pay if the government ran it.

—Anon

As an employer, you have learned the EEOC guidelines and now know all the legal precautions you must take, right? Not so fast, there. Some states have their own regulations on what information employers may use. These restrictions can be more restrictive than the federal EEOC guidelines.

Okay, here comes the obligatory legal caveat. Ready? The following information is true to the best of our knowledge and research. However, these restrictions can change in the blink of a legislator's eye on the last day of the session. Some of the information is a matter of interpretation. In addition, there is always the chance—however slight—that a mistake has been made. So, before treating the following information as gospel, first review the more detailed information in the state profiles section and seek legal advice.

States That Prohibit the Use of Arrest Records (i.e., non-conviction records)

Several states have made a legislative decision that certain arrest records are irrelevant and should not be considered by employers when making employment decisions. They are addressing the credibility issue, i.e., did the individual actually commit the action he is being accused of? This issue was discussed in the EEOC section.

States that have made this decision regarding arrest records have addressed the issue by restricting their state from releasing the information, by prohibiting employers from using the information, or a combination of both.

At the time of this writing, the following states prohibit employers from reviewing arrest records without a resulting conviction unless the charge is pending, or they restrict the release of non-conviction records. So…

- If an arrest has been made and the individual is not convicted, then the information should not be reviewed by an employer.

- If an arrest has been made and there is no disposition yet, then the arrest may be reviewed because the result is pending.

Please note that even here there are shades of prohibition. Some states' laws clearly prohibit the practice, while others pre-employment Inquiry Guides note that it is "improper." This is a complex and occasionally contradictory area. The same state may have laws prohibiting the use of arrest information while in another area requiring "all" records of the past seven years to be reviewed. Details and citations are provided in the state profiles section.

The following attempts to generally summarize when there are arrest restrictions. The states that have some type of prohibition against employers reviewing arrest records (either through restricting release or employer use) not connected to a conviction and without a pending charge are—

- **Alaska**

- **California**
  There is an exception for certain arrests when the applicant will be employed at a health facility and have access to patients, drugs or medication.

- **Connecticut**

- **Georgia**
  There are exceptions for certain offenses within employment dealing with children, the elderly, and the mentally ill.

- **Hawaii**

- **Indiana**

- **Illinois**

- **Kentucky**

- **Massachusetts**
  However, facilities caring for the elderly and disabled, and long-term care facilities must obtain all available criminal offender information concerning an individual before hiring.

- **Michigan**
  This prohibition in Michigan only applies to misdemeanor arrests.

- **Minnesota**
  However, there are exceptions for certain employment — from taxicab drivers to doctors.

- **Nevada**
- **New York**
- **Pennsylvania**
- **Rhode Island**
  Unless the applicant is applying for a job in law enforcement
- **Utah**
- **Virginia**
- **Washington**
- **Wisconsin**
  Unless the applicant is applying for a bondable position

State That Prohibit the Use of Misdemeanor Convictions

Several states also restrict the use by employers of misdemeanor convictions.

If the arrest prohibition is an attempt by some states to address the credibility issue, the misdemeanor prohibition is an attempt to address the "job related" issue. These states have decided that in some cases, misdemeanor infractions should not be considered by employers—that they are never "job related."

The states that to some degree limit employers from reviewing misdemeanor records are—

- **California**
  In those cases in which probation has been successfully completed or otherwise discharged and the case has been judicially dismissed. In addition, employers are prohibited from asking about certain less serious marijuana offenses.

- **Hawaii**
  Employers cannot consider misdemeanor convictions for which a jail sentence cannot be imposed. (They are restrictive on felony convictions too.)

- **Massachusetts**
  Employers cannot inquire into or maintain records regarding any misdemeanor conviction where the date of such conviction or completion of incarceration, whichever date is later, occurred five or more years prior to the date of application for employment, unless such person has been convicted of any offense within the five years immediately preceding the date of such application for employment.

- **Minnesota**
  Employers cannot consider misdemeanor convictions for which a jail sentence cannot be imposed.

- **New York**
  Employers may not consider misdemeanor convictions older than 5 years unless the person has also been convicted of some other crime within the past 5 years.

States That Prohibit the Use of Expunged or Sealed Records

An expunged or sealed criminal record is one that a court has ordered to be kept a secret. When ordering a criminal record on an individual, some locales will report that that they may not report the criminal record because it has been sealed or expunged.

This absurdity is along the lines of "they made me promise not to tell you that your dog got ran over by a car, so I won't."

Sealed or expunged criminal records are controversial, but reporting that an individual's criminal record is not available because it has been sealed or expunged seems one tick disingenuous. Especially ludicrous are those records I have seen that report that there is no criminal record by stating "Record Expunged." Crazy, yet it happens. As a result, some states explicitly prohibit the consideration of expunged or sealed records. These states are:

- **California**
- **Colorado**
- **Connecticut**
- **Florida**
  There are several exceptions, see details in state profile.
- **Hawaii**
- **Illinois**
- **Kansas**
- **Ohio**
  Employers are prohibited from inquiring about job applicants' juvenile arrest records that have been expunged.
- **Oklahoma**
- **Oregon**
  Employers cannot refuse to hire based upon a juvenile record that have been expunged.
- **Rhode Island**
- **Texas**
- **Virginia**

A few more states, while not explicitly prohibiting employers from reviewing the records, do allow job applicants to "lawfully deny or fail to acknowledge" sealed or expunged records. Frankly, it is probably unwise to put too fine a point on the legalities of using a sealed or expunged record. An employer using a legally sealed or expunged record to deny employment will probably be challenged, if the reason for the denial is known. Incidentally, if you are using a criminal record vendor, the vendor will probably suppress notations regarding sealed or expunged records.

States that Limit the Use of First Offense Records

Two states give first offenders a mulligan.

- **Georgia**
  Certain first offender crimes in which the offender has been discharged without court adjudication of guilt are not reportable under Georgia law and a notification of discharge and exoneration is to be placed upon the record by the court. The discharge is not considered a conviction of a crime and may not be used to disqualify a person in any application for employment.

- **Massachusetts**
  Employers may not inquire or maintain records related to a first conviction for any of the following misdemeanors: drunkenness, simple assault, speeding, minor traffic violations, affray, or disturbance of the peace. (In other words, aside from the simple assault misdemeanor, it sounds like most college students catch a break.)

States That Restrict the Use of Records Based on Time Periods

Some states restrict the use of criminal records based on their age. A sampling:

- **California**
  A consumer report may contain criminal information older than 7 years.

- **Hawaii**
  Employers may not examine conviction records older than 10 years.

- **Massachusetts**
  Certain misdemeanors (as detailed in the misdemeanor section above) older than five years.

- **Maine**
  In most instances, an employer must only consider the past 3 years.

State Reporting Restrictions

There is a big difference in a state law that restricts the *use* of a criminal record by *employers* and a state law that restricts what a *vendor* can *report*. Several states restrict what a vendor can report, i.e., they have different limitations than the federal FCRA based on time periods. However, there are many exceptions and many of the states are changing their laws to mirror the federal guidelines. (For more information on this complex interrelation, see Chapter 13.)

States that recently still **restricted vendor reporting** of criminal conviction information **to seven years** were California, Colorado, Kansas, Maryland, Massachusetts, Montana, New Hampshire, New Mexico, New York, Texas, and Washington. **However**, Kansas, Maryland Massachusetts, New Hampshire, and Washington waive the time limit if the applicant is reasonably expected to make $20,000 or more annually. In New York, the exception is $25,000. In Colorado and Texas, the figure is $75,000.

Is it any wonder that many employers and vendors concentrate on complying with the federal FCRA?

States That Limit Record Access to Employers Only Within Certain Industries

Finally, in some states, they have tried to do your thinking for you. If you are in an industry they have deemed to be critical (or the industry had good lobbyists,) you are privileged for criminal record access and use from the state repository. These states permit access, by statute, to certain industries such as childcare, nurseries, etc.

If, on the other hand, you are some poor soul trying to eek out a living by running a business in some "non-critical" industry, you may be up a river for state repository access.

However, as discussed earlier, criminal records from the counties will almost certainly be available and the fact that the state prohibits access to its repository should not prove a deterrent to getting the information you need. In fact, as was discussed earlier, county records are superior to statewide records in some respects. For more industry information see the state profiles section.

Legal Concerns Versus Gut Reactions

Employers will find times when their legal concerns conflict with their gut feelings.

I will not tell you what to do if you are the owner of a laundromat hiring an employee to collect the change from your equipment and you find a misdemeanor conviction for theft. I won't even give advice to you if you are running a daycare or hiring a nanny to watch your children, and your state prohibits your use of all available arrest information.

I will tell you to weigh your options and give it some thought. Here is an example:

Example—

I once knew an old, no-nonsense safety director at a huge trucking company. He was a "law and order" man, not given to (or accepting of) most any illegal dalliance you would care to name. He was in charge of screening and hiring the truck drivers. They had terminals in a state that restricted the use of misdemeanor records. We discussed the issue of finding a misdemeanor DWI (driving while intoxicated) on a potential driver.

I educated him on the law. He educated me on what he thought about the law. He ended with this thought that has stuck with me. "Son, I'd much rather be sitting there in the witness box explaining why I didn't hire that driver than be sitting there explaining to the jury why I did hire him after he's killed somebody."

Food for thought.

If You Get Into Trouble

Here in the Land of the Free and Home of the Brave, anyone can sue most anyone for anything.

If you are an employer and order criminal records, chances are, they will keep you out of court one heck of a lot more than they will bring you to court. However, there is always the chance that a prospective or current employee will sue you in relation to ordering a criminal record. If you have ordered a criminal record and taken an "adverse action" against the subject of the report for something you have found on the report, there is a slim chance you will get sued (or more likely, threaten to get sued). There are several reasons criminal record lawsuits are rare.

Consider first that most people do not have criminal records. The percentage of records you will find that contain a criminal record will vary greatly depending on your applicant pool. (You could expect differing percentages for Nuns and pro football players for instance.) A good average to use for illustrative purposes is 13%.

This means that 87% of the time a criminal record is ordered, it will come back with no criminal record activity. We are litigious, but not yet so much so that the 87% will cause any trouble.

That leaves 13%. As we have discussed, you will not take adverse action on all 13% of these individuals. Some of the criminal activity will be minor, non-job-related activity. Let us say you have ordered 1000 criminal records. Of this amount 130 will have criminal records. You may take "adverse action " against 100 of the 130 applicants.

Of the 100 individuals, most who are turned down for employment will apply elsewhere. Whether the applicant goes down the street or gets ticked at you depends on how many other roughly equal opportunities to yours exist. The attorney-folk would ask if the position being applied for is "fungible." The position, and how many similar others there are will influence the applicant's reaction. In my experience, far fewer than 1 in 100 applicants turned down by a job for a criminal record sue or threaten to sue. You can see, though, that even if it *were* 1 in 100 refused applicants, that is only 1 in 1000 criminal records ordered.

Compare this to the damage that could have been caused by even one of the 100 in 1000 applicants you turned away. Truly, the fear of being sued is far greater than the chance of being sued.

If You Do Get Hit by Legal Lightning

When you did *not* use a vendor

The first advice I can give if you get sued is to procure an attorney who specializes in your trouble. Due, at least in part, to the litigious society in which we live, specialties have come about in law. Just as would not go to your general practitioner Doctor to perform a triple bypass on your heart, I would advise you not to hire your tax attorney to handle your criminal record employment case. Find an attorney well versed in employment law.

If you obtained the record from a vendor

If there is a dispute as to the accuracy of the record or a question as to whether the report you received pertains to your applicant (the most two most common reasons for disputes) and you used a vendor, call your vendor. They should be able to direct you to an attorney well versed in Fair Credit Reporting Act (FCRA) protections.

Many attorneys specializing in employment law are not aware of the provisions of the FCRA, and you need to find one who is.

One benefit of this advice is that you are more likely to win your case if it goes to trial. The huge benefit of this advice is that an attorney who knows his stuff in this area will likely short circuit the case long before it goes to trial. Even if you have an in-house employment attorney, or one on retainer, I recommend a consultation with an attorney who knows the FCRA.

Author Tip

What criminal information can be reported by consumer reporting agencies and used by employers is — as mentioned earlier in this chapter — extremely complex and sometimes downright contradictory, even within one state. It does not help that state laws can change and even then, the changes may only apply to certain industries in certain conditions.

Sometimes you may make a mistake. If you do, I have spent a lot of time on employment FCRA cases, sat in many depositions and worked with many attorneys — of the plaintiff and defense varieties. My unsolicited opinion is that the premier attorney (both on keeping you from making a mistake, or bailing you out if you do) on this subject, with over twenty years experience, is:

> Larry Henry of the firm Boone, Smith, Davis Hurst & Dickman.
> Email: Lhenry@Boonesmith.com
> Firm Website: www.Boonesmith.com
> Telephone: (918) 587-0000.

Section 4

Government Agency Profiles

This section has two chapters.

Chapter 16 - State Profiles -
consists of detail pages on each state. Here you will find
information about a state's criminal record agency, the
sexual offender registry, central state incarceration records
agency, and state court system. The agencies are examined
for the following information: access requirements,
restrictions, fees, online modes, policies and procedures.
Special attention is given to employer needs.

Chapter 17 – U.S. District Courts -
presents an overview of criminal record access at the
federal court level. Each District and Division Court is listed,
along with the specific counties served.

Editor's note: The data in Section 4 is provided by BRB Publications, Inc. www.brbpub.com

Alaska

Alaska Statues and Related Employer Restrictions

General Rule - Criminal Justice Information may be provided for any purpose, except it may not be released if the information is nonconviction information or correctional treatment information. AK ST §12.62.160 (b)(8).

Criminal Justice Information, including information relating to a serious offense, may be provided to an interested person if the information is requested for the purpose of determining whether to grant a person supervisory or disciplinary power over a minor or dependent adult. AK ST §12.62.160 (b)(9)

The following information may not be disclosed   AK ST §40.25.120

1) records of vital statistics and adoption proceedings
2) records pertaining to juveniles
3) medical and related public health records
4) records required to be kept confidential by law

Sealed Records of an arrest, charge, conviction, or sentence may be denied by the subject of the record. AK ST §12.62.180 (d). Information that is sealed may only be provided:

a. For record management purposes
b. Criminal justice employment purposes
c. For review by the subject of the record
d. Research and statistical purposes
e. When necessary to prevent imminent harm to a person
f. For a use authorized by statute

Definitions - AK ST §12.62.900

Criminal Justice Information – includes criminal history record, nonconviction information, and correctional treatment information.

Criminal History Record – included past conviction information, current offender information, and criminal identification information.

Past Conviction Information – includes the terms of any sentence, probation, suspended imposition of sentence, discretionary or mandatory parole, and information that a criminal conviction has been reversed, vacated, or set aside.

Serious Offense – a conviction for a violation or an attempt to commit a felony or a crime involving domestic violence.

Interested Person – person that employs, appoints, or permits a person who would have supervisory or disciplinary power over a minor or dependent adult.

Agency guidelines for pre-employment inquiries: Alaska Department of Labor and Workforce Development, Alaska Employer Handbook, "Pre-Employment Questioning" available online at www.labor.state.ak.us/handbook/legal7.htm

Alaska State Criminal Records Agency

Department of Public Safety

Records and Identification

5700 E Tudor Rd

Anchorage, AK 99507

Phone: 907-269-5765

Fax: 907-269-5091

Web: www.dps.state.ak.us/

Total Records:	251,100
Who Can Access:	Records are available to the general public, with limitations.
Search Requirements:	To receive full record, requester must provide verification of status as "Interested Party" defined as person who employs, appoints or permits the subject to have supervisory power over others, primarily in the child care industry. Include the following in your request: set of fingerprints, full name, identifiers such as DOB, SSN, alias, also mailing address and phone. Approximately 62% of records are fingerprint-supported.
	"Any Person" reports are processed for those who are not "Interested Person" qualified and who have a proper letter of explanation and a topic-specific release from the subject. Fingerprints are helpful. The state also has a "Request for Criminal Justice Information Form" (one for the subject and one for third parties) for this purpose, which can be requested by email at tracey_brown@dps.state.ak.us.
What Is Released:	All records are released, including those without dispositions to "Interested Person" requesters. "Any Person" requesters receive criminal records only with dispositions. Records are available for 10 years from the unconditional discharge date of the incident. The following data is not released: sealed records.
Indexing & Storage:	86% of arrests in database have final dispositions recorded; 85% for those arrests in last 5 years.
Access By:	Mail, in person.
Mail Search:	Results of search are also sent to the subject.
In Person Search:	Results are usually returned by mail.
Fee & Payment:	The fee is $35.00 per search. The subject may - in person - request a search for $20.00, without fingerprints. This also applies to government agencies and

3rd parties. If authorized, a requester may also request a national check by the FBI for an additional $24.00. Fee payee: State of Alaska. Prepayment required. Use money order. No check and no credit cards accepted.

Alaska Sexual Offender Registry

Department of Public Safety   **Phone**: 907-269-0396

Permits and Licensing-SOCR Unit,

5700 E Tudor Rd   **Fax**:   907-269-5091

Anchorage, AK 99507   **Web**:   www.dps.state.ak.us/nSorcr/asp/

AS 18.65.087 authorizes the Dept. of Public Safety to maintain a central registry of sex offenders required to register under AS 12.63.010 and to make information about the offender available to the public.

What is released: The following information about those offenders available to the public: name, address, photograph, place of employment, date of birth, crime for which convicted, date of conviction, and place and court of conviction. Only offenders convicted of the sex offenses specified under AS 12.63.100 are required to register. Persons who have been arrested or charged with a sex offense are not required to register unless the arrest or charge results in a conviction. Records are available since August 10, 1994. There are no levels or classes of sexual offenders in this state. All registration forms of offenders who register locally are forwarded to this address. Not available: sealed records.

Access by: Mail, In Person, Online. In person search note: results are usually returned by mail. Online search note: name searching and geographic searching is available at the website.

Search Notes: Mail turnaround time: 2-4 days.

Alaska State Incarceration Records Agency

Alaska Department of Corrections   **Phone:** 907-269-7426

DOC Classification Office   **Fax:**   907-269-7439

4500 Diplomacy Dr, Suite 340   **Web:**   www.correct.state.ak.us

Anchorage, AK 99508-5918

What is released: Location, physical identifiers, charges, bail data, conviction and sentencing data are released. Records are available on current and former inmates. It takes 1 to 2 days before new records are released.

Search Notes: Include in request: full name; DOB and SSN helpful. No fee for search. Mail turnaround time: 1-3 days.

Access by: Mail.

Alaska State Court System

Court Structure: Alaska is not organized into counties, but rather into 15 boroughs (3 unified home rule municipalities that are combination borough and city, and 12 boroughs) and 12 home rule cities, which do not directly coincide with the 4 Judicial Districts into which the judicial system is divided. In other words, judicial boundaries cross borough boundaries. Alaska has a unified, centrally administered, and totally state-funded judicial system. Municipal governments do not maintain separate court systems.

The superior court is the trial court of general jurisdiction. There are 34 superior court judgeships located throughout the state. The district court is a trial court of limited jurisdiction.

Find Felony Records: Superior Courts

Misdemeanor Records: District Courts, Magistrate Courts

Online Access: You may do a name search of a nearly statewide Alaska Trial Courts database index at www.state.ak.us/courts/names.htm. This index gives the name used on the first pleading; no index updates. The index is updated every 90 days. This search in and by itself is not FCRA-compliant for employment screening purposes. Note that the civil/criminal name index is available to anyone who sends a blank CD-ROM each quarter to the Administrative Director. The home web page also gives access to Supreme Court and Appellate opinions.

Searching Hints: The fees established by court rules for Alaska courts are: search fee - $15.00 per hour or fraction thereof; certification fee - $5.00 per document and $2.00 per additional copy of the document; copy fee - $.25 per page.

Magistrate Courts vary widely in how records are maintained and in the hours of operation (some are open only a few hours per week)

Court Administrator: For add'l questions about the state's court system, visit the website at www.state.ak.us/courts/, or contact the Office of the Administrative Director, Alaska Court System, 820 W 4th Ave, Anchorage, AK 99501, Phone: 907-264-8269.

Alabama

Alabama Statues and Related Employer Restrictions

General Rule - The director may open to any person for inspection criminal history information on any individual if the individual has given written permission. AL ST §32-2-61.

Exception - Fingerprints, photographs, and other records of youthful offenders shall not be open to public inspection. A youthful offender is an individual below 21 years of age. AL ST §15-19-7.

Definitions

Criminal History Information – includes arrest, detention, or initiation of criminal proceedings. AL ST §32-2-60.

Person – any individual, partnership, corporation, association, business, government, governmental agency, or any other public or private entity. AL ST §32-2-60.

Alabama State Criminal Records Agency

Alabama Department of Public Safety   **Phone:** 334-395-4340
A.B.I., Identification Unit
PO Box 1511
Montgomery, AL 36102-1511   **Web:**   www.dps.state.al.us

Total Records: 1,077,000

Note: The State Court Administration provides court criminal records online via a state designated vendor. Visit www.alacourt.com for details.

Who Can Access: Records are available to the general public but only with consent of subject.

Search Requirements: The request must be on a state form (call to have copy sent). Include the following in your request: notarized release from subject, date of birth, Social Security Number, full name, race, sex. Fingerprints optional. 100% of the record files have fingerprints.

What Is Released: All records or arrests are released, including those without dispositions. Records are available from 1942 on. The following data is not released: juvenile records.

Indexing & Storage: It takes about 7 days before new records are available for inquiry. 40% of arrests in database have final dispositions recorded, 65% for those arrests in last 5 years.

Access By: Mail, in person.

Mail Search: Turnaround time: 7 days. No self addressed stamped envelope is required.

In Person Search: You may bring in the required release and request form.

Fee & Payment: The fee is $25.00 per name. For a fingerprint search of both the state and FBI records, the fee is $49.00 per name, however FBI search is not available to the public. Prepayment is required. Fee payee: Alabama Bureau of Investigation. Cashier checks and money orders accepted. No personal checks accepted. No credit cards accepted.

Alabama Sexual Offender Registry

AlabamaDepartment of Public Safety   **Phone**:   334-353-1172

Sexual Offender Registry, PO Box 1511   **Fax**:   334-353-2563

Montgomery, AL 36102-1511   **Web**:   www.dps.state.al.us

(courier address: 301 S Ripley, Montgomery, AL 36109.)

Sections 15-20-21 to 37, Code of Alabama 1975, makes it a class C felony for any criminal sex offender to violate most provisions of the Alabama Community Notification Act.

What is released: Records are available from 08/01/98. It takes about 7 days before new records are released. Not available: information on the victim. Records normally destroyed after the death of the offender.

Search Notes: Include in request: name, DOB, and SSN. Mail turnaround time: 7 days.

Access by: Phone, Fax, Mail, In Person, Online. In person search note: time permitting. Online search note: sex offender data and a felony fugitives list are available online at www.dps.state.al.us/public/abi/system. Search by name, ZIP Code or geographic area.

Alabama State Incarceration Records Agency

Alabama Department of Corrections   **Phone:**   334-240-9501

Central Records Office

PO Box 301501   **Web:**   http://doc.state.al.us

Montgomery, Al 36130

What is released: Records are available on current and former inmates by mail; current inmates only online. No information is available on youthful offenders. It takes about 7 days before new records are released. Records normally kept indefinitely.

Search Notes:	Include in request: full name; AIS number helpful, as is DOB and SSN. There is no fee. Mail turnaround time: 2-3 days.
Access by:	Mail, Online. Online search note: only current inmate information is available online at this time. Location, AIS number, physical identifiers, projected release date are released.

Alabama State Court System

Court Structure:	Jefferson County (Birmingham), Madison (Huntsville), Marshall, and Tuscaloosa Counties have separate criminal divisions for Circuit and/or District Courts. Misdemeanors committed with felonies are tried with the felony. The Circuit Courts are appeals courts for misdemeanors. District Courts can receive guilty pleas in felony cases.
Find Felony Records:	Circuit Courts
Misdemeanor Records:	District Courts, Municipal Courts
Online Access:	The state has a remote access program called (SJIS), but it is only open to government agencies. Searchers are now reccommended by this agency to contact a commercial vendor at www.alacourt.com. Note that fees are involved. State Supreme Court and Appellette decisions are available at www.alalinc.net and at website above.
Searching Hints:	Although in most counties Circuit and District courts are combined, each index may be separate. Therefore, when you request a search of both courts, be sure to state that the search is to cover "both the Circuit and District Court records." Several offices do not perform searches. Some offices do not have public access computer terminals.
Court Administrator:	For add'l questions about the state's court system, visit the website at www.alacourt.org, or contact: Director of Courts, 300 Dexter Ave, Montgomery, AL 36104-3741, Phone: 334-242-0300.

Arizona

Arizona Statues and Related Employer Restrictions

General Rule – The director shall authorize the exchange of criminal justice information with any non-criminal justice agency pursuant to a statute, ordinance, or executive order that specifically authorizes it for the purpose of evaluating the fitness of current or prospective licensees, employees, contract employees or volunteers. Fingerprints and appropriate fee must be submitted along with the request.

The director shall authorize the exchange of criminal justice information with any individual for any lawful purpose on submission of the subject of record's fingerprints and appropriate fee. ARS §41-1750(G)(2) and (4).

Definitions - ARS §41-1750(Y)

Criminal History Record – includes notations of arrest, detentions, indictments, and other formal criminal charges, and disposition arising from those actions, sentencing, formal correctional supervisory action, and release. It does not include information relating to juveniles unless they have been adjudicated as adults.

General Rule: Consumer Reports – A consumer reporting agency may furnish a consumer report to a person that it has reason to believe intends to use the information for employment purposes. ARS §44-1692(A)(3)(b)

Consumer Reports Definitions - ARS §44-1691(3)

Consumer Report – any written, oral, or other communications which bear on a consumer's credit worthiness, credit standing, credit capacity, character, general reputation, personal characteristics, or mode of living which is used . . . for . . . employment purposes.

Caveat – A person cannot be disqualified from employment because of a prior conviction for a felony or misdemeanor within or without this state. However, if the offense has a reasonable relationship to the function of the employment or occupation, then employment may be denied. ARS §13-904(E).

Arizona State Criminal Records Agency

Department of Public Safety   **Phone:** 602-223-2223
Applicant Team One   **Fax:**   602-223-2972
PO Box 18430//Mail Code 2250
Phoenix, AZ 85005-8430   **Web:**   www.dps.state.az.us

Total Records: 915,100

Who Can Search: Record access is limited to agencies that have specific authorization by law including employers or pre-employment search firms located in Arizona.

Search Requirements: Fingerprints are required for a search. Include the following in your request: full set of fingerprints plus demographic information on the applicant. Be sure to address requests to Applicant Team One.

What Is Released: All records are released, including those without dispositions. Records are available from 1988.

Indexing & Storage: It takes about 14 days before new records are available for inquiry. 50% of arrests in database have final dispositions recorded. Records are indexed on computer back to 1983; non-automated records may go back as far as 1960's, depending on charge. Records are normally destroyed after age 99 or 2 years after subject's death.

Access By: Mail.

Mail Search: Turnaround time: 2 to 3 days. Arizona employers may call 602-223-2223 to request fingerprint cards and forms. No self addressed stamped envelope is required.

Fee & Payment: The fee is $5.00 per name. Fee payee: Department of Public Safety. Only cashier's checks and money orders accepted. No credit cards accepted.

Arizona Sexual Offender Registry

Department of Public Safety   **Phone**:   602-255-0611

Sex Offender Compliance   **Fax**:   602-223-2915

PO Box 6638//Mail Code 9999

Phoenix, AZ 85005-6638   **Web**:   www.azsexoffender.com

The county sheriff is responsible for registering sex offenders living within their county. Arizona has approximately 12,000 registered sex offenders.

What is released: Records are available on or after June 1,1996 with risk assessment scores of Level 2 (Intermediate) or Level 3 (High).

Access by: Mail, Online. Online search note: searching of level 2 and level 3 offender is available online at the website above. Search for an individual by name, or search by ZIP Code or address for known offenders. The site also lists, with pictures, absconders who are individuals whose whereabouts are unknown.

Search Notes: Mail turnaround time: 2 to 3 days.

Arizona State Incarceration Records Agency

Arizona Department of Corrections   **Phone:** 602-542-5586

Records Department   **Fax:**   602-545-1638

1601 W. Jefferson St.   **Web:**   www.adc.state.az.us

Phoenix, AZ 85007

What is released: Records are available on current and former inmates. It takes about 7 days before new records are released. Records normally destroyed after 25 years.

Search Notes: Include in request: Full name, ADC number, and what you want. DOB, and SSN helpful. Fee is $.25 for every copy. Payee: Arizona Department of Corrections.

Access by: Fax, Online. No searching by mail; mail is returned. For online search, you must provide last name, first initial or ADC number. Location, ADC number, physical Identifiers and sentencing information are released. Inmates admitted and released from 1972 to 1985 may not be searchable on the web. Also available is ADC Fugitives - an alphabetical Inmate Datasearch listing of Absconders and Escapees from ADC. Other Access: a private company offers free web access at www.vinelink.com/index.jsp.

Arizona State Court System

Court Structure: The Superior Court is the court of general jurisdiction. Justice and Municipal courts generally have separate jurisdiction over case types as indicated in the text. Most courts will search their records by plaintiff or defendant. Estate cases are handled by Superior Court. Fees are the same as for civil and criminal case searching.

Find Felony Records: Superior Courts

Misdemeanor Records: Justice of the Peace, Municipal Courts

Online Access: The Arizona Judicial Branch offers Public Access to Court Case Information, a valuable online service providing a resource for information about court cases from 137 out of 180 superior, justice, and municipal courts in Arizona. Access information includes: detailed case information, i.e., case type, charges, filing and disposition dates; the parties in the case, not including victims and witnesses; and the court mailing address and location. Go to www.supreme.state.az.us/publicaccess/.

The Maricopa and Pima county courts maintain their own systems, but will also, under current planning, be part of ACAP. These two counties provide ever-increasing online access to the public.

Searching Hints: Public access to all Maricopa County court case indexes is available at a central location - 1 W Madison Ave in Phoenix. Copies, however, must be obtained from the court where the case is heard.

Many offices do not perform searches due to personnel and/or budget constraints. As computerization of record offices increases across the state, more record offices are providing public access computer terminals.

Fees across all jurisdictions, as established by the Arizona Supreme Court and State Legislature, are as follows as of August 9, 2001: search - Superior Court: $18.00 per name; lower courts: $17.00 per name; certification - Superior Court: $18.00 per document; lower courts: $17.00 per document; copies - $.50 per page. Courts may choose to charge no fees.

Court Administrator: For add'l questions about the state's court system, visit the website at www.supreme.state.az.us, or contact: Administrative Offices of the Courts, Arizona Supreme Court Bldg, 1501 W Washington, Phoenix, AZ 85007-3231, Phone: 602-542-9301.

Arkansas

Arkansas Statues and Related Employer Restrictions

General Rule - Conviction Information shall be available to any non-governmental entity authorized by the subject of the record in writing or by state or federal law to receive such information. ACA §12-12-1009(a)(2).

Non-conviction information shall be made available for non-criminal justice purposes. ACA §12-12-1009(c).

Exceptions to releasing non-conviction information:

- Any person under 16 years of age who was convicted and given a suspended sentence, subsequently received a pardon for the conviction, and has not since been convicted of another criminal offense will have the criminal record expunged ACA §16-90-601.

- Release of criminal history information for non-criminal justice purposes shall be made only by the Identification Bureau of the Department of Arkansas State Police… and such compiled records will not be released or disclosed for non-criminal justice purpose by other agencies in the state. ACA §12-12-1011.

Definitions – ACA §12-12-1001

Conviction Information – criminal history information disclosing that a person has pleaded guilty or nolo contendere to, or was found guilty of a criminal offense in a court of law together with sentencing information.

Criminal History Information – includes notations of arrest, detentions, indictments, disposition of charges, formal criminal charges, as well as notations on correctional supervision and release

Non-conviction Information – arrest without disposition, as well as all acquittals and all dismissals.

Expunge – record or records in question shall be sealed, sequestered, and treated as confidential. ACA §16-90-901.

Arkansas State Criminal Records Agency

Arkansas State Police   **Phone:**   501-618-8500
Identification Bureau   **Fax:**   501-618-8404
#1 State Police Plaza Dr
Little Rock, AR 72209   **Web:**   www.asp.state.ar.us

Total Records: 499,800

Note: Under Act 63 of the 1st Ext Sess of 2003, employers and professional licensing boards are permitted access to felony arrests not yet resulting in disposition. Generally if such arrest is more than three years old, state personnel will research record.

Who Can Access:	Records are available to the general public, but only with consent of subject.
Search Requirements:	You must use the Bureau's request form. Include the following in your request: notarized release from subject, name, date of birth, sex, Social Security Number, driver's license number. Fingerprints are not required, but may be included. 100% of the arrest records are fingerprint-supported.
What Is Released:	Felony records without dispositions are released only to employers and licensing boards, otherwise all records without disposition are not relased. Records are available for the past 25 years. Older records are located in the off-site State Archives. The following data is not released: pardons and juvenile reocrds.
Indexing & Storage:	It takes 2-3 weeks before new records are available for inquiry. 58% of arrests in database have final dispositions recorded, 77% for those arrests in last 5 years. Records are indexed on computer by name, and on fingerprint cards. Records are normally destroyed after it is determined the subject will probably not commit a crime again (i.e.death).
Access By:	Mail, in person, online.
Mail Search:	Turnaround time: 5 to 7 days. A self addressed stamped envelope is required.
In Person Search:	Bring in signed, notarized release. Results of less than 10 request can usually be done as you wait.
Online Search:	Online access is, but only to employers and professional licensing boards. Registration is required. Agents or 3rd party vendors representing employers are blocked from access, per the state legislators. There is an additional $2.00 to the standard $20.00 search fee. Searches are conducted by name. Search results includes registered sex offenders. Accounts must maintain the signed release documents in-house for three years.
Fee & Payment:	The fee is $20.00 per record. Fee payee: Arkansas State Police. Prepayment required. Personal checks accepted, credit or debit cards are not.

Arkansas Sexual Offender Registry

Arkansas Crime Information Center   **Phone**: 501-682-2222

Sexual Offender Registry, One Capitol Mall   **Fax**:   501-682-2269

Little Rock, AR 72201   **Web**:   www.acic.org/Registration/index.htm

Based on information obtained from the risk assessment process, offenders are assigned the following levels: Level 1: Low Risk; Level 2: Moderate Risk; Level 3: High Risk; Level 4: Sexually Violent Predator. Arkansas Code Annotated 12-12-913 requires the Arkansas Crime Information Center to maintain a registry of sex offenders of Level 3 and Level 4 and this registry is made available to the public via the Internet.

What is released: ACIC provides information on registered sex offenders to all law enforcement agencies in the county where the offender resides. Local law enforcement agencies release names of those determined most likely to re-offend. Records are available from August 1, 1997 forward. There are over 3,800 registered sex offenders living in this state.

Access by: Mail, Online. Mail search note: there is no fee. Online search note: searching is available at www.acic.org/soff/index.php. Search by name or location (county). Includes Level 3 and Level 4 offenders. Also, registered sex offenders are indicated on the criminal record online system maintained by the State Police; however, this system, is only available to employers and professional licensing boards.

Search Notes: Mail turnaround time: 1 -2 weeks.

Arkansas State Incarceration Records Agency

Arkansas Department of Corrections   **Phone**: 870-267-6424

Records Supervisor

7500 Collections Circle   **Web**:   www.accessarkansas.org/doc/inmate_info/

Pine Bluff, AR 71603

What is released: Location, ADC number, physical identifiers and sentencing information, release dates are released. Records are available on current and former inmates; however, the online access is limited to current inmates. It takes 2-3 weeks before new records are released.

Search Notes: Include in request: first and last name or ADC number. There is no fee. Mail turnaround time: 5 to 7 days.

Access by: Mail, Online. The online access at the website has many search criteria capabilites. Also, a private company offers free web access at www.vinelink.com/index.jsp, including state, DOC, and many county jail systems.

Arkansas State Court System

Court Structure: Circuit Courts are the courts of general jurisdiction and are arranged in 28 circuits. Circuit courts consist of five subject matter divisions: criminal, civil, probate, domestic relations, and juvenile. The Circuit Clerk handles the records and recordings. District courts, formerly known as municipal courts before passage of Amendment 80 to the Arkansas Constitution, exercise county-wide jurisdiction over misdemeanor cases, and preliminary felony cases. The City Courts operate in smaller communities where District Courts do not exist and exercise city-wide jurisdiction.

Find Felony Records: Circuit Courts

Misdemeanor Records: District, City, Justice of the Peace and Police Courts

Online Access: There is a very limited internal online computer system at the Administrative Office of Courts. The home web page gives online access to Supreme and Appellate opinions.

Searching Hints: Many courts that allow written search requests require an SASE. Fees vary widely across jurisdictions as do prepayment requirements.

Court Administrator: For add'l questions about the state's court system, visit the website at www.courts.state.ar.us, or contact: Administrative Office of Courts, 625 Marshall Street, 1100 Justice Bldg, Little Rock, AR 72201-1078, Phone: 501-682-9400.

California

California Statues & Related Employer Restrictions

Consumer Report: Investigative Reports – An investigative consumer reporting agency shall only furnish an investigative consumer report... to a person it has reason to believe intends to use the information for employment purposes. Cal. Civil Code §1786.12(d)(1).

If an investigative consumer report is sought for employment purposes, the person seeking the report must have provided disclosure in writing to the consumer and the consumer must authorize in writing. Cal. Civil Code §1786.16(a)(2).

An investigative consumer report may not contain 1) bankruptcies which antedate the report by more than 10 years, 2) suit and satisfied judgments, unsatisfied judgments, paid tax liens, accounts placed for collection, records of arrest indictment, information, misdemeanor complaint, or conviction of a crime which antedate the report by more than 7 years, or 3) unlawful detainer actions where the defendant was the prevailing party or where the action is resolved by settlement agreement. Records of arrest, indictment, information, misdemeanor complaint, or conviction of a crime shall no longer be reported if at any time it is learned that a full pardon has been granted or a conviction did not result, except that information may be reported pending pronouncement of a judgment on the particular subject matter of those records. Cal. Civil Code §1786.18(a).

Additionally, an investigative consumer report may not contain information that is adverse to the consumer if it was obtained through a personal interview with a neighbor, friend, or associate of the consumer or with another person with whom the consumer is acquainted, unless the investigative consumer reporting agency has procedure to confirm the information or the person interviewed is the best possible source of the information. Cal. Civil Code §1786.18(d).

Consumer Report: Consumer Credit Report – No consumer credit report may contain 1) bankruptcies which antedate the report by more than 10 years, or 2) suit and judgments, paid tax liens, accounts placed for collection, records of arrest, indictment, information, misdemeanor complaint, or conviction of a crime which antedate the report by more than 7 years, or 3) unlawful detainer actions where the defendant was the prevailing party or where the action is resolved by settlement agreement. Records of arrest, indictment, information, misdemeanor complaint, or conviction of a crime shall no longer be reported if at any time it is learned that a full pardon has been granted or a conviction did not result. Cal. Civil Code §1785.13(a).

Employment – No employer shall ask an applicant for employment to disclose information concerning an arrest or detention that did not result in conviction, or information concerning a referral to, and participation in, any pretrial or posttrial diversion program. An employer in not prevented from asking about an arrest for which the employee or applicant is out on bail or is pending trial. Cal. Civil Code §432.7(a).

Employers are also prohibited from inquiring about 1) misdemeanors that resulted from possession of less than 28.5 grams of marijuana, which may have resulted in a referral to education, treatment, or rehabilitation facility without a court hearing, and 2) possession of more than 28.5 grams of marijuana which may have resulted in imprisonment in county jail.   Cal Hlth & S §11357(b) and (c).

Agency guidelines for pre-employment inquiries: Department of Fair Employment and Housing, "Pre-Employment Inquiry Guidelines." A copy of these guidelines can be found at the California State Univ. at Long Beach website at www.csulb.edu/depts/oed/resources/pubs3b.htm.

California State Criminal Records Agency

Department of Justice   **Phone:**   916-227-3460
Records Search Section
PO Box 903417   **Web:**   www.caag.state.ca.us
Sacramento, CA 94203-4170

Note: SEVERE LIMITATIONS! Penal Code Sec. 11105.3 limits access to searches involving child care, education, the handicaped and mentally impaired. The subject can obtain their own copy.

Total Records:	6,166,000
Search Requirements:	Entities must be pre-appoved before records can be ordered. Include the following in your request: fingerprints, full name; also helpful DOB and SSN. Those entities permitted to obtain records must submit a completed fingerprint card, a letter explaining why the record is needed, and address of the authorized agency where record will be sent.
What Is Released:	If for a statutorily-required employment check, only records with dispositions are released. However, certain social service agencies may be eligible for all arrest records.
Indexing & Storage:	It takes about 70 days before new records are available for inquiry. 75% of arrests in database have final dispositions recorded, 85% for those arrests in last 5 years. Records are indexed on computer indefinitely, though misdemeanors are purged after 10 years if subject has no subsequent arrests. Records are normally destroyed after 99 years or on notification of the person's death.
Access By:	Mail.
Mail Search:	Turnaround time: 6-8 weeks. Send to: "Attention, Records Review Unit."
Fee & Payment:	The fee is $32.00 per name, but the fee can vary depending on the requester. For FBI fingerprint search, add $24.00. Will expedite for $10.00 add'l. Fee payee: California Department of Justice. Money order is requested. May use Visa, American Express

California Sexual Offender Registry

Department of Justice	**Phone**: Fee Search: 900-448-3000; Tracking: 916-227-4199
Sexual Offender Program	**Fax**: 916-227-4345
PO Box 903387	
Sacramento, CA 94203-3870	**Web**: www.caag.state.ca.us

There are over 99,715 registered sexual offenders in CA.

Search Notes: Offender informatiion can be accessed in 3 ways: 1) in person at DOJ offices, sheriff offices, and police departments in cities with population exceeding 200,000; 2) fee-based phone system from DOJ; 3) mail requests to DOJ. Include in request: full name; also helpful DOB and SSN. Mail turnaround time: 3 to 5 business days. Payee: CA Department of Justice.

Access by: Phone, Mail. The public may call the CA Sexual Offender 900 service at 900-448-3000. There is a fee of $10.00 per call for checks on up to two names. Mail search note: mail requests are available to businesses and organizations. Names searches are $4.00 per name and the request must contain 6 names or more.

California State Incarceration Records Agency

California Department of Corrections	**Phone:** 916-557-5933
Communications Office	**Fax:** 916-327-1988
P.O. Box 942883	**Web:** www.corr.ca.gov
Sacramento, CA 94283-0001	

24 Hour Inmate Locator: 916-445-6713; Dept. of Corrections Main: 916-445-7682

Please note that for new or transferring inmates it can take up to seven business days to update location information. Agency prefers to return results via fax.

What is released: Location, conviction and sentencing information, and county of conviction are released. Records are available on current and former inmates. It takes about 70 days before new records are released. Not available: Case specifics should be acquired from the courts.

Search Notes: Include in request: full name, DOB, your fax and phone numbers; also helpful: inmate number. There is no fee. Mail turnaround time: 4-6 days.

Access by: Phone, Fax, Mail. The Inmate Locator help line at 916-445-6713 is open 24 hours daily. Provides an inmate's location, mailing addresses, and relevant phone numbers. The state provides no online searching, however a private company offers free web access to state/DOC records at www.vinelink.com.

California State Court System

Court Structure: In 1998, the judges in individual counties were given the opportunity to vote on unification of superior and municipal courts within their respective counties. By late 2000, all counties had voted to unify these courts. Courts that were formally Municipal Courts are now known as Limited Jurisdiction Superior Courts. In some counties, superior and municipal courts were combined into one superior court. It is important to note that Limited Courts may try minor felonies not included under our felony definition.

Find Felony Records: Superior Court

Misdemeanor Records: Superior Court and Limited Jurisdiction Superior Court

Online Access: There is no statewide online computer access available, internal or external. However, a number of counties have developed their own online access sytems and provide web access at no fee. The site at www.courtinfo.ca.gov offers access to all opinions from the Supreme and Appeals courts from 1850 to present. Opinions not certified for publications are available for last 60 days. This site also contains very useful information about the state court system, including opinions form the Supreme and Appeals courts.

Los Angeles County - As of 2003, all felony and misdemeanor defendant records in Los Angeles County are available online at www.lasuperiorcourt.org/criminalindex. Search fee is $4 to $5. Historical Superior Court felony indices go back to 1973; misdemeanor cases vary - some go back to 1982, others only until 1991. Case disposition data also varies; generally, if the entire criminal case was automated at the time of sentencing, then an accurate case disposition should be included, but if it was not automated or the electronic data was compromised, then the case disposition will not be available online. Keep in mind this is a new system that is still being tested.

Searching Hints: If there is more than one court of a type within a county, where the case is tried and where the record is held depends on how a citation is written, where the infraction occurred, or where the filer chose to file the case.

Some courts now require signed releases from the subject in order to perform criminal searches and will no longer allow the public to conduct such searches.

Although fees are set by statute, courts interpret them differently. For example, the search fee is supposed to be $6.00 per name per year searched, but many courts charge only $5.00 per name. Generally, certification is $6.60 per document and copies are $.50 per page, in some counties $.75 each page, and in Los Angeles county, $.57 each page.

Court Administrator: For add'l questions about the state's court system, visit the website at www.courtinfo.ca.gov, or contact: Administration Office of Courts, Office of Cummunications, 455 Golden Gate Ave, San Francisco, CA 94102-3660, Phone: 415-865-4200.

Colorado

Colorado Statues and Related Employer Restrictions

General Rule – Except for records of official actions, all criminal justice records may be open to inspection by any person. CRSA §24-72-304(1).

Expunged Record – Upon the entry of an order to seal criminal records, the subject of the record may state that no such record exists. CRSA §24-72-308(1)(d).

Consumer Report – A consumer reporting agency may furnish a consumer report to a person which the agency has reason to believe intends to use the information for employment purposes if the applicant or employee is first informed and consented in writing. CRSA §12-14.3-103(1)(c).

No consumer reporting agency may disclose 1) bankruptcies which antedate the report by more than 10 years, or 2) suits and judgments, records of arrest, indictment, or conviction of a crime, any other adverse information which antedates the report by more than 7 years. CRSA §12-14.3-105.3(1).

However, that does not apply to a consumer report used in the connection with the employment of an individual whose salary equals $75,000 or more. CRSA §12-14.3-105.3(2).

Employment – Employers, educational institutes, state and local government agencies shall not in any application or interview require an applicant to disclose any information contained in sealed records. Such applicant may not be denied solely because of the applicant's refusal to disclose arrest and criminal record information that has been sealed. CRSA §24-72-308(1)(f)(1).

Agency guidelines for pre-employment inquiries: Colorado Civil Rights Division, Publications, "Preventing Job Discrimination" is available online at www.dora.state.co.us/civil-rights/Publicatio ns/JobDiscrim2001.pdf.

Colorado State Criminal Records Agency

Bureau of Investigation, State Repository   **Phone:** 303-239-4208
Identification Unit   **Fax:** 303-239-5858
690 Kipling St, Suite 3000   **Web:** http://cbi.state.co.us
Denver, CO 80215   **Total Records:** 970,000

Who Can Access: Records are available to the general public.

Search Requirements: The requester must sign a disclaimer stating "This record shall not be used for the direct solicitation of business for pecuniary gain." Include the following in your request: full name, date of birth, and disclaimer. The SSN, race, and gender are optional. The SSN is optional, but suggested. Fingerprints are optional unless statutorily-required. Records are 100% fingerprint supported. If charged after fingerprinted, the practice of notifying the state is becoming more common, though this not yet statewide.

What Is Released: All records or arrests are released, including those without dispositions. Records are available from 1967 on. Records prior to 1967 are in on-site computer archives. The following data is not released: sealed records, juvenile records and pending mental comps.

Indexing & Storage: It takes less than 72 hours before new records are available for inquiry. 12% of all arrests in database have final dispositions recorded, over 12% for those arrests within last 5 years. Records are indexed on inhouse computer, fingerprint cards. Records are not destroyed or removed.

Access By: Mail, in person, online.

Mail Search: Turnaround time: 3 days. No self addressed stamped envelope is required.

In Person Search: You may request information in person.

Online Search: There is an Internet access at www.cbirecordscheck.com. Requesters must use a credit card, an account does not need to be established. However, account holders may set up a batch system. The fee is $6.85 per record.

Fee & Payment: Name check-$13.00 per name; fingerprint search-$16.50 per fingerprint. A state mandated fingerprint search plus notification of subsequent arrest in CO-$19.50; or nationwide fingerprint search-$22.00. Interent searches are $6.85 each. Fee payee: Colorado Bureau of Investigations (CBI). Prepayment required. No personal checks accepted. Credit cards accepted: MC/Visa.

Colorado Sexual Offender Registry

Colorado Bureau of Investigation   **Phone**: 303-239-4222
SOR Unit, 690 Kipling St, Suite 4000   **Fax**:   303-233-8336
Denver, CO 80215   **Web**:   http://sor.state.co.us

Each police or sheriff's agency is required to maintain a list of convicted sex offenders in their jurisdiction and is required to release that information to any citizen of the jurisdiction who requests it.

What is released: Requesters are screened for purpose, they must be at least 18 years of age.

Search Notes: Include in request: name, address. The CBI may assess reasonable fees for the search, retrieval, and copying of information requested. Mail turnaround time: 5 days. Payee: CBI.

Access by: Mail, In Person, Online. Mail search note: lists of names can be ordered by city or by ZIP Code. In person search note: Lists of names can be ordered by city or by ZIP Code. Online search note: the website gives access to only certain high-risk registered sex offenders in the following categories: Sexually Violent Predator (SVP), Multiple Offenses, and Failed to Register.

Colorado State Incarceration Records Agency

Colorado Department of Corrections   **Phone:** 719-226-4884

Offender Records Customer Support   **Fax:**   719-226-4899

2862 South Cricle Dr., #418   **Web:**   www.doc.state.co.us/index.html

Colorado Springs, CO 80906-4195

Locator Service: 719-226-4880; Offender Records Customer Support, 2862 South Circle Dr. #418

What is released: Sentence information (crime/sentencing court/docket number); location of incarceration; parole eligibility date/approved parole date; and mandatory release date. Records are available on current and former inmates. 4 weeks before new records are released. Records normally destroyed after 10 years.

Search Notes: Include in request: full name, date of birth, signed release (for full information). Fee is $1.00 per page. Mail turnaround time: 2-4 weeks. Prepayment required. No credit cards or personal checks accepted.

Access by: Phone, Fax, Mail. The Locator Service telephone line is open from 8:00 AM to 5:00 PM. Only very basic information is available by phone.

Colorado State Court System

Court Structure: District and County Courts are combined in most counties. Combined courts usually search both civil or criminal indexes for a single fee, except as indicated in the profiles. Municipal courts only have jurisdiction over traffic, parking, and ordinance violations.

Find Felony Records: District Courts

Misdemeanor Records: County Courts

Online Access: There is no official government system, but we can mention a unique commercial system. As a result of an initiative of the Colorado Judicial Branch, all district courts and all county courts are available on the Internet at www.cocourts.com. Court records go as far back as 1995. There is a fee for this subscription Internet access, generally $6.00 per search. There are discounts for volume users. Contact Jeff Mueller, Major Accounts, by telephone at 866-COCOURT, or by email at Jeffm@cocourts.com.

Searching Hints: November 15, 2001, Broomfield City & County came into existence, derived from the counties of Adams, Boulder, Jefferson and Weld. A District and County Court (presumed to be 17th Judicial District) was established.

Court Administrator: For add'l questions about the state's court system, visit the website at www.courts.state.co.us, or contact: State Court Administrator, 1301 Pennsylvania St, Suite 300, Denver, CO 80203-2416, Phone: 303-861-1111.

Connecticut

Connecticut Statues & Related Employer Restrictions

General Rule – Conviction information shall be available to the public for any purpose. CGSA §54-142(k)(b). Any person may authorize in writing an agency holding non-conviction information pertaining directly to such person to disclose it to his attorney at law. CGSA §54-142(k)(d).

Otherwise, non-conviction information may only be release 1) for the purpose of research, or 2) if there is a specific agreement with a criminal justice agency. CGSA §54-142(m).

Definitions - CGSA §54-142(g)

Conviction Information – criminal history record information which has not been erased, and which discloses that a person has pleaded guilty, or nolo contendere to, or was convicted of any criminal offense, and the terms of the sentence.

Non-conviction Information – means 1) criminal history record information that has been erased; 2) information relating to person granted youthful offender status; 3) continuances which are more than thirteen months old.

Expunged Record - Whenever the accused is found not guilty of the charge, or the charge is dismissed, all police records and records of the state attorney pertaining to such charge shall be erased. Erasure does not apply to persons found not guilty by reason of mental disease or guilty but not criminally responsible by reason of mental disease. CGSA §54-142(a). Youthful offenders may have police and court records erased. CGSA §46b-146.

Caveat - No employer may require an employee or prospective employee to disclose erased records. Employers may not deny employment to a prospective employee because of the existence of an erased record. CGSA §31-51i(b) and (d).

Connecticut State Criminal Records Agency

Department of Public Safety
Bureau of Identification
PO Box 2794
Middletown, CT 06757-9294

Phone: 860-685-8480
Fax: 860-685-8361
Web: www.state.ct.us/dps/spbi.htm

Note: Download DPS-846-C Form "State Police Bureau of Identification Request" from the website.

Total Records: 825,600

Who Can Access: Records are available to the general public.

Search Requirements: Records are open to the public using a name search. Fingerprint searches are not available to the public. Pending case information is available. Include the following in your request: date of birth Request forms may be downloaded from the website. Approximately 90% of the records on file are fingerprint supported.

What Is Released: The records released to the public only contain convictions. Nolles are usually released if in conjunction with a conviction. Records are available from the 1950's on. Records were first computerized in 1983. The following data is not released: dismissals or juvenile records.

Indexing & Storage: It takes about 30 days before new records are available for inquiry. 90% of all arrests in database have final dispositions recorded, 90% for those arrests within last 5 years. Records are normally destroyed after subject reaches 100th birthdate.

Access By: mail, in person.

Mail Search: Turnaround time: 7 to 10 days. Records must be in writing.

In Person Search: Request must be on agency form; results are mailed only. If you come in-person, the results are still mailed.

Fee & Payment: The fee is $25.00 per request. Fee payee: Commissioner of Public Safety. Prepayment required. Personal checks accepted. No credit cards accepted.

Connecticut Sexual Offender Registry

Department of Public Safety   **Phone**: 860-685-8060

Sex Offender Registry Unit   **Fax**:   860-685-8349

PO Box 2794

Middletown, CT 06757-9294   **Web**:   www.state.ct.us/dps/Sex_Offender_Registry.htm

It is suggested to visit local law enforcement if you cannot search online.

What is released: Records are available from October 1, 1988. It takes 1 day before new records are released. Not available: names of victims and treatment information. Records normally destroyed after registry term expires.

Search Notes: Include in request: date of birth There is no fee.

Access by: Online. The agency will not honor written requests. Online search note: the website has two searches: those convicted of a CT law, and those offenders who violated a law in a different state but are living in Connecticut. Search by name or location, ZIP Code, or entire list.

Connecticut State Incarceration Records Agency

Connecticut Department of Corrections

Office of Public Information

24 Wolcott Hill Rd

Wethersfield, CT 06109

Phone: 860-692-7780

Fax: 860-692-7783

Web: www.ct.gov/doc/site/default.asp

What is released: Records are open to the public using a name search. Location, conviction and sentencing information, bond, and release dates are released. Records are available on current and former inmates, except for the website which is current only. Computerized records go back to 1970. It takes about 30 days before new records are released.

Search Notes: Include in request: name; DOB and SSN are helpful. There is no fee. Mail turnaround time: 7 to 10 days.

Access by: Phone, Mail, Online. For phone search, use the number listed above. Online search note: current inmates may be searched at www.ctinmateinfo.state.ct.us/searchop.asp.

Connecticut State Court System

Court Structure: The Superior Court is the sole court of original jurisdiction for all causes of action, except for matters over which the probate courts have jurisdiction as provided by statute. The state is divided into 15 Judicial Districts, 20 Geographic Area Courts, and 14 Juvenile Districts. The Superior Court - comprised primarily of the Judicial District Courts and the Geographical Area Courts - has five divisions: Criminal, Civil, Family, Juvenile, and Administrative Appeals. When not combined, the Judicial District Courts handle felony and civil cases while the Geographic Area Courts handle misdemeanors, and some handle small claims.

Find Felony Records: Judicial District Court

Misdemeanor Records: Geographic Area Courts

Online Access: There is currently no online access to criminal records; however, criminal and motor vehicle data is available for purchase in database format through Judicial Information Systems Office at 860-282-6500.

Searching Hints: Mail requests to perform criminal searches should be made to the Department of Public Safety, 1111 Country Club Rd, PO Box 2794, Middletown, CT 06457, 860-685-8480. The search fee is $25.00.

The State Record Center in Enfield, CT is the repository for criminal and some civil records; open 9AM-5PM M-F. Case records are sent to the Record Center from 3 months to 5 years after disposition by the courts. These records are then maintained 10 years for misdemeanors and 20+ years for felonies. If a requester is certain that the record is at the Record Center, it is quicker to direct the request there rather than to the original court of record. Only written requests are accepted. Search requirements: full defendant name, docket number, disposition date, and court action. Fee is $5.00 for each docket. Fee payee is Treasurer-State of Connecticut. Direct Requests to: Connecticut Record Center, 111 Phoenix Ave., Enfield CT 06082, 860-741-3714. Personal checks must have name and address printed on the check; if requesting in person, check must have same address as drivers' license.

Court Administrator: For add'l questions about the state's court system, visit the website at www.jud.state.ct.us, or contact: Chief Court Administrator, 231 Capitol Ave, Hartford, CT 06106, Phone: 860-757-2100.

Delaware

Delaware Statues and Related Employer Restrictions

General Rule – The Bureau may furnish information pertaining to the identification and conviction data of any person to individuals and agencies for the purpose of employment of the person whose record is sought.   11 Del. C §8513(c).

Definitions - 11 Del. C §8502.

Conviction Data – criminal history record information relating to an arrest which has led to a conviction or other disposition adverse to the subject. This also includes dismissal entered after a period of probation, suspension, or deferral of a sentence. It does not include decisions not to prosecute, dismissals, or acquittals.

Disposition – includes trial verdicts of guilty or not guilty, nolle prosequis, Attorney General probations, pleas of guilty or nolo contendere, dismissals, incompetence to stand trial, findings of delinquency or nondelinquency, and initiation and completion of appellate proceedings.

Expungement - If a person is charged with the commission of a crime and is acquitted or nolle prosequi is taken, the person may file a petition requesting expungment of the police and court records. 11 Del. C §4372.

An offense for which records have been expunged shall not have to be disclosed by the person as an arrest for any reason.   11 Del. C §4374(e).

Exception – an employment application as an employee of a law enforcement agency.

Delaware State Criminal Records Agency

Delaware State Police
State Bureau of Identification
PO Box 430
Dover, DE 19903-0430

Phone: 302-739-5880
Fax: 302-739-5888
Web: www.state.de.us/dsp/

Total Records: 490,000

Who Can Access: Records are available to the general public, but only with consent of subject.

Search Requirements: Must have a signed release from the subject for the fingerprint search and release of information. You do not need to use the state's forms. Include the following in your request: fingerprints, full name, signed release.

What Is Released:	If the disposition is not known by this agency, the record will say "disposition not known." Will only release records with dispositions to pre-employment screeners. Records are available from 1935. The following data is not released: traffic ticket information.
Indexing & Storage:	It takes up to 3 days before new records are available for inquiry. 81% of all arrests in database have final dispositions recorded, 92% for those arrests within last 5 years. Records are normally destroyed after expunged, otherwise kept indefinitely.
Access By:	Mail, in person.
Mail Search:	Turnaround time: 14 days. Must have a signed release and full set of fingerprints. A self addressed stamped envelope is requested.
In Person Search:	It can take up to 14 days before records are ready for pickup.
Fee & Payment:	The search fee is $35.00 per request. Fee payee: Delaware State Police. Prepayment required. Funds must be certified or money order. Credit cards accepted for in person searches only

Delaware Sexual Offender Registry

Delaware State Police   **Phone**: 302-739-5882

Sex Offender Central Registry   **Fax**:   302-739-5888
PO Box 430
Dover, DE 19903-0430   **Web**:   www.state.de.us/dsp/sexoff/

There are three Tiers or Levels of offenders in the state. The public is only made aware of Tiers 2 and 3 via the Internet of through public notification programs by local law enforcement. Door-to-door is used for Tier 3 notification.

What is released:	Name searching is not available in the state except through the web page. Records are available from 06/24/94. It takes up to 3 days before new records are released.
Access by:	Online. No searching by mail. Online search note: statewide registry can be searched at the website. The site gives the ability to search by Last Name, Development, and city or ZIP Code. Any combination of these fields may be used; a search cannot be performed if both a city and ZIP are entered.

Delaware State Incarceration Records Agency

Delaware Department of Corrections   **Phone:** 302-739-2091
Probation and Parole   **Fax:**   302-739-7486
Central Records   **Web:**   www.state.de.us/correct/index.htm
511 Maple Parkway, Dover, DE 19901

The Department of Correction does not offer the public access to an automated database of offender information. However, the public may receive basic information about an offender, including whether the individual is incarcerated in Delaware, where the individual is incarcerated, and how to contact an offender by calling the number above.

What is released: Records are available on current and former inmates. It takes up to 5 days before new records are released. Records normally destroyed after three years.

Search Notes: Include in request: name and DOB.

Access by: Phone. Call the Department's Office of Community Relations at 302-739-5601, ext. 246. No searching by mail. Other Access: An escapees list is available online at www.state.de.us/correct/Data/Escapees.htm.

Delaware State Court System

Court Structure: Superior Courts have jurisdiction over felonies and all drug offenses, the Court of Common Pleas has jurisdiction over all misdemeanors.

Find Felony Records: Superior Court

Misdemeanor Records: Court of Common Pleas

Online Access: An online system called CLAD was the first to offer online access to court records. CLAD contains only toxic waste, asbestos, and class action cases, but based on CLAD's success, Delaware pursued development of online availability of other public records by working in conjunction with private information resource enterprises. Now, Chancery, Superior, Common Pleas and Supreme Court opinions and orders are now available free online at http://courts.state.de.us/opinions. Records go back to 2002.

Chancery Court and Supreme Court filings are available at www.virtualdocket.com. Registration and fees required.

Supereme, Superior and Common Pleas Court calendars are available free at http://courts.state.de.us/calendars.

Searching Hints: Criminal histories are available with a signed release from the offender at the Delaware State Police, Criminal Records Section, see above.

Court Administrator: For add'l questions about the state's court system, visit the website at http://courts.state.de.us, or contact: Administrative Office of the Courts, Supreme Court of Delaware, 820 N French, 11th Fl, Wilmington, DE 19801, Phone: 302-577-2480.

District of Columbia

District Statues and Related Employer Restrictions

General Rule – The Mayor shall keep records of general complaint files, records of lost, stolen, or missing property . . . and arrest books which contain information about the offense with which the person was arrested and the disposition of the case. DC ST §5-113.01. Those records shall be open to the public when not in actual use. DC ST §5-113.06.

Exception – It is illegal to make the subject of the record pay to produce the record. Such "arrest records" shall only contain listings of convictions and forfeitures of collateral that have occurred within 10 years of the time at which such record is requested. DC ST §2-1402.66.

District of Columbia Criminal Records Agency

Metropolitan Police Department
Identification and Records Section
300 Indiana Ave NW, Rm 3055
Washington, DC 20001

Phone: 202-727-4245 (Police)
Fax: 202-638-5352
Web: www.mpdc.dc.gov/main.shtm

Note: Records are also available with less restrictions from the Superior Court, Criminal Div. at 500 Indiana NW, Rm 4001, phone 202-879-1373. The court record mail/fax search fee is $10.00; a signed release not required there.

Total Records: 532,000

Who Can Access: Records are available to the general public, but only with consent of subject.

Search Requirements: Include the following in your request: signed, notarized release from subject, full name (with middle initial), date and place of birth, year. The SSN, race, curent address and case number, if known, are helpful. Fingerprints searches are not available.

What Is Released: Neither records location will supply records without dispositions. Records are available for 10 years. Records at Superior Court are indexed in microfilm from 1974 on, index cards from 1970 on, in house computer from 1978 on and Dist. Archives from 1962 on. Police Dept. keeps felony records back to '92, misdemeanors to '97. The following data is not released: pending cases.

Indexing & Storage: It takes 1 day before new records are available for inquiry. 46% of all arrests in database have final dispositions recorded, 84% for those arrests within last 5 years.

Access By:	Mail, in person.
Mail Search:	Turnaround time: 2 to 4 weeks. A self addressed stamped envelope is required.
In Person Search:	Searching permitted at this address. Also, you may search in person for free at Superior Court, Criminal Div., located at 500 Indiana NW, Rm 4001.
Fee & Payment:	The fee is $7.00 per name from the Police Dept.; Search fee at Superior Court is $10.00. Fee payee: Superior Court, Criminal Division Out of state personal checks accepted. No credit cards accepted.

District of Columbia Sexual Offender Registry

Metropolitan Police Department   **Phone**: 202-727-4407

Sex Offender Registry Unit   **Fax**:   202-727-9292

300 Indiana Ave NW, Rm 3009

Washington, DC 20001   **Web**:   www.mpdc.dc.gov/serv/sor/sor.shtm

In general, an offense requiring registration is: a felony sexual assault (regardless of the age of the victim); an offense involving sexual abuse or exploitation of minors; or sexual abuse of wards, patients, or clients.

What is released:	Searchers can visit any police station and inspect a public registry that will contain current information on all registered sex offenders in the District of Columbia. It takes 1 day before new records are released. Not available: pending cases.
Access by:	Fax, In Person, Online. In person search note: records for all classes may be searched at this office and all local police stations in DC. Online search note: a list of Class A & B registered sex offenders is provided on the website.

District of Columbia Incarceration Records Agency

District of Columbia Department of Corrections   **Phone:** 202-673-8136

DC Detention Facility, Office of Records

1901 D. Street, S.E.   **Web:** www.mpdc.dc.gov/main.shtm

Washington, DC 20003

VINE Inmate Information Line: 202-673-8136 option 2; Administration phone: 202-673-8257.

For full information, a subpeona or signed release is required. The reason for the search must be stated in your request. For general "public" information, this agency prefers that you access the VINE telephone locator system.

What is released:	Type of data released varies depending on request. Records are available on current and former inmates. It takes 1 day before new records are released. Records normally never destroyed; records are archived.
Search Notes:	Include in request: first and last name, DOB. SSN and PVID number helpful and requested. Mail turnaround time: 2 to 4 weeks minimum.
Access by:	Mail.

District of Columbia Court System

Court Structure:	The Superior Court in DC is divided into 17 divisions, one of which is criminal.
Find Felony Records:	Superior Court
Misdemeanor Records:	Superior Court
Online Access:	The Superior Court and Court of Appeals offer access to opinions at www.dcbar.org.
Court Administrator:	For add'l questions about the court system, visit the website at www.dcsc.gov, or contact: Executive Office, 500 Indiana Ave NW, Room 1500, Washington, DC 20001, Phone: 202-879-1700.

Florida

Florida Statues and Related Employer Restrictions

General Rule – Persons in the private sector and non-criminal justice agencies may be provided criminal history information upon tender of fees. Access is without regard to quantity or category of criminal history record information requested. FSA §943.053.

Person may not be disqualified from employment by the state, any of its agencies or political subdivisions, nor shall a person whose civil rights have been restored be disqualified to practice, pursue, or engage in any occupation, trade, vocation, profession, or business for which a license, permit, or certificate is required to be issued by the state because of a prior conviction of a crime. FSA §112.011(1)(a) and (b).

> Above rule is not applicable if:
> 1. prior conviction of a felony or first-degree misdemeanor and directly related to the position of employment sought   FSA §112.011(1)(a) and (b).
> 2. Law enforcement or correctional agency   FSA §112.011(2)(a).
> 3. Fire Department   FSA §112.011(2)(b).
> 4. Positions deemed to be critical to security or public safety   FSA §112.011 (2)(c).

Definitions - FSA §943.045

Criminal History Information – includes information about arrests, detentions, indictments, or other formal criminal charges and the disposition thereof.

Expunction of a Criminal Record – court-ordered physical destruction or obliteration of a record.

Sealing of a Criminal Record – preservation of a record in a way that it is secure and inaccessible to any person not having a legal right to access it.

Minors – Minor who is a serious or habitual offender – retain criminal history record for 5 years after offender reaches 21 at which time the record is expunged. FSA §943.0515(1)(a). Minor who is NOT a serious or habitual offender – retain record for 5 years after offender reaches 19 at which time the record is expunged. FSA §943.0515(1)(b).

If person 18 and charged with or convicted of forcible felony and juvenile record has not been destroyed – person's juvenile record is merged and becomes apart of person's adult record. FSA §943.0515(2)(a).

If at any time minor adjudicated as an adult for forcible felony – criminal record prior to the time of adult adjudication is merged with record as an adjudicated adult. FSA §943.0515(2)(b).

Expunction – Any criminal record of a minor or an adult, which is ordered expunged by a court, must be physically destroyed.   FSA §943.0585(4).

The person whose record is expunged may lawfully deny or fail to acknowledge the arrests covered by the expunged record, except 1) a candidate for employment with a criminal justice agency, 2) a defendant in a criminal prosecution, 3) candidate for admission to the Florida Bar, 4) person seeking employment who would have direct contact with children, the developmentally disabled, the aged, or the elderly, or 5) a person seeking employment at a school, any district school board, or any government entity that licenses child care facilities.   FSA §943.0585(4)(a).

Florida State Criminal Records Agency

Florida Department of Law Enforcement   **Phone:**   850-410-8109
User Services Bureau   **Fax:**   850-410-8201
PO Box 1489
Tallahassee, FL 32302   **Web:**   www.fdle.state.fl.us

Total Records: 4,187,200

Who Can Access: Records are available to the general public.

Search Requirements: Include the following in your request: date of birth, race, sex, name. You can submit fingerprints, for the same fee, but it is not required. 100% of the arrest records are fingerprint-supported.

What Is Released: All records are released, including those without dispositions. Effective 10/01/02, the FDLE no longer releases SSN information to public customers using the Internet access program. The SSN is suppressed except for the last 4 digits. Records are available from the early 1930's. The following data is not released: sealed or expunged records, juvenile records prior to 10/94.

Indexing & Storage: It takes 1 day before new records are available for inquiry. 70% of all felony arrests in database have final dispositions recorded; 63% of misdemeanors. 68% of all records within last 5 years include dispositions. Records are indexed on microfilm, NIST Archive inhouse computer.

Access By: Mail, in person, online.

Mail Search: Turnaround time: 5 working days. No SASE is required.

In Person Search: In person requests are treated the same as mail requests; processing takes 5 working days.

Online Search: Criminal history information from 1967 forward may be ordered over the Department Program Internet site at www2.fdle.state.fl.us. The $23.00 fee applies. Juvenile records from 10/1994 forward are also available. Credit card ordering will return records to your screen or via email.

Fee & Payment: The fee is $23.00 per individual. Pre-paid accounts receive turnaround time of two to five working days. Fee payee: Department of Law Enforcement. Prepayment required. Personal checks accepted. Credit cards accepted only for online requests.

Florida Sexual Offender Registry

Florida Department of Law Enforcement   **Phone**: 888-357-7332 850-410-8572

Sexual Offender/Predator Unit, PO Box 1489   **Fax**:   850-410-8599

Tallahassee, FL 32302   **Web**:   http://www3.fdle.state.fl.us/sexual_predators/index.asp

(courier address: 2331 Phillips Rd, Tallahassee, FL 32308.)

Chapter 97-299, Laws of Florida, requires certain sex offenders to directly register with law enforcement or to have information compiled by the Department of Corrections, with the information to be provided to FDLE.

What is released:	Under Chapter 119, Florida Statutes, the Public Records Law, any of the public records of the Department of Law Enforcement are available for review upon request, subject to statutorily-authorized editing of exempt or confidential information. Records are available from 07/01/96. It takes 1 day before new records are released.
Search Notes:	Include in request: name or address. If documents need printing or are sub-standand forms, then fees may be involved. Mail turnaround time: 5 working days.
Access by:	Phone, Fax, Mail, In Person, Online. Mail search note: No SASE required. In person search note: In person requests are treated the same as mail requests; processing takes 5 working days. Online search note: search the registry from the web page. Searching can be done by name or by geographic area.

Florida State Incarceration Records Agency

Florida Department of Corrections   **Phone:** Phone: 850-488-2533

Central Records Office   **Fax:**   850-413-8302

2601 Blair Stone Rd.   **Web:**   www.dc.state.fl.us

Tallahassee, FL 32399-2500

Records: 850-488-1503; Parole Commission: 850-922-0000.

Full records are housed at the individual institutions, though inmate information is available through this agency and the website should sufficiently fullfill most searches.

What is released:	Location, DOC number, physical identifiers, conviction information, and release dates are released. Records are available on current and former inmates. It takes 1 day before new records are released. Paper records normally destroyed after imaging them electronicly.

Search Notes: Include in request: first and last name and DOB. The SSN and DOC number are helpful. Records indexed on paper, then scanned and stored in database. Image database goes back to 1997. Fee is $.15 per copy. There is $12.00 per hour search fee (minimum is $12.00). Mail turnaround time: 14-30 working days. Payee: Florida Department of Corrections.

Access by: Phone, Fax, Mail, In Person, Online. Searching limited to general "public" information is available by phone. In person search note: In person requesters must call for appointment for a Public File Review; please call two weeks in advance. Online search note: Extensive search capabilities are offered from the website. Click on Inmate Population Information Search. Also, a private company offers free web access at www.vinelink.com/index.jsp. Includes state, DOC, and 44 county jail systems. Other Access: the monthly-updated inmate database is available for $83.00.

Florida State Court System

Court Structure: All counties have combined Circuit and County Courts. The Circuit Court is the court of general jurisdiction.

Find Felony Records: Circuit Court

Misdemeanor Records: County Court

Online Access: 53 Florida Clerk of Courts/Recorders give access to index data at www.myflorida.com, a government sponsored website. Supreme Court dockets are available online at http://jweb.flcourts.org/pls/docket/ds_docket_search. There is no statewide, online computer system for external access available for the Circuit and County Courts. The Florida Legislature mandated that court documents must be imaged and available for inspection over a publicly available website, except court records. In response to concerns of identity theft and fraud, the Florida Legislature recently passed new laws concerning privacy of public documents on public websites.

Searching Hints: All courts have one address and switchboard; however, the divisions within the court(s) are completely separate. Requesters should specify which court and which division --e.g., Circuit Civil, County Civil, etc. -- the request is directed to, even though some counties will automatically check both with one request.

                          Fees are set by statute and are as follows as of July 1, 2004: Search Fee - $1.50 per name per year; Certification Fee - $1.50 per document plus copy fee; Copy Fee - $1.00 per page; some county copy fees may vary.

Court Administrator: For add'l questions about the state's court system, visit the website at www.flcourts.org, or contact: Office of State Courts Administrator, Supreme Court Bldg, 500 S Duval, Tallahassee, FL 32399-1900, Phone: 850-922-5082.

Georgia

Georgia Statues and Related Employer Restrictions

General Rule – Georgia Crime Information Center shall make criminal history records available to private persons and businesses. Private individuals and businesses must provide a fingerprint or a signed consent of the person. When identifying information provided is sufficient to identify person whose records are requested electronically, the center may disseminate electronically criminal history records of in-state felony convictions, pleas, and sentences without consent of the person whose records are requested. Records of arrest, charges, and sentences for crimes relating to first offender in which the offender has been exonerated and discharged without court adjudication of guilt may not be released. Ga. Code Ann. §35-3-34(a).

Exception to release of records of exoneration include if the person was exonerated or discharged on or after July 1, 2004, and

1) Person applied for employment with a school, child welfare agency, or entity that provides care for minor children and the record pertained to alleged child molestation, sexual battery, enticing a child for indecent purposes, sexual exploitation of a child, pimping, pandering, or incest; or

2) Person applied for employment with a nursing home, personal care home, or entity which provides care for the elderly and the record pertained to alleged sexual battery, pimping, pandering, or incest; or

3) Person applied for employment with a facility that provides services to the mentally ill and the record pertained to alleged sexual battery, pimping, pandering, or incest. Ga. Code Ann. §35-3-34.1

Caveat – In the event an adverse employment decision is made against the person whose record was obtained, the person must be notified by the business of all the information pursuant to that decision. Ga. Code Ann. §35-3-34(b).

Definitions – Ga. Code Ann. §35-3-30

Criminal History Record Information – includes notations of arrest, detentions, indictments, accusations, information, or other formal charges, and any disposition arising there from, sentencing, correctional supervision, and release.

Georgia State Criminal Records Agency

Georgia Bureau of Investigations
Attn: GCIC
PO Box 370748
Decatur, GA 30037-0748

Phone: 404-244-2639
Fax: 404-244-2878

Web: www.ganet.org/gbi

Note: GCIC is the central repository of criminal records for the State. (Note: anyone may make a record request at any local law enforcement office and the statewide record will be provided. Fees for this may vary; the maximum fee is $20.00.)

Total Records: 2,323,874

Who Can Access: Records are available to employers, government agencies including licensing agencies, and adoption and foster care providers.

Search Requirements: Include the following in your request: name, set of fingerprints, date of birth, sex, race, Social Security Number. Certain law enforcement agencies, who are online, and local agencies may access and retrieve records for investigative/background purposes. These agencies have the option of requesting a signed release from subject or including a set of fingerprints.

What Is Released: Information released includes arrest, disposition, and custodial information for offenses designated as fingerprintable by the State AG. Records without dispositions are released. Records are available from 1972 forward. The following data is not released: juvenile records, traffic ticket information or out-of-state or federal charges.

Indexing & Storage: It takes 1-3 days before new records are available for inquiry. 70% of all arrests in database have final dispositions recorded, 81% for those arrests within last 5 years. Records are normally destroyed after court order.

Access By: Mail, in person.

Mail Search: Turnaround time: 7 to 10 days. No self addressed stamped envelope is required.

In Person Search: In-person requests are returned by mail in about 14 days.

Fee & Payment: Fee is $15.00 per name. If statutues require a FBI check, both state and FBI require one set of fingerprint cards, a total search fee of $24.00 per name is required plus the fingerprints. Agencies may establish an account. Fee payee: Georgia Bureau of Investigations. Prepayment required. Money orders are accepted. No credit cards accepted.

Georgia Sexual Offender Registry

Georgia Bureau of Investigations   **Phone**: 404-244-2835

GCIC - Sexual Offender Registry   **Fax**:   404-212-3028

PO Box 370748

Decatur, GA 30037-0748   **Web**:   www.ganet.org/gbi/disclaim.html

(courier address: 3121 Panthersville Rd, Decatur, GA 30034.)

The website outlines which offenders are in the searchable database at the website.

What is released: As of July 1, 1999, sexual offenders who have more than one prior conviction for an offense listed in O.C.G.A. § 42-1-12, or who have been convicted of an aggravated offense such as aggravated child molestation, will remain on the registry for life. Records are available from 07/01/96. It takes 1-3 days before new records are released. Records normally destroyed after 10 years unless more than one prior or who have been convicted of an aggravated offense such as aggravated child molestation, will remain on the registry for life.

Search Notes: There is no fee. Mail turnaround time: 7 to 10 days.

Access by: Mail, In Person, Online. In person search note: In person requests are returned by mail in about 14 days if lists are involved. Online search note: records may be searched at www.ganet.org/gbi/sorsch.cgi. Earliest records go back to 07/01/96. Searches may be conducted for sex offenders, absconders, and predators.

Georgia State Incarceration Records Agency

Georiga Department of Corrections   **Phone:** 404-656-4593

Inmate Records Office, Eastern Tower   **Fax:**   404-463-6232

2 Martin Luther King, Jr. Drive, S.E.   **Web:**   www.dcor.state.ga.us

Atlanta, GA 30334-4900

What is released: Location, physical identifiers, conviction information, release dates, and inmate number are released. Records are available on current and former inmates. It takes 1-3 days before new records are released. Records normally destroyed after 15 years.

Search Notes: Include in request: name. DOB, inmate number or SSN are helpful. Mail turnaround time: 7 to 10 days.

Access by: Phone, Fax, Mail, In Person, Online. In person search note: use the agency form. Results are available in two days. Online search note: the website has an extensive array of search capabilities. Also, a private company offers free web access to DOC records at www.vinelink.com/index.jsp.

Georgia State Court System

Court Structure: Georgia's Superior Courts are arranged in 49 circuits of general jurisdiction, and these assume the role of a State Court if the county does not have one. The 69 State Courts, like Superior Courts, can conduct jury trials, but are limited jurisdiction. Magistrate Courts can issue arrest warrants and set bond on all felonies. Probate courts can, in certain cases, issue search and arrest warrants, and hear miscellaneous misdemeanors.

Find Felony Records: Superior Court

Misdemeanor Records: Superior, State, Magistrate, and Municipal Courts

Online Access: A few county courts offer Internet access to court records, but there is no online access available statewide, although one is being planned. Supreme Court docket information and opinions are available from the web. A certified copy of a Supreme Court Opinion can be purchased online for $5.00 at www2.state.ga.us/Courts/Supreme/main_pp.html.

Searching Hints: In most Georgia counties, the courts will not perform criminal record searches. An in-person search or the use of a record retriever is required.

Court Administrator: For add'l questions about the state's court system, visit the website at www.georgiacourts.org, or contact: Administrative Office of the Courts, 244 Washington St SW, #300, Atlanta, GA 30334, Phone: 404-656-5171.

Hawaii

Hawaii Statues and Related Employer Restrictions

Employment – A person shall not be disqualified from public office or employment by the State or be disqualified to practice, pursue, or engage in any occupation, trade, vocation, profession or business for which a license, permit, or certificate is required by the State solely by reason of a prior conviction of a crime. HRS 831-3.1(a).

An employer may inquire about and consider an individual's criminal conviction record, within the most recent 10 years, provided that the conviction record bears a rational relationship to the duties and responsibilities of the position. HRS §378-2.5(a).

Inquiry into and consideration of conviction for prospective employee is allowed only after the prospective employee has received a conditional offer of employment.

Expunged Record – The person who has his or her criminal records expunged shall be treated as not having been arrested, and may state no record exists. HRS §831-3.2.

Agency guidelines for pre-employment inquiries: Hawaii Civil Rights Commission "Guide to Pre-Employment Inquiries" is available online at www.state.hi.us/hcrc/forms/pre-empinquire.pdf

Hawaii State Criminal Records Agency

Hawaii Criminal Justice Data Center   **Phone:**   808-587-3106.
Liane Moriyama, Administrator
465 S King St, Rm. 101   **Web:**   www.state.hi.us/hcjdc/
Honolulu, HI 96813

Total Records:	393,000
Who Can Access:	Records are available to the general public.
Search Requirements:	Include the following in your request: any aliases. Also helpful are gender, date of birth, Social Security Number. Submission of fingerprints is an option. 99% of the records are fingerpirnt-supported.
What Is Released:	Only records with convictions is released to the public. Records without dispositions are not released. Records are available from the 1930's.
Indexing & Storage:	It takes 1 to 20 days before new records are available for inquiry. 89% of all arrests in database have final dispositions recorded, 81% for those arrests

within last 5 years. Records are indexed on in an electronic statewide repository of criminal history records.

Access By:	Mail, in person.
Mail Search:	Turnaround time: 5 to 7 days. A self addressed stamped envelope is requested.
In Person Search:	The public may access conviction information by computer on-site.
Fee & Payment:	The search fee for a name-based criminal record search is $15.00. A fingerprint-based search is $25.00. A public access (convictions only) printout, available only in-person at this office or at main police stations, is $10.00. Certification fee: $10.00. Fee payee: Director of Finance, State of Hawaii. Prepayment required. Money orders and cashiers' checks are the only acceptable methods of payment. No credit cards accepted.

Hawaii Sexual Offender Registry

Hawaii Criminal Justice Data Center   **Phone**: 808-587-3106

Sexual Offender Registry, 465 S King St, Room 101

Honolulu, HI 96813   **Web**:   www.state.hi.us/hcjdc/

The sexual offender registration database is not available for name searches. The court will decide if the offender's information is necessary to protect the public.

Hawaii State Incarceration Records Agency

Hawaii Department of Public Safety   **Phone:** 808-587-3100

Hawaii Criminal Justice Data Center

465 South King St, Rm 101   **Web:**   www.hawaii.gov/hcjdc/

Honolulu, HI 96813

What is released:	Records are available on current and former inmates. It takes 1 to 20 days before new records are released.
Search Notes:	Include in request: name. DOB and SSN helpful. Fee for search is $15.00. Mail turnaround time: 7 to 10 days. Payee: Department of Public Safety Money orders and cashiers' checks are the only acceptable methods of payment.
Access by:	Mail only.

Hawaii State Court System

Court Structure: Hawaii's trial level is comprised of Circuit Courts (with Family Courts) and District Courts. These trial courts function in four judicial circuits: First (Oahu), Second (Maui/Molokai/Lanai), Third (Hawaii County), and Fifth (Kauai/Niihau). The Fourth Circuit was merged with the Third in 1943. Circuit Courts are general jurisdiction and handle all jury trials, felony cases, and civil cases over $20,000, also probate and guardianship. The District Court handles criminal cases punishable by a fine and/or less then 1-yr imprisonment. also DUI cases.

Find Felony Records: Circuit Court

Misdemeanor Records: District Court

Online Access: Free online access to all Circuit Court and family court records is available at the website www.courts.state.hi.us (click on "Search Court Records"). Search by name or case number. These records are not considered "official" for FCRA compliant searches. Most courts have access back to mid 1980's. Also, opinions from the Appellate Court are available from the home page.

Searching Hints: Most Hawaii state courts offer a public access terminal to search records at the courthouse.

Court Administrator: For add'l questions about the state's court system, visit the website at www.courts.state.hi.us/index.jsp, or contact: Administrative Director of Courts, 417 S. King St, Honolulu, HI 96813, Phone: 808-539-4900.

Idaho

Idaho Statues and Related Employer Restrictions

General Rule – A person, private or public agency upon written application may obtain a copy of a person criminal history record. A record of an arrest that does not contain a disposition after twelve months from the date of the arrest may only be disseminated by the department to criminal justice agencies, the subject of the record, or a person requesting the criminal history information who has a signed release from the subject of the record. A person, private or public agency shall not disseminate criminal history information to a person that is not a criminal justice agency without a signed release from the subject of the record.   IS ST §67-3008(2)(b).

Definitions – ID ST §67-3001

Criminal History Record – includes arrests, prosecutions, disposition of cases by court, sentencing, probation and parole, and information from correctional agencies.

Agency guidelines for pre-employment inquiries: Idaho Human Rights Commission, "Pre-Employment Inquiries" is available online at www.jobservice.us/lawintvw3.htm

Idaho State Criminal Records Agency

State Repository
Bureau of Criminal Identification
PO Box 700
Meridian, ID 83680-0700

Phone: 208-884-7130.
Fax: 208-884-7193

Web: www.isp.state.id.us

Total Records: 188,700

Who Can Access: Records are available to the general public.

Search Requirements: A signed release is not required, but suggested. Include the following in your request: name, DOB. SSN and alias will aid in identification. Fingerprints are optional but may be required to establish positive identification Fingerprint searches take 5-7 days. 100% of records are fingerprint-supported.

What Is Released: A record of an arrest without disposition after 12 months from date of arrest will only be given if signed release presented. Requests without the release will receive only records with dispositions. Records are available from 1960 to present.

Indexing & Storage: It takes about 3 days before new records are available for inquiry. 61% of all arrests in database have final dispositions recorded, 56% for those arrests within last 5 years. Records are normally destroyed after subject reaches 99.

Access By: Mail, in person.

Mail Search: Turnaround time: 10 to 15 days.

In Person Search: You may request information in person, but results are still mailed.

Fee & Payment: The $10.00 fee per person is applicable for either a name search or a fingerprint search. Fee payee: Idaho State Police Prepayment required. Cashier check or money order is preferred form of payment. No credit cards.

Idaho Sexual Offender Registry

State Repository   **Phone**: 208-884-7305

Central Sexual Offender Registry   **Fax**:   208-884-7193

PO Box 700

Meridian, ID 83680-0700   **Web**:   www.isp.state.id.us

(courier address: 700 S Stratford Dr, Meridian, ID 83642.)

What is released: Requests may be made on a named individual or a list of registered sex offenders by ZIP Code or county. Any person may inquire by submitting a completed SOR-4 Form to the central registry or a local sheriff. Photos may be requested using SOR-5 Form. Records are available from 07/01/93. It takes about 3 days before new records are released.

Search Notes: Include in request: name and either DOB or address. There is a $5.00 fee, plus an additional $5.00 if photo needed. Schools and nonprofit organizations working with youth, women, or other vulnerable populations are exempt from payment of the fee. Mail turnaround time: 5 to 7 days. Payee: BCI. Prepayment required. Cashier check or money order is preferred form of payment. Personal checks are accepted. No credit cards.

Access by: Mail, In Person, Online. In person search note: you may request information from this agency or from any local sheriff's office. Online search note: access from the web page is available to the public. Inquires can be made by name, address, or by county or ZIP Code.

Idaho State Incarceration Records Agency

Idaho Department of Corrections   **Phone:** 208-658-2000

Records Bureau   **Fax:**   208-327-7444

1299 N. Orchard Street, Suite 110   **Web:**   www.corrections.state.id.us

Boise, ID 83706

What is released:	Records are available on current and former inmates. It takes about 3 days before new records are released. Records normally destroyed after 2 years if probation only and not convicted of sex crime. All other records not destroyed but sent to state storage.
Search Notes:	Include in request: first and last name. DOB, SSN, DOC number are helpful. Cost is $2.00 for pulling from state storage, if required. Copies are $.10 per page after 5 pages. Mail turnaround time: 5 to 7 days.
Access by:	Phone, Fax, Mail, In Person, Online. In person search note: the public has right to view records in person upon making a written request to schedule an appointment with records custodian. Online search note: This database search at https://www.accessidaho.org/public/corr/offender/search.html provides information about offenders currently under Idaho Department of Correction jurisdiction: those incarcerated, on probation, or on parole. Names of individuals who have served time and satisfied their sentence will appear - their convictions will not. Also, a private company offers free web access to Idaho DOC at www.vinelink.com/index.jsp.

Idaho State Court System

Court Structure:	The District Court oversees felony and most civil cases.
Find Felony Records:	District Court
Misdemeanor Records:	District Court
Online Access:	Although appellate and supreme court opinions are available from the web, there is no statewide computer system offering external access. ISTARS is a statewide intra-court/intra-agency system run and managed by the State Supreme Court. All counties are on ISTARS, and all courts provide public access terminals on-site.
Searching Hints:	A statewide court administrative rule states that record custodians do not have a duty to "compile or summarize information contained in a record, nor ... to create new records for the requesting party." Under this rule, some courts will not perform searches.
	Many courts require a signed release for employment record searches.
	The following fees are mandated statewide: Search Fee - none; Certification Fee - $1.00 per document plus copy fee; Copy Fee - $1.00 per page. Not all jurisdictions currently follow these guidelines.
Court Administrator:	For add'l questions about the state's court system, visit the website at http://www2.state.id.us/judicial/, or contact: Administrative Director of the Courts, PO Box 83720, Boise, ID 83720-0101, Phone: 208-334-2246.

Illinois

Illinois Statues and Related Employer Restrictions

General Rule – All conviction information shall be open to public inspection in the State of Illinois. All persons, state agencies, and unit of local government shall have access to inspect, examine, and reproduce such information.   20 ILCS 2635/5.

A requestor shall submit a request to the department and maintain on file for at least 2 years a release signed by the individual to whom the information pertains.   20 ILCS 2635/7.

A requester shall only permit the subsequent dissemination of conviction information furnished by the department for a 30-day period immediately following receipt of the info.   20 ILCS 2635/13.

Definitions – 20 ILCS 2635/3

Conviction Information – data reflecting a judgment of guilt or nolo contendere. Includes prior and subsequent criminal history event directly relating to such judgments such as arrest, charges filed, sentence imposed, fine imposed, all related probation, parole, and release information. Information is not conviction information when a judgment of guilt is reversed or vacated.

Requestor – any private individual, corporation, organization, employer, employment agency, labor organization, or non-criminal justice agency that has made a request pursuant to this Act to obtain conviction information.

Illinois State Criminal Records Agency

Illinois State Police
Bureau of Identification
260 N Chicago St
Joliet, IL 60432-4075

Phone: 815-740-5216 x5184
Fax: 815-740-5215

Web: www.isp.state.il.us

Total Records: 3,280,000

Who Can Access: Records are available only with consent of the subject.

Search Requirements: Requester must use the Uniform Conviction Information Form ISP6-405B. Personal requests are honored per Illinois statute. Include the following in your request: name, date of birth, sex, race. Fingerprint cards are an option; a fingerprint search using Form ISP6-404B is recommended in order to assure proper ID. All forms can be ordered (but not downloaded) at the website.

What Is Released: No records are released without a disposition of conviction. Records are available from 1930's on. The following data is not released: records with warrants only, juvenile records unless juvenile convicted by an adult court of law.

Indexing & Storage: It takes 1 to 5 days before new records are available for inquiry. 61% of all arrests in database have final dispositions recorded, 67% for arrests within last 5 years. Records indexed on microfilm, index cards, inhouse computer.

Access By: Mail, in person, online.

Mail Search: Turnaround time: 3 to 4 weeks. No self addressed stamped envelope is required.

In Person Search: An in person search saves mailing time only.

Online Search: Online access costs $10.00 per name. Upon signing an interagency agreement with ISP and establishing an escrow account, users can submit inquiries by email. Responses are sent back in 24 to 48 hours by either email or fax.

Fee & Payment: The search fee is $16.00 per form. A fingerprint search is $20.00. Fee payee: Illinois State Police. Prepayment required. Modem users and ongoing UCIA requesters must prepay for records in groups of 35 at a time. Personal checks accepted. No credit cards accepted.

Illinois Sexual Offender Registry

Illinois State Police, SOR Unit   **Phone**: 217-785-0653

400 Iles Park Place, #140

Springfield, IL 62703-2978   **Web**:   www.isp.state.il.us/sor/frames.htm

Persons required to register as Sex Offenders are persons who have been charged of an offense listed in Illinois Compiled Statutes 730 ILCS 150/2(B). A status fileld indicates if offender listed as "COMPLIANT" are in good standing with the Sex Offender Registration Laws. Offenders listed as "NON-COMPLIANT" have failed to maintain accurate registration information.

What is released: Illinois Compiled Statutes (730 ILCS 152/115 (a) and (b)) mandate that the Illinois State Police ("ISP") establish and maintain a statewide Sex Offender Database, accessible on the Internet. It takes 1 to 5 days before new records are released.

Access by: Online. No searching by mail. In person search note: you may search at local law enforcement agencies throughout the state. Online search note: the website provides an online listing of sex offenders required to register in the State of Illinois. The database is updated daily and allows searching by name, city, county, and ZIP Code. The City of Chicago provides its own search site at http://12.17.79.4.

Illinois State Incarceration Records Agency

Illinois Department of Corrections
Public Information Office
P.O. Box 19277
Springfield, IL 62794-9277

Phone: 217-522-2666 x2008
Fax: 217-522-3568
Web: www.idoc.state.il.us

What is released: Offender information is available to the general public and private organizations. Location, conviction information, physical identifiers, and release dates are reported. Records are available on current and former inmates, except online is current only. It takes 1 to 5 days before new records are released.

Search Notes: Include in request: full name and DOB, IBOC number, gender, race helpful. For a online search, you can provide name or DOB or IDOC number. Mail turnaround time: 1 to 2 weeks. Records are never destroyed; are archived.

Access by: Phone, Mail, Online. Name searching available by phone. Online search note: click on Inmate Search at the website. Also, a private company offers free web access at www.vinelink.com/index.jsp. Includes state, DOC, and county jails. Other Access: a CD-rom of the inmate database can be purchased for $45.00.

Illinois State Court System

Court Structure: Illinois is divided into 22 judicial circuits; 3 are single county: Cook, Du Page (18th Circuit) and Will (12th Circuit). The other 19 circuits consist of 2 or more contiguous counties. The Circuit Court of Cook County is the largest unified court system in the world. Its 2300-person staff handles approximately 2.4 million cases each year.

Find Felony Records: Circuit Court

Misdemeanor Records: Circuit Court

Online Access: The web page offers access to supreme and appellate opinions. While there is no statewide public online system available, a number of Illinois Circuit Courts offer online access. And, Judici.com offers free searching for a growing number of counties; the Judici.com home page also offers a commercial subscription service for multi-county searching.

Searching Hints: The search fee is set by statute and has three levels based on the county population. The higher the population, the larger the fee. In most Illinois courts the search fee is charged on a per name per year basis.

Court Administrator: For add'l questions about the state's court system, visit the website at www.state.il.us/court/, or contact: Administrative Office of Courts, 222 N. LaSalle, 13th Fl, Chicago, IL 60601, Phone: 312-793-3250.

Indiana

Indiana Statues and Related Employer Restrictions

General Rule – Law enforcement agencies shall release or allow inspection of a limited criminal history to non-criminal justice organizations or individuals if the subject of the request has applied for employment with a non-criminal justice organization or individual. IC 10-13-3-27

Limited criminal history records may not be disclosed which are over 15 years old if the person on record petitioned to limit access to his or her limited criminal history. IC 35-38-5-5.

Juvenile - Department may not release a person's juvenile history data to any person or agency unless the requestor is the juvenile of record or the juvenile's parents, guardian, or custodian. IC 10-13-4-12.

Definitions

Criminal History Data – includes notations of arrests, indictments, information or other formal charges, information regarding a sex and violent offender, and any disposition, including sentencing, correctional system intake, transfer, and release. IC 10-13-3-5.

Limited Criminal History – information about any arrest or criminal charge which must include disposition. However it does include information about any arrest or criminal charge that occurred less than one year before the date of a request even if no disposition has been entered.

Indiana State Criminal Records Agency

Indiana State Police   **Phone:** 317-232-8266
Central Records   **Fax:** 317-233-8813
IGCN - 100 N Senate Ave, Rm 302
Indianapolis, IN 46204-2259   **Web:**   www.IN.gov/isp/

Total Records: 998,068

Who Can Access: The release of records is governed by IC 5-2-5. A "Limited Criminal History" is available to designated entites including employers, licensing agencies, schools, and certain other designates.

Search Requirements: Use State Form 8053. Include the following in your request: full name, date of birth, sex, race. Submitting fingerprints is an option. 100% of the records are fingerprint-supported.

What Is Released: Record will show all activity, including arrests, dismissals, and convictions. But, if a charge is over a year old with no disposition, then the record will not be released. Records are available from 1935.

Indexing & Storage: It takes 10 days before new records are available for inquiry. Approximately 10% of all arrests in database have final dispositions recorded, over 50% for those arrests within last 5 years. This agency now is notified when charges are made after fingerprints are submitted. Records are indexed on inhouse computer. Records are normally destroyed after 99 years.

Access By: Mail, in person, online.

Mail Search: Turnaround time: Two weeks. Use State Form 8053, which can be downloaded from the website at www.in.gov/isp/lch/LCHrequest.pdf.

In Person Search: Requester must have picture ID, turnaround time is 15-20 minutes, but the full record is mailed out 24 hours later.

Online Search: The standard online search fee is $17.50 at www.in.gov/isp/lch/. Subcribers to accessIndiana can obtain records for $15.00 per search or for no charge if you are statuatorily exempt, or $7.00 if you have a government exemption.

Fee & Payment: The fee for employers is $7.00 per name for a limited criminal history, and if no fingerprints used. The fee for a fingerprint search is $10.00. If subject requests own record, fee is $10.00, and this is for a FULL record. Fee payee: State of Indiana. Prepayment required. Cash, money orders, and certified checks are accepted. Ongoing requesters may open a monthly billing account. No bills over $10.00 accepted. Credit cards accepted online only.

Indiana Sexual Offender Registry

Sex and Violent Offender Directory Manager   **Phone**: 317-232-1233
Indiana Criminal Justice Institute
One North Capitol, Suite 1000   **Fax**:   317-232-4979
Indianapolis, IN 46204-2038   **Web**:   https://secure.in.gov/serv/cji_sor

Indiana law requires the Indiana Criminal Justice Institute to maintain a directory of individuals who have been convicted of one or more of the sex and violent offenses requiring registration with local sheriff departments. While this state agency will help requesters to a point, most serachers are directed to the local sheriffs' offices or to the web page.

What is released: Records are available from 04/01/89.

Search Notes: Mail turnaround time: 3 - 5 days.

Access by: Phone, Mail, In Person, Online. Online search note: the website has a searching capabilities by name and city or county. Also, an excellent search site is maintained by the Indiana Sheriff's Association at www.indianasheriffs.org/default.asp. The Indiana Sheriffs' Sex Offender Registry presents photographs, addresses, and identifiers of registered sex and violent offenders.

Indiana State Incarceration Records Agency

Indiana Department of Corrections, IGCS   **Phone**: 317-232-5765

Supervisor of Records, Rm E-334   **Fax:**   317-232-5728

302 W. Washington Street   **Web:**   www.in.gov/indcorrection

Indianapolis, IN 46204

What is released: Computerized records go back to 1989. Location, DOC number, physical identifiers, sentencing, and conviction information, and release dates are released. Records are available on current and former inmates. 10 days before new records are released. Records normally destroyed after 10 years.

Search Notes: Include in request: first and last name; the DOB and SSN helpful. To search online provide either full name or inmate number. Fee is $.10 per page. Mail turnaround: 5 to 10 working days. Payee: Dept. of Corrections.

Access by: Phone, Fax, Mail, Online. Limited searching available by phone. Online search note: at the website, click on Offender Search.

Indiana State Court System

Court Structure: There are 92 judicial circuits with Circuit Courts or Combined Circuit and Superior Courts. In addition, there are 48 City Courts and 25 Town Courts. County Courts are gradually being restructured into divisions of the Superior Courts.

Find Felony Records: Circuit or Superior or County Court

Misdemeanor Records: Circuit, Superior, County, City, and Town Courts

Online Access: There is no statewide trial court records service available. However, the website gives free access to an index of docket information for Supreme, Appeals, and Tax Court cases.

Searching Hints: The Circuit Court Clerk/County Clerk in every county is the same individual and is responsible for keeping all county judicial records. However, it is recommended that, when requesting a record, the request indicate which court heard the case (Circuit, Superior, or County).

Many courts are no longer performing searches, especially criminal searches, based on a 7/8/96 statement by the State Board of Accounts.

Certification and copy fees are set by statute as $1.00 per document plus copy fee for certification and $1.00 per page for copies.

Court Administrator: For add'l questions about the state's court system, visit the website at www.in.gov/judiciary/, or contact: State Court Administrator, 200 W Washington St, #312, Indianapolis, IN 46204, Phone: 317-232-2542.

Iowa

Iowa Statues and Related Employer Restrictions

General Rule – The Department may provide copies of Criminal History Data to a person or public or private agency.   ICA §692.2 (1)(b).

Criminal History Data that does not contain any disposition after eighteen month from the date of arrest, or successful completion of probation following a deferred judgment, may only be disseminated by the Department to a person requesting the Criminal History Data with a signed release from the subject of the Criminal History Data.   ICA §692.2 (1)(b)(3) and (4).

Records of acquittals or dismissals by reason of insanity and records of adjudication of mental incompetence to stand trial in cases in which physical or mental injury or an attempt to commit physical or mental injury to another was alleged shall not be disseminated to persons or agencies other than criminal or juvenile justice agencies.   ICA §692.2 (1)(b)(6).

Juvenile - Juvenile court records are confidential and may not be inspected or disclosed.
ICA §232.47(1).

Definitions – ICA §692.1

Criminal History Data – includes arrest data, conviction data, disposition data, correctional data, adjudication data, and custody data.

Custody Data – means information pertaining to the taking into custody a juvenile for a delinquent act which would be a serious or aggravated misdemeanor or felony if committed by an adult, and includes the date, time, place, facts, and circumstances of the delinquent act.

Agency guidelines for pre-employment inquiries: Iowa Civil Rights Commission, "Successfully Interviewing Job Applicants" is available online at www.iowaworkforce.org/region1/succcessinter.htm

Iowa State Criminal Records Agency

Division of Criminal Investigations
Bureau of Identification
502 E 9th, Wallace State Office Bldg
Des Moines, IA 50319

Phone: 515-281-4776.
Fax: 515-242-6297

Web:
www.state.ia.us/government/dps/dci/crimhist.htm

Total Records: 411,000

Who Can Access: Records are available to the general public.

Search Requirements: A signed release or waiver is not required, nor are fingerprints. But if release is included, the reports will show any arrest over 18 months old without a disposition, otherwise if no release is presented then only up to 18 months. Include the following in your request: date of birth, sex, Social Security Number. A signed release is an option. Be sure to give the full name. Request Form A is required for each surname. This form can be obtained from the website, by fax, mail, or in person.

What Is Released: A signed release by subject entitles requester to all records including those without dispositions (up to 4 years old). If the subject's signed release is not presented, then no arrest records over 18 months old without dispositions are released. Records are available until the person is 80 years old or passes away, then records are deleted. There is a computerized index going back to 1935.

Indexing & Storage: It takes up to 10 days before new records are available for inquiry. 91% of all arrests in database have final dispositions recorded, 91% for those arrests within last 5 years. Records are indexed on in house computer (100%). Records are normally destroyed after 4 years if there is no disposition.

Access By: Mail, fax, in person.

Mail Search: Turnaround time: 1 to 2 days. No self addressed stamped envelope is required.

Fax Search: Only those requesters who have opened a pre-paid account, or credit card may fax.

In Person Search: Only the subject or their attorney will receive the record while they wait, within 15 minutes.

Fee & Payment: The fee for a record search is $13.00 per surname checked. The fee is $15 per search if the result is returned by fax. If married and maiden names are checked, the fee would be $26.00. Iowa law requires employers to pay the fee for potential employees' record checks. Fee payee: Iowa Division of Criminal Investigation. Payment is required unless pre-arranged billing has been arranged. Ongoing requesters can set up an account with a $500 deposit. Personal checks accepted. Credit cards accepted: MasterCard, Visa.

Iowa Sexual Offender Registry

Division of Criminal Investigations   **Phone**: 515-281-8716

SOR Unit, Wallace State Office Bldg   **Fax**:   515-242-6297

Des Moines, IA 50319   **Web**:   www.iowasexoffenders.com/

The Iowa Sex Offender Registry became law on July 1, 1995 and is found in Chapter 692A Code of Iowa.

What is released: Records are available from 07/01/95, if online back to 1999. It takes up to 2 days before new records are released.

Search Notes: Include in request: date of birth, address if known, SSN helpful. Mail turnaround time: 1 to 2 days.

Access by: Mail, Online. In person search note: not at this office; see local police or sheriff. Online search note: the website does not contain the entire list of sex offenders registered in Iowa. In accordance with Iowa law, only those registrants who have been assessed as "at risk" to re-offend can be listed.

Iowa State Incarceration Records Agency

Iowa Department of Corrections   **Phone**: 515-242-5707

420 Watson Powell Jr. Way   **Fax**:   515-281-7345, 515-281-4062

Des Moines, IA 50309-1639   **Web**:   www.doc.state.ia.us.

What is released: Computer records go back to 1986. Location, physical identifiers, county of conviction, and conviction information details are released. Records are available on current and former inmates. Deeper records - sentencing information - are also available; please include details of reason for request. It takes up to 10 days before new records are released. Not available: medical or home address data. Records never destroyed.

Search Notes: Include in request: full name and DOB or SSN. Search fee is $12.00 per hour plus postage fee. Copy fee is $.20 per page. Mail turnaround time: 1 to 10 days. Payee: Treasurer, State of Iowa, Dept. of Corrections. Prepayment required. Personal checks accepted. No credit cards accepted.

Access by: Phone, Mail, Online. Name searching for basic information is available by phone. Online search note: click on Public Info for an inmate search. This site seems to be under construction at times. Other Access: bulk records are not available, but should be in the future.

Iowa State Court System

Court Structure: The District Court is the court of general jurisdiction and handles all court matters. There are no limited jurisdiction courts.

Find Felony Records: District Court

Misdemeanor Records: District Court

Online Access: Criminal, civil, probate, traffic and appellate information is now available from all 99 counties in Iowa at www.judicial.state.ia.us/online_records/. The Iowa Courts online site is providing basic case information for no charge; a more extensive fee portion will be available in the near future. Name searches are available on a statewide or specific county basis. While this is an excellent site with much information, there is one important consideration to keep in mind: although records are updated daily, the historical records offered are not from the same starting date on a county-by-county basis. Also, from the home web page one may access supreme and apppellate court opinions.

Searching Hints: In most courts, the Certification Fee is $10.00 plus copy fee. Copy Fee is $.50 per page. Most courts do not do searches and recommend either in person searches or use of a record retriever.

Courts that accept written search requests usually require an SASE. Most courts have a public access terminal for access to that court's records.

Court Administrator: For add'l questions about the state's court system, visit the website at www.judicial.state.ia.us/courtadmin, or contact: State Court Administrator, Judicial Branch Bldg, 111 East Court Ave, Des Moines, IA 50319, Phone: 515-281-5241.

Kansas

Kansas Statues and Related Employer Restrictions

Employment – An employer may require a job applicant or prospective independent contractor to sign a release allowing the employer to access the applicant's criminal history record for determining the applicant's fitness for employment. If denied employment, the information must reasonably bear upon the applicant's trustworthiness or the safety or well being of the employer's employees or customers.   KSA §22-4710

Expunged Record - A person who has had criminal records expunged may state that he or she has never been arrested or convicted of such an offense. KSA §12-4516(g).

Consumer Report - A consumer reporting agency may not disclose 1) bankruptcy that antedates the report by more than 14 years, and 2) suits and judgments, records of arrest, indictment, or conviction of a crime, paid tax liens, accounts placed for collection, or any other adverse item of information that antedate the report by more than 7 years.   KSA §50-704(a).

Exception – Employment of an individual at an annual salary that equals $20,000 or more. KSA §50-704(b)(3).

Agency guidelines for pre-employment inquiries: Kansas Human Rights Commission "Guidelines on Equal Employment Practices: Preventing Discrimination in Hiring" is available online at www.khrc.net/hiring.html

Kansas State Criminal Records Agency

Kansas Bureau of Investigation
Criminal Records Division
1620 SW Tyler, Crim. History Record Sec.
Topeka, KS 66612-1837

Phone: 785-296-8200.
Fax: 785-368-7162
Web: www.accesskansas.org/kbi/

Total Records: 821,000

Who Can Access: Records are available to the general public. Agencies dealing with children, the elderly or disabled clientele may qualify for reduced fees for record checks. These accounts are known as Caretaker accounts.

Search Requirements: The criminal history information maintained by the KBI includes felony and misdemeanor arrests, prosecution data, court dispositions and information of incarceration in state-operated confinement facilities. Include the following in your request: full name, sex, race, date of birth, Social Security Number. Each request must be on a separate "Records Check Request Form." Fingerprints are optional. Approximately 85% of records are fingerprint supported. Turnaround time may be several weeks if the record is not currently automated; approximately 46% of records are automated.

What Is Released: Records of arrests within the past 12 months are also released when the records of disposition have not yet been received. Records release include court convictions for violations of Kansas law that are felonies or class A or class B misdemeanors as well as municipal ordinances or county resolutions that are equivalent to class A or class B misdemeanors under state statute. Class C misdemeanor assaults are also part of the database. Records are available from 1939 to present. The following data is not released: expunged records, non-convictions or juvenile records except to Criminal justice agencies and agencies required by law.

Indexing & Storage: It takes up to 4 days before new records are available for inquiry. 50% of all arrests in database have final dispositions recorded, 57% for those arrests within last 5 years. Records are indexed on Kansas Central Repository database, which is synchronized with the automated fingerprint ID system database. Records are normally destroyed after court-ordered expungement or after subject reaches 100 years of age.

Access By: Mail, fax, online.

Mail Search: Turnaround time: 2 to 4 weeks. A self addressed stamped envelope is requested.

Fax Search: Prior arrangement is required, same criteria as mail.

Online Search: Anyone may obtain non-certified criminal records online at www.accesskansas.org/kbi/criminalhistory/. The system is also available for premium subscribers of accessKansas. The fee is $17.50 per record. The system is unavailable between midnight and 4 AM daily. A Kansas "Mosted Wanted" list is available at www.accesskansas.org/kbi/mw.htm.

Fee & Payment: Fees: $17.50 for a name check, $25.00 if certified; $30.00 for fingerprint search, $40.00 if certified. Check your own record or be a caregiver and fee is $12.50. Caretaker fingerpirnt check is $20.00. Fee payee: KBI Records Fees Fund. Prepayment required. Personal checks and credit cards are accepted.

Kansas Sexual Offender Registry

Kansas Bureau of Investigation   **Phone**: 785-296-8200

Sexual Offender Registry   **Fax**:   785-296-6781

1620 SW Tyler

Topeka, KS 66612-1837   **Web**:   www.accesskansas.org/kbi/ro.shtml

There are over 2,300 offencers registered in the state.

What is released:	Further information on any registered offender in the file can be obtained from the sheriff's office in the registrant's county of residence. Records are available from 4/14/1994 forward. It takes 5 to 10 days before new records are released.
Search Notes:	Include in request: name, DOB. SSN is hepful is a common name. Mail turnaround time: 1 to 2 days.
Access by:	Fax, Mail, In Person, Online. Online search note: searching is available at the website. All open registrants are searchable.

Kansas State Incarceration Records Agency

Kansas Department of Corrections   **Phone:** 785-296-3310

Public Information Officer   **Fax:**   785-296-7023

900 SW Jackson, 4th Fl   **Web:**   http://docnet.dc.state.ks.us

Topeka, KS 66612-1284.

What is released:	Location, KDOC number, physical identifiers, sentencing and conviction information, disciplinary record, and custody or supervision level are released. Records are available on current and former inmates. It takes up to 4 days before new records are released. Not available: medical, mental health, substance abuse. Records normally destroyed after thirty years.
Search Notes:	Include in request: full name, date of birth and Social Security Number helpful. Mail turnaround time: 2 to 4 weeks.
Access by:	Phone, Fax, Mail, Online. Name searching permitted by phone. Online search note: Web access to the database known as KASPER gives information on offenders who are: currently incarcerated; under post-incarceration supervision; and, who have been discharged from a sentence. The database does not have information available about inmates sent to Kansas under the provisions of the interstate compact agreement. Go to http://docnet.dc.state.ks.us/kasper2/default.asp.

Kansas State Court System

Court Structure: The District Court is the court of general jurisdiction. There are 110 courts in 31 districts in 105 counties.

If an individual in Municipal Court wants a jury trial, the request must be filed de novo in a District Court.

Find Felony Records: District Court

Misdemeanor Records: District Court

Online Access: Commercial online access is available for District Court Records in 4 counties - Johnson, Sedgwick, Shawnee, and Wyandotte - through Access Kansas, part of the Information Network of Kansas (INK) Services. Franklin and Finney counties may be available in late 2004. A user can access INK through their Internet site at www.accesskansas.org or via a dial-up system. The INK subscription fee is $75.00, and the annual renewal fee is $60.00. There is no per minute connect charge but there is a transaction fee. Other information from INK includes Drivers License, Title, Registration, Lien, and UCC searches. For additional information or a registration packet, call 800-4-KANSAS (800-452-6727).

The Kansas Appellate Courts offer free online access to case information at www.kscourts.org.

Searching Hints: Five counties - Cowley, Crawford, Labette, Montgomery and Neosho - have two hearing locations, but only one record center.

Many Kansas courts do not do criminal record searches and will refer any criminal requests to the Kansas Bureau of Investigation. The Kansas Legislature's Administrative Order 156 (Fall, 2000) allows Courts to charge up to $12.00 per hour for search services, though courts may set their own search fees, if any.

Court Administrator: For add'l questions about the state's court system, visit the website at www.kscourts.org, or contact: Judicial Administrator, Kansas Judicial Center, 301 SW 10th St, Topeka, KS 66612-1507, Phone: 785-296-4873.

Kentucky

Kentucky Statues and Related Employer Restrictions

General Rule - All public records shall be open for inspection by any person. KRS § 61.872.

Exceptions - Expunged records are not open to the public. KRS §197.025. Proceedings relating to the adjudication of a juvenile as delinquent or in need of supervision cannot be released without a court order. 502 KAR 30:060. Non-conviction data can only be released to 1) criminal justice agencies for criminal justice purposes and criminal justice employment. 502 KAR 30:060.

An employer may request records involving any felony, pornography misdemeanor, sexual offense misdemeanor, controlled substance misdemeanor committed within five years immediately preceding the application, or any conviction for Driving Under the Influence committed within five years immediately preceding the application of a person who applies for employment or volunteers for a position in which he or she would have supervisory or disciplinary power over a minor. KRS §17.10(1).

Definitions - 502 KAR 30:010

Criminal History Record Information – includes information on arrests, detentions, indictments, informations, and other criminal charges, and any disposition arising there from, including sentencing, correctional supervision, and release.

Kentucky State Criminal Records Agency

Kentucky State Police
Records Branch
1250 Louisville Rd
Frankfort, KY 40601

Phone: 502-227-8713.
Fax: 502-227-8734

Web: www.kentuckystatepolice.org

Note: Local Kentucky courts will not do criminal searches. They refer all requesters to the Administrative Office of Courts in Frankfort, KY; phone 502-573-2350.

Total Records: 856,857

Who Can Access: Per statute, requests are accepted for employment purposes for nursing, schools, lottery, EMT, YMCA, daycare, and adoptive/foster parent background searches. Other requesters are advised to submit requests through the court system.

Search Requirements: Include the following in your request: signed release from subject, full name, date of birth, Social Security Number, reason for information request. Fingerprints are not requested. Statistical information about criminal offenses and accidents is available from 1971 on.

What Is Released: Records without dispositions, including pending and dismissed cases, are not released. Records are available from 1952 on for criminal records. The following data is not released: juvenile records.

Indexing & Storage: It takes a minimum of 30 days before new records are available for inquiry. 69% of all arrests in database have final dispositions recorded, 59% for those arrests within last 5 years. Records are indexed on inhouse computer, fingerprint cards. Nearly 75% of records are automated.

Access By: Mail, in person.

Mail Search: Turnaround time: 2 to 3 weeks. Self addressed stamped envelope is requested.

In Person Search: Turnaround time is while you wait. There is a limit of 5 searches.

Fee & Payment: The fee is $10.00 per name. Fee payee: Kentucky State Treasurer. Prepayment required. Personal checks accepted. No credit cards accepted.

Kentucky Sexual Offender Registry

Kentucky State Police   **Phone**: 502-227-8718; Alert Line: 866-564-5652

Criminal identification and Records Branch

1250 Louisville Rd   **Fax**:   502-226-7419

Frankfort, KY 40601   **Web**:   www.kentuckystatepolice.org/sor.htm

What is released: Only offenders convicted of statutorily covered crimes who are convicted after July 15, 1994 or incarcerated or sentenced after July 15, 1998 are listed. Records are available from 7/15/94 forward.

Access by: Phone, Online. Provide your telephone number and up to three ZIP Codes to monitor. You will be notifed if registered sex offender is moving into one of the ZIP Code areas that you entered. No written requests accepted. Online search note: Access available via the website; search by city, ZIP, or county.

Kentucky State Incarceration Records Agency

Kentucky Department of Corrections   **Phone:** 502-564-2433

Offender Information Services   **Fax:**   502-564-1471

P.O. Box 2400   **Web:**   www.corrections.ky.gov

Frankfort, KY 40602-2400

Victim Notification Line: 800-511-1670

What is released: Location, physical identifiers, conviction and sentencing information, and release dates are reported. Records are available on current and former inmates. It takes approximately 30 days before new records are released. Records normally destroyed after 5 years after release (institutional versions) and after 75 years after release from the central office file.

Search Notes: Include in request: full name. DOB and SSN are helpful. Index does not include alias or other names used. Records indexed on computer back to 1979; prior in archives on paper. Copy fee is $.10 per page. There is no search fee, however list searches may be charged a search fee depending on whether the search is for commercial resale purposes. Mail turnaround time: 1 to 2 weeks. Payee: Kentucky Treasurer Prepayment required. Personal checks accepted. Credit cards accepted.

Access by: Fax, Mail, Online. Online search note: the website provides current inmate information on the Kentucky Online Offender Lookup (KOOL) system as a service to the public. It can take as long as 120 days for the data to be current. Also, a private company offers free web access at www.vinelink.com/index.jsp. Include state, DOC, and county jails. Other Access: the IT Department has the database on magnetic tape; this is available to users with compatible systems. For information on tape access, call 502-564-4360.

Kentucky State Court System

Court Structure: The Circuit Court is the court of general jurisdiction and the District Court is the limited jurisdiction court. Most of Kentucky's counties combined the courts into one location and records are co-mingled.

Find Felony Records: Circuit Courts

Misdemeanor Records: District Courts

Online Access: There are statewide, online computer systems called SUSTAIN and KyCourts available for internal judicial/state agency use only, and KY Bar attorneys may register to use the KCOJ court records data at http://courtnetpublic.kycourts.net. No courts offer online access to records. However, you may search daily court calendars by county for free at http://dockets.kycourts.net. Also, you may search online for circuit court dockets (limited) on the supreme court search page at http://162.114.20.136/dockets. These are only the cases open before the Supreme Court.

Searching Hints: Until 1978, county judges handled all cases; therefore, in many cases, District and Circuit Court records go back only to 1978. Records prior to that time are archived.

Many courts refer requests for criminal searches to the Administrative Office of Courts (AOC - 502-573-2350 or 800-928-6381) due to lack of personnel for searching at the court level. AOC maintains records on an internal system called COURTNET, which contains information on opening, closing, proceedings, disposition, and parties to including individual defendants. Felony convictions are accessible back to 1978, and Misdemeanors back five years. The required Release Form is available from the AOC at the numbers above. A check or money order for the search fee of $10.00 per requested individual ($5.00 fee if non-profit or if you are the individual) is payable to the State Treasurer of Kentucky. A SASE and a second postage-attached envelope must accompany the request.

Court Administrator: For add'l questions about the state's court system, visit the website at www.kycourts.net, or contact: Administrative Office of Courts, Pre-trail Services Records Division, 100 Mill Creek Park, Frankfort, KY 40601, Phone: 502-573-1682.

Louisiana

Louisiana Statues & Related Employer Restrictions

General Rule – Any person of the age of majority may inspect or copy any public record. LSA-RS 44:31.

Exception – Disclosure is not required for 1) records pertaining to pending criminal litigation, 2) identity of a confidential source, 3) records of a person's arrest until a final judgment of conviction or the acceptance of a guilty plea. LSA-RS 44:3.

Employment – A person shall not be disqualified to engage in any trade, occupation, or practice solely because of a prior criminal record unless he or she was convicted of a felony that directly relates to the position sought. LSA-RS 37:2950(A).

This rule does not apply to 1) any law enforcement agency, 2) Louisiana State Board of Medical Examiners, 3) Louisiana State Board of Dentistry, 4) Louisiana State Board of Nursing, 5) Louisiana State Board of Practical Nurse Examiners, 6) State Racing Commission, 7) State Athletic Commission, 8) State Bar Association, 9) State Board of Pharmacy, 10) Louisiana Professional Engineering and Land Surveying Board, 11) State Board of Architectural Examiners, 12) State Board of Private Investigator Examiners, 13) State Board of Embalmers and Funeral Directors, and 13) Office of Alcohol and Tobacco Control of the Department of Revenue. LSA-RS 37:2950(D).

Louisiana State Criminal Records Agency

State Police
Bureau of Criminal Identification
7979 Independence Blvd
Baton Rouge, LA 70806-6409

Phone: 225-925-6095.
Fax: 225-925-7005

Web: www.lsp.org

Access to Records is Restricted

Note: Records ARE RESTRICTED and are not available to the public in general. Records are available for employment or licensing purposes as state law dictates.

Total Records: 1,850,000

Search Requirements: Authorized forms are available from this department. Include the following in your request: set of fingerprints, signed release, full name, SSN, and DOB. 100% of the records are fingerprint-supported.

What Is Released: Only records with convictions are released. Records are available from the early 1900's. Records are indexed by name on computer from 1974 to present. The following data is not released: pending records or juvenile records.

Louisiana Sexual Offender Registry

State Police   **Phone**: 225-925-6100 800-858-0551

Sex Offender and Child Predator Registry

PO Box 66614, Box A-6   **Fax**:   225-925-7005

Baton Rouge, LA 70896   **Web**:   www.lasocpr.lsp.org/socpr/

The Sex Offender and Child Predator Registry program is statutorily provided through La. R. S. 15:542 & 15:542.1, et. seq., of the Louisiana Criminal Code.

What is released: Records are available from 6/18/92. It takes 1 to 3 days before new records are released. Records normally destroyed after the registration term expires (varies by nature of record).

Search Notes: Mail turnaround time: 30 days.

Access by: Phone, Fax, Mail, In Person, Online. Request can be delayed due to limited staff. In person search note: This office and local law enforcement will perform searches. Online search note: search by name, ZIP Code, or view the entire list at the website. Also search by city, school area, or parish.

Louisiana State Incarceration Records Agency

Department of Public Safety and Corrections   **Phone:** 225-342-6642

P.O. Box 94304, Attn: Office of Adult Services **Locator:** 225-342-9711

Baton Rouge, LA 70804-9304   **Web:**   www.corrections.state.la.us.

What is released: Location, conviction and sentencing information is released. Records computerized since 1975. Records are available on current and former inmates. It takes 1 to 3 days before new records are released.

Search Notes: Include in request: full name; DOC number helpful. There is no fee. Mail turnaround time: 30 days.

Access by: Phone, Fax, Mail, Online. Limited name searching available by phone. Online search note: access is limited to schedules for upcoming Parole Board hearings, as well as decisions from previous Parole Board hearings.

Go to www.corrections.state.la.us/Offices/paroleboard/paroledockets.htm. Also, a private company offers free web access at www.vinelink.com/index.jsp including state, DOC, and most county jail systems.

Louisiana State Court System

Court Structure: A District Court Clerk in each Parish holds all the records for that Parish. Each Parish has its own clerk and courthouse. A municipality may have a Mayor's Court; the mayor may hold trials, but nothing over $30.00, and there are no records.

Find Felony Records: District Courts

Misdemeanor Records: City and Parish Courts, and the New Orleans City Courts

Online Access: The online computer system named Case Management Information System (CMIS) is operating and development is continuing. It is for internal use only; there is no plan to permit online public access. However, search opinions from the state Supreme Court at www.lasc.org/opinion_search.asp. Online records go back to 1995. There are a number of Parishes that do offer a means of remote online access to the public.

Court Administrator: For add'l questions about the state's court system, visit the website at www.lasc.org, or contact: Judicial Administrator, Judicial Council of the Supreme Court, 1555 Poydras Street, Suite 1540, New Orleans, LA 70112-1814, Phone: 504-568-5747.

Maine

Maine Statues and Related Employer Restrictions

Public Records General Rule – Every person shall have the right to inspect and copy any public record. 1 MRSA § 408. Records of persons detained, except for records of juvenile detention, are public records. 16 MRSA §612-A(3).

Conviction Data may be disseminated to any person for any purpose. 16 MRSA § 615. Non-conviction data may only be disseminated to 1) criminal justice agencies for criminal justice purposes, 2) express authorization by statute, or court order, 3) specific agreement with criminal justice agency to provide services for the criminal justice agency, and 4) research activities. 16 MRSA § 613.

Definitions - 16 MRSA § 611

Conviction Data – means criminal history information other than non-conviction data

Non-conviction Data – means 1) arrests without disposition if one year has elapsed from the date of arrest and no active prosecution charge is pending, 2) information that the police have elected not to refer a matter to the prosecutor, 3) information that the prosecutor has elected not to pursue criminal proceedings, 4) information that the criminal proceedings have been indefinitely postponed, 5) a dismissal, 6) an acquittal, except one because of mental disease, and 7) information disclosing that a person has been granted a full pardon or amnesty.

Employers General Rule – A state licensing agency may take into consideration criminal history record information from Maine or elsewhere which have not been set aside or for which a full and free pardon has not been granted. The existence of such information shall not operate as an automatic bar to being licensed. 5 MRSA § 5301(1).

A licensing agency may use criminal history record information for 1) convictions in which incarceration for one year or more may be imposed, 2) convictions in which incarceration for less that one year may be imposed and which involved dishonesty, was directly related to the trade, or involved sexual misconduct, and 3) convictions in which no incarceration may be imposed but directly relates to the trade or occupation. 5 MRSA §5301(2). Licensing agency may deny, suspend, or revoke a license for one of the previous criminal history record information ONLY if the licensing agency determines that the applicant has not been sufficiently rehabilitated. 5 MRSA § 5302(1).

> ***Limitations*** - Consideration of prior criminal convictions as an element of fitness shall apply for three years. After three years, the applicant must be considered equivalent to applicants with no prior criminal conviction. 5 MRSA § 5303(1).
>
> Applicants to the Board of Medicine, Osteopathic, Dental Examiners, Psychologists, Social Workers, Nursing, Chiropractic, Criminal Justice Agency, Physical Therapy, and Medical

Services Board shall have a ten-year limit for the consideration of prior criminal conviction as an element of fitness. 5 MRSA § 5303(2).

Consumer Reports General Rule – A consumer reporting agency may furnish a consumer report to a person that the consumer reporting agency has reason to believe intends to use the information for employment purposes. 10 MRSA §1313-A(1)(C)(2).

Consumer must authorize in writing the procurement of the report. 10 MRSA §1313-A(2)(B)(2).

A consumer reporting agency may not disclose 1) bankruptcy that antedates the report by more than 10 years and 2) civil suits, civil judgments and records of arrest, paid tax liens, accounts placed for collection, any other adverse item of information, other than records of conviction of crimes that antedate the report by more than 7 years. 10 MRSA § 1313-B(1).

Exception – Employment of an individual at an annual salary that equals $75,000 or more. 10 MRSA § 1313-B(2)

Maine State Criminal Records Agency

Maine State Police
State Bureau of Identification
42 State House Station; 36 Hospital St.
Augusta, ME 04333

Phone: 207-624-7009.
Fax: 207-624-7088
Web: www.state.me.us/dps/

Total Records:	359,500
Who Can Access:	Records are available to the general public.
Search Requirements:	Requests must be in writing. Submit one name per page (otherwise list could be held or sent back). Will not do FBI fingerprint checks. Records are updated as often as courts submit records to this agency, sometimes as much as six months time lag. Include the following in your request: name, date of birth, any aliases. Fingerprints are optional Include maiden name for females. Also include purpose of the inquiry and name and address of requester. 35% of the records are fingerprint-supported. Fingerprints are not submitted with arrest information to this agency by the courts or police.
What Is Released:	All convictions and all pending cases less than 1 year old are reported, or if the case has not yet been adjudicated in court. Records are available from 1937 on. The following data is not released: juvenile records.
Indexing & Storage:	It takes 1 to 2 days before new records are available for inquiry. 90% of all arrests in database have final dispositions recorded, 90% for those arrests within last 5 years. Records are indexed on computer (43%) and court index cards. Records are normally destroyed after 99 years, if no activity within last five years.
Access By:	Mail, fax, in person, online.

Mail Search:	Normal turnaround time is less than one week, those records with "hits" may take slightly longer to process. A self addressed stamped envelope is requested.
Fax Search:	Records are available by fax.
In Person Search:	This only saves mail-in time; records are returned by mail.
Online Search:	One may request a record search at www.informe.org/PCR/. Results are usually returned via email in 2 hours. Fee is $25.00, unless requester is an in-state subscriber to InforME, then fee is $15.00 per record.
Fee & Payment:	The search fee is $25.00 (unless requester is Maine resident ordering online). Fee payee: Treasurer, State of Maine. Personal checks accepted. No credit cards accepted.

Maine Sexual Offender Registry

State Bureau of Investigation   **Phone**: 207-624-7009

36 Hospital St, Attn: SOR,   **Fax**:   207-624-7088

Augusta, ME 04333   **Web**:   www.state.me.us/dps/

What is released:	Internet access is planned for early 2004. Records are available from 06/30/92 to present. It takes 1 to 2 days before new records are released. Not available: juvenile records.
Search Notes:	Include in request: name, date of birth, any aliases. There is no fee. Mail turnaround time: 1-2 days.
Access by:	Phone, Fax, Mail, In Person, Online. In person search note: Record information released for small request amounts. Online search note: search at www.informe.org/sor/. Search by name, town or ZIP Code. Information is only provided for those individuals that are required to register pursuant to Title 34-A MRSA, Chapter 15. Records date to 06/30/92 forward. The date of the last address verification is indicated next to the registrant's address. Other Access: the entire database is for sale.

Maine State Incarceration Records Agency

Maine Department of Corrections   **Phone:** 207-287-2711

111 State House Stationm Inmate Records,   **Fax:**   207-287-4370

Augusta, ME 04333   **Web:**   www.state.me.us/corrections.

Probation info: 207-287-4381; Victim Services/Inmate info: 800-968-6909

What is released: Records are available on current and former inmates. It takes 1 to 2 days before new records are released. Records never destroyed - archived seven years after release.

Search Notes: Include in request: name, date of birth, any aliases. Fingerprints are optional. There is no fee. Mail turnaround time: 1-2 weeks.

Access by: Phone, Fax, Mail, Email. Name searching available by phone, either through the agency main number or through Victim Services. No direct online access is available at this time although it is planned (check website for updated information). Email searching is available at corrections.Webdesk@maine.gov. Include your full name, address, and reasons for the search. Public information is provided. Other Access: database sales/bulk records can be requested and will be reviewed.

Maine State Court System

Court Structure: The Superior Court is the court of general jurisdiction. Both Superior and District Courts handle "misdemeanor" and "felony" cases, with jury trials being held in Superior Court only. Superior Court has exclusive jurisdiction over pleas or trials for murder cases.

Find Felony Records: Superior Court, District Court

Misdemeanor Records: Superior Court, District Court

Online Access: Development of a judicial computer system is in use statewide for all criminal and certain civil case types. The system is initially for judicial and law enforcement agencies and will not include public access in the near term. Some counties are online through a private vendor.

Searching Hints: Per administrative order, Maine Superior and District courts increased their search fees effective September 1st, 2003 as follows: 1) $15.00 for a search- previously, most courts charged $0 for a search; 2) copy fee 1st page is $2.00, $1.00 each additional; 3) If mail requests do not include a self- addressed stamped envelope, then add an additional $5.00. As we go to press, it is not yet clear if additional fees will be charged for certification. Also, there is some confusion at the courts regarding if the $15.00 fee is for a "combined" search of both civil and criminal, or if one fee for civil and one fee for crimianl. The Order, as it appears at the website, makes no mention of the combined fee. Most mail requests of a name search for full criminal history record information are returned to the sender, referring them to the State Bureau of Investigation. Mail requests that make a specific inquiry related to an identified case are responded to in writing, with appropriate copy and attestation fees.

Court Administrator: For add'l questions about the state's court system, visit the website at www.courts.state.me.us, or contact: State Court Administrator, PO Box 4820, Portland, ME 04112, Phone: 207-822-0792.

Maryland

Maryland Statues and Related Employer Restrictions

Public Records General Rule – Except in accordance with applicable federal law and regulations, a criminal justice unit and the central Repository may not disseminate criminal history record information. MD Code §10-219. A person or his or her attorney, with written authorization, may inspect criminal history record information about the person. MD Code §10-222.

A person may not open or review an expunged record, or disclose to another person any information from that record without a court order. MD Code §10-108.

Consumer Reports General Rule – A consumer reporting agency may furnish a consumer report to a person which the agency has reason to believe intends to use the information for employment purposes. MD Code, 14-1202.

A consumer reporting agency may not disclose 1) bankruptcy that antedates the report by more than 10 years and 2) Suits and judgments, paid tax liens, accounts placed for collection, records of arrest, indictment, or conviction of a crime, and any other adverse item of information that antedate the report by more than 7 years. MD Code §14-1203(a). **Exception** – employment of an individual at an annual salary that equals $20,000 or more. MD Code §14-1203(b)(3).

Caveat – An employer may not require a person to inspect or challenge any criminal history record information relating to that person for the purpose of obtaining a copy of the person's record to qualify for employment. MD Code §10-228.

Maryland State Criminal Records Agency

Criminal Justice Information System
Public Safety & Correctional Records
PO Box 5743
Pikeville, MD 21282-5743

Phone: 410-764-4501
Fax: 410-653-5900

Web: www.dpscs.state.md.us

Total Records: 1,503,700

Who Can Access: Records are available to the general public, with restrictions.

Search Requirements: Release of criminal records is restricted. All private parties must first write/fax/phone this office and request a "petition package," then apply for a petition number. Employers are eligible to request a petition number; 3rd parties may not, directly. Include the following in your request: set of fingerprints. A signed release is not necessary but is helpful. When applying for fingerprinting, a photo ID is required. 100% of records are fingerprint-supported. All searches require fingerprints and all require an authorization number including government. Investigators and all 3rd parties are considered as agents of employers and must use employer's authorization.

What Is Released: All records are released to law enforcement; public receives records with conviction data only. Records with dispositions of acquittal are not released to public. Records are available from 1978.

Indexing & Storage: It takes a week if not submitted electornically. before new records are available for inquiry. Approximately 80% of all arrests in database have final dispositions recorded. Records are indexed on in-house computer. Records are normally destroyed after person reaches age 100.

Access By: Mail, in person.

Mail Search: Turnaround time: 10-15 business days. You may mail a request for a petition for authorization to the Customer Service Dept.; they can mail or fax you the necessary petition information.

In Person Search: In person requests are allowed, though signed release and fingerprints are required, and turnaround time is 5 days.

Fee & Payment: The fee is $18.00 per request. If a statutorily-required FBI fingerpint check is required, add $24.00. Fee payee: CJIS. Prepayment required. Money orders and cashier's checks are preferred. Personal checks accepted. No credit cards.

Maryland Sexual Offender Registry

Criminal Justice Information System   **Phone**: 410-585-3649 866-368-8657
SOR Unit, PO Box 5743   **Fax**:   410-653-5690
Pikeville, MD 21282-5743   **Web**:   www.dpscs.state.md.us/sor/

What is released: Copies of registration statements will include the registrant's photograph but will not include fingerprints, SSN, or the victim's date of birth. Records are available from 10/01/95. It takes a week if not submitted electornically. before new records are released.

Search Notes: Records indexed on in-house computer (90+%). Mail turnaround: 1-2 weeks

Access by: Mail, Online, Email. Online search note: online acces is available at www.dpscs.state.md.us/sor/online_view.shtml. Access to the Sexual Offender Registry can be requested by email at sor@dpscs.state.md.us.

Maryland State Incarceration Records Agency

Dept of Public Safety and Correctional Services   **Phone**: 410-585-3351
6766 Reistertown Road, Suite 310   **Fax**:   410-764-4182
Baltimore, MD 21215-2342   **Web**:   www.dpscs.state.md.us/doc

For an inmate's DOC number and location contact Data Processing via methods below or email to cwood@dpscs.state.md.us. To obtain any other information than DOC number you must contact individual institutions.

What is released: Only location and DOC number are released fromthis agency. Records computerized since 1980. Records are available on current and former inmates. It takes 1 to 2 days before new records are released. Not available: medical and certain personal information.

Search Notes: Include in request: inmates race, sex, full name, DOB, and the SSN if known. No fee for search. Mail turnaround time: 1-3 days.

Access by: Phone, Fax, Mail, Online. Name searching available by phone. Search inmates online at http://www1.dpscs.state.md.us/inmate/. The Locator may not list some short sentenced inmates who, although committed to the Commissioner of Correction, are in fact housed at Division of Pretrial and Detention Services facilities. Also, a private company offers free web access at www.vinelink.com, including state, DOC, and a few county jails.

Maryland State Court System

Court Structure: The Circuit Court is the highest court of record. Certain categories of minor felonies are handled by the District Courts. However, all misdemeanors and felonies that require a jury trial are handled by Circuit Courts.

Find Felony Records: Circuit Court, District Court (minor)

Misdemeanor Records: Circuit Court, District Court

Online Access: An online computer system -- see www.courts.state.md.us/dialup.html -- called the Judicial Information System (JIS) or (SJIS) provides dial-up access to civil and criminal case information from the following:

- All District Courts - All civil and all misdemeanors
- Circuit Courts Criminal - Three courts are on JIS - Anne Arundel, Carroll County, and Baltimore City Court

Inquiries may be made to: the District Court traffic system for case information data, calendar information data, court schedule data, or officer schedule data; the District Court criminal system for case information data or calendar caseload data. There is an annual $50.00 for JIS dial-up access, which must be included with the application. For additional information or to receive a registration packet, write or call Judicial Information Systems, Security Administrator, 2661 Riva Rd., Suite 900, Annapolis, MD 21401, 410-260-1031, or visit the website below.

Court Administrator: For add'l questions about the state's court system, visit the website at www.courts.state.md.us, or contact: Administrative Office of the Courts, 580 Taylor Ave, Annapolis, MD 21401, Phone: 410-260-1400.

Massachusetts

Massachusetts Statues & Related Employer Restrictions

General Rule – Any person may examine or inspect any public record. MGLA 66 § 10.

Expunged Record – Records may be sealed by the court when the defendant has been found not guilty, a finding of no probable cause, a nolle prosequi has been entered, or a dismissal has been entered. An applicant with a sealed record on file may answer "no record" with respect to an inquiry of prior arrests or criminal court appearances. MGLA 276 § 100C.

Employment – An employer may not discriminate against an employee for employment purposes regarding 1) an arrest, detention, or disposition in which a conviction did not result, 2) a first conviction for drunkenness, simple assault, speeding, minor traffic violations, affray, or disturbance of the peace, or 3) any conviction of a misdemeanor that occurred 5 years or more from the date of application. MGLA 151B § 4.

Consumer Report – No consumer reporting agency may disclose in a consumer report 1) bankruptcy that antedates the report by more than 14 years and 2) Suits and judgments, paid tax liens, accounts placed for collection, records of arrest, indictment, or conviction of a crime, and any other adverse item of information that antedate the report by more than 7 years. MGLA 93 § 52. *Exception* – employment of an individual at an annual salary that equals $20,000 or more. MGLA 93 § 52(b)(3).

Massachusetts State Criminal Records Agency

Criminal History Systems Board   **Phone:** 617-660-4600.
200 Arlington Street, #2200   **Fax:**   617-660-4613
Chelsea, MA 02150   **Web:**   www.state.ma.us/chsb/

Note: These searches are offered: 1) Personal, 2) Certified Agency, 3) Publicly Accessible (PUBAC). Certified Agency requests are pre-approved via statute or the Board. PUBAC is open to the public; data is limited.

Total Records: 2,530,000

Who Can Access: Records are available to the general public.

Search Requirements: PUBAC requesters are limited to adult records; the crime must include a sentence of 5 years or more OR sentenced and convicted for any term if, at the time of request, the subject is on probation or has been released within 2 years of felony conviction. Include the following in your request: name, date of birth. The Personal request (on one's self) requires a notarized signature. A "certified agency" search may include youth organizations, child care providers, and others approved by CHSB. This agency does not conduct FBI fingerprint searches.

What Is Released: A Certified Agency record includes all conviction and all open or pending actions. A PUBAC record contains only convictions. Records are available for at least 50 years.

Indexing & Storage: It takes 1 day before new records are available for inquiry. 100% of PUBAC records have final dispositions recorded. Records are indexed on inhouse computer, file folders.

Access By: Mail.

Mail Search: Turnaround time: 2 weeks. A self addressed stamped envelope is required.

Fee & Payment: The Personal request is $25.00. The Certified Agency request is $30.00. The PUBAC request is $30.00. No fingerprint requests are permitted, thus no fingerprint fees. In fact, 0% of the records are fingerprint-supported. Fee payee: The Commonwealth of Massachusetts. Prepayment required. Personal checks accepted. No credit cards accepted.

Massachusetts Sexual Offender Registry

Sex Offender Registry Board   **Phone**: 978-740-6400

PO Box 4547   **Fax**:   978-740-6464

Salem, MA 01970   **Web**:   www.state.ma.us/sorb/

The Sex Offender Registry Board estimates that there are nearly 18,000 sex offenders living and/or working in the Commonwealth of Massachusetts. Requests to this office must be in writing. It is suggested to use the state's form that can be downloaded from the Internet site.

What is released: Information about a sex offender is available to the public only subject has been finally classified by the Board as a Level 2 or a Level 3 Offender. In person requests should be conducted at local law enforcement offices. Records are available from 08/01/81.

Search Notes: There is no fee. Mail turnaround time: 1-2 weeks.

Access by: Mail, Online. Online access is planned, but is not yet available per a Restraining Order.

Massachusetts State Incarceration Records Agency

Massachusetts Executive Office of Public Safety   **Phone:** 617-660-4600

Criminal History Systems Board   **Locator:** 877-421-8463;

200 Arlington, #2200   **Web:**   www.state.ma.us/doc

Chelsea, MA 02150

Criminal Histories Systems Board: 617-660-4690

What is released: Records are available on current and former inmates by mail, current inmates only online. It takes about 7 days before new records are released.

Search Notes: Include in request: full name; AIS number helpful. There is no fee. Mail turnaround time: 2-3 days.

Access by: Phone, Mail, Online. Online search note: No searching online is offered by this agency, however a private company offers free web access to DOC offenders at www.vinelink.com/index.jsp. There is also a DOC Most Wanted list at www.state.ma.us/doc/wanted/index.html.

Massachusetts State Court System

Court Structure: The various court sections are called "Departments." While Superior and District Courts have concurrent jurisdiction in civil cases, the practice is to assign cases less than $25,000 to the District Court and those over $25,000 to Superior Court.

In addition to misdemeanors, the District Courts and Boston Municipal Courts have jurisdiction over certain minor felonies.

Find Felony Records: Superior Court, District Court

Misdemeanor Records: District Court, Boston Municipal Court, Housing Court

Online Access: Online access to records on the statewide Trial Courts Information Center website is available to attorneys and law firms at www.ma-trialcourts.org/tcic/welcome.jsp. Contact Peter Nylin by email at nylin_p@jud.state.ma.us. Site is updated daily.

Searching Hints: In July 2003, the state mandated that the certification fee be $2.50 and the copy fee be $1.00 per page for all Superior and District Courts.

Court Administrator: For add'l questions about the state's court system, visit the website at www.state.ma.us/courts/admin/index.html, or contact: Chief Justice for Administration & Management, 2 Center Plaza, Room 540, Boston, MA 02108, Phone: 617-742-8575.

Michigan

Michigan Statues and Related Employer Restrictions

General Rule – A person has the right to inspect, copy, or receive copies of a public record of a public body. MCLA 15.233(1). Investigative records complied for law enforcement purposes may not be released if it would 1) interfere with law enforcement proceedings, 2) deprive a person of a fair trail, 3) constitute an unwarranted invasion of privacy, 4) disclose the identity of a confidential source, 5) disclose law enforcement investigative techniques, or 6) endanger the life or physical safety of law enforcement personnel. MCLA 15.243 (1)(b).

Expunged Record – A person who is convicted of not more than one offense may file an application with the convicting court for the entry of an order setting aside the conviction. MCLA 780.621. If the order is granted, the conviction record becomes non-public except for a few circumstances, such as employment for a law enforcement agency. MCLA 780.623.

Employment – An employer may not request, make, or maintain a record of information regarding a misdemeanor arrest, detention, or disposition where a conviction did not result. MCLA 37.2202(a)(1).

Agency guidelines for pre-employment inquiries: Michigan Civil Rights Commission, "Pre-Employment Inquiry Guide" is available online at http://ses.cmich.edu/ses-new-webpage/seshandbook/student-supervisors'-handbook/MI-Dept-of-Civil-Rights-Inquiry-Guide.htm

Michigan State Criminal Records Agency

Michigan State Police, Ident. Section
Criminal Justice Information Center
7150 Harris Dr
Lansing, MI 48913

Phone: 517-322-1956.
Fax: 517-322-0635

Web: www.michigan.gov/msp

Total Records: 1,259,500

Who Can Access: Records are available to the general public.

Search Requirements: Include the following in your request: full name, sex, race, date of birth. A SSN or maiden name/previous name is very helpful. Records can be searched with or without a fingerprint card.

What Is Released: Records without dispositions are not released. Records are available until the subject's DOB indicates 99 years or a death is reported. The following data is not released: non-conviction information.

Indexing & Storage: It takes up to 30 days before new records are available for inquiry. 76% of all arrests in database have final dispositions recorded. Records are indexed on inhouse computer. Records are normally destroyed after death.

Access By: Mail.

Mail Search: Turnaround time: 4 to 6 weeks.

Fee & Payment: The search fee is $10.00 per name without a fingerprint card, $30.00 with a fingerprint card, and $54.00 with state and FBI fingerprint cards. Registered users may be eligible for a fee waiver. Fee payee: State of Michigan. Prepayment required. Payment required in advance unless a prepaid account has been arranged with Division cashier. Personal checks accepted. Credit cards will be accepted for online access. **Note:** Non-profit and charitable organizations may submit a copy of Federal Form 501C3 in lieu of payment for a name search

Online Notes: Search state police lists of missing persons/children, most wanted, and fugitives at www.michigan.gov/msp/0,1607,7-123-1589_1878---,00.html.

Michigan Sexual Offender Registry

Michigan State Police   **Phone**: 517-322-5098

SOR Unit, 7150 Harris Dr   **Fax**:   517-322-4957

Lansing, MI 48913   **Web**:   www.mipsor.state.mi.us/

Records may be searched at the local law enforcement level. There are over 33,000 registered sex offenders living in Michigan.

What is released: Only those offenders who have been convicted of a listed offense on or after October 1, 1995 or convicted prior to that date who were still incarcerated, on parole or probation for a listed offense on October 1, 1995 are listed. Records are available since 1995. It takes up to 24 hours before new records are released.

Search Notes: Include in request: name and DOB. There is no search fee.

Access by: Online. Mail search requests no longer offered. One may search the registry at the website, there is no charge.

Michigan State Incarceration Records Agency

Michigan Department of Corrections   **Phone:** 517-373-0284

Central Records Office   **Fax:**   517-373-2628

P.O. Box 30003   **Web:**   www.michigan.gov/corrections

Lansing, MI 48909

For record copies, contact Freedom of Information Act Coordinator, FOIA Coordinator: Department of Corrections, 206 E. Michigan Ave, Grandview Plaza, PO Box 30003, Lansing, MI 48909.

What is released: Location, MDOC number, conviction and sentencing information, physical identifiers, and release dates are provided. Records are available on current and former inmates. It takes 2-3 weeks before new records are released. Records normally destroyed after 7 years from discharge. Almost complete computer records go back to 1981. Computer records prior to that year become less complete the further back you search.

Search Notes: Include in request: full name or MDOC number. The DOB and SSN are helpful. There is a fee for copies; usually these are FOIA requests. Mail turnaround time: 5 to 7 days.

Access by: Phone, Fax, Mail, Online. Name searches are available by phone. Online search note: the online access through the main website and at www.state.mi.us/mdoc/asp/otis2.html has many search criteria capabilites. There is also a Michigan DOC Most Wanted list at www.state.mi.us/mdoc/MostWanted/MostWanted.asp. Other Access: bulk sales of database information is available.

Michigan State Court System

Court Structure: The Circuit Court is the court of general jurisdiction. District, Municipal and probate Courts are limited jurisdiction.

                           As of January 1, 1998, the Family Division of the Circuit Court was created. Domestic relations actions and juvenile cases, including criminal and abuse/neglect, formerly adjudicated in the Probate Court, were transferred to the Family Division of the Circuit Court.

                           Six counties (Barry, Berrien, Iron, Isabella, Lake, and Washtenaw) and the 46th Circuit Court are participating in a "Demonstration" pilot project designed to streamline court services and consolidate case management. These courts may refer to themselves as County Trial Courts.

Find Felony Records: Circuit Court

Misdemeanor Records: District Court, Municipal Court

Online Access: There is a wide range of online computerization of the judicial system from "none" to "fairly complete," but there is no statewide court records network. Some Michigan courts provide public access terminals in clerk's offices, and some courts are developing off-site electronic filing and searching capability. A few offer remote online to the public. The Criminal Justice Information Center (CJIC), the repository for MI criminal record info, offers online access, but the requester must be a business. Results are available in seconds; fee is $5.00 per name. For more information, call 517-322-5546. Subscribe to email updates of appellate opinions at http://courtofapp eals.mijud.net/resources/subscribe.htm. There is no fee.

Searching Hints: Court records are considered public unless spcifically made non-public by statute, court rules, caseload, or court order. Courts will, however, affirm that cases exist and provide case numbers.

Some courts will not perform criminal searches. Rather, they refer requests to the State Police.

Note that costs, search requirements, and procedures vary widely because each jurisdiction may create its own administrative orders.

Court Administrator: For add'l questions about the state's court system, visit the website at http://courts.michigan.gov, or contact: State Court Administrator, PO Box 30048, Lansing, MI 48909, Phone: 517-373-2222.

Minnesota

Minnesota Statues & Related Employer Restrictions

General Rule – All government data collected, created, received, maintained, or disseminated by a state agency, political subdivision, or statewide system shall be public unless classified as non-public, protected non-public, private, or confidential. MSA §13.03(1).

Arrest data, such as the charge, arrest, search warrant, date and time for any release from custody or incarceration, and criminal investigative data that has become inactive is open to the public. MSA 13.82(2) and (7).

Correction and detention data on individuals are classified as private to the extent that 1) it would endanger an individual's life, 2) endanger the effectiveness of an investigation, 3) identify a confidential informant, or 4) disclose medical, psychological or financial information not related to their lawful confinement. MSA §13.85.

Expunged Record – Records may be sealed for first time drug offenders and juveniles, and become a not public record. MSA §609A.02.

Employment – No person shall be disqualified from public employment, nor disqualified from pursuing, practicing, or engaging in any occupation for which a license is required solely or in part because of a prior conviction, unless the crime for which convicted directly relates to the position of employment sought. MSA §364.03(1).

A person who has been convicted of a crime that directly relates to the public employment sought shall not be disqualified from consideration if that person can show evidence of sufficient rehabilitation. MSA §364.03(3).

Records of arrest without a valid conviction, convictions which have been annulled or expunged, and misdemeanor convictions for which no jail sentence can be imposed can not be used, distributed, or disseminated by the state of Minnesota in connection with any application for public employment nor in connection with an application for a license. MSA §364.04.

However, that does not apply to applicants seeking admission to the bar, peace officers, fire protection agencies, law enforcement agencies, private detectives, school bus drivers, special transportation service, commercial driver training instructors, emergency medical services personnel, taxicab drivers, and doctors. MSA §364.09.

Consumer Report – A person may not obtain a consumer report on a consumer for employment purposes unless the person clearly and accurately discloses to the consumer that a consumer report may be obtained. This statute does not apply to a consumer report to be used for employment purposes for which the consumer has not specifically applied, or a consumer report used for an investigation of a current violation of a criminal or civil statute by a current employee.   MSA §13C.02(1) and (4).

Agency guidelines for pre-employment inquiries: Minnesota Department of Human Rights, "Hiring, Job Interviews and the Minnesota Human Rights Act" available online at www.humanrig hts.state.mn.us/employer_hiring.html

Minnesota State Criminal Records Agency

Bureau of Criminal Apprehension
Criminal Justice Information Systems
1430 Maryland Ave E
St Paul, MN 55106

Phone: 651-642-0670.
Fax: 651-793-2401
Web: www.bca.state.mn.us

Total Records: 428,607

Who Can Access: Limited ecords are available to the general public. For most requesters, to obtain the entire adult history, including all arrests, you must have a notarized release form signed by person of record. To get a 15-year record of convictions only, a consent form is not required.

Search Requirements: Include the following in your request: name, date of birth, and sex. Fingerprint searches are not permitted. However, 100% of records are fingerprint-supported.

What Is Released: With consent, all records, including those without dispositions, are released. If no consent, then only conviction records released. Targeted misdemeanors (violent, DV, DUI, etc., where a jail sentence may be imposed) are released; other misdemeanors are if received. Records are available from 1924. The following data is not released: juvenile records.

Indexing & Storage: It takes 1 day before new records are available for inquiry. 72% of all arrests in database have final dispositions recorded, 63% for those arrests within last 5 years. Records are indexed on inhouse computer, microfilm and digital disc. Records normally destroyed after subject reaches 100 years of age or death.

Access By: Mail, in person.

Mail Search: Turnaround time: 1 to 2 weeks. A self addressed stamped envelope is requested.

In Person Search: You use the public access terminal for $4.00. For the full adult history the turnaround time is 2 days, unless you are the person of record, then it is immediate.

Fee & Payment: The fee for the full adult history is $15.00, for non-profits the fee is $8.00. The fee for the 15-year public record is $4.00. Non-profits have a reduced fee, call first. Fee payee: BCA. Prepayment required. Business checks, personal checks, money orders and certified funds are accepted. No credit cards accepted.

Minnesota Sexual Offender Registry

Bureau of Criminal Apprehension   **Phone**: 651-793-7070, 888-234-1248

Minnesota Predatory Offender Program   **Fax**:   651-793-7071

1430 Maryland Ave E

St Paul, MN 55106   **Web**:   www.dps.state.mn.us/bca/

This is not a notification state. The state does not permit public access to this information beyond the Level 3 names found on the web page. This means local law enforcement offices cannot give the public access to all names.

What is released: It takes 48 hours before new records are entered into the system.

Search Notes: There is no fee.

Access by: Online. No mail searching. Level 3 offenders may be searched online at www.doc.state.mn.us/level3/Search.asp. Also, you can bring up lists by city, county, or ZIP Code.

Minnesota State Incarceration Records Agency

Minnesota Department of Corrections   **Phone:** 651-642-0200

Records Management Unit   **Fax:**   651-643-3588

450 Energy Park Drive, #200   **Web:**   www.corr.state.mn.us

St. Paul, MN 55108

What is released: Location, OID number, physical identifiers, conviction and sentencing information, and release dates are provided. Records are computerized since 1978. Records are available on current and former inmates is available; however, the online search is limited to those either still in prison or under probation. It takes about 7 days before new records are released. Records normally destroyed after ninety-nine years.

Search Notes: Include in request: name and DOB. There is a $10.00 retrieval fee and a copy fee of $.25 per page. Mail turnaround time: 2-4 days. Personal checks accepted.

Access by: Phone, Fax, Mail, Online. Online search note: search at the web to retrieve public information about adult offenders who have been committed to the Commissioner of Corrections, and who are still under our jurisdiction (i.e. in prison or released from prison and still under supervision). Also, a private company offers free web access at www.vinelink.com/index.jsp, including state, DOC, and most county jail systems.

Minnesota State Court System

Court Structure: There are 97 District Courts comprising 10 Judicial Districts in the state.

Find Felony Records: District Court

Misdemeanor Records: District Court

Online Access: Appellate and Supreme Court opinions are available from the website. There is an online system in place that allows internal and external access, but only for government personnel.

Searching Hints: Statewide certification and copy fees are as follows: Certification Fee: $10.00 per document, Copy Fee: $5.00 per document (not per page).

An exact name is required to search, e.g., a request for "Robert Smith" will not result in finding "Bob Smith." The requester must request both names and pay two search and copy fees.

When a search is permitted by "plaintiff or defendant," most jurisdictions stated that a case is indexed by only the 1st plaintiff or defendant, and a 2nd or 3rd party would not be sufficient to search.

The 3rd, 5th, 8th and 10th Judicial Districts no longer will perform criminal record searches for the public.

Most courts take personal checks. Exceptions are noted.

Court Administrator: For add'l questions about the state's court system, visit the website at www.courts.state.mn.us/home/, or contact: State Court Administrator, 135 Minnesota Judicial Center, 2 Rev ML King Blvd, St Paul, MN 55155, Phone: 651-296-2474.

Missouri

Missouri Statues and Related Employer Restrictions

General Rule – All state, county and municipal records shall at all reasonable times be open for a personal inspection by any citizen of Missouri. VAMS 109.180.

All incident reports and arrest reports shall be open records. Investigative reports of all law enforcement agencies are closed records until the investigation becomes inactive. If any person is arrested and not charged with an offense against the law within 30 days of the person's arrest, the arrest report shall be a closed record. VAMS 610.100. However, arrest records with no charge that are older than 30 days will be available to criminal justice agencies for criminal justice purposes, criminal justice employment, and child, elderly, or disabled care employment. VAMS 610.120.

Definitions – VAMS 610.100

Arrest report – a record of a law enforcement agency of an arrest and any detention or confinement incident and the charge

Incident report – a record of a law enforcement agency consisting of the date, time, specific location, name of the victim, and immediate facts and circumstances surrounding the initial report of a crime.

Expunged Record – Any record of arrest may be expunged if there is no probable cause, no charges will be pursued, subject of the arrest has no prior or subsequent misdemeanor or felony convictions, the subject did not receive a suspended sentence, and no civil action is pending. VAMS 610.122.

The official records shall be closed if a person arrested is charged, but the case is subsequently nolle prossed, dismissed, the accused is found not guilty, or the imposition of sentence is suspended. If the accused is found not guilty due to mental disease, the records shall be closed except to law enforcement agencies, childcare agencies, and in home services provider agencies. VAMS 610.105.

Employment – No board or other agency may deny a license to an applicant upon the basis that a felony or misdemeanor conviction of the applicant precludes the applicant from demonstrating good moral character, where the conviction resulted in the applicant's incarceration and the applicant has been released by pardon, parole, or the applicant has been placed on probation and there in no evidence the applicant has violated his probation. The board or agency may consider the conviction as some evidence of an absence of good moral character, but shall consider other factors when making its decision. VAMS 314.200.

Agency guidelines for pre-employment inquiries: Commission on Human Rights, Missouri Department of Labor and Industrial Relations, "Pre-Employment Inquiries." More information can be found at www.dolir.state.mo.us/index.htm.

Missouri State Criminal Records Agency

Missouri State Highway Patrol   **Phone:** 573-526-6153.
Criminal Record & Identification Division   **Fax:**   573-751-9382
1510 E Elm St
Jefferson City, MO 65102   **Web:**   www.mshp.dps.missouri.gov

Total Records:	1.070,650
Who Can Access:	Records are available to the general public. Youth service providers must have signature of the subject.
Search Requirements:	Include the following in your request: full name, date of birth, sex, race, Social Security Number. Fingerprints are an option. A request form can be downloaded from the website. Records are 100% fingerprint-supported.
What Is Released:	Open records are accessible by the public. These are convictions, or arrests less than 30 days old unless charges are sought, or suspended imposition of sentence during probation period. Certain entities may access closed record files in accordance with state statute, with the submission of fingerprints and required fee. Records are available from 1970 on.
Indexing & Storage:	It takes 5 weeks before new records are available for inquiry. 64% of all arrests in database have final dispositions recorded, 62% for those arrests within last 5 years. Records are indexed on inhouse computer (84%) including images. Records are normally destroyed after (records maintained indefinitely).
Access By:	Mail, in person.
Mail Search:	Turnaround time: 3-4 weeks. No self addressed stamped envelope is required.
In Person Search:	Turnaround time is while you wait for one search only.
Fee & Payment:	The search fee is $5.00 per individual for a name search. Searches by fingerprint cost $14.00 each. Add $24.00 if the fingerprint search to include an FBI fingerprint check. Fee payee: State of Missouri Criminal Record System Fund Prepayment required. Personal checks accepted. No credit cards accepted.

Missouri Sexual Offender Registry

Missouri State Highway Patrol

Sexual Offender Registry,

PO Box 9500

Jefferson City, MO 65102-0568

Phone: 573-526-6153

Fax: 573-751-9382

Web: www.mshp.dps.missouri.gov/

The sex offender registry is not currently available, including mail and online. However, legislation has passed that will permit searching on the Internet. It will take until sometime in late 2004 for funds available and the program to begin. The only information released is the name, address, and offense.

What is released: At present, qualified entities may obtain sex offender info pursuant to Sect. 43.500, RSMO. Registry information is available from the sheriff in the county where the offender resides. The county list may be released to any person upon request. Records are available 07/01/79 to date.

Missouri State Incarceration Records Agency

Missouri Department of Corrections

Probation and Parole

P.O. Box 236

Jefferson City, MO 65101.

Phone: 573-751-8488

Fax: 573-751-8501

Web: www.corrections.state.mo.us

What is released: Location, conviction and sentencing information are released. Records are available on current and former inmates. Will release limited information on former inmates. It takes about 30 days before new records are released.

Search Notes: Include in request: full name, DOB; SSN helpful. There is no fee. Mail turnaround time: 4-6 days.

Access by: Phone, Fax, Mail, Online, Email. Online search note: No internet searching is available from this agency. However, you may email a single request to mocorxns@doc.mo.gov. Spell the full name correctly. An email response will be provided to you, usually within 24 hours of receipt during regular business hours. This only provides general search information and policy information. Department does not provide search information to companies conducting employee background checks. Although this agency provides no direct internet access, a private company offers free web access at www.vinelink.com/index.jsp.

Missouri State Court System

Court Structure: The Circuit Court is the court of general jurisdiction. There are 45 circuits comprised of 114 County Circuit Courts and one independent city court. There are also Associate Circuit Courts with limited jurisdiction and some counties have Combined Courts. Municipal Courts only have jurisdiction over traffic and ordinance violations.

Find Felony Records: Circuit Court

Misdemeanor Records: Associate Circuit Court

Online Access: Casenet, a limited but growing online system, is available at http://casenet.osca.state.mo.us/casenet. The system includes 69 counties (with more projected) as well as the Eastern, Western, and Southern Appellate Courts, the Supreme Court, and Fine Collection Center. Cases can be searched case number, filing date, or litigant name. One may search supreme and appellate court opinions at the home page.

Court Administrator: For add'l questions about the state's court system, visit the website at www.osca.state.mo.us, or contact: Court Administrator, 2112 Industrial Drive - PO Box 104480, Jefferson City, MO 65110, Phone: 573-751-4377.

Mississippi

Mississippi Statues & Related Employer Restrictions

General Rule – All public records are public property and any person has the right to inspect, copy or obtain a reproduction of any public record. MS ST §25-61-5(1).

Unless specifically authorized by statute, records maintained by the Mississippi Justice Information Center Database are exempt from the Public Records Act. MS ST §45-27-19(1).

Expunged Records – If participant completes all requirements imposed upon him by a drug court, and any person who is arrested, issued a citation, or held for any misdemeanor and not formally charged or prosecuted with an offense within 12 months of arrest, or upon dismissal of the charge, may have the matter expunged. MS ST §§99-15-59 and 9-23-23.

If a person successfully completes deferment of a drug or narcotics charge before the age of 26 or the person is a first time offender convicted of a misdemeanor, he or she may petition the court to expunge the record. The effect of the expunged record shall be to restore that person to the status he or she had before the conviction and he or she shall not be guilty of perjury for denying or failure to recite the conviction later. MS ST §§99-19-71(1) and 41-29-150(d)(2).

Employment – State conviction information and arrest information less than one year old, which is contained in the Mississippi Justice Information Center Database, shall be made available to any non-governmental entity or any employer authorized by the subject of the record in writing or by state or federal law. MS ST §45-27-12(1)(b).

Mississippi State Criminal Records Agency

Criminal Information Center   **Phone:** 601-933-2600.
Dept. of Public Safety
PO Box 958
Jackson, MS 39205

Access to Records is Restricted

Note: Mississippi does not permit the public to access their central state repository of criminal records, except for pre-approved entities with purposes provided for by state statute such as health care, banking/finance, military, childcare and schools.

Total Records: 250,000

Search Requirements: They suggest that you obtain information at the county level. The records on file are 100% fingerprint supported. 40% of the records contain dispositions.

Mississippi Sexual Offender Registry

Dept. of Public Safety

Sexual Offender Registry, PO Box 958

Jackson, MS 39205

Phone: 601-368-1740

Web: www.sor.mdps.state.ms.us/

Also, it is suggested to search at the local sheriff's office.

What is released: Records are available from 07/01/95.

Search Notes: Mail turnaround time: 1 to 2 weeks.

Access by: Phone, Mail, Online. Online search note: state Sex Offender Registry can be accesed at the website. Search by last name, city, county, or ZIP Code.

Mississippi State Incarceration Records Agency

Mississippi Department of Corrections

P.O. Box 880, Records Department

Parchman, MS 38738

Phone: 601-359-5608

Web: www.mdoc.state.ms.us

This agency asks that background screening firms direct their phone, fax, and mail requests through the Criminal Information Center of the Dept. of Public Safety (see Statewide Criminal records section).

What is released: Records are available on current and former inmates. It takes less than 72 hours before new records are released. Computer records go back to 1978.

Search Notes: Include in request: provide full name. The inmate number, county of crime and DOB are helpful. There is no fee. Mail turnaround time: 1-2 weeks.

Access by: Phone, Mail, Online. Name searching available via phone. Online search note: search online by name only from the website. Click on Inmate Search. Also, search the Parole Board at www.mpb.state.ms.us/inmatesearch.asp.

Mississippi State Court System

Court Structure: The court of general jurisdiction is the Circuit Court with 70 courts in 22 districts. Justice Courts were first created in 1984, replacing the Justice of the Peace. Prior to 1984, records were kept separately by each Justice of the Peace, so the location of such records today is often unknown.

Find Felony Records: Circuit Court

Misdemeanor Records: County Court, Justice Court, Municipal Court

Criminal Notes: The Administrative Office of Courts offers a statewide search via fax requesting with a 24 hour turnaround time.There is a $25.00 start-up fee and a $5.00 per name search fee. Call 601-354-7449 or fax 601-354-7459 for details.

Online Access: A statewide online computer system is in use internally for court personnel. There are plans underway to make this system available to the public, however this has been put on hold. The website offers searching of the MS Supreme Court and Court of Appeals Decisions, including dockets of the trial courts.

Searching Hints: A number of Mississippi counties have two Circuit Court Districts. A search of either court in such a county will include the index from the other court.

Full name is a search requirement for all courts. DOB and SSN are very helpful for differentiating between like-named individuals.

Court Administrator: For add'l questions about the state's court system, visit the website at www.mssc.state.ms.us, or contact: Court Administrator, Supreme Court, Box 117, Jackson, MS 39205, Phone: 601-354-7406.

Montana

Montana Statues and Related Employer Restrictions

General Rule – Every citizen has a right to inspect and take a copy pf any public writings of this state. MCA 2-6-102. There are no restrictions on the dissemination of public criminal justice information. MCA 44-5-301.

Non-public criminal history information may be disseminated with the consent of the individual, court order, or for statistical purposes. MCA 44-5-302.

An individual may inspect any criminal history record information about that individual or transfer copies of that information to any other person. MCA 44-5-214. Dissemination of confidential criminal justice information is restricted to criminal justice agencies. MCA 44-5-303.

Definitions – MCA 44-5-103

Confidential Criminal Justice Information – means criminal investigative informations, criminal intelligence information, fingerprints and photographs, criminal justice information made confidential by law, and any other criminal justice information not clearly defined as public criminal justice information.

Criminal History Record Information – consists of descriptions and notations of arrest, detentions, filing of complaints, indictments, or informations, and dispositions arising therefrom, sentences, correctional status, and release. Does not include records of traffic offenses or court records.

Disposition – includes conviction at trial, plea of guilty, acquittal, acquittal by reason of mental disease, acquittal by reason of mental incompetence, sentence imposed and all conditions attached, deferred sentence, nolle prosequi, nolo contendere, deferred prosecution, bond forfeiture, death, release, dismissal, revocation of probation or parole, and correctional placement on probation.

Expunged Record – Upon completion of a deferred sentence, the court may allow the defendant to withdraw a plea of guilty or nolo contendere or may strike the verdict of guilty from the record and order that the charge or charges against the defendant be dismissed. After the charge is dismissed, all records and data relating to the charge are confidential criminal justice information, and public access to the information may only be obtained by district court order upon showing good cause. MCA 46-18-204.

Consumer Report – A consumer reporting agency may furnish a consumer report to a person it has reason to believe intends to use the information for employment purposes. MCA 31-3-111(3)(b).

A person may not procure or cause to be prepared or distributed an investigative consumer report on any consumer unless the report is to be used for employment purposes for which the consumer applied. MCA 31-3-113(b).

No consumer reporting agency may report bankruptcies which antedate the report by more that 14 years, nor suits and judgments, paid tax liens, accounts placed for collection or charged to profit and loss, records of arrest, indictments, or conviction of crime, or any other adverse action which antedates the report by more than 7 years. MCA 31-3-112.

Montana State Criminal Records Agency

Department of Justice   **Phone:** 406-444-3625
Criminal Records   **Fax:**   406-444-0689
PO Box 201403
Helena, MT 59620-1403   **Web:**   www.doj.state.mt.us

Total Records:	141,800
Who Can Access:	Records are available to the general public.
Search Requirements:	Include the following in your request: name, date of birth. The Social Security Number and any aliases are helpful. Place written requests on letterhead. Fingerprint searches are optional. 100% of records are fingerprint-supported.
What Is Released:	All felonies and misdemeanors (except traffic violations) are released. Records without dispositions are released; the agency attempts to locate the disposition prior to public release. Deferred impositions that have been dismissed are not released. Records are available from 1950's on and are 100% computerized. The following data is not released: traffic offenses, unless felony driving under the influence of alcohol.
Indexing & Storage:	It takes 1 week to 1 month before new records are available for inquiry. 85% of all arrests in database have final dispositions recorded. Records are normally destroyed after court order.
Access By:	Mail, in person.
Mail Search:	Turnaround time: 5-10 days. A self addressed stamped envelope is requested.
In Person Search:	Turnaround time is usually immediate, unless there is a record or "hit."
Fee & Payment:	The fee is $8.00 per individual for a name check or $8.00 per individual for a fingerprint check; $32.00 for a fingerprint check plus FBI fingerprint check, when required by statute for child care or schools. Account status to approved screening firms. Fee payee: Montana Criminal Records. Prepayment required. Personal checks accepted. No credit cards accepted.

Montana Sexual Offender Registry

Department of Justice

Sexual and Violent Offender Registry

PO Box 201417

Helena, MT 59620

Phone: 406-444-9479

Fax: 406-444-2759

Web: http://svor2.doj.state.mt.us:8010/index.htm

There are over 2,500 registered offenders in the database. There are three Tier Levels of offenders, 1 being the lowest and 3 being the highest. Level 3 also indicates the offender is a sexually violent predator.

What is released: Records are available from 1989 forward. Tier levels were instituted in 1997. It takes 1 week to 1 month before new records are released.

Search Notes: There is no fee to search. Mail turnaround time: 2 to 3 days.

Access by: Phone, Fax, Mail, In Person, Online. Online search note: the state sexual offender list is available at the website. You can search for this information by name, by city or county, or by the type of offense committed.

Montana State Incarceration Records Agency

Montana Department of Corrections

Directors Office

P.O. Box 201301

Helena, MT 59620-1301.

Phone: 406-444-3930

Fax: 406-444-4920

Web: www.cor.state.mt.us

Information Officer: 406-444-7461

What is released: Location, physical identifiers, conviction and sentencing information, and release dates are provided. Computer records go back to 1978. Records are available on current and former inmates, except for the website which is current only. Computerized records go back to 1980. Older records sent to Historical Society. It takes about 30 days before new records are released. Not available: SSN and medical information.

Search Notes: Include in request: name; and DOB. There is no fee. Mail turnaround time: 10 to 40 days.

Access by: Phone, Mail, Online. Name searching is permitted by phone. Online search note: search current or former inmates on the ConWeb system at http://app.discoveringmontana.com/conweb/index.html. Search by ID number or name. Also, a private company offers free web access to DOC records at www.vinelink.com/index.jsp. Other Access: Entire offender database is available for purchase for $100.00; call Discovering Montana, 406-449-3468. Academic or social researchers can acquire the same database of no charge.

Montana State Court System

Court Structure: The District Court is the court of general jurisdiction. There are Limited Jurisdiction Courts (also known as Justice Courts), City Courts and 1 Municipal Court. Many Montana Justices of the Peace maintain case record indexes on their personal PCs, which does speed the retrieval process.

Find Felony Records: District Court

Misdemeanor Records: Limited Jurisdiction Court, City Court, Municipal Court

Online Access: Supreme Courts Opinions, Orders, and recently Filed Briefs may be found at   www.lawlibrary.state.mt.us/dscgi/ds.py/View/Collection-36.   Federal District court records are also available here. A few individual county courts offer online access.

Court Administrator: For add'l questions about the state's court system, visit the website at www.lawlibrary.state.mt.us, or contact: Court Administrator, PO Box 203002, Helena, MT 59620-3002, Phone: 406-444-2621.

Nebraska

Nebraska Statues and Related Employer Restrictions

General Rule – Complete criminal history record information shall be a public record open to inspection and copying by any person. NE ST §29-3520. Posters for apprehending fugitives, police blotters, court records of any judicial proceeding, and records of traffic offenses shall be classified as public records. NE ST §29-3521.

Notations of arrest that antedate a criminal record history request by one year shall not be disseminated unless the subject of record has made a notarized request for the release of such record. NE ST §29-3523(1)(c).

Definitions

Complete – with reference to criminal history record information, complete means that arrest records shall show the subsequent disposition of the case. NE ST §39-3507.

Criminal History Record information – includes arrest warrants, arrests, detentions, indictments, other formal charges, and any disposition arising from such arrest, charges, sentencing, correctional supervision, and release. NE ST §29-3506.

Disposition – information disclosing that criminal proceedings have been concluded, including if the police elect not to refer the matter to a prosecutor or that the prosecutor has elected not to commence criminal proceedings. NE ST §29-3511.

Expunged Record – Any person arrested due to an error of a law enforcement agency may petition the court to expunge the criminal history record information. NE ST §29-3523(2).

Nebraska State Criminal Records Agency

Nebraska State Patrol   **Phone:**   402-479-4924
CID   **Fax:**   402-479-4002
PO Box 94907
Lincoln, NE 68509-4907   **Web:**   www.nsp.state.ne.us

Total Records: 197,600
Who Can Access: Records are available to the general public.
Search Requirements: Include the following in your request: full name, disposition, date of birth, Social Security Number, sex, race. Fingerprints required for certain state

occupation checks; this includes an FBI fingerprint search. State keeps record of requesters and will inform the person of record if asked. 100% of records are fingerprint-supported. Felonies are required to be submitted this agency, though not all misdemeanors are. Agency will refer you to the proper county.

What Is Released: Records without dispositions are not released, except if an arrest without disposition is less than one year old. Records are available from 1937 to present. The following data is not released: juvenile records.

Indexing & Storage: It takes 15 to 60 days before new records are available for inquiry. 64% of all arrests in database have final dispositions recorded. Records are indexed on inhouse computer, fingerprint cards.

Access By: Mail, in person.

Mail Search: Turnaround time: 15 days. No self addressed stamped envelope is required.

In Person Search: They accept requests in person and turnaround is 15 minutes, but they will mail back the report if it is lengthy or incomplete (unless it is the requester's own report).

Fee & Payment: The search fee is $10.00 per name. A fingerprint search including FBI fingerprint check is $33.00. Fee payee: Nebraska State Patrol. Prepayment required. Personal checks accepted. No credit cards accepted.

Nebraska Sexual Offender Registry

Nebraska State Patrol   **Phone**: 402-471-8647

Sexual Offender Registry,

PO Box 94907   **Fax**:   402-471-8496

Lincoln, NE 68509-4907   **Web**:   www.nsp.state.ne.us/sor/

As of January 2004, there were over 1800 active registered sex offenders in the state of Nebraska.

What is released: The public is only granted access to sex offenders who are classified as high risk/Level 3 sex offenders. Records are available from 1997 to present.

Search Notes: Mail turnaround time: 15 days.

Access by: Phone, Mail, Online. Online search note: a Level 3 sexual offender registry search is available at the website. The records may be searched by either ZIP Code, last name, city or county. Search or review the entire name list.

Nebraska State Incarceration Records Agency

Nebraska Department of Correctional Services   **Phone:** 402-479-5765

Central Records Office   **Fax:**   402-479-5913

P.O. Box 94661   **Web:**   www.corrections.state.ne.us

Lincoln, NE 68509-4661

What is released: Location, DOC number, physical identifiers, conviction and sentencing information, and release dates are provided. Records are available on current and former inmates back to 1977. It takes 1 day before new records are released. Records normally destroyed after 3 years.

Search Notes: Include in request: full name or DOC inmate number. The DOB and SSN number are helpful. To search online, only the name is needed. Records indexed on microfilm and books. Mail turnaround time: 2 to 4 weeks.

Access by: Phone, Fax, Mail, Online. Name searching permitted by phone. Online search note: click on Inmate Records at the website for a search of current inmates. Also, a private company offers free web access at www.vinelink.com/index.jsp; includes state, DOC, and county jails.

Nebraska State Court System

Court Structure: The District Court is the court of general jurisdiction. The number of judicial districts went from 21 to the current 12 in July 1992.

Find Felony Records: District Court

Misdemeanor Records: County Court

Online Access: An online access subscription service is available for NE District and County courts, except Douglas County District Court. Case details, all party listings, payments and actions taken for criminal, civil, probate, juvenile, and traffic is available. Users must be registered with Nebrask@ Online, there is a start-up fee. The fee is $.60 per record or a flat rate of $300.00 per month. Go to www.nebraska.gov/faqs/justice for more info and how far back records go per county. Supreme Court opinions are available from http://court.nol.org/opinions/. Also, Douglas, Lancaster, and Sarpy county courts offer internet access with registration and password required.

Searching Hints: Most Nebraska courts require the public to do their own in-person searches and will not respond to written search requests. The State Attorney General has recommended that courts not perform searches because of the time involved and concerns over possible legal liability.

Court Administrator: For add'l questions about the state's court system, visit the website at http://court.nol.org/AOC/index.html, or contact: Court Administrator, PO Box 98910, Lincoln, NE 68509-8910, Phone: 402-471-3730.

Nevada

Nevada Statues and Related Employer Restrictions

General Rule – All public books and public records of a government entity must be open to inspection by any person, and may be copied. NRS 239.101.

No criminal justice agency in Nevada may disseminate any record of criminal history without first making inquiry of the central repository to obtain the most current information available. NRS 179A.090.

Any record, which only reflects conviction or which pertains to an incident for which a person is currently within the system, may be disseminated by a criminal justice agency without any restrictions. NRS 179A.100(1).

No person who receives criminal history information may disseminate it further without express authority of law or court order. NRS 179A.110.

Definitions – NRS 179A.070

Record of Criminal History – identifies the subject and notations of warrants, arrest, citations for misdemeanors, detentions, decisions not to prosecute, indictments, dispositions of the charges, dismissals, acquittals, convictions, sentences, parole, and probation. Does not include information concerning juveniles, court decisions or opinions, records of traffic violations or records of traffic offenses.

Expunged Record – If the court orders a record sealed, all proceedings in the record are deemed to have never occurred and the person may answer accordingly to any inquiry. NRS 179.285(1)(a).

Employment – Any record which only reflects convictions or which pertains to an incident for which a person is currently within the system may be disseminated by a criminal justice agency to a prospective employer. NRS 179A.100(3).

Records may only be disseminated to a prospective employer if the potential employee has given written consent to the release of the information. NRS 179A.100(5)(m).

Consumer Report – A reporting agency shall not disclose bankruptcies, which antedate the report by more than 10 years, or any civil judgment, report of criminal proceedings, or other adverse information that precedes the report by more than 7 years. NRS 598C.150.

Nevada State Criminal Records Agency

DPS, Nevada Highway Patrol
Record & ID Services
808 W Nye Lane
Carson City, NV 89703

Phone: 775-687-1600
Fax: 775-687-1843

Web: www.nvrepository.state.nv.us

Total Records:	334,000
Who Can Access:	Records are available if you provide fingerprints and consent of subject. This agency suggests a court record search instead.
Search Requirements:	This repository maintains all "fingerprintable charges," meaning, essentially, all felony records and misdemeanor offenses including DUI and domestic violence. Include the following in your request: set of fingerprints, signed release, full name. DOB, SSN, sex and race are helpful.
What Is Released:	Records without dispositions are not released, unless an approved waiver is submitted. Records are available from 1987 and are on computer. Records are maintained indefinitely, unless purged due to court order. The following data is not released: sealed records or juvenile records.
Indexing & Storage:	It takes about 6 hours before new criminal records are available for inquiry. 40% of all arrests in database have final dispositions recorded, approximately 25% for those arrests within last 5 years. Records are indexed on computer. Records are normally destroyed after subject reaches 80 years old.
Access By:	Mail, in person.
Mail Search:	Turnaround time: 15 working days. No self addressed stamped envelope is required.
In Person Search:	Records are still returned by mail.
Fee & Payment:	The fingerprint search fee is $21.00 per individual. If the search requires an FBI fingerprint check (for record checks on occupations concerning children or the elderly, per state stutute), the fee is $45.00. Fee payee: Nevada Highway Patrol. Prepayment required. Cash, money order or cashier's check required. No credit cards or personal checks accepted.

Nevada Sexual Offender Registry

Records and Identification Bureau   **Phone**: 775-687-1600 x253

Sex Offender Registry,   **Fax**:   775-687-1844

808 W Nye Lane

Carson City, NV 89703   **Web**:   www.nvsexoffenders.gov

In 1997, the Community Notification of Sex Offenders law was passed (NRS Chapter 179D). There are over 8,700 offenders registered in the state.

What is released: Based upon NRS 179B.250, the Repository is permitted to share only ZIP Code information. Specific home address information on any convicted sex offender is strictly prohibited. There are less restrictions when requesting data at the local level. Records available from 1997 forward on computer.

Search Notes: Include in request: name, DOB, DL or SSN. There is no fee. Mail turnaround time: 1 day. Payee: Nevada Highway Patrol. Prepayment required. Money order or cashier's check required. No credit cards or personal checks accepted.

Access by: Phone, Fax, Mail, In Person, Online. Online search note: information on the website will include the name, aliases, photograph (where available), conviction information and ZIP Code based on the latest registered address. The website does not contain information on all convicted sex offenders. Information is only provided for sex offenders with a risk assessment score of a TIER Level 3 and certain information regarding a TIER Level 2. Search by name, ZIP Code, or even license plate number.

Nevada State Incarceration Records Agency

Nevada Department of Corrections   **Phone:** 775-887-3285

Correctional Case Records   **Fax:**   775-687-6715

P.O. Box 7011   **Web:**   www.doc.nv.gov

Carson City, NV 89702

What is released: Location, conviction and sentencing information, case number, and release dates are released. Records are available on current and former inmates. It takes 1 to 3 days before new records are released. Not available: medical and mental health data, disciplinaries, correspondence, chronos. Records are not destroyed, but are archived after one year. Searches can be done back to 1864, with varing results.

Search Notes: Include in request: full name; DOC number helpful. There is a $.25 fee per page. Mail turnaround time: 30 days.

Access by: Phone, Mail, Online. Limited name searching available by phone. Online search note: There are two ways to access information at the web page. The first is by clicking on Online Inmate Search or www.doc.nv.gov/nc is/search.php. This will allow you to look up information about a particular individual. If you prefer, you may click on Download Information to obtain text files of all the information available via the Inmate Search. This system contains information about current inmates and those discharged in the past 18 months.

Nevada State Court System

Court Structure: There are 17 District Courts within 9 judicial districts. The 45 Justice Courts are named for the township of jurisdiction. Note that, due to their small populations, some townships no longer have Justice Courts.

Find Felony Records: District Court

Misdemeanor Records: District Court, Justice Court

Online Access: Some Nevada Courts have internal online computer systems, but only Clark and Washoe counties offer online access to the public. A statewide court automation system is being implemented. The Supreme Court website gives access to opinions.

Searching Hints: Many Nevada Justice Courts are small and have very few records. Their hours of operation vary widely and contact is difficult. It is recommended that requesters call ahead for information prior to submitting a written request or attempting an in-person retrieval.

Court Administrator: For add'l questions about the state's court system, visit the website at www.nvsupremecourt.us/aoc.html, or contact: Supreme Court of Nevada, Administrative Office of the Courts, 201 S Carson St, #250, Carson City, NV 89701-4702, Phone: 775-684-1700.

New Hampshire

New Hampshire Statues & Related Employer Restrictions

General Rule – Every citizen has the right to inspect all public records. NH ST §91-A:4. Records of grand and petit juries, parole and pardon boards, personal school records of pupils, teacher certification records, records pertaining to preparing and carrying out emergency functions, and otherwise confidential records are exempt from the general rule. NH ST §91-A:5.

Criminal records are not open to the public unless the subject of the record has provided authorization in writing, signed and notarized, allowing the requestor to receive the information. NH ST §106-B:14.

Information available for noncriminal justice purposes is limited to conviction data.
NH ADC SAF-C 5703.04.

Expunged Record – The record of arrest, conviction, and sentence of any person may be annulled by the sentencing court. NH ST §651:5(I). The person whose record is annulled shall be treated in all respects as if he had never been arrested, convicted, or sentenced. NH ST §651:5(X)(a).

Employment – In any application for employment, license, or other civil right or privilege, a person may be questioned about a previous criminal record only in terms such as "Have you ever been arrested for or convicted of a crime that has not been annulled by a court?" NH ST §651:5(X)(c).

Consumer Report – No consumer reporting agency shall disclose 1) bankruptcies which antedate the report by 14 years, or 2) suits and judgments, paid tax liens, accounts placed for collection, records of arrest, indictment, or conviction of a crime, or any other adverse action which antedates the report by more than 7 years. NH ST §359-B:5(I). *Exception* – The reporting prohibition does not apply to the employment of an individual at an annual salary of $20,000 or more. NH ST §359-B:5(II)

New Hampshire State Criminal Records Agency

State Police Headquarters
Criminal Records, James H. Hayes Bldg,
33 Hazen Dr
Concord, NH 03305

Phone: 603-271-2538.
Fax: 603-271-2339

Web: www.state.nh.us/safety/nhsp/cr.html

Total Records: 618,000

Who Can Access: Requester must have "authorization in writing, duly signed and notarized, explicitly allowing the requester to receive such information."

Search Requirements: Specify exactly what information is needed. Statutorily-required fingerprint searches include FBI check. Include the following in your request: notarized release, full name, date of birth, any aliases, sex, race. Fingerprint searches are required for certain occupations, i.e. teachers, per state statute. 75% of the records are fingerprint supported.

What Is Released: Records without convictions are not released. Records are available from circa 1900.

Indexing & Storage: It takes 1 day before new records are available for inquiry. 80% of all arrests in database have final dispositions recorded, 90% for those arrests within last 5 years.

Access By: Mail, in person.

Mail Search: Turnaround time: 1 week. A self addressed envelope is requested.

In Person Search: In person requests are processed immediately.

Fee & Payment: The search fee is $10.00 per name. When required, FBI fingerprint searches are an additional $24.00 Fee payee: NH State Police. Prepayment required. Personal checks accepted. No credit cards accepted.

New Hampshire Sexual Offender Registry

State Police Headquarters   **Phone**: 603-271-2538

Special Investigations Unit-SOR,   **Fax**:   603-271-6479

James H. Hayes Bldg, 33 Hazen Dr

Concord, NH 03305   **Web**:   www.state.nh.us/safety/nhsp/cr.html

A list of all entries in the database can be accessed through local sheriffs' offices.

What is released: The agency prefers requesters go to the local police departments if the requester does not have Internet access. It takes 1 day before new records are released.

Search Notes: There is no search fee.

Access by: Mail, In Person, Online. In person search note: In person requests are processed immediately. Online search note: for web access, click on the Offenders Against Children link. This list only contains certain information about registered offenders who have committed certain criminal offenses against children. The list also contains outstanding arrest warrants for any sexual offender or offender against children who did not register.

New Hampshire State Incarceration Records Agency

New Hampshire Department of Corrections   **Phone:** 603-271-1825

Offender Records Office   **Fax:**   603-271-1867

P.O. Box 14   **Web:**   http://webster.state.nh.us/doc

Concord, NH 03302

What is released: Records are available on current and former inmates. It takes up to 3 days before new records are released. Records normally destroyed after 12 years. Computerized records go back to 1995.

Search Notes: Include in request: full name, DOB helpful. Mail turnaround: 1-2 weeks.

Access by: Phone, Fax, Mail, In Person. Record requests may also be emailed. Call the number above for a phone name search. In person search note: searchers must present ID and release info.

New Hampshire State Court System

Court Structure: The Superior Court is the court of General Jurisdiction. Felony cases include Class A misdemeanors.

Find Felony Records: Superior Court

Misdemeanor Records: District Court

Online Access: While there is no statewide access available for trial court records, the web page has a lot of useful information, including opinions and directives form the Supreme Court, Superior Courts, and District Courts. Click on Search.

Searching Hints: A statutory search fee has been implemented in the District Courts, as follows:

- Computer search is $10.00 for up to 10 names in one request; $25.00 for 10 or more names in one request; $25.00 per hour for search time beyond one hour.

- Manual search is $25.00 per hour.

If the search requires both types, the fee is the total for each.

Note that several District courts have raised the per hour fee to $35.00.

Court Administrator: For add'l questions about the state's court system, visit the website at www.courts.state.nh.us, or contact: Admin. Office of Courts, 2 Noble Dr, Supreme Ct Bldg, Concord, NH 03301-6160, Phone: 603-271-2521.

New Jersey

New Jersey Statues & Related Employer Restrictions

General Rule – A person or non-governmental entity of any state, who seeks to directly engage the services of the subject of the record, is authorized to obtain from the State Bureau of Identification all New Jersey criminal history record information for purposes of determining the subject's qualifications for employment or volunteer work. NJ ADC 13:591.2(a)(2).

Regardless of the subject's age, all records of pending arrests and charges for violations of New Jersey laws will be released, unless such records have been expunged. NJ ADC 13:591.2(a). Expunged records are deemed not to have occurred. NJSA 2C:52-27.

Rights of employees and applicants: Applicant who is disqualified for employment based on criminal record must be given adequate notice and reasonable time to confirm or deny accuracy of information.

New Jersey State Criminal Records Agency

Division of State Police
Records and Identification Section
PO Box 7068
West Trenton, NJ 08628-0068

Phone: 609-882-2000 x2878.
Fax: 609-530-5780

Web: www.njsp.org

Note: For requesters not living in the state, it is advised to contact a NJ-based investigator to obtain the record.

Total Records: 1,587,000

Who Can Access: Criminal records are not open to the public but can be obtained by employers, private investigators, screening firms, attorney firms, and the subject.

Search Requirements: Include the following in your request: date of birth, Social Security Number. A set of fingerprints is optional. The name must match exactly. All requesters, except attorney firms, must submit Form 212 B which must be signed by the subject. Attorney firms require a subpoena. 100% of the records are fingerprint supported.

What Is Released: All records are released, including those without dispositions. Records are available from 1921 forward. The following data is not released: Juvenile records are restricted. Dismissals, acquittals, not-guilty verdicts are also excluded to the general public.

Indexing & Storage: It takes 1 to 5 days before new records are available for inquiry. 85% of all arrests in database have final dispositions recorded, 95% for those arrests within last 5 years. Records are indexed on inhouse computer. Records are normally destroyed after verification that subject is no longer alive.

Access By: Mail, in person.

Mail Search: Turnaround time: 5 to 10 working days.

In Person Search: Walk-in requests do not receive priority; they are treated as mail requests. Results are mailed.

Fee & Payment: The fee is $18.00 for a name check and $30.00 for a full check with fingerprints. Will not do FBI fingerprint checks. Fee payee: Division of State Police-SBI. Prepayment required. No personal checks or credit cards accepted.

New Jersey Sexual Offender Registry

Division of State Police

Sexual Offender Registry,

PO Box 7068

West Trenton, NJ 08628-0068

Phone: 609-882-2000 x2886

Fax: 609-538-0544

Web: www.njsp.org/

Local law enforcement will assist with localized searches.

What is released: It takes 1 to 5 days before new records are released. Records normally destroyed after court order.

Search Notes: Include in request: name, date of birth. Records indexed on inhouse computer.

Access by: Online. No searching by mail. Online search note: data can be searched online at the website. Click on NJ Sex Offender Registry. Search can be done by name, by county, or by physical characteristics.

New Jersey State Incarceration Records Agency

New Jersey Department of Corrections

Central Administrative Offices

P.O. Box 863

Trenton, NJ 08625-0863

Phone: 609-777-5753

Web: www.state.nj.us/corrections/index.html

What is released: Location, DOC number, physical identifiers, conviction information, and release dates are released. Records are available on current and former inmates. It takes 1 day before new records are released. Records normally destroyed after 10 years after release.

Search Notes: Include in request: full name, DOB and SSN helpful. Mail turnaround time: 5 working days.

Access by: Phone, Fax, Mail, Online. Limited telephone searching available; less than three names per request. Online search note: extensive search capabilities are offered from the website; click on "Offender Search" Offenders on Work Release, Furlough, or in a Halfway House are not necessarily reflected as such in their profile.

New Jersey State Court System

Court Structure: Each of the 21 Superior Courts have 2 divisions; one for the Civil Division and another for the Criminal Division. Search requests should be addressed separately to each division.

Find Felony Records: Superior Court

Misdemeanor Records: Municipal Court

Searching Hints: Effective 1/1/95, all court employees became state employees and each section is responsible for its own fees. Note that Cape May County offices are located in the city of "Cape May Court House," and not in the city of "Cape May."

Court Administrator: For add'l questions about the state's court system, visit the website at www.judiciary.state.nj.us/admin.htm, or contact: Administrative Office of Courts, RJH Justice Complex, PO Box 037, Courts Bldg, 7th Floor, Trenton, NJ 08625, Phone: 609-984-0275.

New Mexico

New Mexico Statues & Related Employer Restrictions

General Rule – Every person has a right to inspect public records of this state except records classified as confidential or law enforcement records that would reveal confidential sources. NMSA 1978 §14-2-1.

Records of arrest not followed by a valid conviction and misdemeanor convictions not involving moral turpitude shall not be distributed in connection with an application for any public employment or license. NMSA 1978 §28-2-3(B).

Employment – In determining eligibility for employment with the state or for a license, permit, or certificate to engage in any trade, business or profession, the board may take convictions into consideration. The conviction shall not operate as an automatic bar to obtaining employment or license. NMSA 1978 §28-2-3(A).

Additionally, the state licensing board may refuse to grant a license if the applicant has 1) been convicted of a felony or misdemeanor involving moral turpitude, and the conviction relates directly to the employment sought, 2) been convicted of a felony or misdemeanor involving moral turpitude, and the conviction does not directly relate to the employment sought but the board determines the applicant has not been sufficiently rehabilitated, or 3) the applicant has been convicted of trafficking controlled substances, criminal sexual penetration, related sexual offenses, or child abuse, and the applicant is seeking employment involving children. NMSA 1978 §28-2-4(A).

Consumer Report – A credit bureau may not disclose 1) bankruptcies which antedate the report more than 14 years, or 2) accounts placed for collection, suit and judgments, paid tax liens, arrests and indictment pending trial, conviction of a crime, or any other data not otherwise specified which antedate the report by more than 7 years. NMSA 1978 §56-3-6.

New Mexico State Criminal Records Agency

Department of Public Safety
Records Bureau
PO Box 1628
Santa Fe, NM 87504

Phone: 505-827-9181

Fax: 505-827-3388

Web: www.dps.nm.org

Total Records: 360,000

Who Can Access: Must have a state notarized signed release from person of record authorizing the State of New Mexico to release records to specific requester.

Search Requirements: Except for law enforcement officials, specify which records you want. Include the following in your request: date of birth, Social Security Number, full name. Fingerprint search requests are not available except for checks for childern or elderly-related occupations mandated by state statute, and an FBI search can be done for those groups. Records are 100% fingerprint-supported.

What Is Released: All records are released, including those without dispositions. Records are available from 1935 on.

Indexing & Storage: It takes 2 to 4 weeks before new records are available for inquiry. 33% of all arrests in database have final dispositions recorded, 35% for those arrests within last 5 years. Records are indexed on inhouse computer (93%); historical paper records are added to computer once requested. Records are normally destroyed after 99 years.

Access By: Mail, in person, online.

Mail Search: Turnaround time: 1 to 2 weeks. Turnaround time is for "no record found." If records exist, turnaround time may be 3 to 4 weeks. A self addressed stamped envelope is requested.

In Person Search: If records are found, they may be available in 5 to 7 working days.

Online Search: Online access is available from www.osogrande.com/online-services.html. The fee is $10.00. You must set up an account to receive a password. When a record is found, a signed release from the subject must then be presented (faxed) to DPS in order to receive the detail page. For more information visit the website mentioned or call 505-345-6555.

Fee & Payment: The fee is $7.00 per individual. Fee payee: Department of Public Safety. Prepayment required. Must use cashiers check or money order. No credit cards accepted.

New Mexico Sexual Offender Registry

Department of Public Safety

Records Bureau, PO Box 1628

Santa Fe, NM 87504-1628

Phone: 505-827-9297, 505-827-9193

Fax: 505-827-3388

Web: www.nmsexoffender.dps.state.nm.us

What is released: Records are available from 07/95. The work address belonging to a sex offender is released if he/she will come into direct contact with children. It takes 2 to 4 weeks before new records are released. The following data is not released: SSN. Records normally destroyed after individual moves out of state.

Search Notes: There is no fee. Mail turnaround time: 1 to 2 weeks.

Access by: Phone, Mail, Online. Online search note: the website offers a variety of search methods including by name, county, city, and ZIP Code. The site also offers a complete state list, also an absconder list.

New Mexico State Incarceration Records Agency

New Mexico Corrections Department   **Phone:** 505-827-8674
Central Records Unit   **Fax:**   505-827-8801
P.O. Box 27116   **Web:**   http://corrections.state.nm.us/
Santa Fe, NM 87502

What is released: Location, conviction and sentencing information, behavior, release dates are provided. Records available on current and former inmates. It takes 1-3 days before new records are released. Records normally destroyed after 50 years.

Search Notes: Include in request: name; DOB and SSN are helpful. Fee is $.50 per copy. Mail turnaround time: 7 to 10 days. Payee: NM Department of Corrections.

Access by: Phone, Mail, Online. Online search note: to search at the website, you must first click on Offender Information, then on Offender Search.

New Mexico State Court System

Court Structure: The 30 District Courts in 13 districts are the courts of general jurisdiction.

Find Felony Records: District Court

Misdemeanor Records: Magistrate Court, Bernalillo Metropolitan Court in Bernalillo County.

Online Access: The www.nmcourts.com website offers free access to District and Magistrate Court case information. In general, records are available from June, 1997 forward.

A commercial online service is available for the Metropolitan Court of Bernalillo County. There is a $35.00 set up fee, a connect time fee based on usage. The system is available 24 hours a day. Call 505-345-6555 for info.

Also, a statewide search is available from the DPS at www.osogran de.com/online-services.html. The fee is $10.00. You must set up an account and receive a password. When a record is found, a signed release from the subject must be presented (faxed) to DPS in order to receive the detail page. For more information visit the website mentioned or call 505-345-6555.

Searching Hints: There are some "shared" courts in New Mexico, with one county handling cases arising in another.

Court Administrator: For add'l questions about the state's court system, visit the website at www.nmcourts.com, or contact: Administrative Office of the Courts, 237 Don Gaspar, Rm 25, Santa Fe, NM 87501, Phone: 505-827-4800.

New York

New York Statues & Related Employer Restrictions

General Rule – Each agency shall make available for public inspection and copying all records, except that such agency may deny access to records or portions thereof. NY PUB OFF §87(2).

No agency may disclose any record or personal information unless such disclosure is pursuant to a written request by or the voluntary written consent of the data subject, provided that such request or consent is limited by its terms and specifically describes the personal information requested, the requestor of the information, and the uses of the information requested. NY PUB OFF §96(1)(a).

Expunged Record – All official records relating to a youthful offender are confidential and are not available to any person or public or private agency. NY CRIM PRO §720.35(2).

Employment – It is unlawful for any person, agency, bureau, corporation, or association to deny any license or employment to an individual by reason of his or her being convicted of one or more criminal offenses, or to conclude a lack of "good moral character" based on his or her being convicted of one or more criminal offenses. NY EXEC §296(15).

An employer may consider the conviction if 1) there is a direct relationship between the previous criminal offense and the employment or license sought or 2) the issuance of the license or granting employment would involve unreasonable risk to property or to the safety or welfare of a specific individual or the general public. NY CORRECT §752.

It is also illegal to make inquiry about or to act adversely to the individual involved, any criminal accusation not then pending which was followed by a termination of the criminal action in favor of the individual, in connection with licensing or employing the individual. However, this does not apply to the regulation of deadly weapons, or an application for employment as a police officer. NY EXEC §296(16).

Credit Report – A consumer reporting agency may furnish a consumer report to a person whom it has reason to believe intends to use the information for employment purposes. NY GEN BUS §380-b(a)(3)(ii).

No consumer reporting agency can report information about an arrest or criminal charge unless there has been a criminal conviction or the charges are still pending. NY GEN BUS §380-j(a)(1).

A consumer reporting agency may collect information about a detention of an individual by a retail mercantile establishment providing that the individual admitted wrongdoing, received notice that the information will be reported, and the receiver of the information will only use the information for employment purposes. NY GEN BUS §380-j(b).

No consumer report may disclose 1) bankruptcies which antedate the report by more than 14 years or 2) judgments, paid tax liens, accounts placed for collection, records of criminal convictions, information regarding drug or alcohol addiction, information relating to past confinement in a mental institute, or any other adverse action which antedate the report by more than 7 years. NY GEN BUS §380-j(f)(1). However, the above information is not prohibited from disclosure for the employment of any individual at an annual salary of $25,000 or more. NY GEN BUS §380-j(f)(2).

No person may procure an investigative consumer report unless the consumer has received notice and the consumer has authorized the procurement of the investigative report. NY GEN BUS §380-c(a).

If an applicant refuses to authorize the procurement of an investigative consumer report, the prospective employer may decline to grant employment. NY GEN BUS §380-c(d).

Agency guidelines for pre-employment inquiries: New York State Division of Human Rights, "Rulings on Inquiries (Pre-employment)" available on the SUNY education system website at http://naples.cc.sunysb.edu/Admin/HRSForms.nsf/0/510e45e64ead755885256d2800561042/$FILE/HRSD0010.pdf

New York State Criminal Records Agency

Division of Criminal Justice Services　　　　　**Phone:** 518-457-6043
4 Tower Place　　　　　　　　　　　　　　　　**Fax:** 　 518-457-6550
Albany, NY 12203

Web: www.criminaljustice.state.ny.us

Access to Records is Restricted

Note: Records are only released pursuant to court order, subpoena, to entities authorized by statute, or to person of record. 99% of records are fingerprint supported. The public must search at the county court level.

Total Records:　　　　7,400,000

Search Requirements　Include the following in your request: name, DOB, SSN, and fingerprints 85% of records have dispositions.

What Is Released:　　Misdemeanor convictions older than five years cannot be considered unless another crime has been commited during that time. The following data is not released: sealed records and confidential records pursuant to the Criminal Procedure Law or Family Court Act.

New York Sexual Offender Registry

Division of Criminal Justice Srvs　　　　**Phone**: 518-457-6326 ext.1; **Verification**: 800-262-3257
Sexual Offender Registry,　　　　　　　**Fax**: 　 518-485-5805
4 Tower Place, Rm 604
Albany, NY 12203

Web: www.criminaljustice.state.ny.us/nsor/search_disclaimer.htm

What is released: Records are available back to 01/22/96. It takes 1 day before new records are released.

Search Notes: Include in request: name, SSN, and DOB. There is no fee to use the 800 telephone number. Mail turnaround time: 1 week.

Access by: Phone, Fax, Mail, Online. Lengthy lists must be mailed. Online search note: the sex offender registry Level 3 can be searched at the website. Requesters are required to register.

New York State Incarceration Records Agency

New York Department of Corrective Services   **Phone:** 505-457-5000

1220 Washington Ave., Building 2   **Fax:**   518-485-9502

Albany, NY 12226-2050   **Web:**   www.docs.state.ny.us

What is released: Location, DIN number, conviction and sentencing information, and release dates are provided. Records are available on current and former inmates. It takes 1 to 20 days before new records are released.

Search Notes: Include in request: full name; the DOB, SSN, and DIN (inmate number) are helpful. There is no search fee. Copy fee $.25 per page. Mail turnaround time: 7 to 10 days.

Access by: Phone, Fax, Mail, Online. Limited name searching by phone is available from the agency. For information on the location of a NYS prison inmate, call 518-457-5000 during normal business hours. Online search note: computerized inmate information is available from the Inmate Lookup at http://nysdocslookup.docs.state.ny.us/kinqw00 or follow "Inmate Lookup" link at main site. Records go back to early 1970s. To acquire inmate DIN number, you may call 518-457-5000.

New York State Court System

Court Structure: New York State has two sites for Administration; an Albany office and a New York City office (addresses and phone numbers below).

"Supreme Courts" are the highest trial courts in the state, equivalent to Circuit or District Courts in other states; they are not appeals courts. Many New York City courts are indexed by plaintiff only.

Records for Supreme and County Courts are maintained by County Clerks. In most counties, the address for the clerk is the same as for the court. In at least 20 New York Counties, misdemeanor records are only available at city, town or village courts.

Find Felony Records: Supreme Court, City Court

Misdemeanor Records: City Court, District Court, City of NY Criminal Court, Town and Village Justice Courts

Criminal Notes: The New York State Office of Court Administration-OCA (address below) has mandated that all criminal record requests made to the Supreme Court Clerk be forwarded to this office for processing. The OCA does not wish to have clerks performing county searches. OCA will perform an electronic search for criminal history information from a database of criminal case records from all the boroughs and counties, including Supremem Courts and some city Courts. (Note: At press time, it is not clear which county courts submit misdemeanors to this database.) The fee, payable by check, is $52.00 per name. Mail and in person requests go to: Office of Court Administration (OCA) Criminal History Search, 25 Beaver St, 8th Fll, New York, NY 10004. You may obtain copies of any case dispositions found from the applicable county court.

Online Access: The OCA offers online access to approved requesters for criminal records. Requesters receive information back via email. Call the OCA for details on how to set up an account. The fee is $52.00 per record, the highest statewide record fee in the U.S.

Open Civil Supreme Court case information is available for all 62 counties through the court system's website - http://e.courts.state.ny.us. Select decisions from New York Supreme Criminal Court and other criminal courts are also available. The information is also available at all courts.

Also, you may search for future court dates for defendants in these 21 criminal courts: Bronx Criminal Court, Bronx Supreme Court, Dutchess County Court, Buffalo City Court, Erie County Court, Kings Criminal Court, Kings Supreme Court, Nassau County Court, Nassau District Court, New York Criminal Court, NY Supreme Court, Orange County Court, Putnam County, Queens Criminal Court, Queens Supreme Court, Richmond Criminal Court, Richmond Supreme Court, Rockland County Court, Suffolk County Court, Suffolk District Court, Westchester County Court.

Searching Hints: Supreme and County Court records are generally maintained in the County Clerk's Office, which outside of New York City may index civil cases by defendant, whereas the court itself maintains only a plaintiff index.

Court Administrator: For add'l questions about the state's court system, visit the website at www.courts.state.ny.us, or contact: NY State Office of Court Administration, New York City Office, 25 Beaver St, New York, NY 10004, Phone: 212-428-2100, *or* NY State Office of Court Administration, Empire State Plaza, Agency Bldg #4, Suite 2001, Albany, NY 12223, Phone: 518-473-1196.

North Carolina

North Carolina Statues & Related Employer Restrictions

General Rule – Public records and public information is the property of the people and the people may obtain copies. NCGSA §132-1(b). Records of criminal investigation or criminal intelligence information are not public records. NCGSA §132-1.4(a).

Records and evidence compiled by the director of the Dept. of Justice, State Bureau of Investigation, are not public records and will not be made available to the public unless ordered by a court of competent jurisdiction. 12 NCAC 3B.0401.

The North Carolina Attorney General's Office is responsible for determining what persons or agencies are entitled by law/authorized to receive criminal history record information. 12 NCAC 3B.0502(b). An authorized requestor is any person approved to receive state and national criminal history data by virtue of being 1) a member of an approved law enforcement agency, 2) any person from Division of Criminal Information, or 3) National Crime Information Center authorized non-criminal justice agency. 12 NCAC 4E.0104(3).

Criminal History Record Information disseminated to the requesting person or agency for a purpose other than the administration of justice will consist of arrest data, which includes a final disposition to the arrest, and arrest data without a final disposition if the date of arrest is within one year or less from the date of request. 12 NCAC 3B.0502(g).

Additional persons/agencies authorized by statute to obtain criminal record check if they obtain the individual's consent include:

1) Hospitals and child placing agencies for providers of treatment for services to children, the elderly, mental health patients, the sick and disabled. NCGSA §114-19.3

2) Division of Social Services, Department of Health and Human Services for a prospective foster or adoptive parent. NCGSA §114-19.4

3) Division of Child Development for any child care provider. NCGSA §114-19.5.

4) Department of Health and Human Services or Department of Juvenile Justice and Delinquency Prevention for an applicant for employment or current employee in a position to care for a client, patient, student, resident, or ward of the Department. NCGSA §114-19.6.

5) NC Auctioneers Commission for an applicant for an auctioneer's license. NCGSA §114-19.8.

6) Nursing Homes, Adult Care Homes, Home Care Agencies, Area Mental Health, Developmental, disabilities, and substance abuse services authorities. NCGSA §114-19.10.

7) North Carolina Board of Nursing for any applicant seeking licensure as a registered nurse or licensed practical nurse. NCGSA §114-19.11.

8) Fire Department for a paid or volunteer position. NCGSA §114-19.12.

9) North Carolina Manufactures Housing Board for any applicant for licensure as a manufactured home manufacturer, dealer, salesperson, or set-up contractor. NCGSA §114-19.13.

10) The City for any person seeking employment with the city. NCGSA §114-19.14.

11) North Carolina Locksmith Licensing Board for any applicant seeking licensure as a locksmith or apprentice. NCGSA §114-19.15.

Employment - Employers for the Fire Department, Department of Health and Human Services, or Department of Juvenile Justice and Delinquency Prevention may use a person's conviction of certain felonies and misdemeanors as just cause for not selecting the person for employment, or for dismissing the person from current employment. However, the conviction shall not automatically prohibit employment. The employer must take into consideration the seriousness of the crime, date of the crime, age of the person at the time of conviction, nexus between the crime and the job duties, and the subsequent commission of a crime. NCGSA §§114-19.6(d) and 114-19.12(d).

Expunged Record – No person who has had a record expunged will be guilty of perjury or guilty of otherwise giving a false statement or response to any inquiry made for any purpose, by reason of his failure to recite or acknowledge any expunged records. NCGAS §15A-146(a).

North Carolina State Criminal Records Agency

State Bureau of Investigation   **Phone:** 919-662-4500 x302
Identification Section   **Fax:**   919-662-4380
PO Box 29500
Raleigh, NC 27626   **Web:**   http://sbi.jus.state.nc.us

Access to Records is Restricted

Note: This agency and the Administrative Office of the Courts (AOC) have implemented a computer-to-computer interface, which provides all users with the capability to access statewide Clerk of Court criminal records.

Total Records: 881,983

Who Can Access: Record access is limited to criminal justice and other government agencies authorized by law. Employers are denied access unless subject is in professions mentioned in the above section.

Search Requirements: Contact agency for proper paperwork. Include the following in your request: full name, SSN, DOB. Fingerprints are optional. The state's records are 100% fingerprint supported.

What Is Released: All records are released, including those without dispositions. The following data is not released: There are no restrictions.

North Carolina Sexual Offender Registry

State Bureau of Investigation

Division of Criminal Information-SOR Unit,
PO Box 29500

Raleigh, NC 27626

Phone: 919-662-4500 x6257

Fax: 919-662-4619

Web: http://sbi.jus.state.nc.us

(courier address: 3320 Garner Rd, Raleigh, NC 27626-0500.)

Records are available for public inspection; name, sex, address, physical description, picture, conviction date, offense for which registration was required, the sentence imposed as a result of the conviction, and registration status.

What is released: This office only releases information online. They suggest to submit a written request for the information to the sheriff. The identity of the victim cannot be released. A sheriff may charge a reasonable fee. Records are available 01/01/96. It takes 24 hours before new records are released. Not available: victim information. Records normally destroyed after 105 years.

Search Notes: Mail turnaround time: 24 hours.

Access by: Mail, In Person, Online. Online search note: search Level 3 records at the website. Search by name or geographic region. Other Access: Agency can provide data on CD-Rom.

North Carolina State Incarceration Records Agency

North Carolina Department of Corrections

Combined Records

2020 Yonkers Road, 4226 MSC

Raleigh, NC 27699-4220

Phone: 919-716-3200

Fax: 919-716-3986

Web: www.doc.state.nc.us

What is released: Location, physical identifiers, conviction and sentencing information, and release dates are provided. Records are available on current and former inmates. It takes up to 10 days before new records are released. Records normally destroyed after 10 years (paper copies). Computer records go back to 1973.

Search Notes: Include in request: full name. The DOB, SSN and DOC number are helpful. The fee for copies is $1.00 for first page and $.25 each add'l. Mail turnaround time: 1 to 2 days. Payee: NC Dept of Corrections.

Access by: Phone, Fax, Mail, Online. Name searching available by phone. Online search note: the web access allows searching by name or ID number for public information on inmates, probationers, or parolees since 1973. Also, a private company offers free web access to inmates at www.vinelink.com/index.jsp; including DOC and county jail systems.

North Carolina State Court System

Court Structure: The Superior Court is the court of general jurisdiction, the District Court is limited. The counties combine the courts, thus searching is done through one court, not two, within the county.

Find Felony Records: Superior Court

Misdemeanor Records: District Court

Online Access: While there is no statewide online access; web access to civil and criminal dockets are available at some individual courts.

Access active District/Superior Court criminal calendars on a county or statewide basis at http://www1.aoc.state.nc.us/www/calendars.html. Historical information is not available. Also, appellate and supreme court opinions are available www.aoc.state.nc.us/www/public/html/opinions.htm.

Searching Hints: Many courts recommend that criminal searches be requested in writing (for a $10.00 search fee, which is certified in most jurisdictions). Many courts have archived their records prior to 1968 in the Raleigh State Archives, 919-733-5722. A list of companies offering NC criminal records online is at www.nccourts.org/Citizens/GoToCourt/Default.asp?topic=1.

Court Administrator: For add'l questions about the state's court system, visit the website at www.nccourts.org/Courts/, or contact: Administrative Office of Courts, PO Box 2448, Raleigh, NC 27602-2448, Phone: 919-733-7107.

North Dakota

North Dakota Statues & Related Employer Restrictions

General Rule – Only the bureau may disseminate criminal history record information to parties other than criminal justice agencies, courts, or pursuant to a judicial, legislative, or administrative agency subpoena issued in North Dakota. The dissemination may only be made if the information 1) has not been purged or sealed, 2) the information is of a conviction, or notwithstanding any disposition following a deferred sentence, or information is a reportable event occurring within one year of the request, 3) the request is written and contains sufficient information to identify the subject, and 4) the identifying information does not match more than 1 individual. NDCC 12-60-16.6.

If the bureau disseminates information to a non-criminal justice agency, the bureau must mail notice to the record subject, unless the request was accompanied by an authorization. NDCC 12-60-16.8.

Definitions

Reportable Event – an interaction with a criminal justice agency for which a report is required to be filed. The term includes only those events in which the subject of the event is an adult or a juvenile adjudicated as an adult. NDDC 12-60-16.1.

Reportable Events – each criminal justice agency shall report to the bureau for each felony and reportable offense the following: fingerprints, charges, description of person arrested, decision not to refer the arrest for prosecution, all charges filed, all final dispositions, judgments of not guilt, judgments of guilt and the sentence, discharges, dismissals in the trial court, reverse or remand of a reported conviction, order to vacate or modify sentence, other information concerning the receipt, escape, death, release, pardon, conditional pardon of an individual who has been sentenced to the North Dakota state penitentiary or other correctional facility. NDDC 12-60-16.2.

Employment – A person may not be disqualified to practice, pursue, or engage in any occupation, trade, or profession for which a license, permit, or certificate is required from any state agency, board or commission solely because of a prior conviction. However, the applicant may be denied a license if the licensing board has determined that the applicant has not been sufficiently rehabilitated, or that the offense has a direct bearing upon a person's ability to serve the public in the specific occupation. NDCC 12.1-33-02.1.

Consumer Report – A consumer reporting agency may not provide or sell data or list that include any information that in whole or in part was submitted in conjunction with an insurance inquiry about a consumer's credit information or a request for a credit report or insurance score. NDCC 26.1-25.1-09.

Consumer Report, Definitions - NDCC 26.1-25.1-02

Consumer reporting agency – any person that for a monetary fee regularly engages in whole or in part in the practice of assembling or evaluating consumer credit information for the purposes of furnishing consumer reports to third parties.

Consumer report – any written, oral or other communication of information by a consumer reporting agency bearing on a consumer's creditworthiness, credit standing, or credit capacity which is used or expected to be used for the purpose of serving as a factor to determine personal insurance premiums, eligibility for coverage, or tier placement.

Agency guidelines for pre-employment inquiries: North Dakota Department of Labor, Human Rights Division "Employment Applications and Interviews" is available online at www.state.nd.us/la bor/publications/docs/brochures/005.pdf

North Dakota State Criminal Records Agency

Bureau of Criminal Investigation
Criminal Records Section
PO Box 1054
Bismarck, ND 58502-1054

Phone: 701-328-5500.
Fax: 701-328-5510
Web: www.ag.state.nd.us

Total Records: 230,400

Who Can Access: Records are available to the general public but only with consent of subject.

Search Requirements: Subject will be notified of the request. Include the following in your request: signed release from subject, name, DOB, current address, Social Security Number. Fingerprints optional, for add'l fee, but fingerprint searches are not available to public. 100% of the records are fingerprint-supported.

What Is Released: After one year, only records with convictions are released. Charges that are dismissed or sealed are not released. Records are available from 1930 to present. The following data is not released: cases dismissed or scaled

Indexing & Storage: It takes 6 to 10 days before new records are available for inquiry. 86% of all arrests in database have final dispositions recorded, 78% for those arrests within last 5 years. Records are indexed on computer if DOB is 1940 to present; prior in paper files. Records are maintained indefinitely.

Access By: Mail, in person.

Mail Search: Turnaround time: 3 to 5 days. No self addressed stamped envelope required.

In Person Search: Turnaround time while you wait.

Fee & Payment: The search fee is $30.00 per name. Fee payee: ND Attorney General. Prepayment required. Personal checks accepted. No credit cards accepted.

North Dakota Sexual Offender Registry

Bureau of Criminal Investigation

SOR Unit, PO Box 1054

Bismarck, ND 58502-1054

Phone: 701-328-5500

Fax: 701-328-5510

Web: www.ndsexoffender.com

(courier address: 4205 N State St, Bismarck, ND 58501)

What is released: Offender information may be requested by city, county, or the entire state. Records are available from 1991. It takes 6 to 10 days before new records are released.

Search Notes: There is no fee. Mail turnaround time: 1 to 2 days.

Access by: Phone, Mail, In Person, Online. Online search note: access is available from the website. The online listings include offenders who are identified as lifetime registrants as defined by law, or have been designated as high-risk offenders by the Attorney General's Risk Level Committee.

North Dakota State Incarceration Records Agency

Department of Correction and Rehabilitation

Records Clerk

P.O. Box 5521

Bismarck, ND 58506

Phone: 701-328-6122

Fax: 701-328-6640

Web: www.state.nd.us/docr/

Employees of the Prisons Division may not disclose inmate information except as granted in North Dakota Century Code 12-47-36.

What is released: Location, conviction and sentencing information, and release dates are provided. Records are available on current and former inmates. It takes about 3 days before new records are released. Records normally destroyed after 7 years after discharge.

Search Notes: Include in request: first and last name. DOB is helpful. There is no fee. Mail turnaround time: 5 to 7 days.

Access by: Phone, Fax, Mail.

North Dakota State Court System

Court Structure: In 1995, the County Courts merged with the District Courts statewide. County court records are maintained by the 53 District Court Clerks in the seven judicial districts. We recommend stating "include all County Court cases" in search requests.

Find Felony Records: District Court

Misdemeanor Records: District Court

Online Access: A statewide computer system for internal purposes is in operation in most counties. You may now search North Dakota Supreme Court dockets and opinions at www.ndcourts.com. Search by docket number, party name, or anything else that may appear in the text. Records are from 1991 forward. Email notification of new opinions is also available.

Searching Hints: In Summer, 1997, the standard search fee in District Courts increased to $10.00 per name; the certification fee increased to $10.00 per document. Copy fees remain at $.50 per page, but many courts charge only $.25.

Court Administrator: For add'l questions about the state's court system, visit the website at www.ndcourts.com, or contact: Court Administrator, North Dakota Supreme Court, 600 E Blvd Ave, Dept 180, Bismarck, ND 58505-0530, Phone: 701-328-4216.

Ohio

Ohio Statues and Related Employer Restrictions

General Rule – All public records shall be promptly prepared and made available for inspection to any person. OH ST §149.43(B)(1). Information and materials collected by the superintendent of Criminal Identification and Investigation, such as records of felony convictions, misdemeanor convictions that would be felonies upon a second conviction, photographs, and fingerprints, are not public records. OH ST §109.57(D).

Criminal Record History Information may be disseminated to employers for applicants who have contact with children, mentally retarded, medical patients, and disabled or elderly adults. OH ST §109.57(F)(2)(a).

Expunged Record – Records sealed upon a finding that the person was a first offender or an unruly child may be sealed and considered not to have occurred. OH ST §§2953.32(C)(2) and 2151.358(C).

Employment – The business of pre-employment background investigation means, and is limited to, furnishing for hire, in person or through a partner or employees, the conducting of limited background investigations, in person interviews, telephone interviews, or written inquires that pertain only to a client's prospective employee, and the employee's employment, and that are engaged in with the prior written consent of the prospective employee. OH ST §4749.01(H)(3)(c).

In application for employment, license, or other right or privilege, an applicant may only be questioned about convictions not sealed, and bail forfeitures not expunged or sealed, unless the question bears a direct and substantial relationship to the position sought. OH ST §2953.33(B).

Ohio State Criminal Records Agency

Ohio Bureau of Investigation
Civilian Background Section
PO Box 365
London, OH 43140

Phone: 740-845-2000 (General Information).
Fax: 740-845-2633
Web: www.webcheck.ag.state.oh.us

Total Records: 1,6000,000
Who Can Access: Records are available to the general public but only with consent of subject.
Search Requirements: Include the following in your request: witnessed signed release from subject, fingerprints, name DOB, SSN. 100% of the records are fingerprint supported.

What Is Released: Records without dispositions are not released. Records are available from 1921 on. Records from 1972 on are computerized.

Indexing & Storage: It takes 5 days, 15 with fingerprints before new records are available for inquiry. 62% of all arrests in database have final dispositions recorded. Records are indexed on inhouse computer. Records are normally destroyed after (records maintained indefinitely).

Access By: Mail, online.

Mail Search: Turnaround time: 30 days. No self addressed stamped envelope is required.

Online Search: WebCheck is an Internet-based request program for civilian background checks for school districts, education associations, children's hospitals, and public institutions. Results are NOT retruned via the Internet. Agencies can send fingerprint images and other data via the Internet using a single digit fingerprint scanner and a driver's license magnetic strip reader. Within two business days, the school or daycare center will receive their results of their background check requests.

Fee & Payment: The search fee is $15.00 per record. Stautorily-required checks may include an FBI fingerprint check for an additional $24.00. Fee payee: Treasurer - State of Ohio. Prepayment required. No credit cards accepted.

Ohio Sexual Offender Registry

Ohio Bureau of Investigation

Sexual Offender Registry, PO Box 365

London, OH 43140

Phone: 740-845-2221 740-845-2223

Fax: 740-845-2633

Web: www.esorn.ag.state.oh.us/Secured/p1.aspx

O.R.C. 2950.13 requires that the public eSORN database contain information on every person convicted as an adult and registered in the state registry of sex offenders and child-victim offenders. The individual county sheriff's representatives are best situated to provide local sex offender and registration information.

What is released: The database that contains information regarding all registered sex offenders in the State of Ohio is known as eSORN.

Access by: Online. No searching by mail. Online search note: search online eSORN at www.esorn.ag.state.oh.us/Secured/p1.aspx. Users can search by offender name, zip code, county and / or school district. The site is linked to all 88 of Ohio's sheriff's offices and all 32 Ohio correctional facility records offices

Ohio State Incarceration Records Agency

Ohio Department of Rehabilitation and Correction   **Phone:**   614-752-1076

Bureau of Records Management   **Fax:**   614-752-1086

1050 Freeway Drive, N.   **Web:**   www.drc.state.oh.us

Columbus, OH 43229

What is released: Location, physical identifiers, conviction and sentencing information, and release dates are provided. Records are available on current and former inmates, except online is current only. It takes 1 to 5 days before new records are released. Records normally destroyed after 10 years.

Search Notes: Include in request: first and last name or Offender Number. The DOB and SSN are helpful. Mail turnaround time: 1 to 2 weeks.

Access by: Phone, Fax, Mail, Online. To obtain information on offenders previously under the supervision of the Department, call 614-752-1159 and choose option 3. Online search note: from the website, in the Select a Destination box, select Offender Search. You can search by name or inmate number. The Offender Search includes all offenders currently incarcerated or under some type of Department supervision (parole, post-release control, or transitional control).

Ohio State Court System

Court Structure: The Court of Common Pleas is the general jurisdiction court and County Courts have limited jurisdiction.

Find Felony Records: Court of Common Pleas

Misdemeanor Records: County Court, Municipal Court, Mayor's Court

Online Access: There is no statewide computer system, but a number of Circuits and Municipal courts offer online access. Appellate and Supreme Court case opinions and annoucements are available at the web page.

Court Administrator: For add'l questions about the state's court system, visit the website at www.sconet.state.oh.us, or contact: Admin. Director, Supreme Court of Ohio, 65 S Front Street, Columbus, OH 43215-3431, Phone: 614-387-9000.

Oklahoma

Oklahoma Statues & Related Employer Restrictions

General Rule – All records of public body and officials shall be open to any person for inspection, copying and/or mechanical reproduction. 51 OSA §24A.5.

Law enforcement agencies shall make available for public inspection arrestee description, facts concerning the arrest, conviction information, disposition of all warrants, crime summary, radio logs, and jail registers. 51 OSA §24A.8(A).

Expunged Record – Employers shall not in any application or interview require an applicant to disclose any information contained in sealed records. An applicant may state that no such action ever occurred. 22 OSA §19(F).

Credit Report – A consumer reporting agency may include information on tax liens when the information is obtained directly from the Oklahoma Tax Commission. 24 OSA §86.

Oklahoma State Criminal Records Agency

OK State Bureau of Investigation
Criminal History Reporting
6600 N Harvey
Oklahoma City, OK 73116

Phone: 405-848-6724.
Fax: 405-879-2503

Web: www.osbi.state.ok.us

Total Records:	850,000
Who Can Access:	Records are available to the general public.
Search Requirements:	A record request form is available at the website. Include the following in your request: DOB or approximate age. The SSN, sex or race are helpful and provide a better search, but not required. Fingerprints are optional. 100% of the records are fingerprint-supported.
What Is Released:	Arrest records without dispositions are released if the party was fingerprinted. Computer searches include arrests without dispositions. Records are available from 1925 on. The following data is not released: juvenile records.
Indexing & Storage:	It takes 5 to 7 days before new records are available for inquiry. 35% of all arrests in database have final dispositions recorded, 47% for those arrests within last 5 years. Records are normally destroyed after (records maintained indefinitely).

Access By:	Mail, fax, in person.
Mail Search:	Turnaround time: 2 weeks. A self addressed stamped envelope is requested.
Fax Search:	Use of credit card and their "Credit Card Fax Form" is required. Call to have them fax you the form or download from web.
In Person Search:	Name requests take 20 minutes, fingerprint searches take up to ten days to process.
Fee & Payment:	The fee for a computer name search is $15.00. The fee for the fingerprint search is $19.00. Fingerprint search does not include FBI fingerprint search; agency will not conduct an FBI search. Copies are $.25 per page. Fee payee: O.S.B.I. Prepayment required. Personal checks not accepted. Credit cards accepted: MasterCard, Visa, Discover.

Oklahoma Sexual Offender Registry

Oklahoma Department fo Corrections   **Phone**: 405-962-6104

Sex Offender Registry, PO Box 11400

Oklahoma City, OK 73136-0400   **Web**: www.doc.state.ok.us/DOCS/offender_info.htm

Search Notes:	Mail turnaround time: 1-3 days.
Access by:	Mail, Online. Mail search note: names searches and geographic lists are available by mail. Online search note: searching is available from the website. The Sex Offender Lookup only lists lifetime (habitual and aggravated) sex offenders, all others have not been put on the site yet. There are a number of search options.

Oklahoma State Incarceration Records Agency

Oklahoma Department of Corrections   **Phone:**   405-425-2500

Offender Records   **Fax:**   405-425-2608

P.O. Box 11400, 3400 Martin Luther King Ave.   **Web:**   www.doc.state.ok.us

Oklahoma City, OK 73136-0400

What is released:	Location, DOC number, physical identifiers, conviction and sentencing information, and release dates are provided. Records are available on current and former inmates. Records are maintained indefinitely. It takes 10 days before new records are released. Not available: SSN, offender home address.
Search Notes:	Include in request: provide first and last name, but the DOB, SSN and DOC number helpful. You can search online by either the name or DOC number. Mail turnaround time: 5 to 10 working days.

Access by: Phone, Fax, Mail, Online. Limited phone searching available. Online search note: at the main website, click on Offender Information. The online system is shut down from 3AM until 3:30 AM.

Oklahoma State Court System

Court Structure: There are 80 District Courts in 26 judicial districts. Cities with populations in excess of 200,000 (Oklahoma City and Tulsa) have municipal criminal courts of record. Cities with less than 200,000 do not have such courts.

Find Felony Records: District Court

Misdemeanor Records: District Court, Municipal Court of Record

Online Access: Free Internet access is available for ten District Courts and all Appellate courts at www.oscn.net. Both civil and criminal docket information is available. The counties are Canadian, Cleveland, Comanche, Garfield, Logan, Oklahoma, Payne, Pushmataha, Rogers, and Tulsa.

One can search the Oklahoma Supreme Court Network by single cite or multiple cite (no name searches) from the www.oscn.net Internet site .

Case information is available in bulk form for downloading to computer. For information, call the Administrative Director of Courts, 405-521-2450.

Also, of note is the Oklahoma District Court Records free website at www.odcr.com. Originally twelve District Courts databases, the system has expanded to 31 jurisdictions in 2003. More counties are being added as they are readied; they hope to eventually feature all Okla. District courts.

Court Administrator: For add'l questions about the state's court system, visit the website at www.oscn.net, or contact: Administrative Director of Courts, 1915 N Stiles, #305, Oklahoma City, OK 73105, Phone: 405-521-2450.

Oregon

Oregon Statues and Related Employer Restrictions

General Rule – The Department of State Police shall deliver to the person or agency making the request of criminal offender information the following information, regarding any convictions, and any arrest less than one year old on which the records show no acquittal or dismissal: 1) date of arrest, 2) offenses for which arrest was made, 3) arresting agency, 4) court of origin, and 5) disposition including sentence imposed, date of parole and parole revocations. ORS §181.560(1)(b).

If the department does not have any information on the individual or the information consists only of non-conviction data, the department shall respond that the individual has no criminal record and shall not release any further information. ORS §181.560(2).

Employment - An entity may request from an authorized agency a criminal record check for the purposes of evaluating the fitness of a subject individual as an employee, contractor, or volunteer. ORS §181.533(2).

The employer must first advise the employee or prospective employee that such information might be sought, and shall state upon making the request that the individual has been so advised and the manner in which so advised. ORS §181.555(2)(b).

Except for applicants seeking employment as a teacher or a license with the Health Licensing Office, no licensing board or agency shall deny, suspend, or revoke an occupational or professional license solely for the reason that the applicant or licensee has been convicted of a crime. It may consider the relationship of the facts that support the conviction and all intervening circumstance to the specific occupational or professional standards in determining the fitness of the person to receive or hold the license or certificate. ORS §670.280.

It is an unlawful employment practice for an employer, state agency, or licensing board to refuse to employ or discharge from employment an individual because of a juvenile record that has been expunged. ORS §§659A.030(1)(a) and 670.290.

Agency guidelines for pre-employment inquiries: Oregon Bureau of Labor and Industries, Civil Rights Division, Fact Sheets, "Pre-Employment Inquiries" is available online at www.boli.state.or.us/civil/tarpreemp.html

Oregon State Criminal Records Agency

Oregon State Police, Unit 11　　　　　　　　**Phone:**　503-378-3070.
Identification Services Section　　　　　　　**Fax:**　　503-378-2121
PO Box 4395
Portland, OR 97208-4395　　　　　　　　　**Web:**　　www.osp.state.or.us

Total Records:　　　　1,033,453

Who Can Access:　　Records are available to the general public.

Search Requirements:　Three types of searches exist: open records search, own record search, and statutorily-required search. The latter can include an FBI fingerprint check for an additional $24.00 fee. Include the following in your request: name, date of birth, last known address. Submitting the SSN is helpful, but not required. Fingerprints are required only when subject submits the request. If record exists, person of record will be notified of the request and the record will not be released for 14 additional days.

What Is Released:　Open record information includes all records with convictions and also all arrests within the past year without disposition. Statutorily-required record searches and own record searches include all records. Records are available from 1941 on and are computerized.

Indexing & Storage:　It takes up to 8 days before new records are available for inquiry. Approximately 50% of all arrests in database have final dispositions recorded. Records are indexed on inhouse computer. Records are normally destroyed after (records maintained indefinitely).

Access By:　　Mail, fax, online.

Mail Search:　Turnaround time: 5 days if clean. Records with hits can take as long as 3 weeks to return.

Fax Search:　Requesters must be pre-approved, however records are not returned by fax.

Online Search:　A web based site is available for requesting and receiving criminal records. Website is ONLY for high-volume requesters who must be pre-approved. Results are posted as "No Record" or "In Process" ("In Process" means a record will be mailed in 14 days). Use the "open records" link to get into the proper site. Fee is $15.00 per record. Call 503-373-1808 x230 to receive the application, or visit the website.

Fee & Payment:　Open record search fee is $15.00 per individual name. If someone is submitting a search on oneself, the fee is $12.00 and fingerprints are required. Statutorily-required searches are $12.00 plus FBI fingerprint fee, if required. $5.00 fee to notarize. Fee payee: Oregon State Police. Prepayment required. Personal checks accepted. No credit cards accepted.

Oregon Sexual Offender Registry

Oregon State Police   **Phone**: 503-378-3720

SOR Unit, 255 Capitol St NE, 4th Fl   **Fax**:   503-363-5475

Salem, OR 97310   **Web**:   www.osp.state.or.us

What is released: It takes up to 8 days before new records are released. Records normally destroyed after 1 year after death of the offender.

Search Notes: Include in request: name and DOB There is no fee. Mail turnaround time: up to 3 weeks.

Access by: Phone, Fax, Mail.

Oregon State Incarceration Records Agency

Department of Corrections   **Phone:** 503-570-6900

Offender Information & Sentence Computation   **Fax:**   503-373-1629

PO Box 5670   **Web:**   www.doc.state.or.us

Wilsonville, OR 97070-5670.

What is released: Location, SID number, physical identifiers, conviction and sentencing information, and release dates are provided. Records are available on current and former inmates. It takes up to four days before new records are released. Records normally destroyed after being microfilmed after final discharge.

Search Notes: Include in request: full name; DOB and SID number helpful. Fees are charged for copies as follows: $.50 for paper, $1.25 from microfilm. Mail turnaround time: 2 to 4 weeks.

Access by: Phone, Fax, Mail, Email. Name searching permitted by phone. Online search note: no online offender searching is available from this agency; there is a "Corrections Most Wanted" list in the pull down menu box. A private company offers free web access at www.vinelink.com/index.jsp; includes state, DOC, and most county jails. Also, you may email mary.l.solomon@doc.state.or.us for an inmate lookup.

Oregon State Court System

Court Structure: Effective January 15, 1998, the District and Circuit Courts were combined into "Circuit Courts." At the same time, three new judicial districts were created by splitting existing ones.

Find Felony Records: Circuit Court

Misdemeanor Records: Circuit Court, Justice Court, Municipal Court

Online Access: Online computer access is available through the Oregon Judicial Information Network (OJIN). OJIN Online includes almost all cases filed in the Oregon state courts. Generally, the OJIN database contains criminal, civil, small claims, probate, and some but not all juvenile records. However, it does not contain any records from municipal nor county courts. There is a one-time setup fee of $295.00, plus a monthly usage charge (minimum $10.00) based on transaction type, type of job, shift, and number of units/pages (which averages $10-13 per hour). For further information and/or a registration packet, write to: Oregon Judicial System, Information Systems Division, ATTN: Technical Support, 1163 State Street, Salem OR 97310, or call 800-858-9658, or visit www.ojd.state.or.us/ojin.

Searching Hints: Many Oregon courts indicated that in person searches would markedly improve request turnaround time as court offices are understaffed or spread very thin. Most Circuit Courts that have records on computer do have a public access terminal that will speed up in-person or retriever searches. Most records offices close from Noon to 1PM Oregon time for lunch. No staff is available during that period.

Court Administrator: For add'l questions about the state's court system, visit the website at www.ojd.state.or.us/osca, or contact: Court Administrator, Supreme Court Bldg, 1163 State St, Salem, OR 97301-2563, Phone: 503-986-5500.

Pennsylvania

Pennsylvania Statues & Related Employer Restrictions

General Rule – Criminal History record information shall be disseminated by a state or local police department to any individual or noncriminal justice agency upon request. All notations of arrest, indictments, or other information relating to the initiation of criminal proceedings where 2 years have elapsed from the date of arrest, no conviction occurred, and no proceedings are pending seeking a conviction shall be extracted from the record when disseminated to an individual or noncriminal justice agency. 18 PACSA §9121.

Expunged Record – When no disposition has been received within 18 months of arrest or in certain juvenile delinquency cases, the court may order records expunged. 18 PACSA §§9123 and 9122.

An expunged record is removed so that there is no trace or indication that such information existed, except for maintenance of the record for certain judicial requirements. 18 PACSA §9102.

Employment – An employer may consider felony and misdemeanor convictions only to the extent that they relate to the applicant's suitability for employment in the position for which he or she has applied. 18 PACSA §9125.

A licensing board may consider conviction of the applicant, but the convictions shall not preclude the issuance, certificate, registration, or permit. Records or arrest without conviction, convictions expunged, convictions of a summary offense, conviction which received a pardon, and convictions which do not relate to the applicant's suitability for the license sought shall not be used in consideration of an application for a license by the licensing board. However, a licensing board may refuse to grant or renew, or may suspend or revoke a license because of a felony conviction or a misdemeanor that relates to the trade, occupation or profession for which the license is sought. 18 PACSA §9124.

Agency guidelines for pre-employment inquiries: Pennsylvania Human Relations Commission, Publications, "Pre-Employment Inquiries" is available online at www.phrc.state.pa.us/PA_Exec/PHRC/publications/literature/web_preempqs.htm

Pennsylvania State Criminal Records Agency

State Police Central Repository
1800 Elmerton Ave
Harrisburg, PA 17110-9758

Phone: 717-783-5494.

Web: www.psp.state.pa.us/psp/site/default.asp

Total Records: 1,903,084

Who Can Access: Records are available to the general public.

Search Requirements: Must make request on Request Form SP4-164 or the request will be returned. Include the following in your request: full name, date of birth, Social Security Number, sex, race, any aliases. A release is not required. The record database is 100% fingerprint-supported. Statutorily-required fingerprint searches include an FBI fingerprint search.

What Is Released: Records include felony and misdemeanor convictions, also cases without dispositions less than 3 years old. Records are available from the 1920s. Records are available for all convictions.

Indexing & Storage: It takes 1 day before new records are available for inquiry. 60% of all arrests in database have final dispositions recorded, 31% for those arrests within last 5 years. Records are indexed on fingerprint cards and inhouse computer. Records are normally destroyed after 3 years after individual is confirmed deceased by fingerprints.

Access By: Mail, online.

Mail Search: Turnaround time: 2-3 weeks. Turnaround can be 6 weeks if a record has a hit. No self addressed stamped envelope is required.

Online Search: Record checks are available for approved agencies through the Internet on the Pennsylvania Access to Criminal Histories (PATCH). This is a commercial system, the same $10.00 fee per name applies. PATCH accepts Visa, Discover, Master Card and American Express. Go to https://epatch.state.pa.us or call 717-705-1768 to register.

Fee & Payment: Fee is $10.00 per name search. Add $24.00 if for a statutorily-required FBI fingerprint check. Fee payee: Commonwealth of Pennsylvania. Prepayment required. No personal checks accepted. No credit cards accepted.

Pennsylvania Sexual Offender Registry

State Police Central Repository   **Phone**: 717-783-4363 717-783-9973

Megan's Law Unit, 1800 Elmerton Ave   **Fax**:   717-705-8839

Harrisburg, PA 17110-9758   **Web**:   www.psp.state.pa.us/psp/site/default.asp

This office provides no searches except via email. The public may request information concerning sexually violent predators in a particular community by visiting the law enforcement office in that community, including local State Police offices.

What is released: Records are available from July 8, 2000 forward.

Access by: Online. No searching by mail. Online search note: September 25, 2003 the Pennsylvania Supreme Court interpreted this provision of Megan's Law to require that a specific request be made before this information can be provided via electronic means. To make a specific request for information on Sexually Violent Predators, please email to ra-pspsvp@state.pa.us.

Pennsylvania State Incarceration Records Agency

Pennsylvania Department of Corrections

Inmate Records Office

P.O. Box 598

Camp Hill, PA 17001-0598

Phone: 717-737-6538

Fax: 717-731-7159

Web: www.cor.state.pa.us

What is released: Location, physical identifiers, conviction and sentencing information, and release dates are available. Records are available on current and former inmates. It takes a minimum of 30 days before new records are released. Records normally destroyed after 10 years after maximum sentence date.

Search Notes: Include in request: full name. DOB and SSN are helpful. There is no fee. Mail turnaround time: 1 to 2 weeks.

Access by: Phone, Fax, Mail, Online. Includes historical information on released inmates. Online search note: At the website, click on Inmate Locator for information about each inmate currently under the jurisdiction of the Department of Corrections. The site indicates where an inmate is housed, race, date of birth, marital status and other items. The Inmate Locator does not contain information on inmates not currently residing in a state correctional institution.

Pennsylvania State Court System

Court Structure: The Courts of Common Pleas are the general trial courts, with jurisdiction over both civil and criminal matters and appellate jurisdiction over matters disposed of by the special courts.

It is not necessary to check with each District Court, but rather to check with the Prothonotary for the county.

Find Felony Records: Court of Common Pleas, Philadelphia Municipal Court

Misdemeanor Records: Court of Common Pleas, Philadelphia Municipal Court, Pittsburgh City Magistrate Court, Magisterial District Court (Justice Court)

Online Access: The state's 556 District Justice Courts are served by a statewide, automated case management system; online access to the case management system is not available.

Search by county for Common Pleas criminal docket information by name or docket number for free at http://ujsportal.pacourts.us. Click on "E-Services." This site also provides access to appellate case information. Also, search Appellate Court dockets at http://pacmsdocketsheet.aopc.org.

The Infocon County Access System provides direct dial-up access to court record information for 16 counties - Armstrong, Bedford, Blair, Butler, Clarion, Clinton, Erie, Franklin, Huntingdon, Juaniata, Lawrence, Mercer, Mifflin, Pike, Potter and Susquehanna. Set up entails a $50.00 base set-up fee plus $25.00 per county. The monthly usage fee minimum is $25.00, plus time charges. For Information, call Infocon at 814-472-6066.

Searching Hints: Fees vary widely among jurisdictions. Many courts will not conduct searches due to a lack of personnel or, if they do search, turnaround time may be excessively lengthy. Many courts have public access terminals for in-person searches.

Court Administrator: For add'l questions about the state's court system, visit the website at www.courts.state.pa.us, or contact: Administrative Office of PA Courts, PO Box 229, Mechanicsburg, PA 17055, Phone: 717-795-2000.

Rhode Island

Rhode Island Statues & Related Employer Restrictions

General Rule – All records maintained or kept on file by any public body shall be public records and every person or entity shall have the right to inspect and/or copy those records. RI ST §38-2-3(a).

Expunged Record – In any application for employment, a person whose conviction of a crime has been expunged may state that he or she has never been convicted of the crime, unless the applicant is applying for a teaching certificate, coaching certificate, admission to the bar, or the operator or employee of an early childhood education facility. RI ST §12-1.3-4(b).

All police records relating to the arrest, detention, apprehension, and disposition of any juvenile shall be withheld from public inspection. RI ST §14-1-64(a).

Employment – It is unlawful for any employer to include on any application a question inquiring if the applicant has ever been arrested or charged with a crime, unless the applicant seeks employment with a law enforcement agency. An employer may inquire whether an applicant has ever been convicted of a crime. RI ST §28-5-7(7).

Rhode Island State Criminal Records Agency

Department of Attorney General   **Phone:** 401-274-4400 x2353.
Bureau of Criminal Identification   **Fax:**   401-222-1331
150 S Main Street   **Web:**   www.riag.ri.gov
Providence, RI 02903

Total Records: 240,000

Who Can Access: Rarely are records available to the general public.

Search Requirements: Criminal records are only released to law enforcement agencies, the subject, or, rarely, to those with a signed notarized authorization from the subject. Records should be obtained at the county level. For those who have the authority, include the following in your request: signed notarized release from subject, DOB, picture ID and DOB of the requester. Fingerprints and SSN are optional. They will call the Notary on the authorization for verification. 100% of the records are fingerprint-supported.

What Is Released: All arrests and convictions are reported.

Indexing & Storage:	It takes 1-7 days before new records are available for inquiry. 60% of all arrests in database have final dispositions recorded. Records are normally destroyed after court order or expungment.
Access By:	Mail, in person.
Mail Search:	Turnaround time: up to 2 weeks. A self addressed stamped envelope is required.
In Person Search:	Turnaround time is while you wait.
Fee & Payment:	The fee is $5.00 per name. If required, the FBI fingerprint search is an additional $24.00. Fee payee: Department of Attorney General. Prepayment required. Personal checks accepted. No credit cards or cash accepted.

Rhode Island Sexual Offender Registry

Department of Attorney General   **Phone**: 401-274-4400

BCI Unit, 150 S Main St. Providence, RI 02903   **Web**:   www.riag.state.ri.us

The state's Sexual Offender Registry is not available to the public. Searching must be done at the local level.

Rhode Island State Incarceration Records Agency

Rhode Island Department of Corrections   **Phone:** 401-462-3900

Assistant to the Director   **Fax:**   401-464-2630

40 Howard Avenue, Cranston, RI 02920   **Web:**   www.doc.state.ri.us

What is released:	Location, physical identifiers, conviction and sentencing information, and release dates are provided. Records are available on current and former inmates. It takes 1 to 3 days before new records are released.
Search Notes:	Include in request: full name; DOB helpful. There is no fee. Mail turnaround time: 30 days.
Access by:	Phone, Fax, Mail. Limited name searching available by phone. Online search note: There is no access to inmate records through the agency, however a private company offers free web access to DOC records at www.vinelink.com/index.jsp.

Rhode Island State Court System

Court Structure: Rhode Island has five counties, but only four Superior/District Court Locations (2nd-Newport, 3rd-Kent, 4th-Washignton, and 6th-Prividence/ Bristol Districts). Bristol and Providence counties are completely merged at the Providence location.

Find Felony Records: Superior Court

Misdemeanor Records: District Court

Online Access: The Rhode Island Judiciary offers free Internet access to court criminal records statewide at http://courtconnect.courts.state.ri.us. A word of caution, this website is provided as an informational service only and should not be relied upon as an official record of the court.

Court Administrator: For add'l questions about the state's court system, visit the website at www.courts.state.ri.us, or contact: Court Administrator, Supreme Court, 250 Benefit St, Providence, RI 02903, Phone: 401-222-3272.

South Carolina

South Carolina Statues & Related Employer Restrictions

General Rule – Any person has a right to inspect or copy any public record of a public body. SC ST ANN §30-4-30(a).

Expunged Record – Any person who has a criminal offense discharged, dismissed, or is found guilty can have all records of the arrest destroyed and no evidence of such record shall be retained by any municipal, county, or state law enforcement agency. SC ST ANN §17-1-40.

Employment – A person may not be refused an authorization to practice, pursue, or engage in a regulated profession solely because of a prior criminal conviction unless it relates directly to the profession or occupation. A board may refuse an applicant if based on all the information available, including the applicant's record of prior conviction, it finds the applicant unfit or unsuited to engage in the profession. SC ST ANN §40-1-140.

South Carolina State Criminal Records Agency

South Carolina Law Enforcement Division (SLED)
Criminal Records Section
PO Box 21398
Columbia, SC 29221

Phone: 803-896-7043
Fax: 803-896-7022

Web: www.sled.state.sc.us

Total Records:	1,075,215
Who Can Access:	Records are available to the general public.
Search Requirements:	Criminal records are open without restrictions. Include the following in your request: full name, any aliases, sex, race, and DOB. The SSN is helpful. 100% of the records are fingerprint supported. They will not do fingerprint searches.
What Is Released:	All records are released, including those without dispositions. Records are available from the 1960s.
Indexing & Storage:	It takes 1 to 12 days before new records are available for inquiry. 72% of all arrests in database have final dispositions recorded, 85% for those arrests within last 5 years. Records are indexed on inhouse computer. Records are normally destroyed after (records maintained indefinitely unless expunged).
Access By:	Mail, in person, online.

Mail Search:	Turnaround time: 5 to 7 days. They will return by overnight delivery service if prepaid and materials provided. A self addressed stamped envelope is requested.
In Person Search:	Turnaround time is within minutes for three names or less.
Online Search:	SLED offers commercial access to criminal record history from 1960 forward on the website. Fees are $25.00 per screening or $8.00 if for a charitable organization. Credit card ordering accepted. Visit the website or call 803-896-7219 for details.
Fee & Payment:	The search fee is $25.00 per individual. The fee is $8.00 for non-profit organizations, pre-approval is required. Fee payee: SLED. Prepayment required. Business and company checks are accepted, personal checks are not. No credit cards accepted, except online.

South Carolina Sexual Offender Registry

Sex Offender Registry   **Phone**: 803-896-7043

c/o SLED, PO Box 21398   **Fax**:   803-896-7022

Columbia, SC 29221   **Web**:   www.sled.state.sc.us

All requests are screened as to the age of the offender. Therefore, all requests must be on a state form, which can be downloaded from the Internet.

What is released:	Records are available from 1994 to present. Not available: registrants under 17 unless as required by law. Records normally destroyed after court order.
Search Notes:	Include in request: proper form. There is no fee unless ordered by a business then fee is $17.00 (form can be downloaded from website). Mail turnaround time: 5 to 7 days.
Access by:	Phone, Mail, Online. Online search note: access is available from the website. Click on Sexual Offender Registry. Search by name or ZIP Code, county, or city.

South Carolina State Incarceration Records Agency

Department of Corrections   **Phone:** 803-896-8531

Inmate Records Branch   **Automated Information:** 877-846-3472

4444 Broad River Rd   **Web:**   www.state.sc.us/scdc

Columbia, SC 29221-1787

What is released:	Location, SCDC number, physical identifiers, conviction and sentencing information, FBI number, and release dates are provided. Records are

available on current and former inmates. It takes 1 to 2 days before new records are released.

Search Notes: Include in request: provide full name, DOB, SSN. The SCDC number is helpful. There is no search fee, but there is a copy fee of $.25 per page. Mail turnaround time: 1-2 weeks.

Access by: Phone, Mail, Online. Name searching available by phone. Online search note: the Inmate Search on the Internet is available for free at http://sword.doc.state.sc.us/incarceratedInmateSearch/index.jsp or click on Inmate search at the main website.

South Carolina State Court System

Court Structure: The 46 SC counties are divided among sixteen judicial circuits. The circuit courts are in operation at the county level and consist of a court of general sessions (criminal) and a court of common pleas (civil). The over 300 Magistrate and Municipal Courts (often referred to as "Summary Courts") only handle misdemeanor cases involving a $500.00 fine and/or 30 days or less jail time.

Find Felony Records: Circuit Court

Misdemeanor Records: Circuit Court, Magistrate Court, Municipal Court

Online Access: Appellate and Supreme Court opinions are available from the website. There is no access to statewide trial court records, but several counties offer online access.

Searching Hints: If requesting a record in writing, it is recommended that the words "request that General Session, Common Pleas, and Family Court records be searched" be included in the request.

Most South Carolina courts will not conduct searches. However, if a name and case number are provided, many will pull and copy the record. Search fees vary widely as they are set by each county individually.

Court Administrator: For add'l questions about the state's court system, visit the website at www.sccourts.org, or contact: Court Administration, 1015 Sumter St, 2nd Floor, Columbia, SC 29201, Phone: 803-734-1800.

South Dakota

South Dakota Statues & Related Employer Restrictions

General Rule – The officer required to keep public records shall keep them available and open to public inspection by any person. SDCL §1-27-1. Confidential criminal justice information is not a public record. SDCL §23-5-11.

Any person may examine criminal history information filed with the Attorney General that refers to that person. The person may also authorize the Attorney General to release his criminal history information to other individuals or organizations. SDCL §23-5-12.

Definitions – SDCL §23-5-10

Criminal History information – includes arrest information, conviction information, disposition information, and correction information.

Expunged Record – Upon granting a pardon, the governor shall order all records relating to the criminal offense sealed. No person who has had records sealed will be guilty of perjury or giving a false statement by such person's failure to recite or acknowledge such arrest, indictment, or trial in response to any inquiry made for any purpose. SDCL §24-14-11.

Agency guidelines for pre-employment inquiries: South Dakota Division of Human Rights "Pre-employment Inquiry Guide" is available online at www.state.sd.us/dol/Boards/hr/preemplo.htm

South Dakota State Criminal Records Agency

Division of Criminal Investigation

Identification Section

500 E Capitol

Pierre, SD 57501-5070

Phone: 605-773-3331.

Fax: 605-773-4629

Web: http://dci.sd.gov

Total Records: 175,000

Who Can Access: Records are available to the general public but only with consent of subject.

Search Requirements: Include the following in your request: date of birth, full name, set of fingerprints, signed release form. The form requires identifying information: color of hair and eyes, height, weight, date of birth, Social Security Number.

What Is Released: Records without dispositions are not released, unless the case is still open. Records are available for 10 years for misdemeanors and lifetime for felonies.

The following data is not released: juvenile records, minor traffic violations or out-of-state or federal charges.

Indexing & Storage: It takes 1 day before new records are available for inquiry. 98% of all arrests in database have final dispositions recorded. Records are indexed on inhouse computer (90+%); only older records not computerized. Records are normally destroyed after 10 years if a misdemeanor, generally.

Access By: Mail.

Mail Search: Turnaround time: 5 to 10 working days. Upon receipt of those requirements, they will conduct a search of their files and supply a copy of any criminal history that is found or a statement that there is no criminal history. A self addressed stamped envelope is requested.

Fee & Payment: The fee is $15.00 per name. Statutorily-required fingerprint checks will include an FBI fingerprint check for an additional $24.00. Fee payee: Division of Criminal Investigation. Prepayment required. Personal checks accepted. No credit cards accepted.

South Dakota Sexual Offender Registry

Division of Criminal Investigation   **Phone**: 605-773-3331, 605-773-4614
Identification Section - SOR Unit,   **Fax**:   605-773-2596
500 E Capitol
Pierre, SD 57501-5070   **Web**: http://dci.sd.gov/administration/id/sexoffender/index.asp

This agencies urges the public to visit local law enforcement offices for access to lists.

What is released: Records are available from 1994. It takes 30+ days before new records are released. Records normally destroyed after court order, moved, or deceased.

Access by: Online. No searching by mail. Online search note: searching is available from the website. Note that there is no statewide search, all searches are done on a county basis.

South Dakota State Incarceration Records Agency

South Dakota Department of Corrections   **Phone:** 605-773-3478
Central Records Office   **Fax:**   605-773-3194
3200 E. Highway 34, 500 E. Capitol Ave   **Web:** www.state.sd.us/corrections/corrections.html
Pierre, SD 57501-5070   Sioux Falls Central Records: 605-367-5190

What is released: Location, conviction and sentencing information are available. Records are available on current and former inmates. It takes up to 3 days before new records are released. Not available: medical, treamnet, and disciplinary records. Records normally destroyed after one year from final discharge.

The computerized records system does not track records back further than those inmates who were discharged in 1985.

Search Notes: Include in request: name and DOB or SSN.

Access by: Phone. For phone search, call the Department's Office of Community Relations at 302-739-5601 x246. No searching by mail. Other Access: A Dept. most wanted list is at www.state.sd.us/corrections/most_wanted.htm

South Dakota State Court System

Court Structure: South Dakota has a statewide criminal record search database, administrated by the State Court Administrator's Office in Pierre. All criminal record information from July 1, 1989 forward, statewide, is contained in the database. To facilitate quicker access for the public, the state has designated 10 county record centers to process all mail or ongoing commercial accounts' criminal record requests. All mail requests are forwarded to, and commercial account requests are assigned to one of 10 specific county court clerks for processing a statewide search. Note that walk-in requesters seeking a single or minimum of requests may still obtain a record from their local county court. Five counties (Buffalo, Campbell, Dewey, McPherson, and Ziebach) do not have computer terminals in-house.

The fee is $15.00 per record. State authorized commercial accounts may order and receive records by fax, there is an additional $5.00 fee unless a non-toll free line is used.

Requesters who wish to set up a commercial account are directed to contact Jill Gusso at the Court Administrator's Office in Pierre at the address mentioned below, or at jill.gusso@ujs.state.sd.us.

Find Felony Records: Circuit Court
Misdemeanor Records: Circuit Court, Magistrate Court

Online Access: There is no statewide online access computer system currently available. Larger courts are being placed on computer systems at a rate of 4 to 5 courts per year. Access is intended for internal use only. Smaller courts place their data on computer cards that are sent to Pierre for input by the state office.

Searching Hints: Most South Dakota courts do not allow the public to perform searches, but rather require the court clerk to do them for a fee of $15.00 per name. A special Record Search Request Form must be used. Searches will be returned with a disclaimer stating that the clerk is not responsible for the completeness of the search. Clerks not required to respond to telephone or fax requests. Many courts are not open all day; they prefer written requests.

Court Administrator: For add'l questions about the state's court system, visit the website at www.sdjudicial.com, or contact: State Court Administrator, State Capitol Bldg, 500 E Capitol Ave, Pierre, SD 57501-5059, Phone: 605-773-3474.

Tennessee

Tennessee Statues & Related Employer Restrictions

General Rule – All state, county, and municipal records shall be open for personal inspection by any citizen of Tennessee. TCA §10-7-503(a). The Tennessee Bureau of Investigation shall process requests for criminal background checks from any authorized person, organization or entity permitted by law to seek criminal history background checks on certain persons. TCA §38-6-109(a).

The following organizations and employers may request a criminal history background check:

- A municipality hiring for public transportation. TCA §6-54-128(b)(1).
- Applicant for license to operate an adult-oriented establishment. TCA §7-51-1122(a).
- Applicant for a permit as an entertainer at an adult oriented establishment. TCA §7-51-1122(a).
- Person seeking to obtain a public contract. TCA § 12-4-606.
- Applicant for school bus driver position. TCA §49-6-2117
- Applicants for employment or to volunteer with adult day care centers. TCA §71-2-403(a)(1).
- Person seeking employment as a teacher or for any other position requiring proximity to schoolchildren. TCA §49-5-406.

Expunged Records – Expunged records are confidential and not public. TCA §38-6-118(d).

Tennessee State Criminal Records Agency

Tennessee Bureau of Investigation
Records and Identification Unit
901 R S Gass Blvd.
Nashville, TN 37216

Phone: 615-744-4000.
Fax: 615-744-4653
Web: www.tbi.state.tn.us

Access to Records is Restricted

Note: Records not available to general public. Per statute, fingerprint-based background checks be conducted for paid or volunteer employment or licensing such as such as child care, teachers, security and armed guards, security system contractors, etc.

Total Records: 2,150,000

What Is Released: All records are released to those entitled, including those without dispositions.

Other Onlne Access: The state maintains a website at www.ticic.state.tn.us for searching of sexual offenders, missing children, and people placed on parole who reside in Tennessee.

Tennessee Sexual Offender Registry

Tennessee Bureau of Investigation   **Phone**: 888-837-4170

Sexual Offender Registry,   **Fax**:   615-744-4655

901 R S Gass Blvd.

Nashville, TN 37216   **Web**:   www.ticic.state.tn.us/

Other than the website, records are not open to the public for viewing. While this agency will do a limited phone verification, it is suggested to go to local law enforcement for extensive checks.

What is released: Records are available from 07/01/97 forward. Not available: expunged records. Records normally destroyed after death of the offender.

Search Notes: Include in request: name, DOB; SSN is helpful.

Access by: Phone, Online. Records are not available by mail. Online search note: search sexual offenders at website by name, county or ZIP Code. One may also search for missing children, and people placed on parole who reside in Tennessee.

Tennessee State Incarceration Records Agency

Tennessee Department of Corrections   **Phone:** 615-741-1000

Rachel Jackson Building   **Fax:**   615-532-1497

320 6th Avenue, N. 2nd Fl.   **Web:**   www.state.tn.us/correction

Nashville, TN 37243-0465

What is released: Location, conviction and sentencing information are provided. Records are available on current and former inmates. It takes 7 days before new records are released. Not available: medical information and SSNs. Records normally destroyed after 100 years.

Search Notes: Include in request: first and last name. The SSN and DOB are helpful. Fees apply when hard copies are needed: $10.00 for search, $.20 per page Mail turnaround time: 10 - 15 working days. Payee: State of Tennessee

Access by: Phone, Fax, Mail, Online. Limited phone searching is available. Online search note: extensive search capabilities are offered from the website. Click on FOIL - Inmate Search. Other Access: a CD-Rom is available with only public information from current offender database; nominal fee; contact the Planning & Research Division.

Tennessee State Court System

Court Structure: Criminal cases are handled by the Circuit Courts and General Sessions Courts. Generally, misdemeanor cases are heard by General Sessions, but in Circuit Court if connected to a felony. Combined courts vary by county, and the counties of Davidson, Hamilton, Knox, and Shelby have separate Criminal Courts.

Find Felony Records: Circuit Court

Misdemeanor Records: Circuit Court, General Sessions Court, Criminal Court, Municipal Court

Online Access: The Administrative Office of Courts provides access to Appellate Court opinions at the website www.tsc.state.tn.us. Several counties offer online access to court records.

Court Administrator: For add'l questions about the state's court system, visit the website at www.tsc.state.tn.us, or contact: Administrative Office of the Courts, Nashville City Center, 511 Union St, Suite 600, Nashville, TN 37219, Phone: 615-741-2687.

Texas

Texas Statues and Related Employer Restrictions

General Rule – Criminal history record information maintained by the department is confidential information for the use of the department, and except as provided for, may not be disseminated by the department. TX GOVT §411.083(a).

Any person is entitled to obtain from the Department of Public Safety criminal history record information maintained by the department that relates to the conviction of or grant of deferred adjudication to a person for any criminal offense, including arrest information that relates to the conviction or grant of deferred adjudication. TX GOVT §411.135(a)(2).

A person who obtains information from the department may use the information for any purpose, or release the information to any other person. TX GOVT §411.135(c).

Expunged Records – The release, dissemination, or use of expunged records and files for any purpose, other than criminal justice purposes, is prohibited when the order to expunge records is final. TX CRIM PRO §55.03(1).

The person arrested may deny the occurrence of the arrest and the existence of the expungement order. TX CRIM PRO §55.03(2).

Employment – An agency that licenses or regulates members of a particular trade, occupation, business, vocation, or profession is entitled to obtain from the Department of Public Safety criminal history record information that relates to a person who is an applicant for a license or a holder of a license. TX GOVT §411.122(a).

A licensing authority may suspend, revoke, or disqualify a person from receiving a license on the grounds that the person has been convicted of a felony or misdemeanor that directly relates to the duties and responsibilities of the licensed occupation. TX GOVT 53.021(a).

Consumer Report – A consumer reporting agency may furnish a consumer report to a person the agency has reason to believe intends to use the information for employment purposes. TX BUS & COM §20.02(a)(3)(B).

A consumer reporting agency may not furnish a report that contains 1) bankruptcies that antedate the report by more than 10 years or 2) a suit or judgment, a tax lien, a record of arrest, indictment or conviction of a crime, or another item or event that antedates the report by more than 7 years. TX BUS & COM §20.05(a). However, a consumer reporting agency is not restricted from reporting information if it is provided in connection with the employment of a consumer with a salary of $75,000 or more. TX BUS & COM §20.05(b)(3).

Texas State Criminal Records Agency

Department of Public Safety   **Phone:** 512-424-2427
Crime Records Service, Correspondence Section **Fax:**   512-424-5011
PO Box 15999   **Web:**   http://records.txdps.state.tx.us
Austin, TX 78761-5999

Total Records: 6,400,000

Who Can Access: Conviction only records are available to the general public; for full information, consent of subject is required.

Search Requirements: To obtain ALL arrest information (conviction and non-conviction), must have a signed release and full set of fingerprints from the person of record. To obtain conviction and deferred adjudication data only, submit full name, sex, race, and DOB. The SSN is helpful, but not required. No letter of authorization is needed for the conviction only report.

What Is Released: Fingerprint searches show complete record; name search is conviction only and deferred adjudications. Since 1/1/93, records include complete information regarding charge, disposition, date of conviction, and county. Data prior to this date may not be complete. Records are available from 1930 to present. The following data is not released: juvenile records.

Indexing & Storage: It takes 1 day before new records are available for inquiry. 55% of all arrests in database have final dispositions recorded. Records are indexed on inhouse computer. Records are normally destroyed after a court order, otherwise they are not destroyed.

Access By: Mail, in person, online.

Mail Search: Turnaround time: 2 weeks. No self addressed stamped envelope is required.

In Person Search: Records requested at the Dept. of Public Safety Crime Records Service in Austin usually takes 1-2 business days.

Online Search: Records can be pulled from the website. Requesters may use a credit card or establish an account and pre-purchse credits. The fee established by the Department (Sec. 411.135(b)) is $3.15 per request plus a $.57 handling fee. These checks are instantaneous and provide convictions and deferred adjudications only.

Fee & Payment: The fee is $15.00 for the full search using fingerprints, and $10.00 for a name-based search. If required, the FBI fingerprint check is an additional $24.00. Fee payee: Texas Department of Public Safety. Prepayment required. Credit cards are accepted for online searches only. Personal checks accepted. Credit cards accepted: MasterCard, Visa.

Texas Sexual Offender Registry

Dept of Public Safety   **Phone**: 512-424-2478

Sex Offender Registration, PO Box 4143

Austin, TX 78765-4143   **Web**:   http://records.txdps.state.tx.us

What is released: A sex offender's home telephone number, Social Security Number, drivers license number will not be released. It takes 1 day before new records are released.

Search Notes: A $10.00 fee is charged for mail searches only. Mail turnaround time: 1-2 weeks. Payee: Texas Department of Public Safety. Prepayment required. Personal checks accepted.

Access by: Mail, Online. Online search note: sex offender data is available online at http://records.txdps.state.tx.us/soSearch/soSearch.cfm. There is no charge for a sex offender search. To see which organizations have purchased the sexual offender database, go to http://records.txdps.state.tx.us/forsale.cfm.

Texas State Incarceration Records Agency

Texas Department of Criminal Justice   **Phone:** 936-437-6371

Bureau of Classification and Records   **In State Parole Status line**: 800-535-0283

P.O. Box 99   **Web:**   www.tdcj.state.tx.us

Huntsville, TX 77342-5099

Previous convictions and sex offender registration inquiries should be directed to the Dept. of Public Safety, 5805 N Lamar, Austin, TX 78752, 512-424-2000 or www.txdps.state.tx.us.

What is released: Location, conviction and sentencing information are provided. Records are available on current and former inmates. It takes 1-3 days before new records are released. Records are stored in microfiche archive indefinitely.

Search Notes: Include in request: name and 7-digit TDCJ number or their full name, DOB or SSN, and county of conviction. No fee for information. Mail turnaround time: 7 to 10 days.

Access by: Phone, Mail, Online. An Offender Information Line at 800-535-0283 allows you to check a paroled or incarcerated offender's status. Offender's name and 7-digit TDCJ number or their full name, date of birth or Social Security Number, and county of conviction required. Online search note: no online searching is available direct from this agency, but you may send an email search request to classify@tdcj.state.tx.us. Also, a private company offers free web access at www.vinelink.com/index.jsp.

Texas State Court System

Court Structure: The legal court structure for Texas is explained extensively in the "Texas Judicial Annual Report." Generally, Texas District Courts have general civil jurisdiction and exclusive felony jurisdiction. As of 01/15/04, four additional District Courts were implemented. The County Court structure consists of two forms of courts - "Constitutional" and "at Law. " The Constitional upper claim limit is $100,000 while the At Law upper limit is $5,000. For civil matters up to $5000, we recommend searchers start at the Constitutional County Court as they, generally, offer a shorter waiting time for cases in urban areas. District Courts handle felonies. County Courts handle misdemeanors and general civil cases. Often, a record search is automatically combined for two courts, for example a District and County court or both county courts.

Find Felony Records: District Court

Misdemeanor Records: County Court, Justice of the peace Court, Municipal Court

Online Access: Appellate court case information is searchable for free on the Internet from the website of each appellate court, reached from the website in next paragraph. Find Court of Criminal Appeals opinions at www.cca.courts.state.tx.us. A number of local county courts offer online access to their records, but there is no statewide system of local level court records.

Court Administrator: For add'l questions about the state's court system, visit the website at www.courts.state.tx.us/oca, or contact: Office of Court Administration, PO Box 12066, Austin, TX 78711-2066, Phone: 512-463-1625.

Utah

Utah Statues and Related Employer Restrictions

General Rule – Dissemination of information from a criminal history record or warrant of arrest information from the Criminal Investigation and Technical Services Division is limited to a qualifying entity for employment background checks for their own employees and persons who have applied for employment with the qualifying entity.   UT ST §53-10-108(1)(g).

A qualifying entity is a business, organization, or governmental entity that employs people who deal with national security interest, care, custody, or control of children, fiduciary trust over money, or health care to children or vulnerable adults.   UT ST §53-10-102(19).

Before requesting information, a qualifying entity must obtain a signed waiver from the person whose information is requested.   UT ST §53-10-108(3)(a).

If a person has no prior criminal conviction record, criminal history information contained in the file may not include arrest or disposition data concerning an individual who has been acquitted, his charges dismissed, or when no complaint has been filed against him.   UT ST §53-10-108(5).

Employment – Employers are prohibited from inquiring about arrest records. Employers may ask whether the applicant has been convicted of a felony, however it is advised only if the inquiry is job related.   UAC R606-2(V).

The Division of Occupational and Professional Licensing may refuse to issue a license to an applicant if the applicant has engaged in unprofessional conduct.   UT ST §58-1-401(2)(a).

Unprofessional conduct includes engaging in conduct that results in conviction, a plea of nolo contendere, or a plea of guilty with respect to a crime of moral turpitude or any crime that bears a reasonable relationship to the applicant's ability to safely or competently practice the occupation or profession.   UT ST 58-1-501(2)(c).

Agency guidelines for pre-employment inquiries: Utah Labor Division Anti-Discrimination Rules, Rule R6062. "Pre-Employment Inquiry Guide" is available free at www.rules.utah.gov/publi cat/code/r606/r606-002.htm

Utah State Criminal Records Agency

Bureau of Criminal Identification
Box 148280
Salt Lake City, UT 84114-8280

Phone: 801-965-4445
Fax: 801-965-4749

Web: http://bci.utah.gov

Total Records: 392,800

Who Can Access: Records are not open to the public nor to employers without fingerprints and without the subject's notarized signature.

Search Requirements: Those agencies authorized by law do not need to submit fingerprints, but still must have subject's notarized signature. Include the following in your request: name, DOB, SSN, driver's license number, notarized signature of subject, fingerprints. Records are 100% fingerprint-supported.

What Is Released: All records are released, including those without dispositions. Records are available back to 1950's.

Indexing & Storage: It takes 3 to 7 days before new records are available for inquiry. 62% of all arrests in database have final dispositions recorded, approximately 75% for those arrests within last 5 years. Records are indexed on inhouse computer. Records are normally destroyed after (records maintained indefinitely unless expunged).

Access By: Mail, fax.

Mail Search: Turnaround time: 7-10 days. A SASE is required. Records are available by mail with submission of proper form.

Fax Search: Records are available by fax if fingerprints are not required.

Fee & Payment: The fee is $10.00 per name (authorization required); $15.00 for fingerprint searches. Statutorily-required searches may include an FBI fingerprint search, additional $24.00 fee. Fee payee: Utah Bureau of Criminal Identification Prepayment required. Personal checks accepted. Accepts Visa/MC cards.

Utah Sexual Offender Registry

Sex Offenders Registration Program
14717 S Minuteman Dr, Records Department
Draper, UT 84020

Phone: 801-545-5908
Fax: 801-545-5911
Web: www.corrections.utah.gov/

Utah Code § 77-27-21.5, requires the Utah Dept. of Corrections to operate, and maintain a registry of persons who have either been convicted of or entered a plea in abeyance to certain sex offenses. The offenses are listed in subsection (1)(e)(i) .

What is released: Records are available from 1987 to present.

Search Notes: Include in request: name, DOB or SSN, requester name address and phone number. Mail turnaround time: 10 days.

Access by: Phone, Mail, In Person, Online. Searches may be requested by phone, but results are mailed. Online search note: the Registry may be searched from the website. Records are searchable by name, ZIP Code, or name and ZIP Code. The information released includes photos, descriptions, addresses, vehicles, offenses, and targets. Also, requests nay be emailed to registry@utah.gov.

Utah State Incarceration Records Agency

Utah Department of Corrections

DIQ Records

P.O. Box 250

Draper, UT 84020

Phone: 801-576-7791

Fax: 801-572-7794

Web: www.cr.ex.state.ut.us

What is released: Location, conviction and sentencing information, and release dates are provided. Records are available on current and former inmates. It takes 1 to 20 days before new records are released. Not available: SSN, DOB, and specific prison housing location.

Search Notes: Include in request: full name and DOB. The SSN and inmate number are helpful. There is a $.25 fee per copy. Mail turnaround time: 7 to 10 days. Payee: Utah State Prison.

Access by: Phone, Fax, Mail. This service provides custody status and release dates, and offers notification if an inmate is release or moved.

Utah State Court System

Court Structure: 41 District Courts are arranged in eight judicial districts. Effective July 1, 1996, each Circuit Court (the lower court) was combined with District Court (the higher court) in each county. It is reported that branch courts in larger counties such as Salt Lake which were formerly Circuit Courts have been elevated to District Courts, with full jurisdiction over felony as well as misdemeanor cases. Many misdemeanors are handled at Justice Courts, which are limited jurisdiction.

Find Felony Records: District Court

Misdemeanor Records: District Court, Justice Court

Online Access: Case information from all Utah District Court locations is available through XChange. Fees include $25.00 registration and $30.00 per month plus $.10 per minute for usage over 120 minutes. Records go back 7 to 10 years.

Information about XChange and the subscription agreement can be found at www.utcourts.gov/records/xchange/ or call 801-238-7877.

One may search for supreme or appellate opinions at the website.

Searching Hints: Information on a particular case or the case history of individuals can be acquired from the Utah Administrative Office of the Courts. There is no charge for the first fifteen (15) minutes; $21 for each hour, charged in fifteen (15) minute increments at $5.25 per fifteen (15) minutes.There is also a fee of $ .25 per page for copies of case history information. You may also submit the information by mail to at the address lsited above or fax her at 801-578-3859.

UT Code Rule 4-202.08 sets fees for county record searches at the same rate mentioned above. But, at the county level, there is a wide variance of per hour charges statewide. The standard hourly search fee depends on which office person does the search; the basic clerk is $15.00. Yet, many courts still report their search fee as $10.00 per hour, many without the first 15 minutes free.

Salt Lake, Ogden, Roy, Provo, and Orem District Courts have automated information phone lines that provide court appearance look-up, outstanding fine balance look-up, and judgment/divorce decree lookup. Use these numbers:

Salt Lake District Court - 801-238-7830

Ogden & Roy District Court - 801-395-1111

Provo & Orem District Court - 801-429-1000

Court Administrator: For add'l questions about the state's court system, visit the website at www.utcourts.gov, or contact: Court Administrator, PO Box 140241, Salt Lake City, UT 84114-0241, Phone: 801-578-3800.

Vermont

Vermont Statues and Related Employer Restrictions

General Rule – Any person may inspect or copy any public record or document of a public agency. VSA §316(a). Records, which by law may only be disclosed to specifically designated persons, are exempt from public inspection. VSA §317(c)(2).

Employment – An employer may obtain from the Vermont Criminal Information Center a Vermont criminal record and an out-of-state criminal record for any applicant who has given written authorization on a release form. VSA §2056c(b). (Please note exceptions and definitions below.)

The employer may obtain the criminal record only after a conditional offer of employment has been made to the applicant. VSA §2056c(c).

Definition - Employer means any individual, organization, or governmental body which has one or more individuals performing services within the state and the employer is a qualified entity that provides care or services to vulnerable classes, or the employer is a postsecondary school with student residential facilities. VSA §2056c(a)(3).

Vermont State Criminal Records Agency

State Repository   **Phone:**   802-241-5237
Vermont Criminal Information Center   **Fax:**   802-241-5552
103 S. Main St.
Waterbury, VT 05671-2101   **Web:**   www.dps.state.vt.us

Access to Records is Restricted

Note: Records are *not* publicly available and can only be accessed if authorized by the subject for personal review, and if authorized by law in their state, if indeed statutes apply there. If records are open in that state, then a signed release *may* be sufficient. Those authorized include employers with employees working with children, elderly, or disabled. If not authorized by law, then you must search at the county level.

Total Records: 179,000
Search Requirements: 35% of records are fingerprint supported. 96% of records have dispositions. A sex offender registry is not available online to the public. This agency does not conduct FBI fingerpint checks.

Screening firms and vendors may qualify for access by agreeing to a user agreement, *and* also provide user agreements from end user clients. The agency administrator reports that the only vendor currently approved is ADP.

What Is Released: All records released to law enforcement. Only convictions released to others.

Searching Hints: There is no fee for those authorized by law.

Vermont Sexual Offender Registry

State Repository, Vermont Criminal Information Center   **Phone**: 802-244-8727

103 S. Main St.   **Fax**:   802-241-5552

Waterbury, VT 05671-2101   **Web**: www.dps.state.vt.us/cjs/s_registry.htm

In 1996, with the passage of Vermont Annotated Statutes, 13 VSA, Chapter 167, Subchapter 3, the Vermont Sex Offender Registry was established.

What is released: Records are not publicly available and can only be access by those authorized by law or the subject. Those authorized include employers with employees working with children, elderly, or disabled. Otherwise, requesters must search at local level.

Vermont State Incarceration Records Agency

Vermont Department of Corrections   **Phone:** 802-241-2276

Inmate Information Request   **Fax:**   802-241-2565

103 S. Main Street, Waterbury, VT 05671-1001   **Web:**   www.doc.state.vt.us

What is released: Location, conviction and sentencing information, and release dates are provided. Records are available on current and former inmates. It takes about 3 days before new records are released. Records normally destroyed after six years, depending on the DN. Computerized records go back to 1988.

Search Notes: Include in request: first and last name. DOB and SSN are helpful. Requestor may be asked to pay reproduction and research fees. Mail turnaround time: 5 to 7 days.

Access by: Phone, Fax, Mail, Online. Searching by telephone permitted if request also in writing. Online search note: the website provides an Incarcerated Offender Locator to ascertain where an inmate is located. Click on the link at bottom of main page or go directly to www.doc.state.vt.us:81/cgi-bin/public.cgi. This is not designed to provide complete inmate records nor is it a database of all inmates past and present in the system.

Vermont State Court System

Court Structure: All counties have a diversion program in which first offenders go through a process that includes a letter of apology, community service, etc. and, after 2 years, the record is expunged. These records are never released. The Vermont Judicial Bureau has jurisdiction over Traffic, Municipal Ordinance, and Fish and Game, Minors in Possession, and hazing.

Find Felony Records: District Court

Misdemeanor Records: District Court

Online Access: Court calendars for all Superior, District, and Family courts are shown at the website above, using the Places to Visit drop down box. Supreme Court opinions are available also from the website. In addition, Supreme Court opinions are maintained by the Vermont Department of Libraries at http://dol.state.vt.us. There is no statewide system of local court records.

Searching Hints: There are statewide search, certification and copy fees, as follows: Search fee - $10.00 per name; Certification Fee - $5.00 per document plus copy fee; Copy Fee - $.25 per page with a $1.00 minimum.

Court Administrator: For add'l questions about the state's court system, visit the website at www.vermontjudiciary.org, or contact: Court Administrator, Administrative Office of Courts, 109 State St, Montpelier, VT 05609-0701, Phone: 802-828-3278.

Virginia

Virginia Statues and Related Employer Restrictions

General Rule – Criminal history record information shall be disseminated only to individuals or organizations specifically authorized by statute. Criminal justice information disseminated to non-criminal justice agencies and individuals may not include information concerning the arrest of an individual if a year has passed from the date of arrest, no disposition of the charge has been recorded, and no active prosecution charges is pending. VA ST §19.2-389(2).

Expunged Record – It is unlawful for any person to disclose any information about an expunged record to another person without a court order. VA ST §19.2-392.3(A).

Employment – An employer shall not require an applicant to disclose information concerning any arrest or criminal charge against him that has been expunged. VA ST §19.2-392.4(A).

An applicant for a license from any licensing board may not be denied solely because of the applicant's refusal to disclose information concerning any arrest or criminal charge against him that has been expunged. VA ST §19.2392.4(B).

Virginia State Criminal Records Agency

Virginia State Police , CCRE
PO Box C-85076
Richmond, VA 23261-5076

Phone: 804-674-2084

Fax: 804-323-0861

Web: www.vsp.state.va.us

Total Records: 1,245,900

Who Can Access: Section 19.2-389 Code of Virginia outlines that non-criminal entities can receive conviction only records. Certain agencies may receive complete records. The website gives complete details.

Search Requirements: Include the following in your request: full name, date of birth, Social Security Number, sex, race. Turnaround time is 4-6 weeks. The general public and employers not covered by statute must have a signed release form from person of record, including notarized signatures for both subject and requester. These requesters must use form "SP-167" which is downloadable from website.

What Is Released: Certain agencies receive complete records; non-criminal justice entities receive conviction only records. Records are available from 1966. The following data is not released: dismissals, nolled pressed, whenever the disposition is missing

Indexing & Storage: It takes 1 to 3 days before new records are available for inquiry. 83% of all arrests in database have final dispositions recorded. Records are indexed on inhouse computer.

Access By: Mail, online.

Mail Search: Turnaround time: 8 to 10 business days. General users must use the state form SP-167 which can be downloaded from the web at www.vsp.state.va.us/forms.htm. Also, you can use form SP-24 or SP-230 depending on your exempt status. A self addressed stamped envelope is requested.

Online Search: Certain entities, including screening companies, can apply for online access via the NCJI System. The system is ONLY available to IN-STATE accounts and allows you to submit requests faster. Fees are same as manual submission-$15.00 per record. Username and password required. There is a minimum usage requirement of 25 requests per month. Turnaround time is 24-72 hours.

Fee & Payment: The fee is $15.00 per name; $20 if sex offender registry search included. When required, statutorily-required fingerprint check is $13; $37 if an FBI fingerpirnt check is also required. Fee payee: Virginia State Police. Prepayment required. Pay by certified check or money order. MasterCard and Visa are accepted.

Virginia Sexual Offender Registry

Virginia State Police   **Phone**: 804-323-2153

Sex Offender and Crimes Against Minors Registry   **Fax**: 804-323-0862

PO Box 85076

Richmond, VA 23261-5076   **Web**: http://sex-offender.vsp.state.va.us/cool-ICE/

What is released: There are two searches. One is distinguished as a search for Crimes Against Minors (use form SP-266); the other is a Sex Offender Registry Name Request (use form SP-230 or SP-167). Records are available from 1994 when the Registry was implemented. It takes 1 to 3 days before new records are released. Not available: DOB, SSN. Records normally destroyed after death of offender

Search Notes: Include in request: name, race, sex, DOB; also helpful-SSN, residence address. $15.00 for mail searches, either type of search. No fee for the Internet search. Mail turnaround time: 1 to 2 weeks. No personal checks accepted. Visa/MC accepted.

Access by: Mail, Online. Mail search note: It is suggested to use one of the two forms described above. Online search note: search by name, city, county or ZIP Code from the website.

Virginia State Incarceration Records Agency

Virginia Department of Corrections   **Phone:** 804-323-2153

Central Criminal Records Section   **Fax:**   804-323-0462

PO Box 26963   **Web:**   www.vadoc.state.va.us

Richmond, VA 23225

What is released: Location, conviction and sentencing information, and release dates are provided. Records are available on current and former inmates (only current if request is online). It takes up to 10 days before new records are released. Computer records go back to 1986.

Search Notes: Include in request: full name; DOB and SSN helpful. There is no fee. Mail turnaround time: 1 to 2 days.

Access by: Phone, Mail, Online, Email. For phone search, dial 804-674-3131, press 0 for the operator. Provides inmate location, address, and approximate release date. Online search note: at www.vipnet.org/cgi-bin/vadoc/doc.cgi is an Incarcerated Offender Locator to ascertain where an inmate is located. This is not designed to provide complete inmate records nor is it a database of all inmates past and present in the system. A private company at www.vinelink.com/index.jsp offers free Internet access at DOC records. There is a DOC wanted/fugitives list at www.vadoc.state.va.us/offend ers/wanted/fugitives.htm. Also, requesters can email requests to clasrec@vadoc.state.va.us.

Virginia State Court System

Court Structure: 123 Circuit Courts in 31 districts are the courts of general jurisdiction. There are 123 District Courts of limited jurisdiction. Please note that a district can comprise a county or a city. It is necessary to check both record locations as there is no concurrent database nor index.

Find Felony Records: Circuit Court

Misdemeanor Records: District Court

Online Access: 130 General District Courts (many are combined courts) may be searched free at http://208.210.219.132/courtinfo/vadistrict/select.jsp?court=. Here you can search both active and inactive cases.

Also, Virginia has the growing "Circuit Court Case Information Pilot Project" with free access to Circuit Court records. You may search records from over 85 courts at http://208.210.219.132/courtinfo/vacircuit/select.jsp?court=.

Another option is the statewide public access computer system: the Law Office Public Access System (LOPAS). The system allows remote access to the court case indexes and abstracts from most of the state's courts. Searching is by specific court; there is no combined index. There are no sign-up or other fees to use LOPAS. Access is granted on a request-by-request basis. Anyone wishing to establish an account or receive information on LOPAS must contact the Supreme Court of Virginia, 100 N 9th St, Richmond VA 23219 or by phone at 804-786-6455 or fax at 804-786-4542.

The www.courts.state.va.us site offers access to Supreme Court and Appellate opinions.

Searching Hints: In many jurisdictions, the certification fee is $2.00 per document plus copy fee. The copy fee is $.50 per page.

Court Administrator: For add'l questions about the state's court system, visit the website at www.courts.state.va.us, or contact: Executive Secretary, Administrative Office of Courts, 100 N 9th St, 3rd Floor, Richmond, VA 23219, Phone: 804-786-6455.

Washington

Washington Statues & Related Employer Restrictions

General Rule – The Washington state patrol must furnish a conviction record upon the request of any employer if the employer's purpose for the information is:

- to secure a bond required for employment, or

- conduct a preemployment or postemployment evaluation of an employee or prospective employee who may in the course of their employment have access to information affecting national security, trade secrets, confidential or proprietary business information, money, or items of value, or

- used to investigate employee misconduct that might constitute a criminal offense.

-Wash. Rev. Code § 43.43.815.[1]

If an employer obtains a conviction record, they must notify the employee within 30 days of receiving it, and must allow the employee time to examine it.

If an employer asks an employee or prospective employee about arrests, they must ask whether the arrest occurred within the last ten years and whether the charges are still pending, have been dismissed, or led to a conviction of a crime that would adversely affect job performance. Wash. Admin. Code 162-12-140.

Employers may ask employees or prospective employees about convictions or imprisonment if they are required by business necessity. A business necessity exists if the crimes reasonably relate to the duties of the job and the conviction occurred within the last ten years.

If a conviction record is cleared or vacated, an employee or prospective employee may answer questions as though the conviction never occurred. Wash. Rev. Code §§ 9.94A.640, 9.96.060.

Definitions

"'Conviction record' means criminal history record information relating to an incident which has led to a conviction or other disposition adverse to the subject." Wash. Rev. Code § 10.97.030(3).

---

[1] Note that Wash. Rev. Code § 10.97.050 states that "[c]onviction records may be disseminated without restriction." However, this statute is found in the Title dealing with Criminal Procedure and says nothing about the use of this information for employment purposes.

Washington State Criminal Records Agency

Washington State Patrol
Identification Section
PO Box 42633
Olympia, WA 98504-2633

Phone: 360-705-5100
Fax: 360-570-5275

Web: www.wsp.wa.gov

Total Records: 1,044,880

Who Can Access: Records are available to the general public.

Search Requirements: Two types of records available: General Conviction - all convictions and arrests less than one year pending disposition; and Child & Adult Abuse record - only conviction of crimes against persons, certain drug crimes, and financial esploitation crimes. Include the following in your request: date of birth, Social Security Number, sex, race, name and address of subject. Fingerprints are optional. Records are 100% fingerprint-supported. Mail requests are directed to the WSP or e-mail to crimhis@wsp.gov.

What Is Released: Records without dispositions are not released, unless the arrest is less than 1 year old. Records are available from 1974. Criminal history information is retained at the Identification and Criminal History Section until the offender is age seventy, or ten years from the last date of arrest, whichever is longer. The following data is not released: non-conviction and arrest information over one year old without disposition.

Indexing & Storage: It takes 30 to 45 days if manual; 2 hours if electronic. before new records are available for inquiry. 79% of all arrests in database have final dispositions recorded, 70% for those arrests within last 5 years. Records are indexed on inhouse computer. Records are normally destroyed after a court order.

Access By: Mail, in person, online.

Mail Search: Turnaround time: 2 to 3 weeks. No self addressed stamped envelope is required.

In Person Search: Requests are returned by mail.

Online Search: WSP offers access through a system called WATCH, which can be accessed from their website. The fee per search is $10.00. The exact DOB and exact spelling of the name, and SSN are required. Credit cards are accepted online. To set up a WATCH account, you may call 360-705-5100 or email watch.help@wsp.wa.gov.

Fee & Payment: The fee for a name check is $10.00 per individual. For a fingerprint check, the fee is $25.00 per individual. Will not conduct FBI fingerprint checks. Fee payee: Washington State Patrol. Money orders or cashier's checks preferred.

Washington Sexual Offender Registry

Washington State Patrol   **Phone**: 360-705-5100 x3

SOR, PO Box 42633   **Fax**:   360-570-5275

Olympia, WA 98504-2633   **Web**:   www.wsp.wa.gov

Access by: Online. No searching by mail. Online search note: in cooperation with the Washington Assoc of Sheriffs and Police Chiefs, online access to Level II and Level III sexual offenders is available at www.waspc.org. There is also a link to county sex offender sites at www.waspc.org/wa_sex/index.shtml.

Washington State Incarceration Records Agency

Washington Department of Corrections   **Phone: Basic info:** 360-753-3317

Office of Correctional Operations   **Public Disclosure:** 360-586-3492

410 W. 5th, MS-41118   **Web:**   www.doc.wa.gov

Olympia, WA 98504-1118

What is released: Location, CCO, parole review data, and counselor are released. Records are available on current and former inmates. It takes 1 to 5 days before new records are released. Records ecords not destroyed; they are eventually archived with Secretary of State office.

Search Notes: Include in request: full name, DOB; SSN is helpful. A copy fee is $.20 per page; a postage fee applies to all mailed documents. Mail turnaround time: 1 to 2 weeks.

Access by: Phone, Mail, Email. Email requests can be directed to correspondence@doc1.wa.gov. Other Access: data is available by subscription for bulk users; for information, contact the Contracts Office at 360-664-0867.

Washington State Court System

Court Structure: 39 Superior Courts are organized in 29 Judicial Districts and are the courts of general jurisdiction. The 65 District Courts and 131 Municipal Courts are limited jurisdiction courts. District Courts retain criminal records forever.

Find Felony Records: Superior Court

Misdemeanor Records: District Court, Municipal Court

Online Access: Appellate, Superior, and District Court records are available online. The Superior Court Management Information System (SCOMIS), the Appellate Records System (ACORDS) and the District/Municipal Court Information System (DISCIS) are on the Judicial Information System's JIS-Link. Case records available through JIS-Link from 1977 include criminal, civil, domestic, probate, and judgments. JIS-Link is generally available 24-hours daily. Minimum browser requirement is Internet Explorer 5.5 or Netscape 6.0. There is a one-time installation fee of $100.00 per site, then $.065 charge per transaction. For information or a registration packet, contact: JISLink Coordinator, Administrative Office of the Courts, 1206 S Quince St., PO Box 41170, Olympia WA 98504-1170, 360-357-3365 or visit www.courts.wa.gov/jislink.

Supreme Court and Appellate opinions can be found at www.courts.wa.gov/appellate_trial_courts.

Searching Hints: An SASE is required in most courts that respond to written search requests.

Court Administrator: For add'l questions about the state's court system, visit the website at www.courts.wa.gov, or contact: Administrative Office of Courts, Temple of Justice, PO Box 41174, Olympia, WA 98504-1174, Phone: 360-357-2121.

West Virginia

West Virginia Statues & Related Employer Restrictions

General Rule – Every person has a right to inspect or copy any public record of a public body in this state. WV ST §19B-1-3(1).

Records of law enforcement agencies that deal with the detection and investigation of crime and the internal records and notations of such law enforcement agencies, which are maintained for internal use for matters relating to law enforcement, are exempt from disclosure.   WV ST §29B-1-4(a)(4).

Records of a juvenile proceeding are not public records and shall not be disclosed.   WV ST §495-17(a).

Expunged Records – Upon expungment, the proceedings in the matter shall be deemed to never have occurred. The court and other agencies shall reply to any inquiry that no record exists on the matter. The person whose record was expunged shall not have to disclose the fact of the record or any matter relating to it on an application for employment, credit, or other application.   WV ST §61-11-25(e).

Employment – The following may deny an application for a license, suspend a license, or revoke a license upon proof that the applicant has been convicted of a felony:

> State Board of Accountancy. WV ADC §1-3-4.
> Board of Chiropractic Examiners. WV ADC §4-5-4.
> Board of Hearing Aid Dealers. WV ADC §8-3-4.
> Board of Optometry. WV ADC §14-4-4.
> Board of Physical Therapy. WV ADC §16-3-4.
> Board of Examiners of Psychologists. WV ADC §17-4-4.
> Board of Examiners for Radiologic Technologists. WV ADC §18-4-4.
> Nursing Home Administrator Board. WV ADC §21-2-4.
> Board of Examiners of Land Surveyors. WV ADC §23-1-8.
> Board of Osteopathy. WV ADC §24-6-4.
> Board of Veterinary Medicine. WV ADC§26-2-4.
> Board of Speech-Language Pathology and Audiology. WV ADC §29-4-4.
> Board of Respiratory Care. WV ADC §30-4-3.
> Massage Therapy Licensure Board. WV ADC §194-3-4.
> Board of Registration for Foresters. WV ADC §200-3-4.

Agency guidelines for pre-employment inquiries: Bureau of Employment Programs "Pre-Employment Inquiry Guide" is available at www.state.wv.us/bep/Bepeeo/empinqu.htm

West Virginia State Criminal Records Agency

State Police   **Phone:** 304-746-2277
Criminal Records Section   **Fax:**   304-746-2402
725 Jefferson Rd
South Charleston, WV 25309   **Web:**   www.wvstatepolice.com

Total Records: 501,043

Who Can Access: Records are available to the general public but only with consent of subject.
Note: The state will also sell an "incident report" of a specific criminal action for $20.00, call 304-746-2178. FBI checks only available if there is statutory authorization

Search Requirements: All searches require fingerprints, also FBI fingerprint checks. Include the following in your request: signed release of subject, SSN, DOB, race, sex, and thumbprint. You must use a WV Fingerprint Card and authorization. All records are returned by mail. Search can be initiated in person, results mailed. 100% of the records are fingerprint-supported.

What Is Released: All records are released, including those without dispositions. Records are available from 1938 on computer.

Indexing & Storage: It takes 3 days before new records are available for inquiry. 70% of all arrests in database have final dispositions recorded. Records are indexed on in house computer (100% of names). Approximately 30% of arrest data is computerized. Records normally destroyed after the person reaches age 80.

Access By: Mail.

Mail Search: Turnaround time: 5 to 10 days.

Fee & Payment: The search fee is $20.00 plus $24.00 for an FBI fingerprint check. Certain statutorily-required searches are $10.00, plus the addition FBI fingercheck fee. Fee payee: West Virginia State Police. Prepayment required. Personal checks accepted. No credit cards accepted.

West Virginia Sexual Offender Registry

State Police Headquarters   **Phone**: 304-746-2133

Sexual Offender Registry, 725 Jefferson Rd   **Fax**:   304-746-2403

South Charleston, WV 25309   **Web**:   www.wvstatepolice.com/sexoff/

West Virginia currently has over 1800 registered sex offenders.

What is released: Records are available from 1994.

Access by: Online. This agency prefers no mail requests. Online search note: online searching is available from website, search by county or name.

West Virginia State Incarceration Records Agency

West Virginia Division of Corrections   **Phone:** 304-558-2037

Records Room   **Fax:**   304-558-5934

112 California Ave., 3rd floor   **Web:**   www.wvf.state.wv.us/wvdoc/

Charleston, WV 25305

What is released:	Location, conviction and sentencing information, and release dates are provided. Records are available on current and former inmates. It takes up to 4 days before new records are released.
Search Notes:	Include in request: full name, date of birth and Social Security Number helpful. Mail turnaround time: 2 to 4 weeks.
Access by:	Phone, Fax, Mail. Name searching permitted by phone. There is no online searching available from this agency. However, a private company offers free web access at www.vinelink.com/index.jsp.

West Virginia State Court System

Court Structure:	The 55 Circuit Courts are courts of general jurisdiction, the 55 Magistrate Courts are courts of limited jurisdiction. There are over 120 local Municipal Courts in the state.
Find Felony Records:	Circuit Court
Misdemeanor Records:	Magistrate Court
Online Access:	The state is working towards a statewide system that will allow access to public records, but one is not yet available. Search opinions from the Supreme Court at www.state.wv.us/wvsca/opinions.htm. This is a commercial system, available only to law firms and government agencies, that gives access to case information from six Circuit Courts and all of the Magistrate Courts. Visit www.swcg-inc.com/swcg/index.html for details.
Searching Hints:	There is a statewide requirement that search turnaround times not exceed five business days. However, most courts do far better than that limit. Release of public information is governed by WV Code Sec.29B-1-1 et seq.
Court Administrator:	For add'l questions about the state's court system, visit the website at www.state.wv.us/wvsca, or contact: Administrative Office, State Supreme Court of Appeals, 1900 Kanawha Blvd, Bldg 1, Rm E 100, Charleston, WV 25305-0830, Phone: 304-558-0145.

Wisconsin

Wisconsin Statues & Related Employer Restrictions

General Rule - It is a violation of Wisconsin's civil rights laws to discriminate against a properly qualified employee or prospective employee by reason of their arrest or conviction record.   Wis. Stat. §§ 111.31-111.335.

Employers may not ask about an arrest record except an employer may ask about a pending charge. Wis. Stat. § 111.335.

If a pending charge substantially relates to the circumstances of the particular job, employers may discriminate against an employee or prospective employee on that basis. An employer may also discriminate against an employee or prospective employee because of a conviction record if the charges substantially relate to the circumstances of the particular job or licensed activity, or if the individual is unable to be bonded because of the conviction.

Special Situations - It is not employment discrimination to refuse to employ or revoke the license or permit of an individual that has been convicted of a felony if the employ or license is for an installer of burglar alarms, private security guard, or a private detective.   Wis. Stat. § 111.335.

In addition, it is not employment discrimination to revoke, suspend, or refuse to renew a license or permit involving alcoholic beverages if the individual has been involved in a crime involving the manufacturing, distribution, or delivery of controlled substances.

Definitions

Arrest record - includes, but is not limited to, information indicating that an individual has been questioned, apprehended, taken into custody or detention, held for investigation, arrested, charged with, indicted or tried for any felony, misdemeanor or other offense pursuant to any law enforcement or military authority."   Wis. Stat. § 111.32.

Conviction record - includes, but is not limited to, information indicating that an individual has been convicted of any felony, misdemeanor or other offense, has been adjudicated delinquent, has been less than honorably discharged, or has been placed on probation, fined, imprisoned, placed on extended supervision or paroled pursuant to any law enforcement or military authority."

Agency guidelines for pre-employment inquiries: Wisconsin Department of Workforce Development, Civil Rights Division Publications, "Fair Hiring & Avoiding Loaded Interview Questions" is available at www.dwd.state.wi.us/dwd/publications/212a/ERD-4825-PWEB.pdf

Wisconsin State Criminal Records Agency

Wisconsin Department of Justice
Crime Information Bureau, Record Check Unit
PO Box 2688
Madison, WI 53701-2688

Phone: 608-266-5764
Fax: 608-267-4558

Web: www.doj.state.wi.us

Total Records: 909,000

Who Can Access: Criminal record information is open to the public per statute 3-21-91.

Search Requirements: Include the following in your request: sex, race, full name, date of birth. Fingerprints are optional. All requests must be in writing. Certain statutorily-required searches require fingerprints.

What Is Released: All records are released, including those without dispositions. Records are available from July 1971 (when the agencies were required to save records) and are computerized. The following data is not released: juvenile records.

Indexing & Storage: It takes 4 days before new records are available for inquiry. 76% of all arrests in database have final dispositions recorded, 67% for those arrests within last 5 years. Records are indexed on inhouse computer. Records are maintained indefinitely and not destroyed.

Access By: Mail, fax, in person, online.

Mail Search: Turnaround time: 7 to 10 days. A self addressed stamped envelope is requested.

Fax Search: Incoming fax permitted only for customers with accounts. There must be a supply of return envelopes on hand.

In Person Search: Records are returned by mail.

Online Search: The agency offers Internet access at http://wi-recordcheck.org. An account is required. Records must be "picked up" within 10 days unless requester is a daycare of caregiver.

Fee & Payment: The fee is $18.00 per individual for a name search, and only $15.00 if a fingerprint search. Non-profits made submit name searches for $7.00 per record. If a statutorily-required search also requires an FBI fingerprint check, add $24.00. Fee payee: Wisconsin Department of Justice. Prepayment required. Personal checks accepted. Credit cards accepted at website only.

Wisconsin Sexual Offender Registry

Department of Corrections   **Phone**: 608-240-5830

Sex Offender Registry Program, PO Box 7925   **Fax**:   608-240-3355

Madison, WI 53707-7925   **Web**:   http://offender.doc.state.wi.us/public/

Information stored in the database is accessible on a limited basis to victims, neighborhood watch programs, and the general public. One may also search at the local law enforcement level.

What is released: Records are available from 1998 to present. Not available: victim profile and data, juvenile adjudication, exact residence address. Records normally destroyed after the registration discharge date.

Search Notes: Mail turnaround time: 1-2 weeks.

Access by: Mail, Online. Online search note: search for offenders by name or location at the website. Second website address is http://widocoffenders.org.

Wisconsin State Incarceration Records Agency

Wisconsin Department of Corrections   **Phone:** 608-240-5000

Bureau of Technology Management   **Fax:**   608-240-3385

P.O. Box 8980   **Web:**   www.wi-doc.com

Madison, WI 53708-8980

What is released: Location, conviction and sentencing information, and release dates are provided. Records are available on current and former inmates. It takes 10 days before new records are released. Records normally destroyed after 5 years beyond termination. Computerized records go back to 1961.

Search Notes: Include in request: first and last name and the DOB. Records indexed on inhouse computer. Copies are $.15 per page, there is no search fee. Mail turnaround time: 5 to 10 working days.

Access by: Phone, Fax, Mail. For phone search, call number above. No online searching is available for the public from this agency, however a private company provides free web access at www.vinelink.com/index.jsp.

Wisconsin State Court System

Court Structure: The Circuit Court is the court of general jurisdiction, with 74 courts in 69 circuits. There are over 225 Municipal Courts in the state.

Find Felony Records: Circuit Court

Misdemeanor Records: Circuit Court

Online Access: Wisconsin Circuit Court Access (WCCA) allows users to view circuit court case information at http://wcca.wicourts.gov which is the Wisconsin court system website. Data is available from all counties. Portage County offers probate records only online. Searches can be conducted statewide or county by county. WCCA provides detailed information about circuit cases and for civil cases, the program displays judgment and judgment party information. WCCA also offers the ability to generate reports. In addition, public access terminals are available at each court. Due to statutory requirements, WCCA users will not be able to view restricted cases. Appellate and Supreme Courts opinions are available from http://old.wicourts.gov/wscca/.

Searching Hints: The statutory fee schedule for the Circuit Courts is as follows: Search Fee - $5.00 per name; Copy Fee - $1.25 per page; Certification Fee - $5.00. In about half the Circuit Courts, no search fee is charged if the case number is provided. There is normally no search fee charged for in-person searches.

Court Administrator: For add'l questions about the state's court system, visit the website at http://wicourts.gov, or contact: Director of State Courts, Supreme Court, PO Box 1688, Madison, WI 53701-1688, Phone: 608-266-6828.

Wyoming

Wyoming Statues and Related Employer Restrictions

General Rule - Criminal history record information may be disseminated if the person seeking such information submits proof that the individual whose record is being checked consents to the release of the information to that person, the application is made through a criminal justice agency in Wyoming that is authorized to access criminal history record information, and a fee is paid. Wyo. Stat. §7-19-106(k).

The information may also be accessed in conjunction with a background check into employees of substitute care providers, state institutions, department of family services or department of health who have access to minors, those suffering from mental or developmental disabilities, or the elderly. Wyo. Stat. § 7-19-201.

Definitions

Criminal history record information - means information, records and data compiled by criminal justice agencies on individuals for the purpose of identifying criminal offenders consisting of identifiable descriptions of the offenders and notations or a summary of arrests, detentions, indictments, information, pre-trial proceedings, nature and disposition of criminal charges, sentencing, rehabilitation, incarceration, correctional supervision and release. Criminal history record information is limited to information recorded as the result of the initiation of criminal proceedings. It does not include intelligence data, analytical prosecutorial files, investigative reports and files, or statistical records and reports in which individual identities are not ascertainable, or any document signed by the governor granting a pardon, commutation of sentence, reprieve, remission of fine or forfeiture, or a restoration of civil rights by the governor or restoration of voting rights by the state board of parole. Wyo. Stat. § 7-19-103(a)(ii).

Criminal justice agency - means any agency or institution of state or local government other than the office of the public defender which performs as part of its principal function, activities relating to:

- The apprehension, investigation, prosecution, adjudication, incarceration, supervision, or rehabilitation of criminal offenders;
- The collection, maintenance, storage, dissemination, or use of criminal history record information. Wyo. Stat. §§ 7-19-103(a)(iii).

Wyoming State Criminal Records Agency

Division of Criminal Investigation   **Phone:**   307-777-7523
Criminal Record Unit   **Fax:**   307-777-7252
316 W 22nd St   **Web:**
Cheyenne, WY 82002   http://attorneygeneral.state.wy.us/dci/index.html

Note: A record inquiry includes all reported felonies, high misdemeanors and other specified misdemeanors, but not municipal ordinance violations. If authorized by state law, the check may include federal records held by FBI.

Total Records:	102,678
Who Can Access:	Records are available to the general public but only with signed, notarized consent of the subject.
Search Requirements:	First, obtain a Request for Criminal Record Packet ($15.00) from address above or phone. Include the following in your request: notarized waiver from subject, name, set of fingerprints, date of birth, Social Security Number, number of years to search. Use the Wyoming standard 8" x 8" orange fingerprint card. Must also fill out waiver that is on the back of this office's fingerprint card.
What Is Released:	Records include all felony and major misdemeanor arrests and convictions. Records are available from 1941 on. The following data is not released: juvenile records.
Indexing & Storage:	It takes up to 10 days before new records are available for inquiry. 79% of all arrests in database have final dispositions recorded, 65% for those arrests within last 5 years. Records are indexed on inhouse computer.
Access By:	Mail, in person.
Mail Search:	Turnaround time: 2 to 4 weeks. A self addressed stamped envelope is requested.
In Person Search:	Proper forms are required to be filled out.
Fee & Payment:	The search fee is $15.00 plus an additional $5.00 if this office must perform the fingerprinting. The fee is $10.00 if the applicant is providing volunteer services, plus the fingerprinting fee if applicable. The FBI fingerprint check is an add'l $24.00. Fee payee: Office of the Attorney General. Prepayment required. Money order, cash or certified checks only. No credit cards accepted.

Wyoming Sexual Offender Registry

Division of Criminal Investigation   **Phone**: 307-777-7809

ATTN: WSOR   **Fax**:   307-777-7252

316 W 22nd St

Cheyenne, WY 82002-0001   **Web**: http://attorneygeneral.state.wy.us/dci/index.html

Wyoming law defines a sex offender subject to registration as a person convicted of a sex offense in which the victim was a minor and the offender was at least eighteen (18) years of age or an aggravated sex offense.

What is released: The County Sheriff's Office or other law enforcement agency maintains a file and forwards the information to the Wyoming Division of Criminal Investigation (DCI).

Access by: Online. No searching by mail. Online search note: the Internet is the search method offered by this agency to the public. Search is by county. The website contains offenders found to have a high risk of re-offense. Data includes name, address, date and place of birth, date and place of conviction, crime for which convicted, photograph and physical description.

Wyoming State Incarceration Records Agency

Wyoming Department of Corrections   **Phone:** 307-777-7405

700 W. 21st St.   **Fax:**   307-777-7479

Cheyenne, WY 82002   **Web:**   http://doc.state.wy.us/corrections.asp

What is released: Location, conviction and sentencing information, and release dates are provided. Records are available on current and former inmates. It takes a minimum of 30 days before new records are released. Not available: probation and parole data, medical, and metal health problems.

Search Notes: Include in request: full name. DOB and SSN are helpful. The fee is $.50 per page. Mail turnaround time: 1 to 2 weeks. Prepayment required. Personal checks accepted.

Access by: Phone, Fax, Mail, Email. Name searching available by phone. No searching online direct from this agency; a private company provides access to DOC records at www.vinelink.com/index.jsp. Also, limited search requests honor via email at mbrazz@wdoc.state.wy.us.

Wyoming State Court System

Court Structure: Prior to 2003, for their "lower" jurisdiction court some counties have Circuit Courts and others have Justice Courts. Thus each county has a District Court ("higher" jurisdiction) and either a Circuit or Justice Court.

Effective January 1, 2003 all Justice Courts become Circuit Courts and follow Circuit Court rules.

Three counties have two Circuit Courts each: Fremont, Park, and Sweetwater. Cases may be filed in either of the two court offices in those counties, and records requests are referred between the two courts.

Find Felony Records: District Court

Misdemeanor Records: Circuit Court, Justice of the Peace, Municipal Court

Online Access: Wyoming's statewide case management system is for internal use only. Planning is underway for a new case management system that will ultimately allow public access.

Court Administrator: For add'l questions about the state's court system, visit the website at www.courts.state.wy.us, or contact: Court Administrator, Supreme Court Bldg, 2301 Capitol Ave, Cheyenne, WY 82002, Phone: 307-777-7480.

Chapter 17

U.S. District Courts

Federal criminal records are a result of an individual committing a federal crime. Federal criminal records in the United States result from Federal District Courts and Federal Appellate Courts. There are ninety-four Federal Judicial Districts. A state may have one or more districts, usually designated by geographic direction, i.e. Eastern, Southern, etc. Additionally, a district may be subdivided into divisions, which are designated by the location city name. Please refer to Chapter 7 - *Criminal Records at the Federal Level* for details on how U.S. District Courts organize and maintain records.

How to Access Records by Mail or Phone

The fees for record searching are standard throughout all Judicial Districts. The standard fee for a mailed request is $20.00 per item (one party name or case number). The standard certification fee is $7.00. A few courts will release limited information or docket information by phone. Copies are $.50 a page if done by the court, $.15 if done in-person by the searcher. As a rule, little information is available by telephone. Data appearing on the docket sheet is released by many courts, but you may need to supply the case number.

Online Access to Records

In ninety-three of the ninety-four U.S. Federal Judicial Districts locations, criminal docket sheets are available online. The only Judicial District not offering the records online is South Dakota. Most online access is through PACER via the Internet. However, a small number of District Courts offer records searching online for free. These are:

- Arkansas Western District at www.arwd.uscourts.gov/mailform.html
- Idaho District at www.id.uscourts.gov/wconnect/wc.dll?usdc_racer~main
- Indiana Southern District at www.insd.uscourts.gov/casesearch.htm
- Pennsylvania Eastern District at www.paed.uscourts.gov

PACER Access

As mentioned on page 48, PACER is a service of United States Judiciary. All the basic case information is entered onto docket sheets and into computerized systems like **PACER**. PACER, the acronym for **P**ublic **A**ccess to **E**lectronic **C**ourt **R**ecords, provides docket information online for open cases at most U.S. District courts and all U.S. Bankruptcy courts. Cases for the U.S. Court of Federal Claims are also available.

The PACER Service Center is operated by the Administrative Office of the United States Courts. PACER information and registration is available at the PACER Service Center in San Antonio Texas. This centralized registration, billing, and technical support center can be reached at P.O. Box 780549, San Antonio, TX 78278-0549, 800-676-6856, and on the Internet at http://pacer.psc.uscourts.gov/.

The user fee for PACER on the Internet is $.07 per page. Additionally, PACER is accessible by remote dial-up service. Users of this telephone system are billed $.60 per minute and dial PACER directly using communication software and a modem. The toll-free number for PACER dial-up information is 800-676-6856.

Within PACER, each court maintains its own databases with case information. Because PACER database systems are maintained within each court, each jurisdiction will have a different URL or modem number. Accessing and querying information from each service is comparable; however, the format and content of information provided may differ slightly. U.S. District Courts that offer access to records through PACER, PACER dial-up modem, CM/ECF, or on the Web are noted in the profiles to follow.

U.S. Party/Case Index

To locate a case number, which is essential for searching in the U.S. Court System, the system provides the U.S. Party/Case Index. Access the U.S. Party/Case Index on the internet at http://pacer.uspci.uscourts.gov. To access the U.S. Party/Case Index by dial-up modem, the toll-free dial-up number is 800-974-8896. Or, talk to the PACER Service Center at 800-676-6856. Requests for archived cases must be made at the court where the case was heard.

CM/ECF—Case Management/Electronic Case Files

As described in Chapter 7, Case Management/Electronic Case Files (CM/ECF) is the growing court-sponsored system that enables attorneys and litigants to electronically submit pleadings and docket entries to the court via the Internet. This system is searchable, but *only* includes case information that is filed electronically into the system, thus it does not offer a complete search of the participating court's case files. The key here is that *Document Images* are available, as well as docket sheets. However, this is going away for the general public, as outlined on page 61. For further information on CM/ECF, visit http://pacer.psc.uscourts.gov/cmecf.

Federal Records Centers and the National Archives

After a federal case is closed, the documents are held by Federal Courts themselves for a number of years, then stored at a designated Federal Records Center (FRC). After 20 to 30 years, the records are then transferred from the FRC to the regional archives offices of the National Archives and Records Administration (NARA). The length of time between a case being closed and its being moved to an FRC varies widely by district. Each court has its own transfer cycle and determines access procedures to its case records even after they have been sent to the FRC.

When case records are sent to an FRC, the boxes of records are assigned accession, location and box numbers. These numbers, which are called case locator information, **must be obtained from the originating court in order to retrieve documents from the FRC.** Some courts provide such information over the telephone; others require a written request.

Locations of the U.S. District Courts

Each of the 296 District and Divisional Courts listed below is show with their respective address, telephone, and the counties that comprise the particular division or district. The web site and type of PACER service is indicated at the beginning of each District. Note that all the records for all Divisional Courts within a specific Judicial District are co-mingled.

Alabama

Middle District of Alabama

www.almd.uscourts.gov **Access by:** PACER dial-up, PACER online, CM/ECF.
-Dothan Div. c/o Montgomery Division, PO Box 711, Montgomery, AL 36101 (physical address: 15 Lee St, Montgomery, AL 36104), 334-223-7308. **Counties:** Coffee, Dale, Geneva, Henry, Houston
-Montgomery Div. Records Search, PO Box 711, Montgomery, AL 36101-0711 (physical address: 15 Lee St, Montgomery, AL 36104), 334-223-7308. **Counties:** Autauga, Barbour, Bullock, Butler, Chilton, Coosa, Covington, Crenshaw, Elmore, Lowndes, Montgomery, Pike
-Opelika Div. c/o Montgomery Division, PO Box 711, Montgomery, AL 36101 (physical address: 15 Lee St, Montgomery, AL 36104), 334-223-7308. **Counties:** Chambers, Lee, Macon, Randolph, Russell, Tallapoosa

Northern District of Alabama

www.alnd.uscourts.gov **Access by:** phone, PACER dial-up, PACER online.
-Birmingham Div. Room 104, U.S. Courthouse, 1729 5th Ave N, Birmingham, AL 35203 (physical address: Use mail address for courier delivery), 205-278-1700. **Counties:** Bibb, Blount, Calhoun, Clay, Cleburne, Greene, Jefferson, Pickens, Shelby, Sumter, Talladega, Tuscaloosa
-Florence Div. PO Box 776, Florence, AL 35630 (physical address: 210 Court St, Florence, AL 35631), 205-760-5815. **Counties:** Colbert, Franklin, Lauderdale
-Gadsden Div. c/o Birmingham Division, Room 140, U.S. Courthouse, 1729 5th Ave N, Birmingham, AL 35203 (physical address: Use mail address for courier delivery), 205-278-1700. **Counties:** Cherokee, De Kalb, Etowah, Marshall, St. Clair
-Huntsville Div. Clerk's Office, U.S. Post Office & Courthouse #302, 101 Holmes Ave NE, Huntsville, AL

35801 (physical address: Use mail address for courier delivery), 205-534-6495. **Counties:** Cullman, Jackson, Lawrence, Limestone, Madison, Morgan

-Jasper Div. c/o Birmingham Division, Room 140, U.S. Courthouse, 1729 5th Ave N, Birmingham, AL 35203 (physical address: Use mail address for courier delivery), 205-278-1700. **Counties:** Fayette, Lamar, Marion, Walker, Winston

Southern District of Alabama

www.als.uscourts.gov **Access by:** phone, PACER dial-up, PACER online, CM/ECF, or on the web.

-Mobile Div. Clerk, 113 St Joseph St, Mobile, AL 36602 (physical address: Use mail address for courier delivery), 251-690-2371. **Counties:** Baldwin, Choctaw, Clarke, Conecuh, Escambia, Mobile, Monroe, Washington

-Selma Div. c/o Mobile Division, 113 St Joseph St, Mobile, AL 36602 (physical address: Use mail address for courier delivery), 251-690-2371. **Counties:** Dallas, Hale, Marengo, Perry, Wilcox

Alaska

District of Alaska

www.akd.uscourts.gov **Access by:** phone, PACER dial-up, or on the web.

-Anchorage Div. Room 229, 222 W 7th Ave, Anchorage, AK 99513-7564 (physical address: Use mail address for courier delivery), 907-677-6100, 866-243-3814. **Jurisdictions:** Aleutian Islands-East, Aleutian Islands-West, Anchorage Borough, Bristol Bay Borough, Dillingham, Kenai Peninsula Borough, Kodiak Island Borough, Lake and Peninsula, Matanuska-Susitna Borough, Valdez-Cordova

-Fairbanks Div. Room 332, 101 12th Ave, Fairbanks, AK 99701 (physical address: Use mail address for courier delivery), 907-451-5791, 866-243-3813. **Jurisdictions:** Bethel, Denali, Fairbanks North Star Borough, North Slope Borough, Northwest Arctic Borough, Southeast Fairbanks, Wade Hampton, Yukon-Koyukuk

-Juneau Div. PO Box 020349, 709 W. 9th Ave, Rm 979, Juneau, AK 99802-0349 (physical address: Room 979, Federal Bldg-U.S. Courthouse, 709 W 9th, Juneau, AK 99802), 907-586-7458, 866-243-3812. **Counties:** Haines Borough, Juneau Borough, Prince of Wales-Outer Ketchikan, Sitka Borough, Skagway-Hoonah-Angoon, Wrangell-Petersburg

-Ketchikan Div. 648 Mission St, Room 507, Ketchikan, AK 99901 (physical address: Use mail address for courier delivery), 907-247-7576. **Jurisdictions:** Ketchikan Gateway Borough

-Nome Div. PO Box 130, Nome, AK 99762 (physical address: 2nd Floor, Federal Bldg, Front St, Nome, AK 99762), 907-443-5216. **Jourisdictions:** Nome

Arizona

District of Arizona

www.azd.uscourts.gov **Access by:** phone (dockets or basic info only), PACER dial-up, PACER online.

-Phoenix Div. Sandra Day O'Connor U.S. Courthouse, #130, 401 W. Washington Street, SPC 1, Phoenix, AZ 85025-2118 (physical address: Use mail address for courier delivery), 602-322-7200. **Counties:** Gila, La Paz, Maricopa, Pinal, Yuma. Some Yuma cases handled by San Diego Division of the Southern District of California

-Prescott Div. 101 W Goodwin St, U.S. Post Office Bldg, Prescott, AZ 86303 (physical address: Use mail address for courier delivery), 928-445-6598. **Counties:** Apache, Coconino, Mohave, Navajo, Yavapai

-Tucson Div. U.S. Court House, 405 W. Congress Ste 1500, Tucson, AZ 85701-5010 (physical address: Use mail address for courier delivery), 520-205-4200. **Counties:** Cochise, Graham, Greelee, Pima, Santa Cruz. The Globe Div. was closed effective 1/1994; all case records for that division are now found here

Arkansas

Eastern District of Arkansas

www.are.uscourts.gov **Access by:** phone, PACER dial-up, or on the web.

-Batesville Div. c/o Little Rock Division, PO Box 869, Little Rock, AR 72201-3325 (physical address: 600 W Capital, Room 402, Little Rock, AR 72201), 501-604-5351. **Counties:** Cleburne, Fulton, Independence, Izard, Jackson, Sharp, Stone

-Helena Div. c/o Little Rock Division, 600 W Capital Rm 402, Little Rock, AR 72201-3325 (physical address: 600 W Capital, Room 402, Little Rock, AR 72201), 501-604-5351. **Counties:** Cross, Lee, Monroe, Phillips, St. Francis, Woodruff

-Jonesboro Div. PO Box 7080, Jonesboro, AR 72403 (physical address: Federal Office Bldg, Room 312, 615 S Main St, Jonesboro, AR 72401), 870-972-4610. **Counties:** Clay, Craighead, Crittenden, Greene, Lawrence, Mississippi, Poinsett, Randolph

-Little Rock Div. Room 402, 600 W Capitol, Little Rock, AR 72201 (physical address: Use mail address for courier delivery), 501-604-5351. **Counties:**

Conway, Faulkner, Lonoke, Perry, Pope, Prairie, Pulaski, Saline, Van Buren, White, Yell
-Pine Bluff Div. PO Box 8307, Pine Bluff, AR 71611-8307 (physical address: U.S. Post Office & Courthouse, 100 E 8th St, Room 3103, Pine Bluff, AR 71601), 870-536-1190. **Counties:** Arkansas, Chicot, Cleveland, Dallas, Desha, Drew, Grant, Jefferson, Lincoln

Western District of Arkansas

www.arwd.uscourts.gov **Access by:** phone, fax, PACER dial-up, PACER online, or on the web.
-El Dorado Div. PO Box 1566, El Dorado, AR 71731 (physical address: Room 205, 101 S Jackson, El Dorado, AR 71730), 870-862-1202. **Counties:** Ashley, Bradley, Calhoun, Columbia, Ouachita, Union
-Fayetteville Div. PO Box 6420, Fayetteville, AR 72702 (physical address: Room 510, 35 E Mountain, Fayetteville, AR 72702), 479-521-6980. **Counties:** Benton, Madison, Washington
-Fort Smith Div. PO Box 1547, Fort Smith, AR 72902 (physical address: Judge Isaac C. Parker Federal Bldg #1038, 6th & Rogers Ave, Fort Smith, AR 72901), 479-783-6833. **Counties:** Crawford, Franklin, Johnson, Logan, Polk, Scott, Sebastian
-Hot Springs Div. PO Drawer6486, Hot Springs, AR 71902 (physical address: Federal Bldg Room 347, 100 Reserve, Hot Springs, AR 71901), 501-623-6411. **Counties:** Clark, Garland, Hot Springs, Montgomery, Pike
-Texarkana Div. PO Box 2746, Texarkana, AR 75504-2746 (physical address: 500 State Line Ave, Room 302, Texarkana, AR 71854), 870-773-3381. **Counties:** Hempstead, Howard, Lafayette, Little River, Miller, Nevada, Sevier

California

Central District of California

www.cacd.uscourts.gov **Access by:** fax, PACER dial-up, PACER online, CM/ECF. Opinions available at www.cacd.uscourts.gov.
-Los Angeles (Western) Div. U.S. Courthouse, Attn: Correspondence, 312 N Spring St, Room G-8, Los Angeles, CA 90012 (physical address: Use mail address for courier delivery), 213-894-5261. **Counties:** Los Angeles, San Luis Obispo, Santa Barbara, Ventura
-Riverside (Eastern) Div. U.S. District Court, PO Box 13000, Riverside, CA 92502-3000 (physical address: 3470 12th StRiverside, CA 92501), 909-328-4450. **Counties:** Riverside, San Bernardino

-Santa Ana (Southern) Div. 411 W 4th St Rm 1053, Santa Ana, CA 92701-4516 (physical address: Use mail address for courier delivery), 714-338-4750. **Counties:** Orange

Eastern District of California

www.caed.uscourts.gov **Access by:** phone, PACER dial-up, PACER online, or on the web. Opinions available at www.caed.uscourts.gov.
-Fresno Div. U.S. Courthouse, Room 5000, 1130 "O" St, Fresno, CA 93721-2201 (physical address: Use mail address for courier delivery), 559-498-7483. **Counties:** Fresno, Inyo, Kern, Kings, Madera, Mariposa, Merced, Stanislaus, Tulare, Tuolumne
-Sacramento Div. 501 I St, Sacramento, CA 95814 (physical address: Use mail address for courier delivery), 916-930-4000. **Counties:** Alpine, Amador, Butte, Calaveras, Colusa, El Dorado, Glenn, Lassen, Modoc, Mono, Nevada, Placer, Plumas, Sacramento, San Joaquin, Shasta, Sierra, Siskiyou, Solano, Sutter, Tehama, Trinity, Yolo, Yuba

Northern District of California

www.cand.uscourts.gov **Access by:** phone, PACER dial-up, PACER online, CM/ECF, or on the web.
-Oakland Div. 1301 Clay St, Ste 400S, Oakland, CA 94612-5212 (physical address: Use mail address for courier delivery), 510-637-3530. **Counties:** Alameda, Contra Costa(Note: Cases may be filed here or at San Francisco Div.; records available electronically at either; the 1st number of the case number indicates the file location: 3=SF, 4=Oak., 5=SJ.
-San Francisco Div. 450 Golden Gate Ave, 16th Fl, San Francisco, CA 94102 (physical address: Use mail address for courier delivery), 415-522-2000. **Counties:** Del Norte, Humboldt, Lake, Marin, Mendocino, Napa, San Francisco, San Mateo, Sonoma(Note: Cases may be filed here or at Oakland Div; records available electronically at either; the 1st number of the case number indicates file location: 3=SF, 4=Oak., 5=SJ.
-San Jose Div. Room 2112, 280 S 1st St, San Jose, CA 95113 (physical address: Use mail address for courier delivery), 408-535-5364. **Counties:** Monterey, San Benito, Santa Clara, Santa Cruz

Southern District of California

www.casd.uscourts.gov **Access by:** PACER dial-up, PACER online, or on the web.
-San Diego Div. Clerk of Court, Room 4290, 880 Front St, San Diego, CA 92101-8900 (physical address: Use mail address for courier delivery), 619-

557-5600. **Counties:** Imperial, San Diego. Court also handles some cases from Yuma County, AZ

Colorado

District of Colorado

www.co.uscourts.gov **Access by:** phone, PACER dial-up, PACER online.
-**Denver Div.** U.S. Courthouse, 901 19th Street, Denver, CO 80294-3589 (physical address: Use mail address for courier delivery), 303-844-3433. **Counties:** All counties in Colorado

District of Columbia

www.dcd.uscourts.gov **Access by:** phone, PACER dial-up, PACER online, CM/ECF. Opinions available at www.dcd.uscourts.gov.
-**Washington DC Div.** U.S. Courthouse, Clerk's Office, Room 1225, 333 Constitution Ave NW, Washington, DC 20001 (physical address: Use mail address for courier delivery), 202-727-2947

Connecticut

District of Connecticut

www.ctd.uscourts.gov **Access by:** phone, PACER dial-up, PACER online, CM/ECF.
-**Bridgeport Div.** Office of the clerk, Room 400, 915 Lafayette Blvd, Bridgeport, CT 06604 (physical address: Use mail address for courier delivery), 203-579-5861. **Counties:** Fairfield (prior to 1993). Since January 1993, cases from any county may be assigned to any of the divisions in the district
-**Hartford Div.** 450 Main St, Hartford, CT 06103 (physical address: Use mail address for courier delivery), 860-240-3200. **Counties:** Hartford, Tolland, Windham (prior to 1993). Since 1993, cases from any county may be assigned to any of the divisions in the district
-**New Haven Div.** 141 Church St, New Haven, CT 06510 (physical address: Use mail address for courier delivery), 203-773-2140. **Counties:** Litchfield, Middlesex, New Haven, New London (prior to 1993). Since 1993, cases from any county may be assigned to any of the divisions in the district

Delaware

District of Delaware

www.ded.uscourts.gov **Access by:** phone, PACER dial-up, PACER online. Opinions available at www.lawlib.widener.edu/pages/deopind.htm.

-**Wilmington Div.** U.S. Courthouse, Lock Box 18, 844 N King St, Wilmington, DE 19801 (physical address: U.S. Courthouse, 844 N King St, Clerk's Office, 4th Floor, Room 4209, Wilmington, DE 19801) 302-573-6170. **Counties:** All Delaware counties

Florida

Middle District of Florida

www.flmd.uscourts.gov **Access by:** phone, PACER dial-up, PACER online.
-**Fort Myers Div.** 2110 First St, Room 2-194, Fort Myers, FL 33901 (physical address: Use mail address for courier delivery), 239-461-2000. **Counties:** Charlotte, Collier, De Soto, Glades, Hendry, Lee
-**Jacksonville Div.** PO Box 53558, Jacksonville, FL 32201 (physical address: Suite 9-150, 300 North Hogan St, Jacksonville, FL 32202), 904-549-1900. **Counties:** Baker, Bradford, Clay, Columbia, Duval, Flagler, Hamilton, Nassau, Putnam, St. Johns, Suwannee, Union
-**Ocala Div.** U.S. Court House, 207 NW Second St, Ocala, FL 34475 (physical address: U.S. Court House, 207 NW Second St, Ocala, FL 34475), 352-369-4860. **Counties:** Citrus, Lake, Marion, Sumter
-**Orlando Div.** Room 218, 80 North Hughey Ave, Orlando, FL 32801 (physical address: Use mail address for courier delivery), 407-835-4200. **Counties:** Brevard, Orange, Osceola, Seminole, Volusia
-**Tampa Div.** Office of the clerk, 801 N Florida Ave #223, Tampa, FL 33602-4500 (physical address: Use mail address for courier delivery), 813-301-5400. **Counties:** Hardee, Hernando, Hillsborough, Manatee, Pasco, Pinellas, Polk, Sarasota

Northern District of Florida

www.flnd.uscourts.gov **Access by:** phone, PACER dial-up, PACER online, CM/ECF.
-**Gainesville Div.** 401 SE First Ave, Room 243, Gainesville, FL 32601 (physical address: Use mail address for courier delivery), 352-380-2400. **Counties:** Alachua, Dixie, Gilchrist, Lafayette, Levy. Records for cases prior to July 1996 are maintained at the Tallahassee Division
-**Panama City Div.** 30 W. Government St, Panama City, FL 32401 (physical address: Use mail address for courier delivery), 850-769-4556. **Counties:** Bay, Calhoun, Gulf, Holmes, Jackson, Washington
-**Pensacola Div.** U.S. Courthouse, 1 N Palafox St, #226, Pensacola, FL 32502 (physical address: Use mail address for courier delivery), 850-435-8440. **Counties:** Escambia, Okaloosa, Santa Rosa, Walton

-Tallahassee Div. Suite 122, 111 North Adams St, Tallahassee, FL 32301 (physical address: Use mail address for courier delivery), 850-521-3501. **Counties:** Franklin, Gadsden, Jefferson, Leon, Liberty, Madison, Taylor, Wakulla

Southern District of Florida

www.flsd.uscourts.gov **Access by:** phone (dockets or basic info only), PACER dial-up, PACER online.

-Fort Lauderdale Div. 299 E Broward Blvd, Fort Lauderdale, FL 33301 (physical address: Use mail address for courier), 954-769-5400. **County:** Broward

-Fort Pierce Div. U S Court House, 300 South Sixth Street, Miami, FL 33128 (physical address: Use mail address for courier delivery), 772-595-9691. **Counties:** Highlands, Indian River, Martin, Okeechobee, St. Lucie

-Key West Div. 301 Simonton St, Key West, FL 33040 (physical address: Use mail address for courier delivery), 305-295-8100. **Counties:** Monroe

-Miami Div. Room 150, 301 N Miami Ave, Miami, FL 33128-7788 (physical address: Use mail address for courier delivery), 305-523-5100. **County:** Miami-Dade

-West Palm Beach Div. Room 402, 701 Clematis St, West Palm Beach, FL 33401 (physical address: Use mail address for courier delivery), 561-803-3400. **Counties:** Palm Beach

Georgia

Middle District of Georgia

www.gamd.uscourts.gov **Access by:** phone, PACER dial-up, PACER online.

-Albany/Americus Div. PO Box 1906, Albany, GA 31702 (physical address: Room 106, 345 Broad Ave, Albany, GA 31701), 229-430-8432. **Counties:** Baker, Ben Hill, Calhoun, Crisp, Dougherty, Early, Lee, Miller, Mitchell, Schley, Sumter, Terrell, Turner, Webster, Worth. Ben Hill and Crisp were transferred from the Macon Division as of October 1, 1997

-Athens Div. PO Box 1106, Athens, GA 30603 (physical address: 115 E Hancock Ave, Athens, GA 30601), 706-227-1094. **Counties:** Clarke, Elbert, Franklin, Greene, Hart, Madison, Morgan, Oconee, Oglethorpe, Walton. Closed cases before April 1997 are located in the Macon Division

-Columbus Div. PO Box 124, Columbus, GA 31902 (physical address: Room 216, 120 12th St, Columbus, GA 31901), 706-649-7816. **Counties:** Chattahoochee, Clay, Harris, Marion, Muscogee, Quitman, Randolph, Stewart, Talbot, Taylor

-Macon Div. PO Box 128, Macon, GA 31202-0128 (physical address: 475 Mulberry, Suite 216, Macon, GA 31201), 912-752-3497. **Counties:** Baldwin, Ben Hill, Bibb, Bleckley, Butts, Crawford, Crisp, Dooly, Hancock, Houston, Jasper, Jones, Lamar, Macon, Monroe, Peach, Pulaski, Putnam, Twiggs, Upson, Washington, Wilcox, Wilkinson. Athens Division cases closed before April 1997 are also located here

-Thomasville Div. c/o Valdosta Division, PO Box 68, Valdosta, GA 31601 (physical address: Room 212, 401 N Patterson, Valdosta, GA 31603), 912-226-3651. **Counties:** Brooks, Colquitt, Decatur, Grady, Seminole, Thomas

-Valdosta Div. PO Box 68, Valdosta, GA 31603 (physical address: Room 212, 401 N Patterson, Valdosta, GA 31601), 912-242-3616. **Counties:** Berrien, Clinch, Cook, Echols, Irwin, Lanier, Lowndes, Tift

Northern District of Georgia

www.gand.uscourts.gov **Access by:** phone, PACER dial-up, PACER online, CM/ECF.

-Atlanta Div. 2211 U.S. Courthouse, 75 Spring St SW, Atlanta, GA 30303-3361 (physical address: Use mail address for courier delivery), 404-215-1660. **Counties:** Cherokee, Clayton, Cobb, De Kalb, Douglas, Fulton, Gwinnett, Henry, Newton, Rockdale

-Gainesville Div. Federal Bldg, Room 201, 121 Spring St SE, Gainesville, GA 30501 (physical address: Use mail address for courier delivery), 678-450-2760. **Counties:** Banks, Barrow, Dawson, Fannin, Forsyth, Gilmer, Habersham, Hall, Jackson, Lumpkin, Pickens, Rabun, Stephens, Towns, Union, White

-Newnan Div. PO Box 939, Newnan, GA 30264 (physical address: 18 Greenville St, #352, Newnan, GA 30263), 678-423-3060. **Counties:** Carroll, Coweta, Fayette, Haralson, Heard, Meriwether, Pike, Spalding, Troup

-Rome Div. PO Box 1186, Rome, GA 30162-1186 (physical address: 600 E 1st St, Room 304, Rome, GA 30161), 706-291-5629. **Counties:** Bartow, Catoosa, Chattooga, Dade, Floyd, Gordon, Murray, Paulding, Polk, Walker, Whitfield

Southern District of Georgia

www.gasd.uscourts.gov **Access by:** phone, PACER dial-up, PACER online.

-Augusta Div. PO Box 1130, Augusta, GA 30903 (physical address: Use mail address for courier delivery, 500 E Ford St, First Floor,), 706-849-4400. **Counties:** Burke, Columbia, Dodge, Glascock, Jefferson, Johnson, Laurens, Lincoln, McDuffie,

Montgomery, Richmond, Taliaferro, Telfair, Treutlen, Warren, Wheeler, Wilkes

-Brunswick Div. PO Box 1636, Brunswick, GA 31521 (physical address: Room 220, 801 Glouchester St, Brunswick, GA 31520), 912-280-1330. **Counties:** Appling, Camden, Glynn, Jeff Davis, Long, McIntosh, Wayne

-Savannah Div. PO Box 8286, Savannah, GA 31412 (physical address: Room 306, 125 Bull St, Savannah, GA 31401), 912-650-4020. **Counties:** Atkinson, Bacon, Bulloch, Brantley, Bryan, Candler, Charlton, Chatham, Coffee, Effingham, Emanuel, Evans, Jenkins, Liberty, Pierce, Screven, Tattnall, Toombs, Ware

Guam

www.gud.uscourts.gov **Access by:** PACER online, or on the web.
Office of the Clerk of Court, 520 W Soledad Ave, 4th Fl, U.S. Courthouse, RM 460, Hagatna, Guam 96910, 671-473-9100. **Counties:** Guam. Address Bankruptcy requests to the Guam Bankruptcy Division.

Hawaii

www.hid.uscourts.gov **Access by:** PACER dial-up, PACER online. **Counties:** All counties
-Honolulu Div. 300 Ala Moana Blvd, Rm C-338, Honolulu, HI 96850 (physical address: Use mail address for courier delivery), 808-541-1300.

Idaho

www.id.uscourts.gov **Access by:** phone, fax, or on the web. Opinions available at www.id.uscourts.gov.
-Boise Div. MSC 039, Federal Bldg, 550 W Fort St, Room 400, Boise, ID 83724 (physical address: Use mail address for courier delivery), 208-334-1361 1-800-448-6172. **Counties:** Ada, Adams, Blaine, Boise, Camas, Canyon, Cassia, Elmore, Gem, Gooding, Jerome, Lincoln, Minidoka, Owyhee, Payette, Twin Falls, Valley, Washington
-Coeur d' Alene Div. c/o Boise Division, MSD 039, Federal Bldg, 550 W Fort St, Room 400, Boise, ID 83724 (physical address: Use mail address for courier delivery), 208-334-1361. **Counties:** Benewah, Bonner, Boundary, Kootenai, Shoshone
-Moscow Div. c/o Boise Division, PO Box 039, Federal Bldg, 550 W Fort St, Boise, ID 83724 (physical address: Use mail address for courier delivery), 208-334-1074. **Counties:** Clearwater, Latah, Lewis, Nez Perce
-Pocatello Div. c/o Boise Division, 801 E Sherman, Pocatello, ID 83201 (physical address: Use mail

address for courier delivery), 208-334-1074 1-800-448-6172. **Counties:** Bannock, Bear Lake, Bingham, Bonneville, Butte, Caribou, Clark, Custer, Franklin, Fremont, Idaho, Jefferson, Lemhi, Madison, Oneida, Power, Teton

Illinois

Central District of Illinois

www.ilcd.uscourts.gov **Access by:** phone, PACER dial-up, PACER online.
-Danville/Urbana Div. 201 S Vine, Room 218, Urbana, IL 61802 (physical address: Use mail address for courier delivery), 217-373-5830. **Counties:** Champaign, Coles, Douglas, Edgar, Ford, Iroquois, Kankakee, Macon, Moultrie, Piatt, Vermilion
-Peoria Div. U.S. District Clerk's Office, 309 Federal Bldg, 100 NE Monroe St, Peoria, IL 61602 (physical address: Use mail address for courier delivery), 309-671-7117. **Counties:** Bureau, Fulton, Hancock, Knox, Livingston, McDonough, McLean, Marshall, Peoria, Putnam, Stark, Tazewell, Woodford
-Rock Island Div. U.S. District Clerk's Office, Room 40, U.S. Court House, 211 19th St, Rock Island, IL 61201 (physical address: Use mail address for courier delivery), 309-793-5778. **Counties:** Henderson, Henry, Mercer, Rock Island, Warren
-Springfield Div. Clerk, 151 U.S. Courthouse, 600 E Monroe, Springfield, IL 62701 (physical address: Use mail address for courier delivery), 217-492-4020. **Counties:** Adams, Brown, Cass, Christian, De Witt, Greene, Logan, Macoupin, Mason, Menard, Montgomery, Morgan, Pike, Sangamon, Schuyler, Scott, Shelby

Northern District of Illinois

www.ilnd.uscourts.gov **Access by:** phone (dockets or basic information only), PACER dial-up, PACER online, CM/ECF.
-Chicago (Eastern) Div. 20th Floor, 219 S Dearborn St, Chicago, IL 60604 (physical address: Use mail address for courier delivery), 312-435-5698. **Counties:** Cook, Du Page, Grundy, Kane, Kendall, Lake, La Salle, Will
-Rockford Div. Room 211, 211 S Court St, Rockford, IL 61101 (physical address: Use mail address for courier delivery), 815-987-4355. **Counties:** Boone, Carroll, De Kalb, Jo Daviess, Lee, McHenry, Ogle, Stephenson, Whiteside, Winnebago

Southern District of Illinois

www.ilsd.uscourts.gov **Access by:** phone, PACER dial-up, PACER online, CM/ECF.

-Benton Div. 301 W Main St, Benton, IL 62812 (physical address: Use mail address for courier delivery), 618-439-7760. **Counties:** Alexander, Clark, Clay, Crawford, Cumberland, Edwards, Effingham, Franklin, Gallatin, Hamilton, Hardin, Jackson, Jasper, Jefferson, Johnson, Lawrence, Massac, Perry, Pope, Pulaski, Richland, Saline, Union, Wabash, Wayne, White, Williamson. Cases mayalso be allocated to the Benton Division

-East St Louis Div. PO Box 249, East St Louis, IL 62202 (physical address: 750 Missouri Ave, East St Louis, IL 62201), 618-482-9371. **Counties:** Bond, Calhoun, Clinton, Fayette, Jersey, Madison, Marion, Monroe, Randolph, St. Clair, Washington. Cases for these counties may be allocated to the Benton Division

Indiana

Northern District of Indiana

www.innd.uscourts.gov **Access by:** phone, PACER dial-up, PACER online, CM/ECF.

-Fort Wayne Div. Room 1108, Federal Bldg, 1300 S Harrison St, Fort Wayne, IN 46802 (physical address: Use mail address for courier delivery), 260-424-7360. **Counties:** Adams, Allen, Blackford, DeKalb, Grant, Huntington, Jay, Lagrange, Noble, Steuben, Wells, Whitley

-Hammond Div. Room 101, 507 State St, Hammond, IN 46320 (physical address: Use mail address for courier), 219-937-5235. **Counties:** Lake, Porter

-Lafayette Div. PO Box 1498, Lafayette, IN 47902 (physical address: 230 N 4th St, Lafayette, IN 47901), 765-420-6250. **Counties:** Benton, Carroll, Jasper, Newton, Tippecanoe, Warren, White

-South Bend Div. Room 102, 204 S Main, South Bend, IN 46601 (physical address: Use mail address for courier delivery), 574-246-8000. **Counties:** Cass, Elkhart, Fulton, Kosciusko, La Porte, Marshall, Miami, Pulaski, St. Joseph, Starke, Wabash

Southern District of Indiana

www.insd.uscourts.gov **Access:** CM/ECF, or the web.

-Evansville Div. 304 Federal Bldg, 101 NW Martin Luther King Blvd, Evansville, IN 47708 (physical address: Use mail address for courier delivery), 812-434-6410. **Counties:** Daviess, Dubois, Gibson, Martin, Perry, Pike, Posey, Spencer, Vanderburgh, Warrick

-Indianapolis Div. Clerk, Room 105, 46 E Ohio St, Indianapolis, IN 46204 (physical address: Use mail address for courier delivery), 317-229-3700. **Counties:** Bartholomew, Boone, Brown, Clinton, Decatur, Delaware, Fayette, Fountain, Franklin, Hamilton, Hancock, Hendricks, Henry, Howard, Johnson, Madison, Marion, Monroe, Montgomery, Morgan, Randolph, Rush, Shelby, Tipton, Union, Wayne

-New Albany Div. Room 210, 121 W Spring St, New Albany, IN 47150 (physical address: Use mail address for courier delivery), 812-542-4510. **Counties:** Clark, Crawford, Dearborn, Floyd, Harrison, Jackson, Jefferson, Jennings, Lawrence, Ohio, Orange, Ripley, Scott, Switzerland, Washington

-Terre Haute Div. 210 Federal Bldg, Terre Haute, IN 47808 (physical address: Use mail address for courier), 812-234-9484. **Counties:** Clay, Greene, Knox, Owen, Parke, Putnam, Sullivan, Vermillion, Vigo

Iowa

Northern District of Iowa

www.iand.uscourts.gov **Access by:** phone, PACER dial-up, PACER online, CM/ECF.

-Cedar Rapids (Eastern) Div. Court Clerk, PO Box 74710, Cedar Rapids, IA 52407-4710 (physical address: Federal Bldg, U.S. Courthouse, 101 1st St SE, Room 313, Cedar Rapids, IA 52401), 319-286-2300. **Counties:** Allamakee, Benton, Black Hawk, Bremer, Buchanan, Cedar, Chickasaw, Clayton, Delaware, Dubuque, Fayette, Floyd, Grundy, Hardin, Howard, Iowa, Jackson, Jones, Linn, Mitchell, Tama, WinneshiekThis court also has records for the Dubuque Branch.

-Sioux City (Western) Div. Room 301, Federal Bldg, 320 6th St, Sioux City, IA 51101 (physical address: Use mail address for courier delivery), 712-233-3900. **Counties:** Buena Vista, Butler, Calhoun, Carroll, Cerro Gordo, Cherokee, Clay, Crawford, Dickinson, Emmet, Franklin, Hamilton, Hancock, Humboldt, Ida,Kossuth, Lyon, Monona, O'Brien, Osceola, Palo Alto, Plymouth, Pocahontas, Sac, Sioux, Webster, Winnebago, Woodbury, Worth, WrightThis court also has records for the Ft. Dodge, Independence, and Mason City Divisions. Court is held occasionally held in Ft. Dodge, but records are here at Sioux City.

Southern District of Iowa

www.iasd.uscourts.gov **Access by:** phone, PACER dial-up, PACER online, or on the web.

-Council Bluffs (Western) Div. PO Box 307, Council Bluffs, IA 51502 (physical address: Room 313, 8 S 6th St, Council Bluffs, IA 51502), 712-328-

0283. **Counties:** Audubon, Cass, Fremont, Harrison, Mills, Montgomery, Page, Pottawattamie, Shelby
-Davenport (Eastern) Div. PO Box 256, Davenport, IA 52805 (physical address: Room 215, 131 E 4th St, Davenport, IA 52801), 563-322-3223. **Counties:** Henry, Johnson, Lee, Louisa, Muscatine, Scott, Van Buren, Washington
-Des Moines (Central) Div. PO Box 9344, Des Moines, IA 50306-9344 (physical address: 123 E. Walnut St, Rm. 300, Des Moines, IA 50306-9344), 515-284-6248. **Counties:** Adair, Adams, Appanoose, Boone, Clarke, Clinton, Dallas, Davis, Decatur, Des Moines, Greene, Guthrie, Jasper, Jefferson, Keokuk, Lucas, Madison, Mahaska, Marion, Marshall, Monroe, Polk, Poweshiek, Ringgold, Story, Taylor, Union, Wapello, Warren, Wayne

Kansas

District of Kansas

www.ksd.uscourts.gov **Access by:** phone (dockets or basic information only), PACER dial-up, PACER online, CM/ECF.
-Kansas City Div. Clerk, 500 State Ave, Kansas City, KS 66101 (physical address: Use mail address for courier delivery), 913-551-6719. **Counties:** Atchison, Bourbon, Brown, Cherokee, Crawford, Doniphan, Johnson, Labette, Leavenworth, Linn, Marshall, Miami, Nemaha, Wyandotte
-Topeka Div. Clerk, U.S. District Court, Room 490, 444 SE Quincy, Topeka, KS 66683 (physical address: Use mail address for courier delivery), 785-295-2610. **Counties:** Allen, Anderson, Chase, Clay, Cloud, Coffey, Dickinson, Douglas, Franklin, Geary, Jackson, Jewell, Lincoln, Lyon, Marion, Mitchell, Morris, Neosho, Osage, Ottawa, Pottawatomie, Republic, Riley, Saline, Shawnee, Wabaunsee, Washington, Wilson, Woodson
-Wichita Div. 204 U.S. Courthouse, 401 N Market, Wichita, KS 67202-2096 (physical address: Use mail address for courier delivery), 316-269-6491. **Counties:** All counties in Kansas. Cases may be heard from counties in the other division

Kentucky

Eastern District of Kentucky

www.kyed.uscourts.gov **Access by:** phone, PACER dial-up, PACER online, CM/ECF.
-Ashland Div. Suite 336, 1405 Greenup Ave, Ashland, KY 41101 (physical address: Use mail address for courier delivery), 606-329-8652. **Counties:** Boyd, Carter, Elliott, Greenup, Lawrence, Lewis, Morgan, Rowan
-Covington Div. Clerk, PO Box 1073, Covington, KY 41012 (physical address: U.S. Courthouse, Room 201, 35 W 5th St, Covington, KY 41011), 859-392-7925. **Counties:** Boone, Bracken, Campbell, Gallatin, Grant, Kenton, Mason, Pendleton, Robertson
-Frankfort Div. Room 313, 330 W Broadway, Frankfort, KY 40601 (physical address: Use mail address for courier delivery), 502-223-5225. **Counties:** Anderson, Carroll, Franklin, Henry, Owen, Shelby, Trimble
-Lexington Div. PO Box 3074, Lexington, KY 40588 (physical address: Room 206, 101 Barr St, Lexington, KY40588-3074), 859-233-2503. **Counties:** Bath, Bourbon, Boyle, Clark, Estill, Fayette, Fleming, Garrard, Harrison, Jessamine, Lee, Lincoln, Madison, Menifee, Mercer, Montgomery, Nicholas, Powell, Scott, Wolfe, Woodford. Lee and Wolfe counties were part of the Pikeville Divisionbefore 10/31/92. Perry became part of Pikeville after 1992
-London Div. PO Box 5121, London, KY 40745-5121 (physical address: 124 U.S. Courthouse, 310 S Main, London, KY 40741), 606-877-7910. **Counties:** Bell, Clay, Harlan, Jackson, Knox, Laurel, Leslie, McCreary, Owsley, Pulaski, Rockcastle, Wayne, Whitley
-Pikeville Div. Office of the clerk, 203 Federal Bldg, 110 Main St, Pikeville, KY 41501 (physical address: Use mail address for courier delivery), 606-437-6160. **Counties:** Breathitt, Floyd, Johnson, Knott, Letcher, Magoffin, Martin, Perry, Pike. Lee and Wolfe Counties were part of this division until 10/31/92, when they were moved to the Lexington Division.

Western District of Kentucky

www.kywd.uscourts.gov **Access by:** phone, PACER dial-up, PACER online, CM/ECF. Opinions available at www.kywd.uscourts.gov.
-Bowling Green Div. U.S. District Court, 241 E Main St, Room 120, Bowling Green, KY 42101-2175 (physical address: Use mail address for courier delivery), 270-389-2500. **Counties:** Adair, Allen, Barren, Butler, Casey, Clinton, Cumberland, Edmonson, Green, Hart, Logan, Metcalfe, Monroe, Russell, Simpson, Taylor, Todd, Warren
-Louisville Div. Clerk, U.S. District Court, 601 Broadway, Rm106, Louisville, KY 40202 (physical address: Use mail address for courier delivery), 502-625-3500. **Counties:** Breckinridge, Bullitt, Hardin,

Jefferson, Larue, Marion, Meade, Nelson, Oldham, Spencer, Washington
-Owensboro Div. Federal Bldg, Room 126, 423 Frederica St, Owensboro, KY 42301 (physical address: Use mail address for courier delivery), 270-689-4400. **Counties:** Daviess, Grayson, Hancock, Henderson, Hopkins, McLean, Muhlenberg, Ohio, Union, Webster
-Paducah Div. 501 Broadway, Ste127, Paducah, KY 42001 (physical address: Use mail address for courier delivery), 270-415-6400. **Counties:** Ballard, Caldwell, Calloway, Carlisle, Christian, Crittenden, Fulton, Graves, Hickman, Livingston, Lyon, McCracken, Marshall, Trigg

Louisiana

Eastern District of Louisiana

www.laed.uscourts.gov **Access by:** phone (dockets or basic info only), PACER dial-up, PACER online.
-New Orleans Div. Clerk, 500 Poydras St, New Orleans, LA 70130 (physical address: Use mail address for courier delivery), 504-589-7650. **Parishes:** Assumption Parish, Jefferson Parish, Lafourche Parish, Orleans Parish, Plaquemines Parish, St. Bernard Parish, St. Charles Parish, St. James Parish, St. John the Baptist Parish, St. Tammany Parish, Tangipahoa Parish, Terrebonne Parish, Washington Parish

Middle District of Louisiana

www.lamd.uscourts.gov **Access by:** phone, PACER dial-up, PACER online.
-Baton Rouge Div. PO Box 2630, Baton Rouge, LA 70821-2630 (physical address: 777 Florida St, #139, Baton Rouge, LA 70801), 225-389-3500. **Parishes:** Ascension Parish, East Baton Rouge Parish, East Feliciana Parish, Iberville Parish, Livingston Parish, Pointe Coupee Parish, St. Helena Parish, West Baton Rouge Parish, West Feliciana Parish

Western District of Louisiana

www.lawd.uscourts.gov **Access by:** phone, PACER dial-up, PACER online, CM/ECF.
-Alexandria Div. PO Box 1269, Alexandria, LA 71309 (physical address: 515 Murray, Alexandria, LA 71301), 318-473-7415. **Parishes:** Avoyelles Parish, Catahoula Parish, Concordia Parish, Grant Parish, La Salle Parish, Natchitoches Parish, Rapides Parish, Winn Parish
-Lafayette Div. Room 113, Federal Bldg, 705 Jefferson St, Lafayette, LA 70501 (physical address: Use mail address for courier delivery), 337-593-5000. **Parishes:** Acadia Parish, Evangeline Parish, Iberia Parish, Lafayette Parish, St. Landry Parish, St. Martin Parish, St. Mary Parish, Vermilion Parish
-Lake Charles Div. 611 Broad St, Suite 188, Lake Charles, LA 70601 (physical address: Use mail address for courier delivery), 337-437-3870. **Parishes:** Allen Parish, Beauregard Parish, Calcasieu Parish, Cameron Parish, Jefferson Davis Parish, Vernon Parish
-Monroe Div. PO Drawer 3087, Monroe, LA 71210 (physical address: Room 215, 201 Jackson St, Monroe, LA 71201), 318-322-6740. **Parishes:** Caldwell Parish, East Carroll Parish, Franklin Parish, Jackson Parish, Lincoln Parish, Madison Parish, Morehouse Parish, Ouachita Parish, Richland Parish, Tensas Parish, Union Parish, West Carroll Parish.
-Shreveport Div. U.S. Courthouse, Suite 1167, 300 Fannin St, Shreveport, LA 71101-3083 (physical address: Use mail address for courier delivery), 318-676-4273. **Parishes:** Bienville Parish, Bossier Parish, Caddo Parish, Claiborne Parish, De Soto Parish, Red River Parish, Sabine Parish, Webster Parish

Maine

District of Maine

www.med.uscourts.gov **Access by:** phone, PACER dial-up, PACER online, CM/ECF.
-Bangor Div. Court Clerk, PO Box 1007, Bangor, ME 04402-1007 (physical address: Room 357, 202 Harlow St, Bangor, ME 04401), 207-945-0575. **Counties:** Aroostook, Franklin, Hancock, Kennebec, Penobscot, Piscataquis, Somerset, Waldo, Washington
-Portland Div. Court Clerk, 156 Federal St, Portland, ME 04101 (physical address: Use mail address for courier delivery), 207-780-3356. **Counties:** Androscoggin, Cumberland, Knox, Lincoln, Oxford, Sagadahoc, York

Maryland

Northern District of Maryland

www.mdd.uscourts.gov **Access by:** phone, PACER dial-up, PACER online, CM/ECF. Opinions available at www.mdd.uscourts.gov.
-Baltimore Div. Clerk, 4th Floor, Room 4415, 101 W Lombard St, Baltimore, MD 21201 (physical address: Use mail address for courier delivery), 410-962-2600. **Counties:** Allegany, Anne Arundel, Baltimore, City of Baltimore, Caroline, Carroll, Cecil, Dorchester, Frederick, Garrett, Harford, Howard, Kent, Queen Anne's, Somerset, Talbot, Washington, Wicomico, Worcester

Southern District of Maryland

www.mdd.uscourts.gov **Access by:** phone, fax, PACER dial-up, PACER online, CM/ECF. Opinions available at www.mdd.uscourts.gov.
-Greenbelt Div. Clerk, Room 240, 6500 Cherrywood Lane, Greenbelt, MD 20770 (physical address: Use mail address for courier delivery), 301-344-0660. **Counties:** Calvert, Charles, Montgomery, Prince George's, St. Mary's

Massachusetts

District of Massachusetts

www.mad.uscourts.gov **Access by:** PACER dial-up, PACER online, CM/ECF.
-Boston Div. U.S. Courthouse, 1 Courthouse Way Ste 2300, Boston, MA 02210 (physical address: Use mail address for courier delivery), 617-748-9152. **Counties:** Barnstable, Bristol, Dukes, Essex, Middlesex, Nantucket, Norfolk, Plymouth, Suffolk
-Springfield Div. 1550 Main St, Springfield, MA 01103 (physical address: Use mail address for courier delivery), 413-785-0015. **Counties:** Berkshire, Franklin, Hampden, Hampshire
-Worcester Div. 595 Main St, Room 502, Worcester, MA 01608 (physical address: Use mail address for courier delivery), 508-929-9900. **Counties:** Worcester

Michigan

Eastern District of Michigan

www.mied.uscourts.gov **Access by:** phone, PACER dial-up, PACER online, CM/ECF.
-Ann Arbor Div. PO Box 8199, Ann Arbor, MI 48107 (physical address: 200 E Liberty St, Room 120, Ann Arbor, MI 48104), 734-741-2380. **Counties:** Jackson, Lenawee, Monroe, Oakland, Washtenaw, Wayne. Civil cases in these counties are assigned randomly to the Detroit, Flint or Port Huron Divisions. Case files are maintained where the case is assigned
-Bay City Div. 1000 Washington Ave Rm 304, PO Box 913, Bay City, MI 48707 (physical address: Use mail address for courier delivery), 989-894-8800. **Counties:** Alcona, Alpena, Arenac, Bay, Cheboygan, Clare, Crawford, Gladwin, Gratiot, Huron, Iosco, Isabella, Midland, Montmorency, Ogemaw, Oscoda, Otsego, Presque Isle, Roscommon, Saginaw, Tuscola
-Detroit Div. 231 W Lafayette Blvd, Detroit, MI 48226 (physical address: Use mail address for courier delivery), 313-234-5005. **Counties:** Macomb, St. Clair, Sanilac. Civil cases for these counties are assigned randomly among the Flint, Ann Arbor and Detroit divisions. Port Huron cases may be assigned here. Case files are kept where the case is assigned.
-Flint Div. Clerk, Federal Bldg, Room 140, 600 Church St, Flint, MI 48502 (physical address: Use mail address for courier delivery), 810-341-7840. **Counties:** Genesee, Lapeer, Livingston, Shiawassee. This office handles all criminal cases for these counties. Civil cases are assigned randomly among the Detroit, Ann Arbor and Flint divisions

Western District of Michigan

www.miwd.uscourts.gov **Access by:** phone, PACER dial-up, PACER online, CM/ECF.
-Grand Rapids Div. PO Box 3310, Grand Rapids, MI 49501 (physical address: Gerald Ford Federal Building, 110 Michigan St NW, Rm 399, Grand Rapids, MI 49503), 616-456-2381. **Counties:** Antrim, Barry, Benzie, Charlevoix, Emmet, Grand Traverse, Ionia, Kalkaska, Kent, Lake, Leelanau, Manistee, Mason, Mecosta, Missaukee, Montcalm, Muskegon, Newaygo, Oceana, Osceola, Ottawa, Wexford. The Lansing and Kalamazoo Divisions also handle cases from these counties
-Kalamazoo Div. 410 W Michigan, Rm B-35, Kalamazoo, MI 49007 (physical address: Use mail address for courier delivery), 269-337-5706. **Counties:** Allegan, Berrien, Calhoun, Cass, Kalamazoo, St. Joseph, Van Buren. Also handle cases from the counties in the Grand Rapids Division
-Lansing Div. 113 Federal Building, 315 W Allegan, Rm 101, Lansing, MI 48933 (physical address: Use mail address for courier delivery), 517-377-1559. **Counties:** Branch, Clinton, Eaton, Hillsdale, Ingham. Also handle cases from the counties in the Grand Rapids Division
-Marquette-Northern Div. PO Box 698, Marquette, MI 49855 (physical address: 202 W Washington, Room 229, Marquette, MI 49855), 906-226-2117. **Counties:** Alger, Baraga, Chippewa, Delta, Dickinson, Gogebic, Houghton, Iron, Keweenaw, Luce, Mackinac, Marquette, Menominee, Ontonagon, Schoolcraft

Minnesota

District of Minnesota

www.mnd.uscourts.gov **Access by:** phone, PACER dial-up, PACER online, CM/ECF.
-Duluth Div. Clerk's Office, 417 Federal Bldg, 515 W. 1st St, Duluth, MN 55802-1397 (physical address: Use mail address for courier delivery), 218-529-3500. **Counties:** Aitkin, Becker*, Beltrami*, Benton, Big Stone*, Carlton, Cass, Clay*, Clearwater*, Cook,

Crow Wing, Douglas*, Grant*, Hubbard*, Itasca, Kanabec, Kittson*, Koochiching, Lake, Lake of the Woods*, Mahnomen*, Marshall*, Mille Lacs, Morrison, Norman*, OtterTail,* Pennington*, Pine, Polk*, Pope*, Red Lake*, Roseau*, Stearns*, Stevens*, St. Louis, Todd*, Traverse*, Wadena*, Wilkin*. From March 1, 1995, to 1998, cases from the counties marked with an asterisk (*) were heard here.Before and after that period, cases were and are allocated between St. Paul and Minneapolis

-Minneapolis Div. Court Clerk, Room 202, 300 S 4th St, Minneapolis, MN 55415 (physical address: Use mail address for courier delivery), 612-664-5000. **Counties:** All counties not covered by the Duluth Division. Cases are allocated between Minneapolis and St Paul

-St Paul Div. 700 Federal Bldg, 316 N Robert, St Paul, MN 55101 (physical address: Use mail address for courier delivery), 651-848-1100. **Counties:** All counties not covered by the Duluth Division. Cases are allocated between Minneapolis and St Paul

Mississippi

Northern District of Mississippi

www.msnd.uscourts.gov **Access by:** phone (dockets or basic info only), PACER dial-up, PACER online. Opinions available at http://sunset.backbone.olemis s.edu/~llibcoll/ndms.

-Aberdeen-Eastern Div. PO Box 704, Aberdeen, MS 39730 (physical address: 301 W Commerce, Room 310, Aberdeen, MS 39730), 662-369-4952. **Counties:** Alcorn, Attala, Chickasaw, Choctaw, Clay, Itawamba, Lee, Lowndes, Monroe, Oktibbeha, Prentiss, Tishomingo, Winston

-Clarksdale/Delta Div. c/o Oxford-Northern Division, PO Box 727, Oxford, MS 38655 (physical address: Suite 369, 911 Jackson Ave, Oxford, MS 38655), 662-234-1971. **Counties:** Bolivar, Coahoma, De Soto, Panola, Quitman, Tallahatchie, Tate, Tunica

-Greenville Div. PO Box 190, Greenville, MS 38702-0190 (physical address: U.S. Post Office & Federal Bldg, 305 Main, Greenville, MS 38701), 662-335-1651. **Counties:** Carroll, Humphreys, Leflore, Sunflower, Washington

-Oxford-Northern Div. PO Box 727, Oxford, MS 38655 (physical address: Suite 369, 911 Jackson Ave, Oxford, MS 38655), 662-234-1971. **Counties:** Benton, Calhoun, Grenada, Lafayette, Marshall, Montgomery, Pontotoc, Tippah, Union, Webster, Yalobusha

Southern District of Mississippi

www.mssd.uscourts.gov **Access by:** phone (dockets or basic info only), PACER dial-up, PACER online.

-Biloxi-Southern Div. Room 243, 725 Dr. Martin Luther King Jr. Blvd, Biloxi, MS 39530 (physical address: Use mail address for courier delivery), 228-432-8623. **Counties:** George, Hancock, Harrison, Jackson, Pearl River, Stone

-Eastern Div. c/o Jackson Division, Suite 316, 245 E Capitol St, Jackson, MS 39201 (physical address: Use mail address for courier delivery), 601-965-4439. **Counties:** Clarke, Jasper, Kemper, Lauderdale, Neshoba, Newton, Noxubee, Wayne

-Hattiesburg Div. Suite 200, 701 Main St, Hattiesburg, MS 39401 (physical address: Use mail address for courier delivery), 601-583-2433. **Counties:** Covington, Forrest, Greene, Jefferson Davis, Jones, Lamar, Lawrence, Marion, Perry, Walthall

-Jackson Div. Suite 316, 245 E Capitol St, Jackson, MS 39201 (physical address: Use mail address for courier delivery), 601-965-4439. **Counties:** Amite, Copiah, Franklin, Hinds, Holmes, Leake, Lincoln, Madison, Pike, Rankin, Scott, Simpson, Smith

-Western Div. c/o Jackson Division, Suite 316, 245 E Capitol St, Jackson, MS 39201 (physical address: Use mail address for courier delivery), 601-965-4439. **Counties:** Adams, Claiborne, Issaquena, Jefferson, Sharkey, Warren, Wilkinson, Yazoo

Missouri

Eastern District of Missouri

www.moed.uscourts.gov **Access by:** phone, PACER dial-up, PACER online, CM/ECF.

-Cape Girardeau Div. 339 Broadway, Room 240, Cape Girardeau, MO 63701 (physical address: Use mail address for courier delivery), 573-335-8538. **Counties:** Bollinger, Butler, Cape Girardeau, Carter, Dunklin, Madison, Mississippi, New Madrid, Pemiscot, Perry, Reynolds, Ripley, Scott, Shannon, Stoddard, Wayne

-St Louis Div. 111 S. 10th St, Ste 3.300, St Louis, MO 63102 (physical address: Use mail address for courier delivery), 314-244-7900. **Counties:** Adair, Audrain, Chariton, Clark, Crawford, Dent, Franklin, Gasconade, Iron, Jefferson, Knox, Lewis, Lincoln, Linn, Macon, Maries, Marion, Monroe, Montgomery, Phelps,Pike, Ralls, Randolph, Schuyler, Scotland, Shelby, St. Charles, St. Francois, St. Louis, St. Louis City, Ste. Genevieve, Warren, Washington,This court also holds records for the Hannibal Division.

- ### Western District of Missouri

www.mow.uscourts.gov **Access by:** phone, PACER dial-up, PACER online, CM/ECF.

-Jefferson City-Central Div. 131 W High St, Jefferson City, MO 65101 (physical address: Use mail address for courier delivery), 573-636-4015. **Counties:** Benton, Boone, Callaway, Camden, Cole, Cooper, Hickory, Howard, Miller, Moniteau, Morgan, Osage, Pettis

-Joplin-Southwestern Div. c/o Kansas City Division, Charles Evans Whittaker Courthouse, 400 E 9th St, Kansas City, MO 64106 (physical address: Use mail address for courier delivery), 816-512-5000. **Counties:** Barry, Barton, Jasper, Lawrence, McDonald, Newton, Stone, Vernon

-Kansas City-Western Div. Clerk of Court, 201 U.S. Courthouse, Rm 1056, 400 E 9th St, Kansas City, MO 64106 (physical address: Use mail address for courier delivery), 816-512-5000. **Counties:** Bates, Carroll, Cass, Clay, Henry, Jackson, Johnson, Lafayette, Ray, St. Clair, Saline

-Springfield-Southern Div. 222 N John Q Hammons Pkwy, Suite 1400, Springfield, MO 65806 (physical address: Use mail address for courier), 417-865-3869. **Counties:** Cedar, Christian, Dade, Dallas, Douglas, Greene, Howell, Laclede, Oregon, Ozark, Polk, Pulaski, Taney, Texas, Webster, Wright

-St Joseph Div. PO Box 387, 201 S 8th St, St Joseph, MO 64501 (physical address: Use mail address for courier delivery), . **Counties:** Andrew, Atchison, Buchanan, Caldwell, Clinton, Daviess, De Kalb, Gentry, Grundy, Harrison, Holt, Livingston, Mercer, Nodaway, Platte, Putnam, Sullivan, Worth

Montana

District of Montana

www.mtd.uscourts.gov **Access by:** phone, fax, PACER dial-up.

-Billings Div. Clerk, Room 5405, Federal Bldg, 316 N 26th St, Billings, MT 59101 (physical address: Use mail address for courier delivery), 406-247-7000. **Counties:** Big Horn, Carbon, Carter, Custer, Daniels, Dawson, Fallon, Garfield, Golden Valley, McCone, Musselshell, Park, Petroleum, Powder River, Prairie, Richland, Rosebud, Sheridan, Stillwater, Sweet Grass, Treasure, Wheatland, Wibaux, Yellowstone, Yellowstone National Park

-Butte Div. U.S. District Court, 400 North Main, Butte, MT 59701 (physical address: Use mail address for courier delivery), 406-782-0432. **Counties:**

Beaverhead, Deer Lodge, Gallatin, Madison, Silver Bow

-Great Falls Div. Clerk, PO Box 2186, Great Falls, MT 59403 (physical address: 215 1st Ave N, Great Falls, MT 59401), 406-727-1922. **Counties:** Blaine, Cascade, Chouteau, Daniels, Fergus, Glacier, Hill, Judith Basin, Liberty, Phillips, Pondera, Roosevelt, Sheridan, Teton, Toole, Valley

-Helena Div. Paul G. Hatfield Courthouse, 901 Front Street, Helena, MT 59626 (physical address:), 406-441-1355. **Counties:** Broadwater, Jefferson, Lewis and Clark, Meagher, Powell

-Missoula Div. Russell Smith Courthouse, 201 E Broadway, Missoula, MT 59801 (physical address:), 406-542-7260. **Counties:** Flathead, Granite, Lake, Lincoln, Mineral, Missoula, Ravalli, Sanders

Nebraska

District of Nebraska

www.ned.uscourts.gov **Access by:** phone, PACER dial-up, PACER online, CM/ECF.

-Lincoln Div. PO Box 83468, Lincoln, NE 68501 (physical address: 593 Federal Bldg, 100 Centennial Mall N, Lincoln, NE 68508), 402-437-5225. **Counties:** Nebraska cases may be filed in any of the three courts at the option of the attorney, except that filings in the North Platte Division must be during trial session.

-North Platte Div. c/o Lincoln Division, PO Box 83468, Lincoln, NE 68501 (physical address: 593 Federal Bldg, 100 Centennial Mall N, Lincoln, NE 68508), 402-437-5225. **Counties:** Nebraska cases may be filed in any of the three courts at the option of the attorney, except that filings in the North Platte Division must be during trial session. Some case records may be in the Omaha Division as well as the Lincoln Division

-Omaha Div. 111 S 18th Plaza, Ste 1152, Omaha, NE 68102 (physical address: Use mail address for courier delivery), 402-661-7350. **Counties:** Nebraska cases may be filed in any of the three courts at the option of the attorney, except that filings in the North Platte Division must be during trial session.

Nevada

District of Nevada

www.nvd.uscourts.gov **Access by:** phone, PACER dial-up, PACER online.

-Las Vegas Div. Room 4425, 300 Las Vegas Blvd S, Las Vegas, NV 89101 (physical address: Use mail

address for courier delivery), 702-464-5400. **Counties:** Clark, Esmeralda, Lincoln, Nye
-Reno Div. Room 301, 400 S Virginia St, Reno, NV 89501 (physical address: Use mail address for courier delivery), 775-686-5800. **Counties:** Carson City, Churchill, Douglas, Elko, Eureka, Humboldt, Lander, Lyon, Mineral, Pershing, Storey, Washoe, White Pine

New Hampshire

District of New Hampshire

www.nhd.uscourts.gov **Access by:** phone, PACER dial-up, PACER online, CM/ECF.
-Concord Div. Warren B Rudman Courthouse, 55 Pleasant St, #110, Concord, NH 03301 (physical address: Use mail address for courier delivery), 603-225-1423. **Counties:** Belknap, Carroll, Cheshire, Coos, Grafton, Hillsborough, Merrimack, Rockingham, Strafford, Sullivan

New Jersey

District of New Jersey

http://pacer.njd.uscourts.gov **Access by:** phone, PACER dial-up, PACER online, CM/ECF. Opinions at http://lawlibrary.rutgers.edu/fed/search.html.
-Camden Div. Clerk, PO Box 2797, Camden, NJ 08101 (physical address: Room 1050, 4th & Cooper Sts, Camden, NJ 08101), 856-757-5021. **Counties:** Atlantic, Burlington, Camden, Cape May, Cumberland, Gloucester, Salem
-Newark Div. ML King, Jr Federal Bldg. & U.S. Courthouse, 50 Walnut St, Room 4015, Newark, NJ 07101 (physical address: Use mail address for courier delivery), 973-645-3730. **Counties:** Bergen, Essex, Hudson, Middlesex, Monmouth, Morris, Passaic, Sussex, Union. Monmouth County was transferred from Trenton Division in late 1997; closed cases remain in Trenton
-Trenton Div. Clerk, U.S. District Court, Room 2020, 402 E State St, Trenton, NJ 08608 (physical address: Use mail address for courier delivery), 609-989-2065. **Counties:** Hunterdon, Mercer, Ocean, Somerset, Warren. Monmouth County was transferred to Newark and Camden Division in late 1997; closed Monmouth cases remain in Trenton

New Mexico

District of New Mexico

www.nmcourt.fed.us/dcdocs **Access by:** phone, CM/ECF, or on the web.
-Albuquerque Div. 333 Lomas Blvd NW #270, Albuquerque, NM 87102-2274 (physical address: Use mail address for courier delivery), 505-348-2000. **Counties:** All counties in New Mexico. Cases may be assigned to any of its three divisions - Santa Fe (505-988-6481), Las Cruces (505-528-1400), and Roswell (505-625-2388). Santa Fe and Las Cruces have searchable records; Roswell does not.

New York

Eastern District of New York

www.nyed.uscourts.gov **Access by:** PACER dial-up, PACER online, CM/ECF.
-Brooklyn Div. Brooklyn Courthouse, 225 Cadman Plaza E, Room 130, Brooklyn, NY 11201 (physical address: Use mail address for courier delivery), 718-260-2600. **Counties:** Kings, Queens, Richmond. Cases from Nassau and Suffolk may also be filed here (but paper records and cases are heard in Central Islip Div.), but all records are available electronically trhough PACER from this Brooklyn Division.
-Central Islip Div. 100 Federal Plaza, Central Islip, NY 17722-4438 (physical address: Use mail address for courier delivery), 613-712-6000. **Counties:** Nassau, Suffolk. Cases from these counties may be filed in Brooklyn Division, but heard in Central Islip. Central Islip cases can be found on Brooklyn's PACER system.

Northern District of New York

www.nynd.uscourts.gov **Access by:** PACER dial-up, PACER online, CM/ECF.
-Albany Div. 445 Broadway, Room 509, James T Foley Courthouse, Albany, NY 12207-2924 (physical address: Use mail address for courier delivery), 518-257-1800. **Counties:** Albany, Clinton, Columbia, Essex, Greene, Rensselaer, Saratoga, Schenectady, Schoharie, Ulster, Warren, Washington
-Binghamton Div. 15 Henry St, Binghamton, NY 13902 (physical address: Use mail address for courier delivery), 607-773-2893. **Counties:** Broome, Chenango, Delaware, Franklin, Jefferson, Lewis, Otsego, St. Lawrence, TiogaThis court provides the judges for the Watertown Division.
-Syracuse Div. PO Box 7367, Syracuse, NY 13261-7367 (physical address: 100 S Clinton St, Syracuse,

NY 13261-7367), 315-234-8500. **Counties:** Cayuga, Cortland, Fulton, Hamilton, Herkimer, Madison, Montgomery, Onondaga, Oswego, Tompkins
-Utica Div. Alexander Pirnie Bldg, 10 Broad St, Utica, NY 13501 (physical address: Use mail address for courier delivery), 315-793-8151. **Counties:** Oneida

Southern District of New York

www.nysd.uscourts.gov **Access by:** phone (dockets or basic info only), PACER dial-up, CM/ECF. Opinions available at www.nysd.uscourts.gov/courtweb.
-New York City Div. 500 Pearl St, New York, NY 10007 (physical address: Use mail address for courier delivery), 212-805-0136. **Counties:** Bronx, New York. A 2nd courthouse at 40 Centre St is an Appelate Division with some District Cases heard there; search both at Pearl St location. Some cases from the counties in the White Plains Division are also assigned to this New York Division.
-White Plains Div. U.S. Courthouse, 300 Quarropas St, White Plains, NY 10601 (physical address: Use mail address for courier delivery), 914-390-4100. **Counties:** Dutchess, Orange, Putnam, Rockland, Sullivan, Westchester. Some cases may be assigned to New York Division

Western District of New York

www.nywd.uscourts.gov **Access by:** PACER dial-up, PACER online, CM/ECF.
-Buffalo Div. Room 304, 68 Court St, Buffalo, NY 14202 (physical address: Use mail address for courier delivery), 716-551-4211. **Counties:** Allegany, Cattaraugus, Chautauqua, Erie, Genesee, Niagara, Orleans, Wyoming. Prior to 1982, this division included what is now the Rochester Division
-Rochester Div. Room 2120, 100 State St, Rochester, NY 14614 (physical address: Use mail address for courier delivery), 585-263-6263. **Counties:** Chemung, Livingston, Monroe, Ontario, Schuyler, Seneca, Steuben, Wayne, Yates

North Carolina

Eastern District of North Carolina

www.nced.uscourts.gov **Access by:** phone, PACER dial-up.
-Eastern Div. Room 209, 201 S Evans St, Greenville, NC 27858-1137 (physical address: Use mail address for courier delivery), 252-830-6009. **Counties:** Beaufort, Carteret, Craven, Edgecombe, Greene, Halifax, Hyde, Jones, Lenoir, Martin, Pamlico, Pitt

-Northern Div. c/o Raleigh Division, PO Box 25670, Raleigh, NC 27611 (physical address: Room 574, 310 New Bern Ave, Raleigh, NC 27601), 919-856-4370. **Counties:** Bertie, Camden, Chowan, Currituck, Dare, Gates, Hertford, Northampton, Pasquotank, Perquimans, Tyrrell, Washington
-Southern Div. Alton Lennon Fed. Bldg, `2 Princess Street, Wilmington, NC 28401 (physical address: Room 239, 2 Princess St, Wilmington, NC 28401), 910-815-4663. **Counties:** Bladen, Brunswick, Columbus, Duplin, New Hanover, Onslow, Pender, Robeson, Sampson
-Western Div. Clerk's Office, PO Box 25670, Raleigh, NC 27611 (physical address: Room 574, 310 New Bern Ave, Raleigh, NC 27601), 919-645-1700. **Counties:** Cumberland, Franklin, Granville, Harnett, Johnston, Nash, Vance, Wake, Warren, Wayne, Wilson

Middle District of North Carolina

www.ncmd.uscourts.gov **Access by:** phone (dockets or basic info only), PACER dial-up, PACER online.
-Greensboro Div. Clerk's Office, PO Box 2708, Greensboro, NC 27402 (physical address: Room 401, 324 W Market St, Greensboro, NC 27401), 336-332-6000. **Counties:** Alamance, Cabarrus, Caswell, Chatham, Davidson, Davie, Durham, Forsyth, Guilford, Hoke, Lee, Montgomery, Moore, Orange, Person, Randolph, Richmond, Rockingham, Rowan, Scotland, Stanly, Stokes, Surry, Yadkin

Western District of North Carolina

www.ncwd.uscourts.gov **Access by:** phone, PACER dial-up, PACER online.
-Asheville Div. Clerk of the Court, Room 309, U.S. Courthouse Bldg, 100 Otis St, Asheville, NC 28801-2611 (physical address: Use mail address for courier delivery), 828-771-7200. **Counties:** Avery, Buncombe, Haywood, Henderson, Madison, Mitchell, Transylvania, Yancey
-Bryson City Div. c/o Asheville Division, Clerk of the Court, Room 309, U.S. Courthouse, 100 Otis St, Asheville, NC 28801-2611 (physical address: Use mail address for courier delivery), 828-771-7200. **Counties:** Cherokee, Clay, Graham, Jackson, Macon, Swain
-Charlotte Div. Clerk, Room 210, 401 W Trade St, Charlotte, NC 28202 (physical address: Use mail address for courier delivery), 704-350-7400. **Counties:** Anson, Gaston, Mecklenburg, Union
-Shelby Div. c/o Asheville Division, Clerk of the Court, Room 309, U.S. Courthouse, 100 Otis St, Asheville, NC 28801-2611 (physical address: Use mail

address for courier delivery), 828-771-7200. **Counties:** Burke, Cleveland, McDowell, Polk, Rutherford

-Statesville Div. PO Box 466, Statesville, NC 28687 (physical address: Room 205, 200 W Broad St, Statesville, NC 28687), 704-883-1000. **Counties:** Alexander, Alleghany, Ashe, Caldwell, Catawba, Iredell, Lincoln, Watauga, Wilkes

North Dakota

District of North Dakota

www.ndd.uscourts.gov **Access by:** phone, PACER dial-up, PACER online.

-Bismarck-Southwestern Div. PO Box 1193, Bismarck, ND 58502 (physical address: 220 E Rosser Ave, Room 476, Bismarck, ND 58501), 701-530-2300. **Counties:** Adams, Billings, Bowman, Burleigh, Dunn, Emmons, Golden Valley, Grant, Hettinger, Kidder, Logan, McIntosh, McLean, Mercer, Morton, Oliver, Sioux, Slope, Stark

-Fargo-Southeastern Div. PO Box 870, Fargo, ND 58107 (physical address: 655 1st Ave N, Fargo, ND 58102), 701-297-7000. **Counties:** Barnes, Cass, Dickey, Eddy, Foster, Griggs, La Moure, Ransom, Richland, Sargent, Steele, Stutsman. Rolette County cases prior to 1995 may be located here

-Grand Forks-Northeastern Div. c/o Fargo-Southeastern Division, 102 N 4th St, Grand Forks, ND 58201 (physical address: 655 1st Ave N, Fargo, ND 58102), 701-772-0511. **Counties:** Benson, Cavalier, Grand Forks, Nelson, Pembina, Ramsey, Towner, Traill, Walsh

-Minot-Northwestern Div. c/o Bismarck Division, PO Box 1193, Bismarck, ND 58502 (physical address: 100 1st St SW, Minot, ND 58701), 701-839-6251. **Counties:** Bottineau, Burke, Divide, McHenry, McKenzie, Mountrail, Pierce, Renville, Rolette, Sheridan, Ward, Wells, Williams. Case records from Rolette County prior to 1995 may be located in Fargo-Southeastern Division

Ohio

Northern District of Ohio

www.ohnd.uscourts.gov **Access by:** phone, PACER dial-up, PACER online, CM/ECF.

-Akron Div. 568 U.S. Courthouse, 2 S Main St, Akron, OH 44308 (physical address: Use mail address for courier delivery), 330-375-5705. **Counties:** Carroll, Holmes, Portage, Stark, Summit, Tuscarawas, Wayne. Cases filed prior to 1995 for counties in the Youngstown Division may be located here

-Cleveland Div. 801 West Superior Ave, Cleveland, OH 44114-1830 (physical address: Use mail address for courier delivery), 216-357-7000. **Counties:** Ashland, Ashtabula, Crawford, Cuyahoga, Geauga, Lake, Lorain, Medina, Richland. Cases prior to July 1995 for the counties of Ashland, Crawford, Medina and Richland are located in the Akron Division. Cases filed prior to 1995 from the counties in theYoungstown Division may be located here

-Toledo Div. 114 U.S. Courthouse, 1716 Spielbusch, Toledo, OH 43624 (physical address: Use mail address for courier delivery), 419-259-6412. **Counties:** Allen, Auglaize, Defiance, Erie, Fulton, Hancock, Hardin, Henry, Huron, Lucas, Marion, Mercer, Ottawa, Paulding, Putnam, Sandusky, Seneca, Van Wert, Williams, Wood, Wyandot

-Youngstown Div. 337 Federal Bldg, 125 Market St, Youngstown, OH 44503-1780 (physical address: Use mail address for courier delivery), 330-746-1906. **Counties:** Columbiana, Mahoning, Trumbull. This division was re-activated in the middle of 1995. Older cases will be found in Akron or Cleveland

Southern District of Ohio

www.ohsd.uscourts.gov **Access by:** phone, PACER dial-up, PACER online, CM/ECF.

-Cincinnati Div. Clerk, U.S. District Court, Potter Stewart Courthouse Rm 324, 100 E 5th St, Cincinnati, OH 45202 (physical address: Use mail address for courier delivery), 513-564-7500. **Counties:** Adams, Brown, Butler, Clermont, Clinton, Hamilton, Highland, Lawrence, Scioto, Warren

-Columbus Div. Office of the clerk, Room 260, 85 Marconi Blvd, Columbus, OH 43215 (physical address: Use mail address for courier delivery), 614-719-3000. **Counties:** Athens, Belmont, Coshocton, Delaware, Fairfield, Fayette, Franklin, Gallia, Guernsey, Harrison, Hocking, Jackson, Jefferson, Knox, Licking, Logan, Madison, Meigs, Monroe, Morgan, Morrow, Muskingum, Noble, Perry, Pickaway, Pike, Ross, Union, Vinton,Washington

-Dayton Div. Federal Bldg, 200 W 2nd, Room 712, Dayton, OH 45402 (physical address: Use mail address for courier delivery), 937-512-1400. **Counties:** Champaign, Clark, Darke, Greene, Miami, Montgomery, Preble, Shelby

Oklahoma

Eastern District of Oklahoma

www.oked.uscourts.gov **Access by:** phone, PACER dial-up.

-Muskogee Div. Clerk, PO Box 607, Muskogee, OK 74401 (physical address: 101 N 5th, Muskogee, OK 74401), 918-684-7920. **Counties:** Adair, Atoka, Bryan, Carter, Cherokee, Choctaw, Coal, Haskell, Hughes, Johnston, Latimer, Le Flore, Love, McCurtain, McIntosh, Marshall, Murray, Muskogee, Okfuskee, Pittsburg, Pontotoc, Pushmataha, Seminole, Sequoyah, Wagoner

Northern District of Oklahoma

www.oknd.uscourts.gov **Access by:** phone, PACER dial-up, PACER online, CM/ECF, or on the web.

-Tulsa Div. 411 U.S. Courthouse, 333 W 4th St, Tulsa, OK 74103 (physical address: Use mail address for courier delivery), 918-699-4700. **Counties:** Craig, Creek, Delaware, Mayes, Nowata, Okmulgee, Osage, Ottawa, Pawnee, Rogers, Tulsa, Washington

Western District of Oklahoma

www.okwd.uscourts.gov **Access by:** phone, PACER dial-up, PACER online, CM/ECF.

-Oklahoma City Div. Clerk, Room 1210, 200 NW 4th St, Oklahoma City, OK 73102 (physical address: Use mail address for courier delivery), 405-609-5000. **Counties:** Alfalfa, Beaver, Beckham, Blaine, Caddo, Canadian, Cimarron, Cleveland, Comanche, Cotton, Custer, Dewey, Ellis, Garfield, Garvin, Grady, Grant, Greer, Harmon, Harper, Jackson, Jefferson, Kay, Kingfisher, Kiowa, Lincoln, Logan, McClain, Major, Noble,Oklahoma, Payne, Pottawatomie, Roger Mills, Stephens, Texas, Tillman, Washita, Woods, Woodward

Oregon

District of Oregon

www.ord.uscourts.gov **Access by:** phone, PACER dial-up, PACER online, CM/ECF, or on the web.

-Eugene Div. 100 Federal Bldg, 211 E 7th Ave, Eugene, OR 97401 (physical address: Use mail address for courier), 541-465-6423. **Counties:** Benton, Coos, Deschutes, Douglas, Lane, Lincoln, Linn, Marion

-Medford Div. 201 James A Redden U.S. Courthouse, 310 W 6th St, Medford, OR 97501 (physical address: Use mail address for courier delivery), 541-776-3926. **Counties:** Curry, Jackson, Josephine, Klamath, Lake. Court set up in April 1994; Cases prior to that time were tried in Eugene

-Portland Div. Clerk, 740 U.S. Courthouse, 1000 SW 3rd Ave, Portland, OR 97204-2902 (physical address: Use mail address for courier delivery), 503-326-8000. **Counties:** Baker, Clackamas, Clatsop, Columbia, Crook, Gilliam, Grant, Harney, Hood River, Jefferson, Malheur, Morrow, Multnomah, Polk, Sherman, Tillamook, Umatilla, Union, Wallowa, Wasco, Washinton, Wheeler, Yamhill

Pennsylvania

Eastern District of Pennsylvania

www.paed.uscourts.gov **Access by:** PACER dial-up, PACER online, CM/ECF, or on the web. Opinions available at www.paed.uscourts.gov/contents.shtml.

-Allentown/Reading Div. c/o Philadelphia Division, Room 2609, U.S. Courthouse, 601 Market St, Philadelphia, PA 19106-1797 (physical address: Use mail address for courier), 215-597-7704. **Counties:** Berks, Lancaster, Lehigh, Northampton, Schuylkill

-Philadelphia Div. Room 2609, U.S. Courthouse, 601 Market St, Philadelphia, PA 19106-1797 (physical address: Use mail address for courier delivery), 215-597-7704. **Counties:** Bucks, Chester, Delaware, Montgomery, Philadelphia

Middle District of Pennsylvania

www.pamd.uscourts.gov **Access by:** phone (dockets or basic information only), fax, PACER dial-up, PACER online, CM/ECF, or on the web.

-Harrisburg Div. PO Box 983, Harrisburg, PA 17108-0983 (physical address: U.S. Courthouse & Federal Bldg, 228 Walnut St, Harrisburg, PA 17108), 717-221-3920. **Counties:** Adams, Cumberland, Dauphin, Franklin, Fulton, Huntingdon, Juniata, Lebanon, Mifflin, York

-Scranton Div. Clerk's Office, William J Nealon Fedearl Bldg & U.S. Courthouse, PO Box 1148, Scranton, PA 18501 (physical address: 235 N Washington Ave, Room 101, Scranton, PA 18503), 570-207-5680. **Counties:** Bradford, Carbon, Lackawanna, Luzerne, Monroe, Pike, Susquehanna, Wayne, Wyoming

-Williamsport Div. PO Box 608, Williamsport, PA 17703 (physical address: Federal Bldg, ROom 218, 240 W 3rd St, Williamsport, PA 17701), 570-323-6380. **Counties:** Cameron, Centre, Clinton, Columbia, Lycoming, Montour, Northumberland, Perry, Potter, Snyder, Sullivan, Tioga, Union

Western District of Pennsylvania

www.pawd.uscourts.gov **Access by:** phone, PACER dial-up, PACER online.
-Erie Div. PO Box 1820, Erie, PA 16507 (physical address: 102 U.S. Courthouse, 617 State St, Erie, PA 16501), 814-453-4829. **Counties:** Crawford, Elk, Erie, Forest, McKean, Venango, Warren
-Johnstown Div. Penn Traffic Bldg, Room 208, 319 Washington St, Johnstown, PA 15901 (physical address: Use mail address for courier delivery), 814-533-4504. **Counties:** Bedford, Blair, Cambria, Clearfield, Somerset
-Pittsburgh Div. U.S. Post Office & Courthouse, Room 829, 7th Ave & Grant St, Pittsburgh, PA 15219 (physical address: Use mail address for courier delivery), 412-208-7500. **Counties:** Allegheny, Armstrong, Beaver, Butler, Clarion, Fayette, Greene, Indiana, Jefferson, Lawrence, Mercer, Washington, Westmoreland

Puerto Rico

www.prd.uscourts.gov **Access by:** PACER dial-up, PACER online, or on the web. Address: Clemente-Ruiz-Nazario U.S. Courthouse, 150 Carlos Chardon St, Hato Rey, Puerto Rico 00918, 787-772-3000. **Counties:** All counties.

Rhode Island

District of Rhode Island

www.rid.uscourts.gov **Access by:** phone, PACER dial-up, PACER online.
-Providence Div. Clerk's Office, One Exchange Terrace, Federal Bldg, Providence, RI 02903 (physical address: Use mail address for courier delivery), 401-752-7200. **Counties:** All counties in Rhode Island

South Carolina

District of South Carolina

www.scd.uscourts.gov **Access by:** PACER dial-up, PACER online. Opinions are available online at www.law.sc.edu/dsc/dsc.htm.
-Anderson Div. c/o Greenville Division, PO Box 10768, Greenville, SC 29603 (physical address: 300 E Washington St, Greenville, SC 29601), 864-241-2700. **Counties:** Anderson, Oconee, Pickens
-Beaufort Div. c/o Charleston Division, PO Box 835, Charleston, SC 29402 (physical address: 85 Broad St, Hollings Judicial Center, Charleston, SC 29401), 843-579-1401. **Counties:** Beaufort, Hampton, Jasper

-Charleston Div. PO Box 835, Charleston, SC 29402 (physical address: 85 Broad St, Hollings Judicial Center, Charleston, SC 29401), 843-579-1401. **Counties:** Berkeley, Charleston, Clarendon, Colleton, Dorchester, Georgetown
-Columbia Div. 1845 Assembly St, Columbia, SC 29201 (physical address: Use mail address for courier delivery), 803-765-5816. **Counties:** Kershaw, Lee, Lexington, Richland, Sumter
-Florence Div. PO Box 2317, Florence, SC 29503 (physical address: 401 W Evans St, McMillan Federal Bldg, Room 361, Florence, SC 29501), 843-676-3820. **Counties:** Chesterfield, Darlington, Dillon, Florence, Horry, Marion, Marlboro, Williamsburg
-Greenville Div. PO Box 10768, Greenville, SC 29603 (physical address: 300 E Washington St, Greenville, SC 29601), 864-241-2700. **Counties:** Greenville, Laurens
-Greenwood Div. c/o Greenville Division, PO Box 10768, Greenville, SC 29603 (physical address: 300 E Washington St, Greenville, SC 29601), 864-241-2700. **Counties:** Abbeville, Aiken, Allendale, Bamberg, Barnwell, Calhoun, Edgefield, Fairfield, Greenwood, Lancaster, McCormick, Newberry, Orangeburg, Saluda
-Spartanburg Div. c/o Greenville Division, PO Box 10768, Greenville, SC 29603 (physical address: 300 E Washington St, Greenville, SC 29601), 864-241-2700. **Counties:** Cherokee, Chester, Spartanburg, Union, York

South Dakota

District of South Dakota

www.sdd.uscourts.gov **Access by:** PACER dial-up, PACER online, CM/ECF, or on the web.
-Aberdeen Div. c/o Pierre Division, Federal Bldg & Courthouse, 225 S Pierre St, Room 405, Pierre, SD 57501 (physical address: Use mail address for courier delivery), 605-224-5849. **Counties:** Brown, Campbell, Clark, Codington, Corson, Day, Deuel, Edmunds, Grant, Hamlin, McPherson, Marshall, Roberts, Spink, Walworth. Judge Battey's closed case records are located at the Rapid City Division
-Pierre Div. Federal Bldg & Courthouse, Room 405, 225 S Pierre St, Pierre, SD 57501 (physical address: Use mail address for courier delivery), 605-224-5849. **Counties:** Buffalo, Dewey, Faulk, Gregory, Haakon, Hand, Hughes, Hyde, Jackson, Jerauld, Jones, Lyman, Mellette, Potter, Stanley, Sully, Todd, Tripp, Ziebach
-Rapid City Div. Clerk's Office, Room 302, 515 9th St, Rapid City, SD 57701 (physical address: Use mail address for courier delivery), 605-343-3744. **Counties:**

Bennett, Butte, Custer, Fall River, Harding, Lawrence, Meade, Pennington, Perkins, Shannon. Judge Battey's closed cases are located here.
-Sioux Falls Div. P.O. Box 5060, Sioux Falls, SD 57117-5060 (physical address: Room 128, U.S. Courthouse, 400 S Phillips Ave, Sioux Falls, SD 57104-6851), 605-330-4447. **Counties:** Aurora, Beadle, Bon Homme, Brookings, Brule, Charles Mix, Clay, Davison, Douglas, Hanson, Hutchinson, Kingsbury, Lake, Lincoln, McCook, Miner, Minnehaha, Moody, Sanborn, Turner, Union, Yankton

Tennessee

Eastern District of Tennessee

www.tned.uscourts.gov **Access by:** phone, PACER dial-up, PACER online, CM/ECF.
-Chattanooga Div. Clerk's Office, PO Box 591, Chattanooga, TN 37401 (physical address: Room 309, 900 Georgia Ave, Chattanooga, TN 37402), 423-752-5200. **Counties:** Bledsoe, Bradley, Hamilton, McMinn, Marion, Meigs, Polk, Rhea, Sequatchie
-Greeneville Div. U.S. District Court, 220 West Depot Street, Ste 200, Greenville, TN 37743 (physical address: Use mail address for courier delivery), 423-639-3105. **Counties:** Carter, Cocke, Greene, Hamblen, Hancock, Hawkins, Johnson, Sullivan, Unicoi, Washington
-Knoxville Div. Clerk's Office, 800 Market St Ste 130, Knoxville, TN 37902 (physical address: Use mail address for courier delivery), 865-545-4228. **Counties:** Anderson, Blount, Campbell, Claiborne, Grainger, Jefferson, Knox, Loudon, Monroe, Morgan, Roane, Scott, Sevier, Union
-Winchester Div. PO Box 459, Winchester, TN 37398 (physical address: 200 S Jefferson St, Room 201, Winchester, TN 37397), 931-967-1444. **Counties:** Bedford, Coffee, Franklin, Grundy, Lincoln, Moore, Van Buren, Warren

Middle District of Tennessee

www.tnmd.uscourts.gov **Access by:** PACER dial-up, PACER online, CM/ECF.
-Columbia Div. c/o Nashville Division, 800 U.S. Courthouse, 801 Broadway, Nashville, TN 37203 (physical address: Use mail address for courier delivery), 615-736-5498. **Counties:** Giles, Hickman, Lawrence, Lewis, Marshall, Maury, Wayne
-Cookeville Div. c/o Nashville Division, 800 U.S. Courthouse, 801 Broadway, Nashville, TN 37203 (physical address: Use mail address for courier delivery), 615-736-5498. **Counties:** Clay, Cumberland,

De Kalb, Fentress, Jackson, Macon, Overton, Pickett, Putnam, Smith, White
-Nashville Div. 800 U.S. Courthouse, 801 Broadway, Nashville, TN 37203 (physical address: Use mail address for courier delivery), 615-736-5498. **Counties:** Cannon, Cheatham, Davidson, Dickson, Houston, Humphreys, Montgomery, Robertson, Rutherford, Stewart, Sumner, Trousdale, Williamson, Wilson

Western District of Tennessee

www.tnwd.uscourts.gov **Access by:** phone, PACER dial-up, PACER online, CM/ECF.
-Jackson Div. Rm 26, U.S. Courthouse 262, 111 S Highland, Jackson, TN 38301 (physical address: Use mail address for courier delivery), 731-421-9200. **Counties:** Benton, Carroll, Chester, Crockett, Decatur, Gibson, Hardeman, Hardin, Haywood, Henderson, Henry, Lake, McNairy, Madison, Obion, Perry, Weakley
-Memphis Div. Federal Bldg, Room 242, 167 N Main, Memphis, TN 38103 (physical address: Use mail address for courier delivery), 901-495-1200. **Counties:** Dyer, Fayette, Lauderdale, Shelby, Tipton

Texas

Eastern District of Texas

www.txed.uscourts.gov **Access by:** phone, PACER dial-up, PACER online, CM/ECF.
-Beaumont Div. PO Box 3507, Beaumont, TX 77704 (physical address: Room 104, 300 Willow, Beaumont, TX 77701), 409-654-7000. **Counties:** Delta*, Fannin*, Hardin, Hopkins*, Jasper, Jefferson, Lamar*, Liberty, Newton, Orange, Red River. Counties marked with an asterisk are called the Paris Division, whose case records are maintained here.
-Lufkin Div. 104 N. Third St, Lufkin, TX 75901 (physical address: Use mail address for courier delivery), 936-632-2739. **Counties:** Angelina, Houston, Nacogdoches, Polk, Sabine, San Augustine, Shelby, Trinity, Tyler
-Marshall Div. PO Box 1499, Marshall, TX 75671-1499 (physical address: 100 E Houston, Marshall, TX 75670), 903-935-2912. **Counties:** Camp, Cass, Harrison, Marion, Morris, Upshur
-Sherman Div. 101 E Pecan St Rm112, Sherman, TX 75090 (physical address: Use mail address for courier delivery), 903-892-2921. **Counties:** Collin, Cooke, Denton, Grayson.
-Texarkana Div. Clerk's Office, 500 State Line Ave, Room 301, Texarkana, TX 75501 (physical address:

Use mail address for courier delivery), 903-794-8561.
Counties: Bowie, Franklin, Titus
-Tyler Div. Clerk, Room 106, 211 W Ferguson, Tyler, TX 75702 (physical address: Use mail address for courier delivery), 903-590-1000. **Counties:** Anderson, Cherokee, Gregg, Henderson, Panola, Rains, Rusk, Smith, Van Zandt, Wood

Northern District of Texas

www.txnd.uscourts.gov **Access by:** phone, PACER dial-up, PACER online, CM/ECF.
-Abilene Div. PO Box 1218, Abilene, TX 79604 (physical address: Room 2008, 341 Pine St, Abilene, TX 79601), 915-677-6311. **Counties:** Callahan, Eastland, Fisher, Haskell, Howard, Jones, Mitchell, Nolan, Shackelford, Stephens, Stonewall, Taylor, Throckmorton
-Amarillo Div. 205 E 5th St, Amarillo, TX 79101 (physical address: Use mail address for courier delivery), 806-324-2352. **Counties:** Armstrong, Briscoe, Carson, Castro, Childress, Collingsworth, Dallam, Deaf Smith, Donley, Gray, Hall, Hansford, Hartley, Hemphill, Hutchinson, Lipscomb, Moore, Ochiltree, Oldham, Parmer, Potter, Randall, Roberts, Sherman, Swisher, Wheeler
-Dallas Div. Room 1452, 1100 Commerce St, Dallas, TX 75242 (physical address: Use mail address for courier delivery), 214-753-2200. **Counties:** Dallas, Ellis, Hunt, Johnson, Kaufman, Navarro, Rockwall
-Fort Worth Div. Clerk's Office, 501 W Tenth St, Room 310, Fort Worth, TX 76102 (physical address: Use mail address for courier delivery), 817-978-3132. **Counties:** Comanche, Erath, Hood, Jack, Palo Pinto, Parker, Tarrant, Wise
-Lubbock Div. Clerk, Room 209, 1205 Texas Ave, Lubbock, TX 79401 (physical address: Use mail address for courier delivery), 806-472-7624. **Counties:** Bailey, Borden, Cochran, Crosby, Dawson, Dickens, Floyd, Gaines, Garza, Hale, Hockley, Kent, Lamb, Lubbock, Lynn, Motley, Scurry, Terry, Yoakum
-San Angelo Div. Clerk's Office, Room 202, 33 E Twohig, San Angelo, TX 76903 (physical address: Use mail address for courier delivery), 325-655-4506. **Counties:** Brown, Coke, Coleman, Concho, Crockett, Glasscock, Irion, Menard, Mills, Reagan, Runnels, Schleicher, Sterling, Sutton, Tom Green
-Wichita Falls Div. PO Box 1234, Wichita Falls, TX 76307 (physical address: Room 203, 1000 Lamar, Wichita Falls, TX 76301), 940-767-1902. **Counties:** Archer, Baylor, Clay, Cottle, Foard, Hardeman, King, Knox, Montague, Wichita, Wilbarger, Young

Southern District of Texas

www.txsd.uscourts.gov **Access by:** phone, PACER dial-up, PACER online, CM/ECF.
-Brownsville Div. 600 E Harrison St Rm 101, Brownsville, TX 78520-7114 (physical address: Use mail address for courier delivery, 600 E Harrison St #101,), 956-548-2500. **Counties:** Cameron, Willacy
-Corpus Christi Div. Clerk's Office, 1133 N. Shoreline Blvd, #208, Corpus Christi, TX 78401 (physical address: Use mail address for courier delivery), 361-888-3142. **Counties:** Aransas, Bee, Brooks, Duval, Jim Wells, Kenedy, Kleberg, Live Oak, Nueces, San Patricio
-Galveston Div. Clerk's Office, PO Box 2300, Galveston, TX 77553 (physical address: 601 Rosenberg, Room 411, Galveston, TX 77550), 409-766-3530. **Counties:** Brazoria, Chambers, Galveston, Matagorda
-Houston Div. PO Box 61010, Houston, TX 77208 (physical address: Room 1217, 515 Rusk, Houston, TX 77002), 713-250-5500. **Counties:** Austin, Brazos, Colorado, Fayette, Fort Bend, Grimes, Harris, Madison, Montgomery, San Jacinto, Walker, Waller, Wharton
-Laredo Div. PO Box 597, Laredo, TX 78042-0597 (physical address: Room 319, 1300 Matamoros, Laredo, TX 78040), 956-723-3542. **Counties:** Jim Hogg, La Salle, McMullen, Webb, Zapata
-McAllen Div. Suite 1011, 1701 W Business Hwy 83, McAllen, TX 78501 (physical address: Use mail address for courier delivery), 956-618-8065. **Counties:** Hidalgo, Starr
-Victoria Div. Clerk U.S. District Court, PO Box 1638, Victoria, TX 77902 (physical address: Room 406, 312 S Main, Victoria, TX 77901), 361-788-5000. **Counties:** Calhoun, De Witt, Goliad, Jackson, Lavaca, Refugio, Victoria

Western District of Texas

www.txwd.uscourts.gov **Access by:** phone, PACER dial-up, PACER online.
-Austin Div. Room 130, 200 W 8th St, Austin, TX 78701 (physical address: Use mail address for courier delivery), 512-916-5896. **Counties:** Bastrop, Blanco, Burleson, Burnet, Caldwell, Gillespie, Hays, Kimble, Lampasas, Lee, Llano, McCulloch, Mason, San Saba, Travis, Washington, Williamson
-Del Rio Div. Room L100, 111 E Broadway, Del Rio, TX 78840 (physical address: Use mail address for courier delivery), 830-703-2054. **Counties:** Edwards, Kinney, Maverick, Terrell, Uvalde, Val Verde, Zavala

-El Paso Div. U.S. District Clerk's Office, Room 350, 511 E San Antonio, El Paso, TX 79901 (physical address: Use mail address for courier delivery), 915-534-6725. **Counties:** El Paso

-Midland Div. Clerk, U.S. District Court, 200 E Wall St, Rm 107, Midland, TX 79701 (physical address: Use mail address for courier delivery), 432-686-4001. **Counties:** Andrews, Crane, Ector, Martin, Midland, Upton

-Pecos Div. U.S. Courthouse, 410 S Cedar St, Pecos, TX 79772 (physical address: Use mail address for courier delivery), 432-445-4228. **Counties:** Brewster, Culberson, Hudspeth, Jeff Davis, Loving, Pecos, Presidio, Reeves, Ward, Winkler

-San Antonio Div. U.S. Clerk's Office, 655 E Durango Blvd, Suite G-65, San Antonio, TX 78206 (physical address: Use mail address for courier delivery), 210-472-6550. **Counties:** Atascosa, Bandera, Bexar, Comal, Dimmit, Frio, Gonzales, Guadalupe, Karnes, Kendall, Kerr, Medina, Real, Wilson

-Waco Div. Clerk, Room 303, 800 Franklin, Waco, TX 76701 (physical address: Use mail address for courier delivery), 254-750-1501. **Counties:** Bell, Bosque, Coryell, Falls, Freestone, Hamilton, Hill, Leon, Limestone, McLennan, Milam, Robertson, Somervell

Utah

District of Utah

www.utd.uscourts.gov **Access by:** phone, PACER dial-up, PACER online, CM/ECF.
Clerk's Office, Room 150, 350 S Main St, Salt Lake City, UT 84101-2180 (physical address: Use mail address for courier delivery), 801-524-6100. **Counties:** All counties in Utah. Although all cases are heard here, the district is divided into Northern and Central Divisions. The Northern Division includes the counties of Box Elder, Cache, Rich, Davis, Morgan and Weber, and the Central Division includes allother counties

Vermont

District of Vermont

www.vtd.uscourts.gov **Access by:** phone, PACER dial-up, or on the web.
-Burlington Div. Clerk's Office, PO Box 945, Burlington, VT 05402-0945 (physical address: Room 506, 11 Elmwood Ave, Burlington, VT 05401), 802-951-6301. **Counties:** Caledonia, Chittenden, Essex, Franklin, Grand Isle, Lamoille, Orleans, Washington.

However, cases from all counties in the state are assigned randomly to either Burlington or Brattleboro. Brattleboro is a hearing location only, not listed here
-Rutland Div. PO Box 607, Rutland, VT 05702-0607 (physical address: 151 West St, Rutland, VT 05701), 802-773-0245. **Counties:** Addison, Bennington, Orange, Rutland, Windsor, Windham. However, cases from all counties in the state are randomly assigned to either Burlington or Brattleboro. Rutland is a hearing location only, not listed here

Virginia

Eastern District of Virginia

www.vaed.uscourts.gov **Access by:** phone, PACER dial-up, PACER online.
-Alexandria Div. 401 Courthouse Square, Alexandria, VA 22314 (physical address: Use mail address for courier delivery), 703-299-2100. **Counties:** Arlington, Fairfax, Fauquier, Loudoun, Prince William, Stafford, City of Alexandria, City of Fairfax, City of Falls Church, City of Manassas, City of Manassas Park

-Newport News Div. Clerk's Office, PO Box 494, Newport News, VA 23607 (physical address: U.S. Post Office Bldg, Room 201, 101 25th St, Newport News, VA 23607), 757-247-0784. **Counties:** Gloucester, James City, Mathews, York, City of Hampton, City of Newport News, City of Poquoson, City of Williamsburg

-Norfolk Div. U.S. Courthouse, Room 193, 600 Granby St, Norfolk, VA 23510 (physical address: Use mail address for courier delivery), 757-222-7204. **Counties:** Accomack, City of Chesapeake, City of Franklin, Isle of Wight, City of Norfolk, Northampton, City of Portsmouth, City of Suffolk, Southampton, City of Virginia Beach

-Richmond Div. Lewis F Powell, Jr Courthouse Bldg, 1000 E Main St, Room 305, Richmond, VA 23219-3525 (physical address: Use mail address for courier delivery), 804-916-2200. **Counties:** Amelia, Brunswick, Caroline, Charles City, Chesterfield, Dinwiddie, Essex, Goochland, Greensville, Hanover, Henrico, King and Queen, King George, King William, Lancaster, Lunenburg, Mecklenburg, Middlesex, New Kent, Northumberland, Nottoway, City ofPetersburg, Powhatan, Prince Edward, Prince George, Richmond, City of Richmond, Spotsylvania, Surry, Sussex, Westmoreland, City of Colonial Heights, City of Emporia, City of Fredericksburg, City of Hopewell

Western District of Virginia

www.vawd.uscourts.gov **Access by:** phone, fax, PACER dial-up, PACER online, CM/ECF.

-Abingdon Div. Clerk's Office, PO Box 398, Abingdon, VA 24212 (physical address: 180 W Main St, Abingdon, VA 24210), 276-628-5116. **Counties:** Buchanan, City of Bristol, Russell, Smyth, Tazewell, Washington

-Big Stone Gap Div. PO Box 490, Big Stone Gap, VA 24219 (physical address: 322 Wood Ave E, Room 204, Big Stone Gap, VA 24219), 276-523-3557. **Counties:** Dickenson, Lee, Scott, Wise, City of Norton

-Charlottesville Div. Clerk, Room 304, 255 W Main St, Charlottesville, VA 22902 (physical address: Use mail address for courier delivery), 434-296-9284. **Counties:** Albemarle, Culpeper, Fluvanna, Greene, Louisa, Madison, Nelson, Orange, Rappahannock, City of Charlottesville

-Danville Div. PO Box 1400, Danville, VA 24543-0053 (physical address: Dan Daniel Post Office Bldg, Room 202, 700 Main St, Danville, VA 24541), 434-793-7147. **Counties:** Charlotte, Halifax, Henry, Patrick, Pittsylvania, City of Danville, City of Martinsville, City of South Boston

-Harrisonburg Div. Clerk, PO Box 1207, Harrisonburg, VA 22803 (physical address: Post Office Bldg, 116 N Main St, Room 314, Harrisonburg, VA 22802), 540-434-3181. **Counties:** Augusta, Bath, Clarke, Frederick, Highland, Page, Rockingham, Shenandoah, Warren, City of Harrisonburg, City of Staunton, City of Waynesboro, City of Winchester

-Lynchburg Div. Clerk, PO Box 744, Lynchburg, VA 24505 (physical address: Room 212, 1100 Main St, Lynchburg, VA 24504), 434-847-5722. **Counties:** Amherst, Appomattox, Bedford, Buckingham, Campbell, Cumberland, Rockbridge, City of Bedford, Buena Vista City, Lexington City, City of Lynchburg

-Roanoke Div. Clerk, PO Box 1234, Roanoke, VA 24006 (physical address: 210 Franklin Rd SW, Roanoke, VA 24011), 540-857-5100. **Counties:** Alleghany, Bland, Botetourt, Carroll, Craig, Floyd, Franklin, Giles, Grayson, Montgomery, Pulaski, Roanoke, Wythe, City of Covington, City of Clifton Forge, City of Galax, City of Radford, City of Roanoke, City of Salem

Washington

Eastern District of Washington

www.waed.uscourts.gov **Access by:** PACER dial-up, PACER online.

-Spokane Div. PO Box 1493, Spokane, WA 99210-1493 (physical address: Room 840, W 920 Riverside, Spokane, WA 99201), 509-353-2150. **Counties:** Adams, Asotin, Benton, Chelan, Columbia, Douglas, Ferry, Franklin, Garfield, Grant, Lincoln, Okanogan, Pend Oreille, Spokane, Stevens, Walla Walla, Whitman. Also, some cases from Kittitas, Klickitat and Yakima are heard here

-Yakima Div. PO Box 2706, Yakima, WA 98907 (physical address: Room 215, 25 S 3rd St, Yakima, WA 98901), 509-575-5838. **Counties:** Kittitas, Klickitat, Yakima. Cases assigned primarily to Judge McDonald are here. Some cases from Kittitas, Klickitat and Yakima are heard in Spokane.

Western District of Washington

www.wawd.uscourts.gov **Access by:** phone, PACER dial-up, PACER online, CM/ECF.

-Seattle Div. Clerk of Court, 215 U.S. Courthouse, 1010 5th Ave, Seattle, WA 98104 (physical address: Use mail address for courier delivery), 206-553-5598. **Counties:** Island, King, San Juan, Skagit, Snohomish, Whatcom

-Tacoma Div. Clerk's Office, Room 3100, 1717 Pacific Ave, Tacoma, WA 98402-3200 (physical address: Use mail address for courier delivery), 253-593-6313. **Counties:** Clallam, Clark, Cowlitz, Grays Harbor, Jefferson, Kitsap, Lewis, Mason, Pacific, Pierce, Skamania, Thurston, Wahkiakum

West Virginia

Northern District of West Virginia

www.wvnd.uscourts.gov **Access by:** phone, PACER dial-up, PACER online.

-Clarksburg Div. PO Box 2857, Clarksburg, WV 26302-2857 (physical address: 500 W Pike St, Rm 301, Clarksburg, WV 26301), 304-622-8513. **Counties:** Braxton, Calhoun, Doddridge, Gilmer, Harrison, Lewis, Marion, Monongalia, Pleasants, Ritchie, Taylor, Tyler

-Elkins Div. PO Box 1518, Elkins, WV 26241 (physical address: 2nd Floor, 300 3rd St, Elkins, WV 26241), 304-636-1445. **Counties:** Barbour, Grant, Hardy, Mineral, Pendleton, Pocahontas, Preston, Randolph, Tucker, Upshur, Webster

-Martinsburg Div. Room 207, 217 W King St, Martinsburg, WV 25401 (physical address: Use mail address for courier delivery), 304-267-8225. **Counties:** Berkeley, Hampshire, Jefferson, Morgan

-Wheeling Div. Clerk, PO Box 471, Wheeling, WV 26003 (physical address: 12th & Chapline Sts, Wheeling, WV 26003), 304-232-0011. **Counties:** Brooke, Hancock, Marshall, Ohio, Wetzel

Southern District of West Virginia

www.wvsd.uscourts.gov **Access by:** phone, fax, PACER dial-up, PACER online.

-Beckley Div. PO Drawer 5009, Beckley, WV 25801 (physical address: 110 N. Heber, Beckley, WV 25801), 304-253-7481. **Counties:** Fayette, Greenbrier, Raleigh, Sumners, Wyoming

-Bluefield Div. Clerk's Office, PO Box 4128, Bluefield, WV 24701 (physical address: 601 Federal St, Bluefield, WV 24701), 304-327-9798. **Counties:** McDowell, Mercer, Monroe

-Charleston Div. PO Box 3924, Charleston, WV 25339 (physical address: 300 Virginia St E, #2400, Charleston, WV 25339), 304-347-3000. **Counties:** Boone, Clay, Jackson, Kanawha, Lincoln, Logan, Mingo, Nicholas, Putnam, Roane

-Huntington Div. Clerk of Court, PO Box 1570, Huntington, WV 25716 (physical address: Room 101, 845 5th Ave, Huntington, WV 25701), 304-529-5588. **Counties:** Cabell, Mason, Wayne

-Parkersburg Div. Clerk of Court, PO Box 1526, Parkersburg, WV 26102 (physical address: Room 5102, 425 Julianna St, Parkersburg, WV 26101), 304-420-6490. **Counties:** Wirt, Wood

Wisconsin

Eastern District of Wisconsin

www.wied.uscourts.gov **Access by:** phone, PACER dial-up, PACER online, CM/ECF.

-Milwaukee Div. Clerk's Office, Room 362, 517 E Wisconsin Ave, Milwaukee, WI 53202 (physical address: Use mail address for courier delivery), 414-297-3372. **Counties:** Brown, Calumet, Dodge, Door, Florence, Fond du Lac, Forest, Green Lake, Kenosha, Kewaunee, Langlade, Manitowoc, Marinette, Marquette, Menominee, Milwaukee, Oconto, Outagamie, Ozaukee, Racine, Shawano, Sheboygan, Walworth, Washington, Waukesha, Waupaca, Waushara, Winnebago

Western District of Wisconsin

www.wiw.uscourts.gov **Access by:** phone, PACER dial-up, PACER online.

-Madison Div. PO Box 432, Madison, WI 53701 (physical address: 120 N Henry St, Madison, WI 53703), 608-264-5156. **Counties:** Adams, Ashland, Barron, Bayfield, Buffalo, Burnett, Chippewa, Clark, Columbia, Crawford, Dane, Douglas, Dunn, Eau Claire, Grant, Green, Iowa, Iron, Jackson, Jefferson, Juneau, La Crosse, Lafayette, Lincoln, Marathon, Monroe, Oneida, Pepin, Pierce, Polk,Portage, Price, Richland, Rock, Rusk, Sauk, Sawyer, St. Croix, Taylor, Trempealeau, Vernon, Vilas, Washburn, Wood

Wyoming

District of Wyoming

www.ck10.uscourts.gov/wyoming/district/index.html **Access by:** PACER dial-up, PACER online, CM/ECF.

-Cheyenne Div. 2120 Capitol Ave, Room 2141, Cheyenne, WY 82001 (physical address: Room 2141, 2120 Capitol Ave, Cheyenne, WY 82001), 307-433-2120. **Counties:** All counties in Wyoming. Some criminal records are held in Casper, but all are available electronically here.

Section 5

Appendix

Appendix 1: State Charts

   - State Membership in Compacts

   - State Criminal Records - Required Data to be
        Submitted to State Criminal Record Agencies

Appendix 2: Fair Credit Reporting Act Summaries

Appendix 3: Title VII EEOC Notices

Appendix 4: Common Criminal Record Terms

Appendix 5: Common Criminal Record Abbreviations

Appendix 1

State Membership in Compacts

There are three information sharing compacts that a state may participate in:
1. The Interstate Identification Index, or III. 2. The National Crime Prevention Compact.
3. National Fingerprint File, or NFF.

"X" indicates that state is a participating member.

State	III - Interstate ID Index	Nat. Crime Prevention Compact	NFF	State	III - Interstate ID Index	Nat. Crime Prevention Compact	NFF
Alabama	X			Missouri			
Alaska	X			Montana	X	X	
Arizona	X			Nebraska	X		
Arkansas	X			Nevada	X	X	
California	X			New Hampshire	X		
Colorado	X	X		New Jersey	X		X
Connecticut	X	X		New Mexico	X		
Delaware	X			New York	X		
Dist. of Columbia				North Carolina	X		X
Florida	X	X	X	North Dakota	X		
Georgia	X	X		Ohio	X		
Hawaii				Oklahoma	X		
Idaho	X			Oregon	X		X
Illinois	X			Pennsylvania	X		
Indiana	X			Rhode Island	X		
Iowa	X	X		South Carolina	X	X	
Kansas		X		South Dakota	X		
Kentucky				Tennessee			
Louisiana				Texas	X		
Maine		X		Utah	X		
Maryland				Vermont			
Massachusetts	X			Virginia	X		
Michigan	X			Washington	X		
Minnesota	X			West Virginia	X		
Mississippi	X			Wisconsin	X		
				Wyoming	X		

Appendix 1, Part 2

State Criminal Records - Required Data to be Submitted to State Criminal Record Agencies

By state statute or agreement, certain data related to criminal records must be submitted for entry into the state central criminal records system.

"X" indicates that the data is required to be submitted to the state criminal records agency.

State	Prosecutor Declinations	Court felony dispositions w/ felony jurisdiction	Admission/ Release of felons - state prisons	Admission/ Release of felons - local jails	Probation Information	Parole information
Alabama		X	X	X		
Alaska	X	X	X	X	X	X
Arizona	X	X	X		X	X
Arkansas	X	X	X	X		X
California	X	X	X	X		X
Colorado		X			X	X
Connecticut		X	X	X	X	X
Delaware	X	X	X	X	X	X
Dist. of Columbia					X	X
Florida	X	X	X		X	X
Georgia	X	X	X		X	X
Hawaii		X			X	
Idaho		X	X	X	X	X
Illinois	X	X	X	X	X	X
Indiana		X	X			
Iowa	X	X	X			
Kansas	X	X	X		X	X
Kentucky	X	X				
Louisiana	X	X	X	X	X	
Maine	X	X				

State	Prosecutor Declinations	Court felony dispositions w/ felony jurisdiction	Admission/ Release of felons - state prisons	Admission/ Release of felons - local jails	Probation Information	Parole information
Maryland	X	X	X	X		
Massachusetts		X			X	X
Michigan	X	X	X		X	X
Minnesota	X	X	X	X	X	X
Mississippi	X	X	X	X	X	X
Missouri	X	X	X		X	X
Montana	X	X			X	
Nebraska	X	X	X	X	X	X
Nevada	X	X				
New Hampshire		X	X			
New Jersey	X	X	X	X	X	X
New Mexico			X	X		
New York	X	X	X	X	X	X
North Carolina	X	X	X		X	X
North Dakota	X	X	X	X	X	X
Ohio	X	X	X	X		
Oklahoma	X	X	X	X	X	X
Oregon		X				
Pennsylvania	X	X			X	X
Rhode Island	X	X				
South Carolina		X	X	X	X	
South Dakota	X	X	X	X	X	X
Tennessee	X	X	X		X	X
Texas	X	X				
Utah	X	X	X	X	X	X
Vermont		X			X	X
Virginia	X	X	X		X	X
Washington	X	X	X			
West Virginia		X	X			
Wisconsin		X	X	X	X	X
Wyoming	X	X	X	X	X	X

Appendix 2

Prescribed Summary of Consumer Rights Appendix A to Part 601

The prescribed form for this summary is as a separate document, on paper no smaller than 8x11 inches in size, with text no less than 12-point type (8-point for the chart of federal agencies), in bold or capital letters as indicated. The form in this appendix prescribes both the content and the sequence of items in the required summary. A summary may accurately reflect changes in numerical items that change over time (e.g., dollar amounts, or phone numbers and addresses of federal agencies), and remain in compliance.

A Summary of Your Rights Under the Fair Credit Reporting Act

The federal Fair Credit Reporting Act (FCRA) is designed to promote accuracy, fairness, and privacy of information in the files of every "consumer reporting agency" (CRA). Most CRAs are credit bureaus that gather and sell information about you -- such as if you pay your bills on time or have filed bankruptcy -- to creditors, employers, landlords, and other businesses. You can find the complete text of the FCRA, 15 U.S.C. 1681-1681u, at the Federal Trade Commission's web site (*http://www.ftc.gov*). The FCRA gives you specific rights, as outlined below. You may have additional rights under state law. You may contact a state or local consumer protection agency or a state attorney general to learn those rights.

- **You must be told if information in your file has been used against you.** Anyone who uses information from a CRA to take action against you -- such as denying an application for credit, insurance, or employment -- must tell you, and give you the name, address, and phone number of the CRA that provided the consumer report.

- **You can find out what is in your file.** At your request, a CRA must give you the information in your file, and a list of everyone who has requested it recently. There is no charge for the report if a person has taken action against you because of information supplied by the CRA, if you request the report within 60 days of receiving notice of the action. You also are entitled to one free report every twelve months upon request if you certify that (1) you are unemployed and plan to seek employment within 60 days, (2) you are on welfare, or (3) your report is inaccurate due to fraud. Otherwise, a CRA may charge you up to eight dollars.

- **You can dispute inaccurate information with the CRA.** If you tell a CRA that your file contains inaccurate information, the CRA must investigate the items (usually within 30 days) by presenting to its information source all relevant evidence you submit, unless your dispute is frivolous. The source must review your evidence and report its findings to the CRA. (The source also must advise national CRAs -- to which it has provided the data -- of any error.) The CRA must give you a written report of the investigation, and a copy of your report if the investigation results in any change. If the CRA's investigation does not resolve the dispute, you may add a brief statement to your file. The CRA must normally include a summary of your statement in future reports. If an item is deleted or a dispute statement is filed, you may ask that anyone who has recently received your report be notified of the change.

- **Inaccurate information must be corrected or deleted.** A CRA must remove or correct inaccurate or unverified information from its files, usually within 30 days after you dispute it. **However, the CRA is not required to remove accurate data from your file unless it is outdated (as described below) or cannot be verified.** If your dispute results in any change to your report, the CRA cannot reinsert into your file a disputed item unless the information source verifies its accuracy and completeness. In addition, the CRA must give you a written notice telling you it has reinserted the item. The notice must include the name, address and phone number of the information source.

- **You can dispute inaccurate items with the source of the information.** If you tell anyone -- such as a creditor who reports to a CRA -- that you dispute an item, they may not then report the information to a CRA without including a notice of your dispute. In addition, once you've notified the source of the error in writing, it may not continue to report the information if it is, in fact, an error.

- **Outdated information may not be reported.** In most cases, a CRA may not report negative information that is more than seven years old; ten years for bankruptcies.

- **Access to your file is limited.** A CRA may provide information about you only to people with a need recognized by the FCRA -- usually to consider an application with a creditor, insurer, employer, landlord, or other business.

- **Your consent is required for reports that are provided to employers, or reports that contain medical information.** A CRA may not give out information about you to your employer, or prospective employer, without your written consent. A CRA may not report medical information about you to creditors, insurers, or employers without your permission.

- **You may choose to exclude your name from CRA lists for unsolicited credit and insurance offers.** Creditors and insurers may use file information as the basis for sending you unsolicited offers of credit or insurance. Such offers must include a toll-free phone number for you to call if you want your name and address removed from future lists. If you call, you must be kept off the lists for two years. If you request, complete, and return the CRA form provided for this purpose, you must be taken off the lists indefinitely.

- **You may seek damages from violators.** If a CRA, a user or (in some cases) a provider of CRA data, violates the FCRA, you may sue them in state or federal court.

The FCRA gives several different federal agencies authority to enforce the FCRA:

FOR QUESTIONS OR CONCERNS REGARDING:	PLEASE CONTACT:
CRAs, creditors and others not listed below	Federal Trade Commission Consumer Response Center - FCRA Washington, DC 20580 202-326-3761
National banks, federal branches/agencies of foreign banks (word "National" or initials "N.A." appear in or after bank's name)	Office of the Comptroller of the Currency Compliance Management, Mail Stop 6-6 Washington, DC 20219 800-613-6743
Federal Reserve System member banks (except national banks, and federal branches/agencies of foreign banks)	Federal Reserve Board Division of Consumer & Community Affairs Washington, DC 20551 202-452-3693
Savings associations and federally chartered savings banks (word "Federal" or initials "F.S.B." appear in federal institution's name)	Office of Thrift Supervision Consumer Programs Washington, DC 20552 800-842-6929
Federal credit unions (words "Federal Credit Union" appear in institution's name)	National Credit Union Administration 1775 Duke Street Alexandria, VA 22314 703-518-6360
State-chartered banks that are not members of the Federal Reserve System	Federal Deposit Insurance Corporation Division of Compliance & Consumer Affairs Washington, DC 20429 800-934-FDIC
Air, surface, or rail common carriers regulated by former Civil Aeronautics Board or Interstate Commerce Commission	Department of Transportation Office of Financial Management Washington, DC 20590 202-366-1306
Activities subject to the Packers and Stockyards Act, 1921	Department of Agriculture Office of Deputy Administrator - GIPSA Washington, DC 20250 202-720-7051

Prescribed Notice of Furnisher Responsibilities Appendix B to Part 601

This appendix prescribes the content of the required notice.

NOTICES TO FURNISHERS OF INFORMATION: OBLIGATIONS OF FURNISHERS UNDER THE FCRA

The federal Fair Credit Reporting Act (FCRA), as amended, imposes responsibilities on all persons who furnish information to consumer reporting agencies (CRAs). These responsibilities are found in Section 623 of the FCRA. State law may impose additional requirements. All furnishers of information to CRAs should become familiar with the law and may want to consult with their counsel to ensure that they are in compliance. The FCRA, 15 U.S.C. 1681-1681u, is set forth in full at the Federal Trade Commission's Internet web site (*http://www.ftc.gov*). Section 623 imposes the following duties:

General Prohibition on Reporting Inaccurate Information:

The FCRA prohibits information furnishers from providing information to a consumer reporting agency (CRA) that they know (or consciously avoid knowing) is inaccurate. However, the furnisher is not subject to this general prohibition if it clearly and conspicuously specifies an address to which consumers may write to notify the furnisher that certain information is inaccurate. *Sections 623(a)(1)(A) and (a)(1)(C)*

Duty to Correct and Update Information:

If at any time a person who regularly and in the ordinary course of business furnishes information to one or more CRAs determines that the information provided is not complete or accurate, the furnisher must provide complete and accurate information to the CRA. In addition, the furnisher must notify all CRAs that received the information of any corrections, and must thereafter report only the complete and accurate information. *Section 623(a)(2)*

Duties After Notice of Dispute from Consumer:

If a consumer notifies a furnisher, at an address specified by the furnisher for such notices, that specific information is inaccurate, and the information is in fact inaccurate, the furnisher must thereafter report the correct information to CRAs. *Section 623(a)(1)(B)*

If a consumer notifies a furnisher that the consumer disputes the completeness or accuracy of any information reported by the furnisher, the furnisher may not subsequently report that information to a CRA without providing notice of the dispute. *Section 623(a)(3)*

Duties After Notice of Dispute from Consumer Reporting Agency:

If a CRA notifies a furnisher that a consumer disputes the completeness or accuracy of information provided by the furnisher, the furnisher has a duty to follow certain procedures. The furnisher must:

Conduct an investigation and review all relevant information provided by the CRA, including information given to the CRA by the consumer. *Sections 623(b)(1)(A) and (b)(1)(B)*

Report the results to the CRA, and, if the investigation establishes that the information was, in fact, incomplete or inaccurate, report the results to all CRAs to which the furnisher provided the information that compile and maintain files on a nationwide basis. *Sections 623(b)(1)(C) and (b)(1)(D)*

Complete the above within 30 days from the date the CRA receives the dispute (or 45 days, if the consumer later provides relevant additional information to the CRA). *Section 623(b)(2)*

Duty to Report Voluntary Closing of Credit Accounts:

If a consumer voluntarily closes a credit account, any person who regularly and in the ordinary course of business furnishes information to one or more CRAs must report this fact when it provides information to CRAs for the time period in which the account was closed. *Section 623(a)(4)*

Duty to Report Dates of Delinquencies:

If a furnisher reports information concerning a delinquent account placed for collection, charged to profit or loss, or subject to any similar action, the furnisher must, within 90 days after reporting the information, provide the CRA with the month and the year of the commencement of the delinquency that immediately preceded the action, so that the agency will know how long to keep the information in the consumer's file. *Section 623(a)(5)*

Prescribed Notice of User Responsibilities Appendix C to Part 601

This appendix prescribes the content of the required notice.

NOTICE TO USERS OF CONSUMER REPORTS: OBLIGATIONS OF USERS UNDER THE FCRA

The federal Fair Credit Reporting Act (FCRA) requires that this notice be provided to inform users of consumer reports of their legal obligations. State law may impose additional requirements. This first section of this summary sets forth the responsibilities imposed by the FCRA on all users of consumer reports. The subsequent sections discuss the duties of users of reports that contain specific types of information, or that are used for certain purposes, and the legal consequences of violations. The FCRA, 15 U.S.C. 1681-1681u, is set forth in full at the Federal Trade Commission's Internet web site (*http://www.ftc.gov*).

I. OBLIGATIONS OF ALL USERS OF CONSUMER REPORTS

A. Users Must Have a Permissible Purpose

Congress has limited the use of consumer reports to protect consumers' privacy. All users must have a permissible purpose under the FCRA to obtain a consumer report. Section 604 of the FCRA contains a list of the permissible purposes under the law. These are:

- As ordered by a court or a federal grand jury subpoena. *Section 604(a)(1)*

- As instructed by the consumer in writing. *Section 604(a)(2)*

- For the extension of credit as a result of an application from a consumer, or the review or collection of a consumer's account. *Section 604(a)(3)(A)*

- For employment purposes, including hiring and promotion decisions, where the consumer has given written permission. *Sections 604(a)(3)(B) and 604(b)*

- For the underwriting of insurance as a result of an application from a consumer. *Section 604(a)(3)(C)*

- When there is a legitimate business need, in connection with a business transaction that is initiated by the consumer. *Section 604(a)(3)(F)(i)*

- To review a consumer's account to determine whether the consumer continues to meet the terms of the account. *Section 604(a)(3)(F)(ii)*

- To determine a consumer's eligibility for a license or other benefit granted by a governmental instrumentality required by law to consider an applicant's financial responsibility or status. *Section 604(a)(3)(D)*

- For use by a potential investor or servicer, or current insurer, in a valuation or assessment of the credit or prepayment risks associated with an existing credit obligation. *Section 604(a)(3)(E)*

- For use by state and local officials in connection with the determination of child support payments, or modifications and enforcement thereof. *Sections 604(a)(4) and 604(a)(5)*

In addition, creditors and insurers may obtain certain consumer report information for the purpose of making unsolicited offers of credit or insurance. The particular obligations of users of this "prescreened" information are described in Section V below.

B. Users Must Provide Certifications

Section 604(f) of the FCRA prohibits any person from obtaining a consumer report from a consumer reporting agency (CRA) unless the person has certified to the CRA (by a general or specific certification, as appropriate) the permissible purpose(s) for which the report is being obtained and certifies that the report will not be used for any other purpose.

C. Users Must Notify Consumers When Adverse Actions Are Taken

The term "adverse action" is defined very broadly by Section 603 of the FCRA. "Adverse actions" include all business, credit, and employment actions affecting consumers that can be considered to have a negative impact -- such as unfavorably changing credit or contract terms or conditions, denying or canceling credit or insurance, offering credit on less favorable terms than requested, or denying employment or promotion.

1. Adverse Actions Based on Information Obtained From a CRA

If a user takes any type of adverse action that is based at least in part on information contained in a consumer report, the user is required by Section 615(a) of the FCRA to notify the consumer. The notification may be done in writing, orally, or by electronic means. It must include the following:

> The name, address, and telephone number of the CRA (including a toll-free telephone number, if it is a nationwide CRA) that provided the report.

> A statement that the CRA did not make the adverse decision and is not able to explain why the decision was made.

> A statement setting forth the consumer's right to obtain a free disclosure of the consumer's file from the CRA if the consumer requests the report within 60 days.

> A statement setting forth the consumer's right to dispute directly with the CRA the accuracy or completeness of any information provided by the CRA.

2. Adverse Actions Based on Information Obtained From Third Parties Who Are <u>Not</u> Consumer Reporting Agencies

If a person denies (or increases the charge for) credit for personal, family, or household purposes based either wholly or partly upon information from a person other than a CRA, and the information is the type of consumer information covered by the FCRA, Section 615(b)(1) of the FCRA requires that the user clearly and accurately disclose to the consumer his or her right to obtain disclosure of the nature of the information that was relied upon by making a written request within 60 days of notification. The user must provide the disclosure within a reasonable period of time following the consumer's written request.

3. Adverse Actions Based on Information Obtained From Affiliates

If a person takes an adverse action involving insurance, employment, or a credit transaction initiated by the consumer, based on information of the type covered by the FCRA, and this information was obtained from an entity affiliated with the user of the information by common ownership or control, Section 615(b)(2) requires the user to notify the consumer of the adverse action. The notification must inform the consumer that he or she may obtain a disclosure of the nature of the information relied upon by making a written request within 60 days of receiving the adverse action notice. If the consumer makes such a request, the user must disclose the nature of the information not later than 30 days after receiving the request. (Information that is obtained directly from an affiliated entity relating solely to its transactions or experiences with the consumer, and information from a consumer report obtained from an affiliate are not covered by Section 615(b)(2).)

II. OBLIGATIONS OF USERS WHEN CONSUMER REPORTS ARE OBTAINED FOR EMPLOYMENT PURPOSES

If information from a CRA is used for employment purposes, the user has specific duties, which are set forth in Section 604(b) of the FCRA. The user must:

> Make a clear and conspicuous written disclosure to the consumer before the report is obtained, in a document that consists solely of the disclosure, that a consumer report may be obtained.

> Obtain prior written authorization from the consumer.

> Certify to the CRA that the above steps have been followed, that the information being obtained will not be used in violation of any federal or state equal opportunity law or regulation, and that, if any adverse action is to be taken based on the consumer report, a copy of the report and a summary of the consumer's rights will be provided to the consumer.

Before taking an adverse action, provide a copy of the report to the consumer as well as the summary of the consumer's rights. (The user should receive this summary from the CRA, because Section 604(b)(1)(B) of the FCRA requires CRAs to provide a copy of the summary with each consumer report obtained for employment purposes.)

III. OBLIGATIONS OF USERS OF INVESTIGATIVE CONSUMER REPORTS

Investigative consumer reports are a special type of consumer report in which information about a consumer's character, general reputation, personal characteristics, and mode of living is obtained through personal interviews. Consumers who are the subjects of such reports are given special rights under the FCRA. If a user intends to obtain an investigative consumer report, Section 606 of the FCRA requires the following:

> The user must disclose to the consumer that an investigative consumer report may be obtained. This must be done in a written disclosure that is mailed, or otherwise delivered, to the consumer not later than three days after the date on which the report was first requested. The disclosure must include a statement informing the consumer of his or her right to request additional disclosures of the nature and scope of the investigation as described below, and must include the summary of consumer rights required by Section 609 of the FCRA. (The

user should be able to obtain a copy of the notice of consumer rights from the CRA that provided the consumer report.)

The user must certify to the CRA that the disclosures set forth above have been made and that the user will make the disclosure described below.

Upon the written request of a consumer made within a reasonable period of time after the disclosures required above, the user must make a complete disclosure of the nature and scope of the investigation that was requested. This must be made in a written statement that is mailed, or otherwise delivered, to the consumer no later than five days after the date on which the request was received from the consumer or the report was first requested, whichever is later in time.

IV. OBLIGATIONS OF USERS OF CONSUMER REPORTS CONTAINING MEDICAL INFORMATION

Section 604(g) of the FCRA prohibits consumer reporting agencies from providing consumer reports that contain medical information for employment purposes, or in connection with credit or insurance transactions, without the specific prior consent of the consumer who is the subject of the report. In the case of medical information being sought for employment purposes, the consumer must explicitly consent to the release of the medical information in addition to authorizing the obtaining of a consumer report generally.

V. OBLIGATIONS OF USERS OF "PRESCREENED" LISTS

The FCRA permits creditors and insurers to obtain limited consumer report information for use in connection with unsolicited offers of credit or insurance under certain circumstances. *Sections 603(l), 604(c), 604(e), and 615(d)* This practice is known as "prescreening" and typically involves obtaining a list of consumers from a CRA who meet certain pre-established criteria. If any person intends to use prescreened lists, that person must (1) before the offer is made, establish the criteria that will be relied upon to make the offer and to grant credit or insurance, and (2) maintain such criteria on file for a three-year period beginning on the date on which the offer is made to each consumer. In addition, any user must provide with each written solicitation a clear and conspicuous statement that:

- Information contained in a consumer's CRA file was used in connection with the transaction.

- The consumer received the offer because he or she satisfied the criteria for credit worthiness or insurability used to screen for the offer.

- Credit or insurance may not be extended if, after the consumer responds, it is determined that the consumer does not meet the criteria used for screening or any applicable criteria bearing on credit worthiness or insurability, or the consumer does not furnish required collateral.

The consumer may prohibit the use of information in his or her file in connection with future prescreened offers of credit or insurance by contacting the notification system established by the CRA that provided the report. This statement must include the address and toll-free telephone number of the appropriate notification system.

VI. OBLIGATIONS OF RESELLERS

Section 607(e) of the FCRA requires any person who obtains a consumer report for resale to take the following steps:

- Disclose the identity of the end-user to the source CRA.

- Identify to the source CRA each permissible purpose for which the report will be furnished to the end-user.

- Establish and follow reasonable procedures to ensure that reports are resold only for permissible purposes, including procedures to obtain:

  1. the identity of all end-users;

  2. certifications from all users of each purpose for which reports will be used; and

  3. certifications that reports will not be used for any purpose other than the purpose(s) specified to the reseller. Resellers must make reasonable efforts to verify this information before selling the report.

VII. LIABILITY FOR VIOLATIONS OF THE FCRA

Failure to comply with the FCRA can result in state or federal enforcement actions, as well as private lawsuits. *Sections 616, 617, and 621.* In addition, any person who knowingly and willfully obtains a consumer report under false pretenses may face criminal prosecution. *Section 619* .

For More Information About FCRA—

The Federal Trade Commission web site is filled with information, including Staff Opinion Letters, Educational Materials, and a complete copy of the act. Visit http://www.ftc.gov/os/statutes/fcrajump.htm

Title VII EEOC Notices

The Appendix contains copies of four important notices written by the EEOC. These notices have set the bar so to speak on what an employer and cannot do with criminal records.

- Notice N-915.043 (July, 1989)
- Notice N-915-061 (9/7/90)
- Notice N-915 (7/29/87)
- Notice N-915 (2/4/87)

For more information about the EEOC, visit their web site at www.eeoc.gov.

Notice N-915.043 (July, 1989)

1. SUBJECT: Job Advertising and Pre-Employment Inquiries Under the Age Discrimination In Employment Ace (ADEA).

2. PURPOSE: This policy guidance provides a discussion of job advertising and pre-employment inquiries under the ADEA. Additionally, certain defenses are discussed that may be proffered by respondents when impermissible practices appear to be involved.

3. EFFECTIVE DATE: Upon receipt.

4. EXPIRATION DATE: As an exception to EEOC Order 205.001, Appendix B, Attachment 4, § a(5), this Notice will remain in effect until rescinded or superseded.

5. ORIGINATOR: ADEA Division, Office of the Legal Counsel.

6. INSTRUCTIONS: File behind § 801 of Volume II of the Compliance Manual.

7. SUBJECT MATTER:

I. JOB ADVERTISING

A: GENERAL

The ADEA makes it unlawful, unless a specific exemption applies, for an employer to utilize job advertising that discriminates on account of age against persons 40 years of age or older. Specifically, sec. 4(e) of the ADEA provides as follows:

It shall be unlawful for an employer, labor organization, or employment agency to print of publish, or cause to be printed or published, any notice or advertisement relating to employment by such an employer or membership in or any classification or referral for employment by such a labor organization, or relating to any classification or referral for employment by such an employment agency, indicating any preference, limitation, specification, or discrimination, based on age.   29 USC. § 623(e).

The commission interpretative regulation further develops the statutory language by providing the following guidance.

> When help wanted notices or advertisements contain terms and phrases such as "age 25 to 35," "young," "college student," "recent college graduate," "boy," "girl," or others of a similar nature, such a term or phrase a violation of the Act, unless one of the exceptions applies. Such phrases as "40 to 50," "age over 65," "retired persons," or "supplement your pension" discriminate against others within the protected group and, therefore, are prohibited unless one of the exceptions applies. 29 C.F.R. S 1625.4(a).

Former Secretary of Labor, Willard Wirtz, in his 1965 report to Congress on age discrimination in employment was among the first to recognize a need to carefully assess employers' job advertisements, to assure that older workers are not arbitrarily discriminated against.

> The most obvious kind of discrimination in employment takes the form of employer policies of not haring people over a certain age, without consideration of a particular applicant's individual qualifications. These restrictive practices appear in announced employer policies (e.g., in help-wanted advertisements; or in job orders filed with employment agencies) or in dealing with applicants when they appear in the hiring office.[1]

Congress responded to this concern, in part, by enacting sec. 4(e). Covered entities are limited by sec. 4(e) of the ADEA with respect to the content of their job notices and advertisements. They must be careful to avoid not only explicit age based limitations, but also advertisements that implicitly deter older persons from applying. For example, a "job description can exert a subtle form of discrimination by setting qualifications of education that are completely appropriate for the young employee and completely irrelevant for someone with 30 years experience."[2]

Although the language of sec. 4(e) is relatively straightforward, and judicial and Commission interpretations have added insight as to its application, generally there remains the need for a careful, case-by-case assessment as to whether a particular job advertisement runs afoul of sec. 4(e). The analysis requires an examination not only of the language used in the advertisement but also the context in which it is used to determine whether persons in the protected age group would be discouraged from applying.

In Hodgson v. Approved Personnel Service Inc., 529 F.2d 760 (4th Cir. 1975), the court examined over fifty advertisements published by the defendant, an employment agency. The court held that some of the advertisements violated the ADEA while others did not. The defendant's advertisements used such words and phrases as: "recent college graduate." "those unable to continue in college," "1-2 years out of college," "excellent first job," "any recent degree," "recent high school grad," "young executive," recent technical school grad," "junior secretary," "junior accountant," "athletically inclined," "career girls," "young office group," and "all American type."

---

[1] *The Older American Worker, Age Discrimination In Employment, Report of the Secretary of Labor to the Congress Under Section 715 of the Civil Rights Act of 1964, 6 (1965)*
[2] *Improving The Age Discrimination Law: A Working Paper, Senate Special Committee on Aging,* 93d Cong., 1st Sess. 6 (1973).

The court's analysis of each phrase involved close scrutiny of the advertisement in its entirety to determine whether sec. 4(e) had been violated. Specifically the court stated, "we are inclined to think that the discriminatory effect of an advertisement is determined no solely by "trigger words" but rather by its context."[3] In order to determine from its context whether the advertisement is in fact discriminatory, one must read the ad in its entirety, taking into consideration the results of the ad on the employer's hiring practices. The mere presence of "trigger words: does not constitute a violation of the ADEA.

Those words and phrases found by the Hodgson court not to violate the ADEA are as follows: 1) "young executive seeks," refers to the age of the employer and does not state an age requirement for job applicants or suggest that older persons will not be considered; 2) "young office group," certainly carries an implication that an older person might not fit in but it tells the older applicant something he may want to know: that those already employed who will be his work associates are young; 3) "Athletically inclined" or "all American type," state qualifications relating to personal appearance and physical characteristics which can exist in persons at any age; 4) "junior," this adjective when applied to an employee's job description designates the scope of his duties and responsibilities. And does not carry connotations of youth prohibited by the Act; Hodgson at page 767 (Appendix). Of course, in a different context, the outcome with respect to any of the foregoing words and phrases might be different. As stated in the text, a case-by-case fact specific analysis is always required.

Read in context, "trigger words" may be innocent in some advertisements and clearly discriminatory in others. Hodgson at 765. The above concepts are demonstrated by the following examples.

EXAMPLE 1 = CP, a 65 year old, saw an ad in the newspaper for a cashier at a local supermarket ®. R's advertisement specified that "applicant must be young, energetic, and posses excellent customer relations skills. Applicants who are selected would be required to stand long periods of time and to lift 20-30 pounds." CP contacted the Commission to institute a charge against R, local supermarket. In this case the Commission would find a violation. By use of the word "young" the ad specifically indicates a preference, limitation, specification or discrimination based on age. Such an ad would almost certainly deter many qualified older persons from applying. Note that if the same ad appeared with only the word "young" deleted, it would probably be acceptable. Persona of all ages can be energetic and possess excellent customer relations skills. Further, the need to stand for long periods and to lift 20-30 pounds are not age related criteria and, in any event, appear to be legitimate requirements for the job in question.

EXAMPLE 2 – CP, a 57 year old graphic artist, claims that R, Advertising Firm, has discriminated against him based on age by publishing an advertisement which he feels clearly deters older persons from applying. R's ad stated, "Young-thinking, 'new wave' progressive advertising firm has openings for entry level position for graphic artist with no more than 3 years experience. We specialize in music videos and broadcast productions for a youthful audience. Our main focus is in the area of animation. Our clients include famous rock stars. If you have fresh, innovative ideas, and can relate to our audience, send your resume." While the ad does not contain explicit age limitations, read in its entirety, it does appear that persons in the protected age group would be discouraged from applying for the position. The employer contends that it does not discriminate against older persons and

---

[3] *Hodgson v. Approved Personnel Serv.* At 765.

would hire a 75 year old applicant if he or she is qualified and willing to work for an entry level salary. However, on further investigation it was found that the employer has no employees over 30 years of age. It was also revealed that the firm recently turned down two fully qualified graphic artists X and Y, ages 47 and 67, who were willing to work at an entry level salary, though both possessed more that 3 years of experience. In this context the Commission would probably take the position that the ad is designed to deter older persons from applying. The Commission would seek to have R change the ad to read "young-thinking persons of any age with at least 3 years experience and willing to work at an entry level salary." The Commission would also attempt to contact X and Y to investigate the circumstances surrounding the denial of employment for the advertised position. The Commission has provided further specific guidance for investigating such incidents of "subtle" discriminatory advertising. See Volume I, Investigative Procedures Manual, § 8.6(b)(3)(i).

As indicated in sec. 1625.4(a), younger persons in the protected age group, for example, those individuals older than 40 but not old enough to retire, may be victimized by job advertising favoring older persons within the protected age group. The following example illustrates how this situation may occur.

EXAMPLE 3 – CP, a 42 year old individual who is actively seeking part-time employment, contends that she was deterred from applying for a position because of the employer's ad. R, a local Laundromat, advertised in the newspaper as follows: "Opening for a person seeking to supplement pension. Part-time position available for Laundromat Attendant from 9:00 am – 2:00 PM, Monday-Thursday. Responsibilities include dispensing products sold on premises, maintaining washer, dryer, and vending machines. Retired persons preferred." This ad limits the applicant pool by indicating a preference based on age. Persons rarely receive pensions or attain retirement status before 55 and frequently not until age 65. Thus, the ad deters younger persons within the protected age group from applying. Therefore it is a violation of sec. 4(e) unless one of the exceptions to the Act applies.

Note, however, that the Commission would be unlikely to find a violation in situations where an age-neutral advertisement encourages individuals within the protected age group to actively seek the position(s) available.[4]

EXEMPLE 4 – In response to a acute labor shortage that exists throughout the southeast region of the country, R, a large home improvement chain publishes the following advertisement:

WANTED; Individuals of all ages. Day and evening hours available. Full and part-time positions. All inquiries welcomed. Excellent secondary source of income for retirees.

While the ad mentions "retirees," the Commission would not find an illegal age-based discriminatory advertising practice in this instance. Individuals of all ages are welcomed for the employment

---

[4] Section 2(b) of the ADEA states in pertinent part that "[I]t is therefore the purpose of this Act to promote employment of older persons based on their ability rather than age." See also EEOC Opinion Letter – 1, December 13, 1983 (ADEA rights of retirees).

opportunity. The reference to retirees in the ad does not, on its face, indicate a preference for this sub-grouping of the protected age group. Rather, it notifies them of an opportunity and invites them to participate. The language in this ad differs from the language used in Example 3 which suggests that only retired, pension eligible persons are considered for employment.

B. EMPLOYMENT AGENCY ADVERTISEMENTS

Some courts have fashioned an exception to the general rules when the advertising in question is done by an employment agency and is intended to acquaint persons with the agency's services.[5] The Hodgson court held that when employment agencies use such phrases as "recent grad," or others of a similar nature to appeal acquaint such individuals with the agency's services, the ADEA is not violated. However, such an advertisement would seem to clearly indicate a preference, limitation, specifications, or discrimination based on age which is prohibited by the ADEA. The Commission, therefore, would not agree with the exception fashioned in the Hodgson decision. As a general enforcement principle, the Commission will closely scrutinize all ads that use words and phrases that would deter older persons from applying, including those used by employment agencies to inform the public of their services. An employment agency could as easily advertise generally for persons looking for employment by including in the advertisement language making it clear that both young and older applicants are wanted.[6]

In summary, a careful analysis of job advertising practices, whether by an employer or employment agency, is required in determining whether a violation of sec. 4(e) of the ADEA has occurred. If an ADEA charge/complaint raises the issue of an illegal age-based discriminatory advertising practice the following analytical scheme of investigation is suggested.

In some instances an advertisement may use a term or phrase which is listed in 29 C.F.R. § 1625.4(a). If an employer or employment agency resorts to the use of such terminology the advertising practice is per se illegal and a finding of a violation of sec. 4(e) of the ADEA is warranted, unless an exception (e.g., BFOQ) applies.

In many cases, however, the challenged advertisement will not contain direct age-based prohibited specifications or preferences and as such the legality of the advertising practice will depend upon the overall context, application and effect of discouraging individuals within the protected age group from applying or, in the alternative, generally limits, classifies or otherwise discriminates against an individual based on age. Specific attention in such instances should be given but not limited to charging party's/complainant's (1) explanation of why the ad served to discourage him or her from applying; (2) respondent's overall hiring practices, or; (3) a comparative analysis of respondent's applicant flow data with similar size employers using nondiscriminatory advertising practices. See generally Volume I, Investigative Procedures Manual, § 8.6(b)(3)(i)(ii).

---

[5] See Hodgson at 766.

[6] C. Edelman & I. Sigler, Federal Age Discrimination in Employment Law, Slowing Down the Gold Watch, 96 (1978). The Commission, for example, would encourage the use of such phrases as "state of the art knowledge" in lieu of "recent college graduate" or recommend to employment agencies the use of a specific disclaimer such as, "While we are skilled in assisting recent grads in finding positions, we encourage applicants of all ages and levels of experience – neither this agency nor any of our clients discriminate on the basis of an applicant's age."

C. BONA FIDE OCCUPATIONAL QUALIFICATION DEFENSE

Where an ad is per se discriminatory on the basis of age, a respondent may seek to invoke the :bona fide occupational qualification" defense, hereinafter referred to as "BFOQ," to justify the use of the ad.[7] If, because of the requirements of a job, an employer believes it must limit, specify, or discriminate based on age, an employer has the burden of proving that the position is a BFOQ.[8]

There are several elements which must be met in establishing a BFOQ defense. Whenever this defense is raised an employer must always show that :the age limit is reasonably necessary to the essence of the business."[9] In proving that age must be used as a proxy for ability to perform the job, an employer must next show that either "all or substantially all individuals excluded from the job are in fact disqualified,"[10] or "some of the individuals so excluded possess a disqualifying trait that cannot be ascertained except by reference to age."[11]

Unless the employer can establish the existence of a BFOQ, the ad would have to be modified to eliminate any limitations based upon age.

> EXAMPLE 5 – CP, a 43 year old fashion model, contends that she has been discriminated against based on age. R, a modeling agency, advertised in the newspaper as follows:" Experienced models between 20-30 for upcoming spring collection of 'junior sportswear.' Applicants must bring a portfolio and references to our New York Office. Only those persons in the specified age category need apply." CP auditioned and was rejected when the company found out her age. During the investigation, R raises the BFOQ defense and states that the "junior collection requires applicants who have a youthful appearance. R further alleges that traditionally the "junior" fashions are targeted to younger women, generally between 20-30. However, while CP is 43, she appears to be 23. In fact, R was in the process of completing the paperwork necessary to hire CP when its personnel manager noticed the date of birth on her driver's license. R is not able to prove that persons 40 or older have a disqualifying trait that cannot be ascertained except by reference to age. R has not established the existence of a BFOQ and its discriminatory ad must be changed. R has also violated the Act by its failure to hire CP on account of her age.

In sum, the employer has the burden of proving a bona fide occupational qualification. The Commission and the courts construe this defense very narrowly. If, however, the employer satisfies the requirements of the exemption, it can continue to express appropriate age limitations in its job ads.

---

[7] Section 4(f)(l) of the ADEA permits an employer "to take any action otherwise prohibited under subsection (a), (b), (c), or (e) of this section where age is a bona fide occupational qualification reasonably necessary to the normal operation of the particular business."

[8] 29 C.F.R.S 1625.6(b)
[9] 29 C.F.R. S 1625.6(b)(3)

[10] 29 C.F.R.S 1625.6(b)(2)

[11] 29 C.F.R. S 1625.6(b)(1)

II. PRE-EMPLOYMENT INQUIRIES

Pursuant to sec. 4(a)(1) of the ADEA, 29 U. S. C. § 623(A)(1), "[I]t shall be unlawful for an employer to fail or refuse to hire or to discharge any individual or otherwise discriminate against any individual with respect to his compensation, terms, conditions, or privileges of employment, because of such individual's age." Although it is almost always unlawful to make employment decisions based on age, a pre-employment inquiry on the part of an employer for information such as "Date of Birth" or :State Age" on an application form is not, in itself, a violation of the ADEA.

However, because the request that an applicant state his age may tend to deter older applicants from applying, pre-employment inquires which request such information will be closely scrutinized by the Commission to assure that the request is for a permissible purpose and not for a purpose proscribed by the Act. There must be legitimate, non-discriminatory reasons for seeking the information and the information must not be used for an impermissible purpose.

The Commission has addressed the issue of pre-employment inquiries concerning age in two separate provisions. The first provision, 29 C.F.R. § 1625.4(b), Specifically addresses requests in help-wanted notices or advertisements for age or date of birth. The Commission's position in regard to help-wanted notices and advertisements is that although inquiries regarding age will be closely scrutinized, such inquiries are not per se violations of the Act.

The second provision, 29 C.F.R. § 1625.5, focuses on requests for age on employment application forms. The Commission regulation at 29 C.F.R. § 1625.5 provides in part:

> A request on the art of an employer for information such as "Date of Birth" or "State Age" on an application form is not, in itself, a violation of the Act. But because the request that an applicant state his age may tend to deter older applicants or otherwise discriminate based on age, employment application forms which request such information will be closely scrutinized to assure that the request is for a permissible purpose and not for purposes proscribed by the Act. That the purpose is not one proscribed by the statute should be made known to the applicant. The term "employment applications" refers to all written inquiries about employment or application for employment or promotion including, but not limited to, resumes or other summaries of the applicant's background. It relates not only to written pre-employment inquiries, but to inquiries concerning terms, conditions, or privileges of employment as specified in section 4 of the Act.

The purpose of section 1625.5 is to insure that older applicants are judged on ability rather than age. To assure applicants in the protected age group that an inquiry as to age is for a permissible purpose, employers should include a reference on the application form stating that the employer does not discriminate on the basis of age. Another option would be to explain to each applicant the specific reason why the information concerning age is being requested. Most importantly, of course, employers must not use age related inquiries for an impermissible purpose.

> EXAMPLE 6 – CP, a 55 year old radio announcer, sent a resume to R, WZAB, for the position of Program Director. WZAB's format is "hard rock." R responded by forwarding CP an employment application and scheduling an interview. The application requested CP to state his age, and also stated the statutory prohibition against age discrimination in employment. At the interview CP was introduced to the staff, all of whom appeared to be between the ages of 18 and 35. During the interview, CP discussed his past experience and talked at length about how the radio business had changed since he had begun his career. R

asked CP if he would be opposed to having a younger supervisor and whether or not CP enjoyed working with younger people. Two days lager CP received a rejection letter from R. CP alleges that he was discriminated against based on age. It was later found that X, a 23 year old who was hired for the position of Program Director, did not submit an application and no inquiry was made as to her age. This evidence conflicted with R's statement that it was a standard practice to ascertain the age of all applicants. Despite the presence of the statutory prohibition against age discrimination on the application form, it would appear that in this particular instance, the inquiry about age was not applied uniformly and was used only to disqualify CP. Thus, even if an employer sets forth the statutory prohibition against age discrimination on the application form, when an age related inquiry is challenged, the employer must show that it has legitimate non-discriminatory reasons for seeking the information.

III. CASE RESOLUTION

The Commission's position is that employment related inquiries requesting an applicant's age or date of birth will be closely scrutinized on a case-by-case basis to assure that they are for a lawful purpose.

Pre-employment inquiries as to age which are used for the purpose of disqualifying persons in the protected age group are prohibited. When the employer's inquiry does not serve any legitimate purpose, or the practice is not uniformly adhered to, it is quite likely that the information is being sought for purposes proscribed by the ADEA.[12]13

[Signed by Clarence Thomas on 07-02-89]

Date: _____   Signed:_____

                                           Clarence Thomas

                                             Chairman

---

[12]The ADEA principles and the BFOQ defense discussed in the text apply equally to Title VII. <u>See</u>, e.g., 29 C.F.R. S 1604.7. It should be noted, however, that the BFOQ defense under Title VII is limited to religion, sex, and national origin.

Notice N-915-061 (9/7/90)

1. <u>SUBJECT</u>:   Policy Guidance on the Consideration of Arrest Records in Employment Decisions under Title VII of the Civil Rights Act of 1964, as amended, 42 USC. § 2000e <u>et seq.</u> (1982).

2. <u>PURPOSE</u>:   This policy guidance sets forth the Commission's procedure for determining whether arrest records may be considered in employment decisions.

3. <u>EFFECTIVE DATE</u>:   September 7, 1990.

4. <u>EXPIRATION DATE</u>:   As an exception to EEOC Order 205.001, Appendix B, Attachment 4, § a(5), this Notice will remain in effect until rescinded or superseded.

5. <u>ORIGINATOR</u>:   Title VII/EPA Division, Office of the Legal Counsel.

6. <u>INSTRUCTIONS</u>:   File behind the last Policy Guidance § 604 of Volume II of Compliance Manual.

7. <u>SUBJECT MATTER</u>:

I. Introduction

The question addressed in this policy guidance is "to what extent may arrest records be used in making employment decisions?" The Commission concludes that since the use of arrest records as a absolute bar to employment has a disparate impact on some protected groups, such records alone cannot be used to routinely exclude persons from employment. However, conduct which indicates unsuitability for a particular position is a basis for exclusion. Where it appears that the applicant or employee engaged in the conduct for which he was arrested and that the conduct is job-related and relatively recent, exclusion is justified.

The analysis set forth in this policy guidance is related to two previously issued policy statements regarding the consideration of conviction records in employment decisions: "Policy Statement on the Issue of Conviction Records under Title VII of the Civil Rights Act of 1964, as amended 42 U.S.C. § 2000e <u>et seq.</u> (1982)" (hereinafter referred to as the February 4, 1987 Statement) and "Policy Statement on the use of statistics in charges involving the exclusion of individuals with conviction records from employment" (hereinafter referred to ad July 29, 1987 Statement). The February 4, 1987 Statement states that nationally, Blacks and Hispanics are convicted in numbers which are disproportionate to Whites and that barring people from employment based on their conviction records will therefore disproportionately exclude those groups.[1] Due to this adverse impact, an employer may not base an employment decision on the conviction record of an applicant

---

[1] The July 29 Statement notes that despite national statistics showing adverse impact, an employer may refute this <u>prima facie</u> showing by presenting statistics which are specific to its region or applicant pool. If these statistics demonstrate that the policy has no adverse impact against a protected group, the plaintiff's <u>prima facie</u> case has been rebutted and the employer need not show any business necessity to justify the use of the policy. Statistics relating to arrests should be used in the same manner.

or an employee absent business necessity.[2] Business necessity can be established where the employee or applicant is engaged in conduct which is particularly egregious or related to the position in question.

Conviction records constitute reliable evidence that a person engaged in the conduct alleged since the criminal justice system requires the highest degree of proof ("beyond a reasonable doubt") for a conviction. In contract, arrests alone are not reliable evidence that a person has actually committed a crime. Schware v. Board of Bar Examiners, 353 US 232, 241 (1957) ("[t]he mere fact that a [person] has been arrested has very little, if any, probative value in showing that he has engaged in misconduct.") Thus, the Commission concludes that to justify the use of arrest records, an additional inquiry must be made. Even where the conduct alleged in the arrest record is related to the job at issue, the employer must evaluate whether the arrest record reflects the applicant's conduct. It should, therefore, examine the surrounding circumstances, offer the applicant or employee an opportunity to explain, and, if he or she denies engaging in the conduct, make the follow-up inquiries necessary to evaluate his/her credibility. Since using arrests as a disqualifying criteria can only be justified where it appears that the applicant actually engaged in the conduct for which he/she was arrested and that conduct is job related, the Commission further concludes that an employer will seldom be able to justify making broad general inquiries about an employee's or applicant's arrests.

The following discussion is offered for guidance in determining the circumstances under which an employer can justify excluding an applicant or an employee on the basis of an arrest record.

II. Discussion

A. Adverse Impact of the Use of Arrest Records

The leading case involving an employer's use of arrest records is Gregory v. Litton Systems, 316 F. Supp. 401, 2 EPD ¶ 10,264 (C.D. Cal. 1970), modified on other grounds, 472 F.2d 631, 5 EPD ¶ 8089 (9th Cir. 1972). Litton held that nationally, Blacks are arrested more often than are Whites. Courts and the Commission have relied on the statistics presented in Litton to establish a prima facie case of discrimination against Blacks where arrest records are used in employment decisions.[3] There are, however, more recent statistics, published by the US Department of Justice, Federal Bureau of

---

[2] The policy statements on convictions use the term "business necessity," as used by courts prior to the Supreme Court's decision in Wards Cove Packing Co. v. Atonio, 109 S. Ct. 2115 (1989). In Atonio, the Supreme Court adopted the term "business justification" in place of business necessity, but noted that "although we have phrased the query differently in different cases...the dispositive issue is whether a challenged practice serves, in a significant way, the legitimate employment goals of the employer, "citing, inter alia, Griggs v. Duke Power Co., 401 US 424 (1971). 109 S. Ct. at 2125-2126.

[3] US v. City of Chicago, 385 F. Supp. 543, 556-557 (N.D. Ill. 1974), adopted by reference, 411 F. Supp. 218, aff'd in rel. part, 549 F.2d 415, 432 (7th Cir. 1977); City of Cairo v. Illinois Fair Employment Practice Commission, et al., 8 EPD ! 9682 (Ill. App. Ct. 1974); Commission Decision Nos. 78-03, 77-23, 76-138, 76-87, 76-39, 74-92, 74-90, 74-83, 74-02, CCH EEOC Decisions (1983) !! 6714, 6710, 6700, 6665, 630, 6424, 6423, 6414, 6386 and Commission Decisions Nos. 72-1460, 72-1005, 72-094 and 71-1950, CCH EEOC Decisions (1973) !! 6341, 6357 and 6274 respectively.

Investigation, which are consistent with the Litton finding.[4] It is desirable to use the most current available statistics. In addition, where local statistics are available, it may be helpful to use them, as the court did in Reynolds v. Sheet Metal Workers Local 102, 498 F. Supp. 952, 22 EPD ¶ 30,739 (D.C. 1980), aff'd., 702 F.2d 221, 25 EPD ¶ 31,706 (D.C. Cir. 1981). In Reynolds, the court found that the use of arrest records in employment decisions adversely affected Blacks since the 1978 Annual Report of the Metropolitan Police of Washington, D.C., stated that 85.5% of persons arrested in the District of Columbia were nonwhite while the nonwhite population constituted 72.4% of the total population. 498 F. Supp. At 960. The Commission has determined that Hispanics are also adversely affected by arrest record inquiries. Commission Decisions Nos. 77-23 and 76-03, CCH EEIC Decisions (1983) ¶¶ 6714 and 6598, respectively.[5] However, the courts have not yet addressed this issue[6] and the FBI's Uniform Crime Reporting Program does not provide information on the arrest records (see July 29, 1987 Statement), the employer may rebut by presenting statistics which are more current, accurate and/or specific to its region or applicant pool than are the statistics presented in the prima facie case.

B. Business Justification

If adverse impact is established, the burden of producing evidence shifts to the employer to show a business justification for the challenged employment practice. Wards Cove Packing Co. v. Atonio, 109 S.Ct. 2115, 2126 (1989).[7] As with conviction records, arrest records may be considered in the employment decision as evidence of conduct which may render an applicant unsuitable for a particular position. However, in the case of arrests, not only must the employer consider the relationship of the charges to the position sought, but also the likelihood that the applicant actually committed the conduct alleged in the charges. Gregory v. Litton Systems, 316 F. Supp. 401; Carter

---

[4] The FBI's Uniform Crime Reporting Program reported that in 1987, 29.5% of all arrests were of Blacks. The US. Census reported that Blacks comprised 11.7% of the national population in 1980 and projected that the figure would reach 12.2% in 1987. Since the national percentage of arrest for Blacks is more that twice the percentage of their representation in the population (whether considering the 1980 figures or the 1987 projections), the Litton presumption of adverse impact, at least nationally, is still valid.

[5] The statistics presented in Decision No. 77-23 pertain only to prison populations in the Southwestern United States. This data would, therefore, probably not constitute a prima facie case of discrimination for other regions of the country. In fact, there is no case law to indicate whether courts would accept this data as evidence of adverse impact for arrest records, even for cases arising in the Southwest, since all arrests do not result in incarceration. Decision No. 76-03 noted that Hispanics are arrested more frequently that are Whites, but no statistics were presented to support this statement.

[6] Cf. EEOC v. Carolina Freight Carriers, 723 F. Supp. 734, 751, 52 EPD ¶ 39, 538 (S.D. Fla. 1989) (EEOC failed to provide statistics for the relevant labor market to prove that trucking company's exclusion of drivers with, convictions for theft crimes had an adverse impact on Hispanics at a particular job site).

[7]Under Atonio, the burden of producing evidence shifts to the employer, but the burden of persuasion remains with the plaintiff at all stages of the Title VII case. 109 S.Ct. at 2116. Atonio thus modifies Griggs and its progeny.

v. Gallagher, 452 F.2d 315, 3 EPD ¶ 8335 (8th Cir. 1971), cert. Denied, 406 U.S. 950, 4 EPD ¶ 7818 (1972); Reynolds v. Sheet Metal Workers Local 102, 498 F. Supp. 952; Dozier v. Chupka, 395 F. Supp. 836 (D.C. Ohio 1975); US. V. City of Chicago, 411 F. Supp. 218 (N.D. Ill. 1974), aff'd. in rel. part, 549 F.2d 415 (7th Cir. 1977); City of Cairo v. Illinois Fair Employment Practice Commission et al., 8 EPD ¶ 9682 (Ill. App. Ct. 1974); Commission Decisions Mos. 78-03, 77-23, 76-138, 76-87, 76-54, 76-39, 76-17, 74-92, 74-83, 76-03, 74-90, 78093, 74025, CCH EEOC Decisions (1983) ¶¶ 6714, 6710, 6700, 6665, 6639, 630, 612, 6424, 6414, 6598, 6423, 6400 and Commission Decisions Nos. 72-0947, 72-1005, 72-1460, CCH EEOC Decisions (1973) ¶¶ 6357, 6350 and 6341, respectively.

1. A Business Justification Can Rarely Be Demonstrated for Blanket Exclusions on the Basis of Arrest Records

Since business justification rests on issues of job relatedness and credibility, a blanket exclusion of people with arrest records will almost never withstand scrutiny. Gregory v. Litton Systems, 316 F. Supp. 401. Litton held that employer's policy of refusing to hire anyone who had been arrested "on a number of occasions" violated Title VII because the policy disproportionately excluded Blacks from consideration and was not justified by business necessity. In Litton, an applicant for a position as a sheet metal worker was disqualified because of this arrest record. The court found no business necessity because the employer had failed to establish a business necessity for its discriminatory policy, it was enjoined from basing future hiring decisions on arrest records. Accord Carter v. Gallagher, 452 F.2d 315 (firefighter); Dozier v. Chupka, 395 F. Supp. 836 (firefighter); City of Cairo v Illinois Fair Employment Practice Commission, et al, 8 EPD ¶ 9682 (police officer).

The Commission has consistently invalidated employment policies which create a blanket exclusion of persons with arrest records. Commission Decision Nos. 78-03, 76-87, 76-39, 76-17, 76-03, 74-90, 74-25, 72-0947, 72-1005, CCH EEOC Decisions (1983) ¶¶ 6714 (laborer), 6665 (police officer), 6630 (cashier), 6612 (credit collector), 6598 (catalogue clerk), 6423 (uniformed guard commissioned by police department), 6400 (firefighter), 6357 (line worker) and 6350 (warehouse worker or driver). In several decisions, it appears that the arrest record inquiry was made on a standard company application which was used by the employer to fill various positions and there was no mention of any particular position sought. Commission Decision Nos. 76-138, 76-54, 74-82, 74-83, 74-02 and 72-1460, CCH EEOC Decisions (1983) ¶¶ 6700, 639, 6424, 6414, 6386 and 6341 and Commission Decision No. 71-1950, CCH EEOC Decisions (1973) ¶ 6274, respectively. An employer may not routinely exclude persons with arrest records based on the assumption that an arrest record will prevent an applicant from obtaining necessary credentials to perform a job without giving the applicant an opportunity to obtain those credentials. For example, in Decision 76-87, the Commission rejected an employer's assertion that employees' arrest records might hinder its ability to maintain fidelity (bond) insurance since it offered no proof to this effect.

Even where there is no direct evidence that an employer used an arrest record in an employment decision, a pre-employment inquiry regarding arrest records may violate Title VII. It is generally presumed that an employer only asks questions which he/she deems relevant to the employment decision. Gregory v. Litton Systems, 316 F. Supp. At 403-404. Noting that information which is obtained is likely to be used, the court in Litton enjoined the employer from making any pre-employment inquiries regarding arrests which did not result in convictions. Id.[8] But see EEOC f.

---

[8] Furthermore, potential applicants who have arrest records may be discouraged from applying for positions which require them to supply this information, thus creating a "chilling effect" on the

Local 638, 532 F.2d 821 (2d Cir. 1976) (inquiry not invalidated where there was no evidence that union actually rejected applicants who had been arrested but not convicted); Jimerson v. Kisco, 404 F. Supp. 338 (E.D. Mo. 1975) (court upheld discharge for falsifying information regarding arrest record on a pre-employment application without considering the inquiry itself violated Title VII).[9] Numerous states have specifically prohibited or advised against pre-employment inquiries in their fair employment laws due to the possible misuse of this information.[10]

2. The Alleged Conduct Must Be Related to the Position Sought

As discussed above, an arrest record may be used as evidence of conduct upon which an employer makes an employment decision. An employer may deny employment opportunities to persons based on any prior conduct which indicates that they would be unfit for the position in question, whether that conduct is evidenced by an arrest, conviction or other information provided to the employer. It is the conduct, not he arrest or conviction per se, which the employer may consider in relation to the position sought. The considerations relevant to the determination of whether the alleged Conduct demonstrates unfitness for the particular job were set forth in Green v. Missouri Pacific Railroad Co., 549 F.2d 1158, 1160, 13 EPD ¶ 11, 579 (8th Cir. 1977) and reiterated in the February 4, 1987 Statement on Convictions, page 2:

1. the nature and gravity of the offense or offenses;

2. the time that has passed since the conviction[11] (or in this case, arrest) .; and

3. the nature of the job held or sought.

See also Carter v. Maloney Trucking and Storage Inc., 631 F.2d 40, 43, 24 EPD ¶ 31,348 (5th Cir. 1980) (employer refused to rehire an ex-employee who had murdered a co-worker, not solely

---

Black applicant pool. Carter v. Gallagher, 452 F.2d at 330-331; Reynolds v. Sheet Metal Workers, Local 102, 498 F. Supp. At 964 n.12, 966 n.13, 967, 973; Commission Decision Nos. 76-138, 76-87, 76-17, 74-90, 74-25 and 74-02, CCH EEOC Decisions (1983) !! 6700, 6665, 612, 6423, 6400, 6386 and Commission Decision Nos. 74-1005 and 71-1950, CCH EEOC Decisions (1973) !! 6350 and 6274, respectively.

9 Note also that in Walls v. City of Petersburg, 895 F.2d 188, 52 EPD ! 39,602 (4th Cir. 1990), the court upheld an employer's policy of making an employment inquiry regarding the arrest records of employees' immediate family members. The court determined that under Atonio, the plaintiff was obligated to show not only that Blacks were more likely to have "negative" responses to this question, but also that the employer made adverse employment decisions based on such responses.

[10] New York, Hawaii, Oregon, Wisconsin, New Jersey, Ohio, Virginia, District of Columbia, California, Maryland, Minnesota, Utah, Washington, West Virginia, Arizona, Colorado, Idaho, Massachusetts, Michigan, Mississippi.

[11] But see EEOC v. Carolina Freight Carriers, 723 F. Supp. At 753 (court upheld trucking company's lifetime bar to employment of drivers who had been incarcerated for theft crimes since EEOC did not produce evidence that a 5-10 year bar would be an equally effective alternative). Note also that the court in Carolina Freight specifically rejected the Eighth Circuit's reasoning in Green, cautioning that Green could be construed too broadly. 723 F. Supp. At 752.

because of his conviction, but because he was a dangerous person and friends of the murdered man might try to retaliate against him while he was on the job); Osborne v. Cleland, 620 F.2d 195, 22 EPD on a charge of "sexual procurement" was unfit to be a nursing assistant in a psychiatric ward); Lane v. Inman, 509 F.2d 184 (5th Cir. 1975) (city ordinance which prohibited the issuance of taxicab driver permits to persons convicted of smuggling marijuana was "so obviously job related" that "it could not be held to be unlawful race discrimination," irrespective of any adverse impact); EEOC v. Carolina Freight, 723 F. Supp. 734, 52 EPD ¶ (S.D. Fla. 1989) (criminal history was related to position of truck driver who transported valuable property); McCray v. Alexander, 30 EPD ¶ 33,219 (D. Colo. 1982), aff'd 38 EPD ¶35,509 (10th Cir. 1985) (supervisory guard was discharged for killing a motorist, while off-duty, in a traffic dispute because employer concluded that, despite his acquittal, the conduct showed poor judgment on the use of deadly force).

Where the position sought is "security sensitive," particularly where it involves enforcing the law or preventing crime, courts tend to closely scrutinize evidence of prior criminal conduct of applicants. US. V. City of Chicago, 411 F. Supp. 217, 11 EPD ¶ 10,597 (N.D. Ill. 1976), aff'd in rel. part, 549 F.2d 415, 13 EPD ¶ 11,380 (7th Cir. 1977), on remand, 437 F. Supp. 256 (N.D. Ill. 1977) (applicants for the police department were disqualified for prior convictions for "serious" offenses); Richardson v. Hotel Corporation of America, 332 F. Supp. 519, 4 EPD ¶ 7666 (E.D. La. 1971), aff'd mem., 468 F.2d 951, 4 EPD ¶ 7666 (5th Cir. 1972) (bellman was discharged after his conviction for theft and receipt of stolen goods was discovered since bellmen had access to guests; rooms and was not subject to inspection when carrying packages); Haynie v. Chupka, 17 FEP Cases 267, 271 (S.D. Ohio 1976) (police department permissibly made inquires regarding arrest records and other evidence of prior criminal conduct).[12] (See Examples 3 and 4.)

Even where the employment at issue is not a law enforcement position or one which gives the employee easy access to the possessions of others, close scrutiny of an applicant's character and prior conduct is appropriate where an employer is responsible for the safety and/or well being of other persons. Osborne v. Cleland, 620 F.2d 195 (8th Cir. 1975) (psychiatric nursing assistant); Lane v. Inman, 509 F.2d 184 (taxi driver). In these instances, the facts would have to be examined closely in order to determine the probability that an applicant would pose a threat to the safety and well being of others. (See Examples 5 and 6).

3. Evaluating the Likelihood that the Applicant Engaged in the Conduct Alleged

The cases cited above illustrate the job-relatedness of certain conduct to specific positions. In cases alleging race discrimination based on the use of arrest records as opposed to convictions, courts have generally required not only job-relatedness, but also a showing that the alleged conduct was actually committed. In City of Cairo v. Illinois Fair Employment Practice Commission, et al., 8 EPD ¶ 9682, the court held that where applicants sought to become police officers, they could not be absolutely barred from appointment solely because they had been arrested, as distinguished from convicted. See also Commission Decision No. 76-87, CCH EEOC Decisions (1983) ¶ 6665 (potential police officer could not be rejected based on one arrest five years earlier for riding in a stolen car since there was no conviction and the applicant asserted that he did not know that the car was stolen).

---

[12] See also Quarrels v. Brown, 48 EPD ! 38,641 (D.C. Mich. 1988) (recent conviction was related to position of corrections officer). Note however, that this action was brought under 42 USC. S 1983, rather than Title VII, and plaintiff alleged that he was discriminated against because he was an ex-offender, not because the policy adversely affected a protected group.

Similarly, in Decision No. 74083, CCH EEOC Decision (1983) ¶ 6424, the Commission found no business justification for an employer's unconditional termination of all employees with arrest records (all five employees terminated were Black), purportedly to cut down on thefts in the workplace. The employer could produce no evidence that the employee had been involved in any of the thefts or that persons who are arrested, but not convicted, are prone toward crime. Commission Decision No. 74-92, CCH EEOC Decisions (1983) ¶ 6424.

An arrest record does no more than raise a suspicion that an applicant may have engaged in a particular type of conduct.[13] Thus, the investigator must determine whether the applicant is likely to step because it requires the employer either to accept the employee's denial or to attempt to obtain additional information and evaluate his/her credibility. An employer need not conduct an informal "trial" or an extensive investigation to determine an applicant's or employee's guilt or innocence. However, the employer may not perfunctorily "allow the person an opportunity to explain" and ignore the explanation where the person's claims could easily be verified by a phone call, i.e., to a previous employer or a police department. The employer is required to allow the person a meaningful opportunity to explain the circumstances of the arrest(s) and to make a reasonable effort to determine whether the explanation is credible before eliminating him/her from employment opportunities.[14] (See Examples 1, 4, 5 and 6.)

III. Examples

The following examples are provided to illustrate the process by which arrest record charges should be evaluated.

Example 1: Wilma, a Black female, applies to Buss Inc. in Highway City for a position as a bus driver. In response to a pre-employment inquiry, Wilma states that she was arrested two years earlier for driving while intoxicated. Bus Inc. rejects Wilma, despite her acquittal after trial. But Inc. does not accept her denial of the conduct alleged and concludes that Wilma was acquitted only because the breatholizer test which was administered to her at the time of her arrest was not administered in accordance with proper police procedures and was therefore inadmissible at trial. Witnesses at Wilma's trial testified that after being stopped for reckless driving, Wilma staggered from the car and had alcohol on her breath. Wilma's rejection is justified because the conduct underlying the arrest, driving while intoxicated, is clearly related to the safe performance of the duties of a bus driver; it occurred fairly recently; and there was no indication of subsequent rehabilitation.

Contrast Example Number 1 with the facts below.

Example 2: Lola, a Black female, applies to Buss Inc. for a position as a bus driver. In response to an inquiry whether she had ever been arrested, Lola states that she was arrested five years earlier for fraud in unemployment benefits. Lola admits that she committed the crime alleged. She explains that she received unemployment benefits shortly after her husband died and her expenses increased. During this period, she worked part-time for minimum wage because her unemployment check amounted to slightly less than the

---

[13] The employer's suspicion may be raised by an arrest record just as it would be negative comments about an applicant's conduct made by a previous employer or a personal reference.

[14] Although the number of arrests is not determinative (see Litton), it may be relevant in making a credibility determination.

monthly rent for her meager apartment. She did not report the income to the State Unemployment Board for fear that her payments would be reduced and that she would not be able to feed her three young children. After her arrest, she agreed to, and did, repay the state. Bus Inc. rejected Lola. Lola's rejection violated Title VII. The commission of fraud in the unemployment system does not constitute a business justification for the rejection of an applicant for the position of bus driver. The type of crime which Lola committed is totally unrelated to her ability to safely, efficiently and/or courteously drive a bus. Furthermore, the arrest is not recent.

Example 3: Tom, a Black male, applies to Lodge City for a position as a police officer. The arrest rate for Blacks is substantially disproportionate to that of Whites in Lodge City. In response to an arrest record inquiry, Tom states that he was arrested three years earlier for burglary. Tom is interviewed and asked to explain the circumstances surrounding his arrest. Tom admits that although the burglary charge was dismissed for lack of sufficient evidence, he did commit the crime. He claims, however, that he is a changed man, having matured since then. Lodge City rejects Tom. Police officers are: 1) entrusted with protecting the public; 2) authorized to enter nearly and dwelling under the appropriate circumstances; and 3) often responsible for transporting valuables which are confiscated as evidence. The department is, therefore, justified in declining to take the chance that Tom has reformed. Even if the department is completely satisfied that Tom has reformed, it may reject him because his credibility as a witness in court could be severely damaged if he were asked about his own arrest and the surrounding circumstances while testifying against a person whom he has arrested. Since an essential element of police work is the ability to effect an arrest and to credibly testify against the defendant in court, the department would have two separate business justifications for rejecting Tom.

The above example is contracted with circumstances under which an arrest record would not constitute ground for rejection.

Example 4: John, a Black male, applies to Lodge City for the same position as does Tom. John was arrested three years earlier for burglary. The charges were dismissed. Lodge City eliminates John from consideration without further investigation and will not consider the surrounding circumstances of the arrest. If allowed to explain, John could establish that his arrest was a case of mistaken identity and that someone else, who superficially fit John's description, was convicted of the crime for which John was initially charged. Since the facts indicate that John did not commit the conduct alleged in the arrest record, Lodge City has not carried its burden of proving a business justification for John's rejection.

Example 5: David, a Black male, applies for a teaching position in West High School. In response to a pre-employment inquiry, David states that he was arrested two years earlier for statutory rape, having been accused of seducing a seventeen-year old student in his class when he taught at another high school The charges were dismissed. West High rejects David. David relies on Litton to establish a prima facie case of race discrimination, and West High is unable to rebut the case with more current, ac curate or specific statistics. David denies that there is any truth to the charge. West High decides to conduct a further investigation and learns that David was arrested after another teacher found him engaged in sexual activity with Ann, one of his students, in the school's locker room. This event occurred on Ann's eighteenth birthday, but in the confusion of the arrest, no one realized that Ann had just reached the age of majority. Ann's parents and other teachers believed that David had seduced Ann, who has a schoolgirl "crush" on him, prior to her eighteenth birthday. However, since Ann would not testify against David, the charges had been dismissed. West High may reject David. Irrespective of Ann's age, West High is justified in attempting to protect its students from teachers who may make sexual advances toward them. Although he might not have been guilty of statutory rape, his conduct was unbefitting a teacher.

The above example is contracted to the following circumstances.

Example 6: Paul, a Black male, applies for the same position as does David. Paul was arrested two years earlier for statutory rape, having been accused of seducing a seventeen year old student in his class at another high school. West High eliminates Paul from consideration without further investigation and refuses to consider the surrounding circumstances of the arrest. When filing his complaint, Paul states that when he taught at the other high school, he befriended a troubled student in his class, Alice, who was terrified of her disciplinarian parents. Paul insists that he never touched Alice in any improper manner and that on the day before his arrest, Alice confided in him that she had become pregnant by her seventeen-year old boyfriend, Peter, and was afraid to tell her parents for fear that her father would kill him. Paul states that the charges were dismissed because the district attorney did not believe Alice's statements. The district attorney and the principal of the high school, Ms. P., confirm Paul's assessment of Alice. Ms. P; states that Peter confided in her that he was the father of Alice's baby and that Alice had assured him that nothing sexual had ever happened between her and Paul. Ms. P. states that there were indications that Alice's father was abusive, that he had beaten her into giving him the name of someone to blame for the pregnancy and that Alice thought that Paul could handle her father better than could Peter. Since Paul denied committing the conduct alleged and his explanation was well supported by the district attorney and his former employer, West High has not demonstrated a business justification for rejecting Paul.

The examples discussed above demonstrate that whereas an employer may consider a conviction as conclusive evidence that a person has committed the crime alleged, arrests can only be considered as a means of "triggering" further inquiry into that person's character or prior conduct. After considering all of the circumstances, if the employer reasonably concludes that the applicant's or employee's conduct is evidence that he or she cannot be trusted to perform the duties of the position in question, the employer may reject or terminate that person.

_____   Approved: _____

Date   Evan J Kemp, Jr.

                                         Chairman

Notice N-915 (7/29/87)

1.   <u>SUBJECT</u>: Policy statement on the use of statistics in charges involving the exclusion of individuals with conviction records from employment

2.   <u>PURPOSE</u>: This policy statement sets forth the commission's view as to the appropriate statistics to be used in evaluating an employer's policy of refusing to hire individuals with conviction records.

3.   <u>EFFECTIVE DATE</u>: July 29, 1987

4.   <u>EXPIRATION DATE</u>: January 29, 1988

5.   <u>ORIGINATOR</u>: title VII.EPA Division, Office of Legal Counsel.

6.   <u>INSTRUCTIONS</u>: insert behind §S 604 of EEOC Compliance Manual, Volume II

7.   <u>SUBJECT MATTER</u>:

INTRODUCTION

<u>Green v. Missouri Pacific Railroad Company</u>, 523 F.2d 1290, 10 EPD ¶ 10,314 (8th Cir. 1975), is the leading Title VII case on the issue of conviction records. In <u>Green</u>, the court held that the defendant's policy of refusing employment to any person convicted of a crime other than a minor traffic offense had an adverse impact on Black applicants and was not justified by business necessity. In a second appeal following remand, the court upheld the district court's injunctive order prohibiting the defendant from using an applicant's conviction record as an absolute bar to employment but allowing it to consider a prior criminal record as long as it constituted a business necessity. <u>Green v. Missouri Pacific Railroad Company</u>, 549 F.2d 1158, 1160, 13 EPD ¶ 11,579 (8th Cir. 1977). <u>See</u> <u>also</u> Commission Decision No. 72-1497, CCH EEOC Decisions (1973) ¶ 6352, and Commission Decision Nos. 74-89, 78-10, 78-35, and 80-10, CCH EEOC Decisions (1983) ¶¶ 6418, 6715, 6720, and 6822, respectively.

It is the Commission's position that an employer's policy or practice of excluding individuals from employment on the basis of their conviction records has an adverse impact on Blacks [1]/ and Hispanics [2]/ in light of statistics showing that they are convicted at a rate disproportionately greater than their representation in the population. Policy Statement on the Issue of Conviction Records Under Title VII (February 4, 1987). However, when the employer can present more narrowly drawn statistics showing

Either that Blacks and Hispanics are <u>not</u> convicted at a disproportionately greater rate or that there is no adverse impact in its own hiring process resulting from the convictions policy, then a no cause determination would be appropriate.

---

[1] <u>See</u>, <u>e.g.</u>, Commission Decision No. 72-1497, CCH EEOC Decisions (1973) ! 6352, and Commission Decision Nos. 74-89, 78-10, 78-35, and 80-10, CCH EEOC Decisions (1983) !! 6418, 6715, 6720, and 6822 respectively.

[2] <u>See</u> Commission Decision No. 78-03, CCH EEOC Decisions (1983) ¶ 6714.

1. Where the Employer's Policy is Not Crime-Specific

An employer's policy of excluding from employment all persons convicted of any crime is likely to create an adverse impact for Blacks and Hispanics based on national and regional conviction rate statistics. However, it is open to the respondent/employer to present more narrow local, regional, or applicant flow data, showing that the policy probably will not have an adverse impact on its applicant pool and/or in fact does not have an adverse impact on the pool. As Supreme Court stated,

> Although a statistical showing of disproportionate impact need not always be based on an analysis of the characteristics of actual applicants, Dothard v. Rawlinson, 433 U.S. 321, 330, evidence showing that the figures for the general population might not accurately reflect the pool of qualified job applicants undermines the significance of such figures. Teamsters v. United States, 431 U.S. 324, 340 n. 20.

New York City Transit Authority v. Beazer, 440 U.S. 568, 586 n. 29, 19 EPD ¶ 9027 at p. 6315 (1979). See also Costa v. Markey, 30 EPD ¶ 33,173 at p. 27,638 (1st Cir. 1982), vacated on other grounds, 706 F.2d 796, 32 EPD ¶ 32,622 (1st Cir.), cert. denied, 104 S. Ct. 547, 32 EPD ¶ 33,955 (1983).

If the employer provides applicant flow data, information should be sought to assure that the employer's applicant pool was not artificially limited by discouragement. For example, if many Blacks with conviction records did not apply for a particular job because they knew of the employer's policy and they therefore expected to be rejected, then applicant flow data would not be an accurate reflection of the conviction policy's actual effect. See Dothard v. Rowlinson, 433 US 321, 330 (1977). (Section 608, Recruitment, of Volume II of the Compliance Manual will provide a more detailed discussion of when and how to investigate for discouragement.

2. Where the Employer's Policy is Crime-Specific

In the past, when the Commission has evaluated an employer's "no convictions' policy dealing with a subcategory of crimes; e.g., theft, robbery, or drug-related crimes; the Commission has relied upon national or regional conviction statistics for crimes as a whole. See, e.g., Commission Decision No. 73-0257, CCH EEOC Decisions (1973) ! 6372, and Commission Decision Nos. 76-110 and 80-17, CCH EEOC Decisions (1983) !! 6676 and 6809, respectively. However, these statistics only show a probability of adverse impact for Blacks and Hispanics, while more narrow data may show no adverse impact.

If the employer can present more narrow regional or local data on conviction rates for all crimes showing that Blacks and Hispanics are not convicted at disproportionately higher rates, then a no cause determination would be proper. [3]/ Alternatively, the employer may present national, regional, or local data on conviction rates for the particular crime which is targeted in its crime-specific convictions policy. If such data shows no adverse impact, then a no cause determination would be appropriate. Finally, the employer can use applicant flow data to demonstrate that its conviction policy has not resulted in the exclusion from employment of a disproportionately high number of Blacks and Hispanics.

[Signed July 29, 1987 by Clarence Thomas]

---

[3] However, if even more narrow statistics, such as regional or local crime-specific data, show adverse impact, then a cause finding would be appropriate absent a justifying business necessity.

Notice N-915 (2/4/87)

1. SUBJECT: Policy Statement on the Issue of Conviction Records under Title VII of the Civil Rights Act of 1964, as amended, 42 U.S.C. § 2000e et seq. (1982).

2. PURPOSE: This policy statement sets forth the Commission's revised procedure for determining the existence of a business necessity justifying, for purposes of Title VII, the exclusion of an individual from employment on the basis of a conviction record.

3. EFFECTIVE DATE: February 27, 1987.

4. EXPIRATION DATE: September 15, 1987.

5. ORIGINATOR: Office of Legal Counsel.

6. INSTRUCTIONS: File behind page 604- 36 of EEOC Compliance Manual, Volume II, Section 604, Theories of Discrimination.

7. SUBJECT MATTER:

At the Commission meeting of November 26, 1985, the Commission approved a modification of its existing policy with respect to the manner in which a business necessity is established for denying an individual employment because of a conviction record. The modification, which is set forth below, does not alter the Commission's underlying position that an employer's policy or practice of excluding individuals from employment on the basis of their conviction records has an adverse impact on Blacks[1] and Hispanics[2] in light of statistics showing that they are convicted at a rate disproportionately greater than their representation in the population. Consequently, the Commission has held and continues to hold that such a policy or practice is unlawful under Title VII in the absence of a justifying business necessity. [3]

However, the Commission has revised the previous requirements for establishing business necessity [4] in the following manner. Where a charge involves an allegation that the Respondent employer [5]

---

[1] See, e.g., Commission Decision No. 72-1497, CCH EEOC Decisions (1973) ¶ 6352, and Commission Decision Nos. 74-89, 78-10, 78-35, and 80-10, CCH EEOC Decisions (1983) ¶¶ 6418, 6715, 6720, and 6822, respectively.

[2] See Commission Decision No. 78-03, CCH EEOC Decisions (1983) ¶ 6714.

[3] See, e.g., Commission decisions cited supra notes 1-2.

[4] Prior to this modification, for an employer to establish a business necessity justifying excluding an individual from employment because of a conviction record, the evidence had to show that the offense for which the applicant or employee was convicted was job-related. If the offense was not job-related, a disqualification based on the conviction alone violated Title VII. However, even if the offense were determined to be job-related, the employer had to examine other relevant factors to determine whether the conviction affected the individual's ability to perform the job in a manner consistent with the safe and efficient operation of the employer's business. The factors identified by the Commission to be considered by an employer included:

failed to hire or terminated the employment of the Charging Party as a result of a conviction policy or practice that has an adverse impact on the protected class to which the Charging Party belongs, The Respondent must show that it considered these three factors to determine whether its decision was justified by business necessity:

1. The nature and gravity of the offense or offenses:

2. The time that has passed since the conviction and/or completion of the sentence; and

3. The nature of the job held or sought. [6]

Footnote 4 continued:

1. The number of offenses and the circumstances of each offense for which the individual was convicted;

2. The length of time intervening between the conviction for the offense and the employment decision;

3. The individual's employment history; and

4. The individual's efforts at rehabilitation.

See, e.g., Commission Decision No. 78-35, CCH EEOC Decisions (1983) ! 6720.

Thus, under the previous procedure, business necessity was established by means of a two-step process: first, by showing that the conviction was job-related; then, by separately demonstrating that the conviction would affect the individual's ability to safety and efficiently perform the job upon consideration of the four factors enumerated above.

[5] Although the term "employer" is used herein, the Commission's position on this issue applies to all entities covered by Title VII. See e.g., Commission Decision No. 77-23, CCH EEOC Decisions (1983) ¶ 6710 (union's policy of denying membership to persons with conviction records unlawfully discriminated against Blacks).

[6] The Commission's revised business necessity analysis follows a decision by the United States Court of Appeals for the Eighth Circuit in the Green v. Missouri Pacific Railroad Company case. Green, 523 F.2d 1290, 10 EPD ¶ 10,314 (8th Cir. 1975), it the leading Title VII case on the issue of conviction records. In that case, the court held that the defendant's absolute policy of refusing employment to any person convicted of a crime other than a minor traffic offense had an adverse impact on Black applicants and was not justified by business necessity. On a second appeal in that case, following remand, the court upheld the district court's injunctive order prohibiting the defendant from using an applicant's conviction record as an absolute bar to employment but allowing it to consider a prior criminal record as a factor in making individual hiring decisions as long as the defendant took into account "the nature and gravity of the offense or offenses, the time that has passed since the conviction and/or completion of sentence, and the nature of the job for which the applicant has applied. Green v. Missouri Pacific Railroad Company, 549 F.2d 1158, 1160, 13 EPD ¶ 11,579 (8th Cir. 1977).

This procedure condenses the Commission's previous standard for business necessity, substituting a one-step analysis for the prior two-step procedure and retaining some but not all of the factors previously considered. [7] The modification principally eliminates the need to consider an individual's employment history and efforts at rehabilitation. However, consideration is still given to the job-relatedness of a conviction, covered by the first and third factors, and to the time frame involved, covered by the second factor. Moreover, the first factor encompasses consideration of the circumstances of the offense(s) for which an individual was convicted as well as the number of offenses.

The Commission continues to hold that, where there is evidence of adverse impact, an absolute bar to employment based on the mere fact that an individual has a conviction record is unlawful under Title VII. [8] The Commission's position on this issue is supported by the weight of judicial authority [9]

It should be noted that the modified procedure does not affect charges alleging disparate treatment on a prohibited basis in an employer's use of a conviction record as a disqualification for employment. A charge brought under the disparate treatment theory of discrimination is one where, for example, an employer allegedly rejects Black applicants who have conviction records but does not reject similarly situated White applicants.

With respect to conviction charges that are affected by this modification—that is, those raising the issue of adverse impact—Commission decisions that apply the previous standard are no longer available as Commission decision precedent for establishing business necessity. To the extent that such prior decisions are inconsistent with the position set forth herein, they are expressly overruled.

Questions concerning the application of the Commission's revised business necessity standard to the facts of a particular charge should be directed to the Regional Attorney for the Commission office in which the charge was filed.

[Signed 2-4-87 by Clarence Thomas]

_____   Approved:_____

Date   Clarence Thomas

                                                Chairman

---

[7] See discussion supra note 4.

[8] See, e.g., Commission Decision No. 78-35, CCH EEOC Decisions (1983) ¶ 6720.

[9] See Green, 523 F.2d at 1298; Carter v. Gallagher, 452 F.2d 315, 3 EPD ¶ 8335 (8th Cir. 1971), cert. denied, 406 US 950, 4 EPD ¶ 7818 (1972) (brought under 42 U.S.C. §§ 1981 and 1983); and Richardson v. Hotel Corporation of America, 332 F. Supp. 519, 4 EPD ¶ 7666 (E.D. La. 1971), aff'd mem., 468 F.2d 951, 5 EPD ¶ 8101 (5th Cir. 1972). See also Hill v. United States Postal Service, 522 F. Supp. 1283 (S.D.N.Y. 1981); Craig v. Department of Health, Education, and Welfare, 508 F. Supp. 1055 (W.D. Mo. 1981); and Cross v. United States Postal Service, 483 F. Supp. 1050 (E.D. Mo. 1979), aff'd in relevant part, 639 F.2d 409, 25 EPD ¶ 31,594 (8th Cir. 1981).

Appendix 4

Common Criminal Record Terms

Archaeological Dig Uncovers Ancient Race of
Skeleton People

— Headline from *The Onion*

Sometimes like white bones in black rock, criminal record information is right there in black and white. A criminal record is obtained, there is some activity on the report, but terms used are unfamiliar or the information is so abbreviated that the bare bones information must be fleshed out. With thousands of criminal record jurisdictions using thousands of terms, some unique, interpretation of information can present a challenge.

What follows are two glossaries:

- Definitions of Criminal Record Terms
- Common Abbreviations Found on Criminal Records

Many of these terms and abbreviations are taken from the Department of Justice Uniform Crime Reporting program that created the National Incident-Based Reporting System (NIBRS). NIBRS has the following goals:

1. To enhance the quantity, quality, and timeliness of crime statistical data collected by the law enforcement community.

2. To improve the methodology used for compiling, analyzing, auditing, and publishing the collected crime data.

Notwithstanding the above, this list should be used only as a guide in interpreting criminal record information. Some jurisdictions interpret some of the terms provided differently. Further, this list is obviously not all-inclusive. If you have a question on any term you find, check with your record provider, the jurisdiction from which the record was received or your legal counsel.

Criminal Records Offense Glossary

Most of definitions below reflect or use NIBRS standards. Others were obtained through law dictionaries. You should consider the context in which the word is used and also watch for the use of "degrees," such as: first, second, and third; voluntary or involuntary; and petty or grand. In many cases, these are assigned for purposes of applying fines or punishment and may be relevant to you in making your employment decision.

A

Abduction .... Taking away by violence or fraud and persuasion; kidnapping. Usually a female or wife, child or ward.

Abet .... See Aiding and Abetting.

Abstraction .... Taking away with intent to harm or deceive.

Accessory .... Not the perpetrator of the crime but in some way involved without being present in the commission of the crime.

Accessory After the Fact .... One who helps a criminal to elude arrest.

Accessory Before the Fact .... One who induces another to commit a crime.

Acquittal .... A not-guilty verdict absolving an accused party of guilt. Release or absolution.

Adjudication .... The legal process by which a case or claim is settled. May also be the final pronouncement of judgment in a case or claim.

Adjudication Withheld .... The court will withhold a decision until a future date. Usually some sort of probation is added and if the defendant complies with the conditions for a specified period of time, the case will be dismissed.

Affidavit .... A voluntarily, written statement of fact, confirmed by oath.

Affray .... Brawl or disturbance. Not premeditated.

Aggravated (assault, battery, arson, etc.) ...... Circumstances surrounding the commission of a crime or tort which increase or add to its injurious consequences.

Aiding and Abetting .... To assist and/or incite another to commit a crime.

Alias .... False name used in substitution of a legal name on official documents and for official purposes. Nicknames are not considered aliases. May be noted as AKA (Also Known As) on criminal records.

Antitrust Acts or Laws .... Laws to protect trade and commerce from unlawful practice.

Appeal .... A complaint to a superior court to review the decision of a lower court.

Appellant.. One who makes a complaint to a superior court to review the decision of a lower court.

Appellate Court... A court having jurisdiction of appeal and review. Not a trial court.

Appropriate .... To take something from another for one's own use or benefit.

Archive/Archives .... The place where records are stored after a certain specified period of time. The period of time a record is held at a court of record may differ between courts and states.

Arraignment... A call to the accused to come before the court to hear charges or enter a plea.

Arrest .... The taking of an individual into custody by law enforcement personnel for the purpose of charging them with an illegal act.

Arrest Record... An official form completed by the police department when a person is arrested. Also, a cumulative record of all instances in which a person has been arrested.

Arson... To unlawfully and intentionally damage or attempt to damage any real or personal property by fire or incendiary device.

Assault .... An unlawful attack by one person upon another.

    Aggravated Assault   An unlawful attack by one person upon another wherein the offender uses a weapon or displays it in a threatening manner, or the victim suffers obvious severe or aggravated bodily injury involving apparent broken bones, loss of teeth, possible internal injury, severe laceration, or loss of consciousness. This also included assault with a disease (as in cases when the offender is aware that he/she is infected with a deadly disease and deliberately attempts to inflict the disease by biting, spitting, etc.). This usually includes offenses such as Pointing and Presenting a Firearm, Brandishing a Firearm, etc. A severe laceration is one that should receive medical attention. A loss of consciousness must be the direct result of force inflicted on the victim by the offender.

    Simple Assault................................. An unlawful physical attack by one person upon another where neither the offender displays a weapon, nor the victim suffers obvious severe or aggravated bodily injury involving apparent broken bones, loss of teeth, possible internal injury, severe laceration, or loss of consciousness.

    Intimidation .... To unlawfully place another person in reasonable fear of bodily harm through the use of threatening words and/or other conduct but without displaying a weapon or subjecting the victim to actual physical attack. (This offense includes stalking).

B

Bad Checks .... Knowingly and intentionally writing and/or negotiating checks drawn against insufficient or nonexistent funds.

Bail .... An amount of money set by a judge at an initial appearance to ensure the return of the accused at subsequent proceedings.

Battery .... Non-consensual, unlawful contact, such as touching, beating or wounding of another. See Assault.

Bench Trial .... Trial by judge, without jury.

Bench Warrant .... A process delivered by the court directing a law enforcement agency to bring a specified individual before the court.

Bind Over .... To put under bond to appear in court. The term is also used when a case is shifted from a lower court to a higher court.

Blackmail .... An illegal demand for money or property under threat of harm or exposure of undesirable acts.

Bond .... A certificate of obligation, either unsecured or secured with collateral, to pay a specified amount of money within a specified period of time.

Bond Forfeiture .... Bond forfeiture occurs when a case has been disposed and a fine is to be, or has been paid. If it is a first offense, it is listed on the record but not classified as a conviction; any other time it is classified as a conviction.

Bookmaking .... An operation with the purpose of placing, registering, paying off or collecting debts for bets.

Bribery .... The offering, giving, receiving, or soliciting of anything of value (i.e., a bribe, gratuity, or kickback) to sway the judgment or action of a person in a position of trust or influence.

Burglary/Breaking and Entering .... The act of entering a premises, without the privilege to enter, with the purpose of committing a crime. States may classify as first, second, or third degree burglary.

C

Capias .... The Latin meaning is "That You Take". This is the name for several types of writs which require that a law enforcement official take a named defendant into custody.

Capital Case/Crime .... Case or crime for which the death penalty may be imposed.

Capital Punishment .... Punishment by death for capital crime.

Carnal.. Sexual, sensual. Carnal knowledge is sexual intercourse.

Cause of Action................................... One or more related charges combined and made against a defendant for wrongs committed.

Charge.. In criminal law, a charge is an allegation that an individual has committed a specific offense.

Citation.. An order issued by a law enforcement officer requiring appearance in court to answer a charge. Bail is not accepted in lieu of appearance.

Circuit.. Judicial division of the United States or of an individual state.

Circuit Courts..................................... Courts whose jurisdiction extends over several counties or districts. (There are thirteen judicial circuits wherein the U.S. Courts of Appeals reside).

City Court.. Courts that try persons accused of violating municipal ordinances. City courts may have jurisdiction over minor civil or criminal cases, or both.

Civil Disorder..................................... A violent public disturbance by three or more people which causes danger, damage or injury to property or persons.

Co-defendant....................................... One of a group of two or more people charged in the same crime.

Coercion... The use of physical force or threats to compel someone to commit an act against their will.

Compounding Crime............................ The receipt by an individual of consideration in exchange for an agreement not to prosecute or inform on someone who they know has committed a crime.

Concurrent Sentences........................ Two or more terms of imprisonment served simultaneously.

Conditional Discharge....................... A conviction. Court issues the discharge from the jail and requires defendant to comply with some conditions. Regardless whether defendant complies with rules or not, he/she is still convicted (GUILTY) and case can never be expunged.

Conditional Release .... The release from a correctional facility before full sentence has been served which is conditioned on specific behavior. If conditions are not met, the individual may be returned to the facility.

Consecutive Sentences...................... Multiple sentences, served one after the other.

Conspiracy .... The coming together of two or more people for the purpose of committing an unlawful act or to commit a lawful act by unlawful means.

Contempt of Court .... An act committed which serves to obstruct the court in its administration or authority.

Controlled Substance .... A drug whose availability is restricted by law.

Conversion .... The unauthorized taking of another's property.

Conviction .... Guilty verdict in a criminal trial.

Count/Charge .... An offense named in a cause of action. A cause of action may contain multiple counts or charges, each relating to the others but identifying a separate offense.

Counterfeiting/Forgery .... The altering, copying, or imitation of something, without authority or right, with the intent to deceive or defraud by passing the copy or thing altered or imitated as that which is original or genuine or the selling, buying or possession of an altered, copied, or imitated thing with the intent to deceive or defraud.

Court of Record .... The court where the permanent record of all proceedings is held.

Credit Card Fraud .... Use, or attempted use of a credit card to purchase goods or services with the intent to avoid payment of such.

Crime Against Nature .... Deviate sexual intercourse.

Criminal Nonsupport .... Failure to pay child support

Culpability .... Blame, or degree of responsibility for a crime. This may be in degrees of purposeful, knowingly, recklessly or by negligence.

Cumulative Sentence .... A sentence that takes effect after a prior sentence is completed for crimes tried under the same cause of action.

Curfew/Loitering/Vagrancy .... The violation of a court order, regulation, ordinance, or law requiring the withdrawal of persons from the streets or other specified areas; prohibiting persons from remaining in an area or place in an idle or aimless manner; or prohibiting persons from going from place to place without visible means of support. (Includes begging.)

D

Dangerous Weapon .... Something that is capable, though not designed to cause serious injury or death.

De Novo .... Latin for "anew" or "afresh". Usually used as Trial De Novo. New trial or one that is held for a second time, as if there had been no previous trial or decision.

Dead Docket .... The case never went to trial. The case can be reopened if new evidence is submitted.

Deadly Weapon .... A weapon designed to cause serious injury or death.

Defendant... A person against whom a cause of action is taken.

Deferred Adjudication of Guilt .... The final judgment is delayed for a period of time. Can be likened to probation before a final verdict. If "probation" is completed without incident, the charges are usually dropped and the case is dismissed. During the "probationary period" the disposition is not necessarily considered a conviction.

Deferred Discharge .... Dismissed and considered a non-conviction.

Deferred Probation .... The judge doesn't make a finding of guilt; he assigns probation. If probation is completed without incident, the charges are usually dropped.

Deferred Sentence .... Postponement of the pronouncement of the sentence.

Defraud .... Knowingly misrepresenting facts to cheat or trick.

Degree (First, Second, or Third, A, B or C).. Classification assigned to a crime, depending on circumstances, for purposes of determining punishment. First degree is considered most serious than third; A is more serious than C. Degrees may be assigned to the actual crime (IE: murder in the first or second degree) or the class of crimes (IE: felony or misdemeanor).

Destruction/Damage/Vandalism of Property To willfully or maliciously destroy, damage, deface, or otherwise injure real or personal property without the consent of the owner or the person having custody or control of it. (The crime of arson is not included in this definition.)

Directed Verdict... A determination by a jury, made at the direction of the judge. A directed verdict happens in cases where there has been a lack of evidence, an overwhelming amount of evidence, or where the law is in favor of one of the parties.

Dismissal... Finally disposing of the cause without further consideration. May be voluntary or involuntary. When involuntary, there is usually lack of prosecution or failure to produce sufficient evidence.

Dismissal Without Leave After Deferred
Prosecution.. Charges dismissed after specified time (90 days to 1 year) provided certain conditions have been met such as participating in specified program of anger control or drug counseling or providing community service, etc.

Disorderly Conduct...................................... Any behavior that tends to disturb the public peace or decorum, scandalize the community, or shock the public sense of morality.

Disposed/Disposition .... The final settlement in the matter. Examples of disposed cases are those with a finding of guilt (conviction), innocence, or acquittal.

Diversion Program .... To set aside. A court direction which calls a defendant, who has been found guilty, to attend a work or educational program as part of probation.
May include some type of anger management, drug rehab, etc. If the condition of program is met, charge may be considered non-conviction.

Diversity of Citizenship .... A crime or claim which extends between citizens of different states. This is one of the grounds that can be used to invoke the jurisdiction of the U.S. Federal District Court.

Docket Record .... A court's official record of proceedings and calendar of upcoming cases.

Driving Under the Influence .... Driving or operating a motor vehicle or common carrier while mentally or physically impaired as the result of consuming an alcoholic beverage or using a drug or narcotic. Complete intoxication is not required. Individual state statutes specify the blood alcohol content at which a person is presumed to be under the influence of intoxicating liquor.

Drug/Narcotic Offenses .... The violation of laws prohibiting the production, distribution, and/or use of certain controlled substances and the equipment or devices utilized in their preparation and/or use. This may include the unlawful cultivation, manufacture, distribution, sale, purchase, use, possession, transportation, or importation of any controlled drug or narcotic substance.

Drunkenness.. To drink alcoholic beverages to the extent that one's mental faculties and physical coordination are substantially impaired. This includes Drunk and Disorderly.

Due Diligence .... A reasonable and expected measure of attention taken for a particular action. Not measurable by an absolute standard, but dependant on the situation.

Due Process of Law .... Procedures followed by law enforcement and courts to insure the protection of an individual's rights as assigned by the Constitution.

E

Embezzlement .... The unlawful misappropriation by an offender to his/her own use or purpose of money, property, or some other thing of value entrusted to his/her care, custody, or control, usually through employment.

Ex parte .... Means on one side only. When an act is one for one party only. For example, in an Ex parte proceeding, only one party to the case is heard.

Expunge/Expunged .... When a record of an offense is expunged it will not appear on a released criminal history. The record may be destroyed or sealed after a certain period of time. Records may be expunged in juvenile cases, or upon satisfactory completion of a court-ordered probation and/or class(s).

Extortion/Blackmail .... To unlawfully obtain money, property, or any other thing of value, either tangible or intangible, through the use of threat of force, misuse of authority, threat of criminal prosecution, threat of destruction or reputation or social standing, or through other coercive means.

Extradition .... The surrender of an individual accused or convicted of a crime by one state to another.

F

Family Offenses, Nonviolent .... Unlawful, nonviolent acts by a family member (or legal guardian) that threaten the physical, mental, or economic well-being or morals of another family member and that are not classifiable as other offenses such as Assault, Incest, Statutory Rape, etc. Examples include: Abandonment, Desertion, Neglect and nonsupport.

Felonious .... Describing an offense which is done with malicious, villainous criminal intent. IE: felonious assault.

Felony .... A serious offense carrying a penalty of incarceration from one year to life in a state prison, to the death penalty.

Felony Conversion
(Fraudulent Conversion) .... Similar to embezzlement or theft. An example of felony conversion is if someone sold goods for a company, and kept the money instead of turning it in to the company. (North Carolina)

Forcible Entry .... Entering or taking possession of property with force, threats or menacing conduct.

Fraud .... The intentional perversion of the truth for the purpose of inducing another person or other entity in reliance upon it to part with something of value or to surrender a legal right.

False Pretenses/Swindle/Confidence Game—The intentional misrepresentation of existing fact or condition or the use of some other deceptive scheme or device to obtain money, goods, or other things of value.

Credit Card/Automatic Teller Machine Fraud—The unlawful use of a credit (or debit) card or automatic teller machine for fraudulent purposes.

Impersonation—Falsely representing one's identity or position and acting in the character or position thus unlawfully assumed to deceive others and thereby gain a profit or advantage, enjoy some right or privilege, or subject another person or entity to an expense, charge, or liability that would not have otherwise been incurred.

Welfare Fraud—The use of deceitful statement, practices, or devices to unlawfully obtain welfare benefits.

Wire Fraud—The use of an electric or electronic communications facility to intentionally transmit a false and/or deceptive message in furtherance of a fraudulent activity.

G

Gambling Offenses .... To unlawfully bet or wager money or something else of value; assist, promote, or operate a game of chance for money or some other stake; possess or transmit wagering information; manufacture, sell, purchase, possess, or transport gambling equipment, devices, or goods; or tamper with the outcome of a sporting event or contest to gain a gambling advantage.

Betting/Wagering—To unlawfully stake money or something else of value on the happening of an uncertain event or on the ascertainment of a fact in dispute.

Operating/Promoting/Assisting Gambling—To unlawfully operate, promote, or assist in the operation of a game of chance, lottery, or other gambling activity.

Gambling Equipment Violations—To unlawfully manufacture, sell, buy, possess, or transport equipment, devices, and/or goods used for gambling purposes.

Sports Tampering—To unlawfully alter, meddle in, or otherwise interfere with a sporting contest or event for the purpose of gaining a gambling advantage.

Grand Jury .... A body of persons with the authority to investigate and accuse, but not to try cases. The grand jury will listen to and review evidence to see if it there are sufficient grounds to bring an individual to trial.

Grand Larceny .... The theft of property over a specified value. Dollar amounts vary by state.

Gross .... Flagrant, out of measure.

Gross Misdemeanor .... Serious misdemeanor.

Guilt/Guilty .... Final disposition. Having committed a crime.

H

Habeas Corpus .... A writ requesting a trial or the release of a prisoner.

Habitual Violator .... To have committed the same offence three times. Can also be charged as a habitual offender.

Hijacking .... To take control of a vehicle by intimidation, force or threatened force. Also, the theft of goods while in transit, as when transported in trucks.

Homicide .... The killing of another human being by another. . "Justifiable homicide" occurs in cases such as during the enforcement of law, and/or occurs without evil intent. "Excusable homicide" may occur by accident or in self-defense. "Felonious homicide" is the killing of another without justification. This type has two degrees – manslaughter and murder, depending on circumstances or intent. See Manslaughter; Murder.

Hung Jury .... A hung jury is one in which all jurors cannot reach a consensus required for a verdict.

I

Illicit .... Prohibited or unlawful.

Incendiary .... One who intentionally set fires. Arsonist.

Incorrigible .... One who is incapable of reform.

Indictment .... A formal, written accusation made by the grand jury.

Infraction .... Violation of local ordinance or state statute usually resulting in a fine or limited period of incarceration. Term usually used in traffic offenses.

Injunction .... A court order which prohibits a person from doing a specified act for a specified period of time.

Intent .... The frame of mind or attitude of the person at the time an act was committed. See Culpability.

Intoxicate, Intoxication .... Reduction of physical or mental capabilities caused by the ingestion of an intoxicating substance such as alcohol or drugs.

Involuntary Dismissal .... Dismissed due to lack of prosecution or lack of evidence.

J

Judgment... The final decision of the court regarding a claim or case.

Jurisdiction.. The power of a court to question facts, apply law, make decisions and judgments.

K

Kidnapping/Abduction................................ The unlawful seizure, transportation, and/or detention of a person against his/her will or of a minor without the consent of his/her custodial parent(s) or legal guardian.

L

Larceny .... The unlawful taking of another person's property. Larceny is commonly classified as "petty" or "grand" depending on the value of the property. Dollar values to establish classifications of "petty" and "grand" may vary from state to state.

Pocket-picking—The theft of articles from another person's physical possession by stealth where the victim usually does not become immediately aware of the theft.

Purse-snatching—The grabbing or snatching of a purse, handbag, etc., from the physical possession of another person.

Shoplifting—The theft by someone other than an employee of the victim of goods or merchandise exposed for sale.

Theft from Motor Vehicle—The theft of articles from a motor vehicle, locked or unlocked.

Legal Malice .... An act, committed without just cause or excuse, intended to inflict harm or cause death.

Lewd and Lascivious .... Obscene, indecent.

Libel.. Defamation of another person through print, pictures, or signs.

Lis Pendens .... A pending suit.

M

Magistrate .... Public officials, including judicial officers who have limited jurisdiction in criminal cases and civil causes.

Mail Fraud.. The use of the mail system to commit a fraud.

Malice Aforethought.................................... Planning to commit an unlawful act without just cause or excuse.

Manslaughter.. The unpremeditated killing of a person. Can be voluntary or involuntary, determined by circumstances. The feature distinguishing involuntary manslaughter from voluntary is the absence of intent to cause death or commit an act that might be expected to produce death or harm.
Voluntary manslaughter is homicide that is committed during an act in the heat of passion.

Negligent Manslaughter—The killing of another person through negligence.

Mayhem .... The intentional infliction of injury on another which causes amputation, disfigurement or impairs the function of any part of the body.

Mistrial.. A trial which is terminated or declared invalid. Reasons for mistrial include misconduct on the part of the jury, defense team or the court, or illness on the part of the judge, jury or defendant. May be followed by a retrial on the same charges.

Motor Vehicle Theft..................................... The theft of a motor vehicle. This includes a self propelled vehicle that runs on the surface of land and not on rails and that fits one of the following property descriptions: automobiles, buses, recreational vehicles, trucks, and other vehicles such as motorcycles, snowmobiles or golf carts.

Murder .... Unlawful killing with malice aforethought. Murder is willful, deliberate and premeditated, or done during the commission of a crime. This classification of crime is generally divided by degrees, murder in the first degree and murder in the second degree, for the purpose of imposing penalties.

N

Negligence .... Flagrant and reckless disregard of the safety of others. Willful indifference.

Negotiated Plea .... See Plea Bargain.

No Bill or No True Bill .... The decision by a grand jury that it will not bring indictment against the accused on the basis of the allegations and evidence presented by the prosecutor.

No Contest .... A plea in which the defendant does not contest the charge. This has the same effect as a guilty plea except the conviction cannot be used against the defendant in a civil suit.

No Papered... Charges were not pursued. (This is a legal term in Washington, D.C.)

No Probable Cause....................................... There was not sufficient reason to bring case to trial.

Nolle Pros or Nolle Prosequi........................ Latin phrase used by the district attorney or plaintiff when they do not wish to prosecute or proceed with the action.

Nolo Contendre... Latin phrase used by a defendant to say "I do not wish to contest." This plea in a criminal case has the legal effect of pleading guilty. See No Contest.

O

Obtain Property under False Pretense .... The misrepresentation of the value of something. Passing bad check.

P

Pander .... To provide products or services which cater to the sexual gratification of others. To entice another into prostitution.

Parole .... To release from confinement after serving part of a sentence, usually with terms and conditions provided in the parole order.

Parole Violation .... An act that does not conform to the terms of parole.

Peeping Tom .... To secretly look through a window, doorway, keyhole, or other aperture for the purpose of voyeurism.

Perjury.. Intentionally making a false statement under oath.

Plea.. The defendant's formal answer to a charge.

Plea Bargain .... A plea of guilt to a lesser offense in return for a lighter sentence.

Pornography/Obscene Material..................... The violation of laws or ordinances prohibiting the manufacture, publishing, sale, purchase, or possession of sexually explicit material, e.g., literature or photographs.

Prayer for Judgment, 1st Offense (NC).......... Asking the court to give leniency. No finding of guilt by the court.

Pre-Trial Intervention .... An extensive background check to help determine if charges will be pressed.

Probation .... Relief of all or part of a sentence on the promise of proper conduct.

Prostitution .... To unlawfully engage in sexual relations for profit.

Q

Quash/Quashed .... Declined to prosecute but with the option to reopen the case.

R

Racketeering .... An organized conspiracy for the purpose of committing crimes of extortion or coercion.

Rape .... Sex without consent. May be forcible or by intoxication, with a person who is underage and unable to give consent, or with a person with diminished mental and/or physical capabilities.

Reckless Endangerment .... An act which does or could cause injury to another, not necessarily with intent.

Refused .... Charges were not accepted by the District Attorney's Office.

Remand .... To return an individual to custody pending further trial, or to return a case from an appellate to a lower court for further proceedings.

Restraining Order .... An order prohibiting a specified action until such time that a hearing on an application for an injunction can be held.

Retired (as Disposition) .... The case can be brought up within the next year if the individual is arrested for anything. It is the judge's decision and only he can take action. If the individual remains "clean," then the case can be dismissed.

RICO Act .... Racketeer Influenced and Corrupt Organizations Act.

Robbery .... The taking or attempting to take anything of value under confrontational circumstances from the control, custody, or care of another person by force or threat or violence and/or by putting the victim in fear of immediate harm.

S

Secreting Lien Property .... Hiding property that has a lien filed against it.

Sedition .... Advocating the overthrow or reform of a government by unlawful means.

Sentence .... A judgment of punishment for a criminal act.

Serious Misdemeanor .... Having a more severe penalty than other misdemeanors.

Slander .... Defamation verbal communication. Making false and malicious statements about another.

Sodomy .... Oral or anal sexual intercourse with another person, forcibly and/or against that person's will or not forcibly against the person's will in instances where the victim is incapable of giving consent because of his/her youth or because or his/her temporary or permanent mental or physical incapacity.

Solicitation .... Asking, urging or enticing.

Status: Closed.. No further action will occur on this case; cannot be reopened at later date.

Statutory Rape... Sexual activity by an adult with a person under the age of consent.

Stricken .... To eliminate or expunge.

Suspended Sentence.................................... Deferment of punishment usually over a period of probation.

T

Theft of Services .... Obtaining services without consent through deception, threat, tampering, etc.

Theft/unauthorized....................................... Means the person used someone else's information, credit card, check, or something similar.

Trespassing .... To unlawfully enter land, a dwelling, or other real property.

Truncated Files.. Destroyed or partially destroyed. Unable to obtain more information.

U

Under the Influence of Intoxicating
Liquor or Drugs.. Any condition where the nervous system, brain or muscles are impaired to an appreciable degree by an intoxicating substance.

Usury... Charging more interest than is permitted by law for a loan.

Unlawful Entry... Entry without force and without permission by means of fraud or other wrongful act.

Uttering .... To forge another's name.

V

Vacate (Judgment) .... To make void; to cancel.

Vehicular Homicide .... Death of another caused by the intentional, unlawful or negligent operation of a motor vehicle.

Venue.. The geographic area where the case or claim occurred, within which a court with jurisdiction can hear and determine a case. A change of venue, or the moving of a case from one court to another may be granted for such reasons as when the court does not think the defendant can get a fair trial in that area or for the convenience of the parties in a civil case.

Verdict .... The formal, final decision or finding made by a jury or judge.

Voluntary Dismissal.................................... The court or district attorney dismisses the charges.

W

Waiver by Magistrate.................................... Charges are waived after the defendant agrees to pay a fine. The defendant is not prosecuted on this charge.

Waiver of Jury.. The right to a jury trial is waived and the judge makes the decision of guilt or innocence.

Wanton... Reckless, malicious. Without regard for the rights of others, indifferent to consequences to health, life or the reputation of another. Usually done without intent, but an act so unreasonable the perpetrator should know that harm will result.

Warrant .... Court order authorizing a law enforcement official to arrest or perform search and seizure.

Weapons Offenses... The unlawful sale, distribution, manufacture, alteration, transport, possession or use of a deadly or dangerous weapon.

With Specifications .... When W/S is listed after a charge, it is usually followed with a description of violence involved with the charge.

Withheld... Adjudication withheld.

Writ .... A written court order, or a judicial process.

Wrongful Entrustment.................................. Allowing an unlicensed driver to operate a motor vehicle.

Y

Youthful Offender... Classification of youths and young adults, generally older then juveniles. In the 18 to 25 year age group, these individuals are sometimes given special sentencing consideration for the purpose of rehabilitation, sometimes through education and counseling.

Youthful Training Act................................... Usually a non-conviction. Used for juvenile first-time offenders. It may be reported on a criminal record. If the juvenile complies with the sentence, case will be dropped from the record when the offender reaches adulthood.

Appendix 5

Common Criminal Record Abbreviations

> *I've got two words for you: "Keep it real!" And that's two because "it" is just an abbreviation!*
>
> — Ali G in the movie *Ali G Indahouse*

Especially mystifying — and aggravating — is obtaining a criminal record and the offense appears to be an acronym or abbreviation. The challenge is more than simply understanding the definition of the offense, but understanding what offense to which they are referring.

What follows are some of the more common abbreviations, but keep in mind two things:

1. The abbreviations shown below are not universally used and agreed upon by different jurisdictions. For example if you obtain a criminal record with an offense of "A" as shown below, do not automatically assume it is referring to an "assault" if there is no supporting evidence. Some jurisdictions abbreviate burglary as "B." Some jurisdictions abbreviate "B" as "Breaking." Contact your record provider or the jurisdiction to investigate unclear abbreviations.

2. There are many more abbreviations in use that provided here.

- a -

A	Assault
A ARMED	Assault, Armed
A INT MAIM	Assault with Intent to Maim
A TO K (or MAIM, MUR, RAPE, ROB)	Assault to Kill (or Maim, Murder, Rape, Rob)
A & B	Assault and Battery
A & ROB (armed)	Assault and Robbery (armed)
AA/DW	Aggravated Assault with a Deadly Weapon
AA/PO	Aggravated Assault Police Officer (Dallas County)
AA/SBI	Aggravated Assault / Serious Bodily Injury
AAWW	Aggravated Assault With Weapon

ABC Act	Alcohol Beverage Control Act
ABD	Abduction
ABNDN or ABNDNT	Abandon or Abandonment
ABST	Abstraction
ABUS LANG	Abusive Language
ABWIK	Assault and Battery With Intent to Kill
ACAF	Accessory After the Fact
ACBF	Accessory Before the Fact
ACC	Accessory
ACC AFT FACT REC	Accessory After the Fact, Receiving
ACC BURG	Accessory to Burglary
ACC TO ISS CHK	Accessory to Issuing Check
ACC TO JL BRK	Accessory to Jail Break
ACC TO L	Accessory to Larceny
ACC TO MUR	Accessory to Murder
ACC TO ROB	Accessory to Robbery
ACCOMP DD	Accompanying Drunken Driver
ACCPL	Accomplice
ACCPT BRB	Accepting a Bribe
ADJ	Adjudication
ADLTY	Adultery
ADW	Assault with Deadly Weapon
ADW/FIREARM	Assault with Deadly Weapon/Firearms
AFA	Alien Firearms Act
AFCF	After Former Conviction of a Felony
AFDVT	Affidavit
AFFR	Affray
AFFR WDW	Affray With Deadly Weapon
AFO	Assaulting a Federal Officer
AGG A	Aggravated Assault
AID & ABET LOTT	Aiding and Abetting Lottery
AID & HAR ESC PR	Aiding and Harboring an Escaped Prisoner
AID PR TO ESC	Aiding a Prisoner to Escape
AIDA	Automobile Information Disclosure Act
AKA	Also Known As
ALIEN POSS FIREARMS	Alien in Possession of Firearms
ALLOW DR W/O PRMT	Allowing One to Drive Without a Permit

ALT	Altering
ANNOY & SOL	Annoying and Soliciting
APC	Actual Physical Control
APCV	Actual Physical Control of a Vehicle
APIPOCC	Appropriating Property In Possession Of Common Carrier
APP. CT.	Appellate Court
APPROP	Appropriating
APO	Assaulting Police Officer
AR	Anti-Racketeering
ARD	Accelerated Rehabilitation Disposition
ARL	Antiriot Laws
ARMED WDW	Armed With Dangerous Weapon
ARSON OF PERS PROP	Arson of Personal Property
ASLT	Assault
ASLT TO RA	Assault to Rob Armed
ASMB	Assembling
ASST	Assisting
ASST ATT TO RAPE	Assisting in Attempt to Commit Rape
ASST PROST	Assisting Prostitution
ATL	Antitrust Law
ATPT	Attempt
ATT	Attempt or Attempted
ATT RA	Attempted Robbery Armed
ATTEMPT	Attempt to Steal, Commit, etc.
AUTO H & R	Auto – Hit and Run
AUTO NO LIC	Auto – No License
AVIN	Altered Vehicle Identification Number
AWDW	Assault with Deadly Weapon
AWDWIKISI	Assault with a Deadly Weapon with Intent to Kill or Inflict Serious Injury
AWOL	Absent Without Leave

- b -

B	Breaking
B	Battery (FBI definition)
B & E	Breaking and Entering
B of P	Breach of Peace (FBI definition)
B/F	Bond Forfeiture

BAIL JUMPG	Bail Jumping
BATT	Battery
BB	Bank Burglary
BC	Bad Check or Bogus Check
BF & E	Bank Fraud and Embezzlement
BI	Bodily Injury
BKMKG	Bookmaking
BL	Bank Larceny
BLKML	Blackmail
BOND FORF	Bond Forfeiture
BOP	Breach of Peace
BORD	Bill of Review Denied
BORG	Bill of Review Granted
BR	Bank Robbery
BRBG	Bribing
BRBY	Bribery
BRCSP	Buying, Receiving, Concealing Stolen Property
BTCP	Probation Following Boot Camp Incarceration
BTG	Beating
BNID	Burglary Not In a Dwelling
BURG	Burglary
BURN DEST INS PROP	Burning, Destroying, etc., Insured Property
BURN INT INJ INS	Burning, Intent to Injure Insurer

- C -

C & F	Stands for call and failed, which means voluntary dismissal by judge or court
C to D of M	Contributing to the Delinquency of a Minor
CAID	Criminal Activity In Drugs
CAR B	Car Breaking
CAR PROWL	Car Prowling
CC ABUSE/USE	Credit Card Abuse
CCDW	Carrying Concealed Deadly Weapon
CCF	Carrying Concealed Firearm
CCW	Carry Concealed Weapon
CD	Conditional Discharge
CDW	Carrying Dangerous Weapon
CIT	Citation Code (Georgia State)

CK...(Check) can also mean Carnal Knowledge (FC: Female child)
CL ....Complied with Law
CMPT...Contempt
CNSP ....Conspiracy to Commit
CNTY CRT..County Court
COC ....Contempt of Court
COMM IND ACT..Committing Indecent Act
COMN ....Common (used with assault, cheat, drunk, etc.)
COMP FEL..Compounding a Felony
CONC EVID..Concealing Evidence
CONSP..Conspiracy
CONT DA..Controlled Dangerous Substance
CONV ....Conversion
CPCS...Criminal Possession of a Controlled Substance
CPDD..Criminal Possession of Dangerous Drugs
CPSP ....Criminal Possession of Stolen Property
CR B ....Criminal – B (Not Felony)
CR to ANI..Cruelty to Animals
CR to CHDN...Cruelty to Children
CRIM CRLESS...Criminal Carelessness
CRLESS DR ....Careless Driving
CRNL..Carnal
CRNL KNLDG...Carnal Knowledge (of FC – Female Child)
CRSP...Criminal Receiving Stolen Property
CRV ....Conditional Release Violator
CSA...Controlled Substance Act
CSCS...Criminal Sale of Controlled Substances
CTFG or CTFT ....Counterfeiting or Counterfeit
CW ....Concealed Weapons
CW W/O PRMT OR LIC...............................Carrying Weapon Without Permit or License
CWIK...Cutting With Intent to Kill

- d -

D & D(C) ....Drunk and Disorderly (Conduct)
D & S ....Dangerous and Suspicious
DA..Drug Abuse
DAA W/O OP ....Driving Away Auto Without Owner's Permission

DAMV	Destruction of Aircraft or Motor Vehicles
DAR	Driving After Revocation
DC	Disorderly Conduct
DCI	Driving Car Intoxicated
DCI (-D or -L)	Driving Car Intoxicated (-Drugs or -Liquor)
DCMW	Drunk in Control of Motor Vehicle
DE	Deferred
DEAL IN LOTT POL	Dealing in Lottery Police
DECEPTIVE PRACTICE	Writing Bad Checks
DEF BLDG	Defacing Building
DEF BRAKES	Defective Brakes
DEF GPVT BONDS	Defacing Government Bonds
DEF OR DEST PERS PROP	Defacing or Destroying Personal Property
DEF OR DEST PUB PROP	Defacing or Destroying Public Property
DEFR	Defrauding
DELIN	Delinquent
DEP	Deportation
DEPOS IN US PO THRT	Depositing in U.S. Post Office Threat to Injure Person or Property of Addressee
DESER	Desertion or Deserter
DESTR OF IP	Destruction of Interstate Property
DGP	Destruction of Government Property
DH	Disorderly House
DIP	Drunk In Public
DIS	Disorderly
DISCH FIREARMS	Discharging Firearms
DISM	Charge Dismissed
DISP MTG PROP	Disposing of Mortgaged Property
DISP STLN PROP	Disposing of Stolen Property
DIST	Disturbance
DIST PEACE	Disturbing the Peace
DISTIL	Distilling
DISTR	Distributing
DIV	Diverting
DL	Drug Law
DMG PROP	Damaging Property
DOF	Desecration of Flag

DP .... Disorderly Person
DR W/O PRMT .... Driving Without Permit
DRK .... Drunk
DRUG/MOP SCH.. Drugs Manufactured or Possessed Near a School
DRW CHK W/O FDS .... Drawing Check Without Funds
DRW OR EXH FIREARMS........................... Drawing or Exhibiting Firearms
DSMD.. Dismissed
DSPLY VOID OP LIC .... Displaying Void Operator's License
DUI (L) .... Driving Under Influence (of Liquor)
DUS .... Driving Under Suspension
DV.. Domestic Violence
DW.. Dangerous Weapon
DWA... Dangerous Weapon Act
DWAI .... Driving While Ability Impaired
DWD (-D or -L) .... Driving While Drunk (-Drugs or -Liquor)
DWI .... Driving While Impaired
DWLG .... Dwelling
DWLS .... Driving While License Suspended
DWLS/SR .... Driving While License Suspended/Sentence Reduced
DYN.. Dynamiting
DYN INH BLDG.. Dynamiting Inhabited Building

- e -

EAR .... Escape and Rescue
ECT.. Extortionate Credit Transactions
EFP.. Escaped Federal Prisoner
EGP... Embezzlement of Government Property
EID.. Explosives and Incendiary Devices
EL.. Election Laws
ELIM... Elimination
EMBZ .... Embezzlement or Embezzling
ENDANG... Endangering
ENDANG L OR H OF CHILD...................... Endangering the Life or Health of a Child
ENT (or E) .... Entering
ENTIC.. Enticing
ENTIC FEM U AGE..................................... Enticing Females Under Age
ENTIC INTO IMM PLACE .... Enticing Into Immoral Place

ESC	Escaped
ESC CONV	Escaped Convict
ESC FED CUST	Escaping Federal Custody
ESC LAW FRAUD VIOLATION	Employment Security Commission Law Fraud Violation (Welfare Fraud)
ESP	Espionage
EV	Evasion or Evading
EV TAX L	Evasion of Tax Law
EVSDRP	Eavesdropping
EXH	Exhibiting
EXPLSV	Explosives
EXPOS	Exposing
EXT	Extortion

- f -

F1 – F6	Felonies with F1 being the most serious type of offense
FACL	Facilitation Of
FAG	Fraud Against Government
FAIL	Failure
FAIL ANS SUM	Failure to Answer Summons
FAIL ASST AFT CAUS WRK	Failure to Assist After Causing Wreck
FAIL TO APP	Failure to Appear
FAIL TO OBT LIC OR PRMT	Failure to Obtain a License or Permit
FAIL TO PROV	Failure to Provide
FAIL RPT ACC	Failure to Report and Accident
FAIL RPT FEL	Failure to Report a Felony
FAIL SRV LEG PROC	Failure to Serve Legal Process
FAIL TO AID	Failure to Stop and Render Aid
FALSE	Pretenses Writing Insufficient Check
FCC	False Claiming U.S. Citizenship
FCR	Fines, Costs and Restitution
FEL RED	Felony Reduction
FERIC	False Entries in Records of Interstate Carriers
FF	Fugitive File
FFA	Federal Firearms Act
FFJ	Fugitive from Justice
FFST	Fail to File State Taxes
FHA	Federal Housing Administration

FHIF	Frequenting House of Ill Fame
FICT	Fictitious
FIREARMS A	Firearms Act
FJDA	Federal Juvenile Delinquency Act
FLS	False
FLS ADV	False Advertising
FLS CL	False Claims
FLS FIRE ALA	False Fire Alarm
FLS POL ALA	False Police Alarm
FMFR	Failure to Maintain Financial Responsibility
FOA	Fugitive Other Authorities
FORC ENT	Forcible Entry
FORF	Forfeiture, Forfeiting
FORG	Forged, Forgery
FORG & PASS	Forging and Passing
FORG DR PRESC	Forging Doctor's Prescription
FORG US OBLI	Forging U.S. Obligations
FORN	Fornication
FP	False Pretenses
FR	False Report
FRA	Federal Reserve Act
FRD	Fraud, Fraudulent
FTA/TP CST	Failure to Appear to Pay Fine and Cost
FSRA	Failure to Stop and Render Aid after a Collision
FUDE	Fugitive Deserter
FUUSTC	Forging and Uttering U.S. Treasury Check

- g -

GA	Guilty in Absentia
GAMB	Gambling
GL (A)	Grand Larceny (Auto)
GLFR	Grand Larceny from Retailer
GR BOD INJ	Gross Bodily Injury
GRD THFT or GT(A)	Grand Theft (Auto)
GROSS CHT	Gross Cheat
GROSS INJ	Gross Injury

- h -

H of IF	House of Ill Fame
H of PROST	House of Prostitution
HAB	Habitual
HAB DRK	Habitual Drunk
HARB CRIM	Harboring Criminals
HB	Housebreaking
HLDP	Holdup
HLDP DW	Holdup with Deadly Weapon
HVSW	Health Violation Solid Waste
HWY ROB	Highway Robbery

- I -

ICC	Indirect Criminal Contempt
IGA	Interstate Gambling Activities
IGB	Illegal Gambling Business
ILL MFNG USE SALE emblems/Insignia	Illegal Manufacturing Use – Possession – Sale – Emblems - Insignia
ILLEG BUSN	Illegal Business
ILLEG COHAB	Illegal Cohabitation
ILLEG ENT US	Illegal Entry to U.S.
ILL PRAC MED	Illegal Practice of Medicine
ILLIC	Illicit
ILLIC DISTIL	Illicit Distilling
IMM	Immoral
IMM ENTNMT	Immoral Entertainment
IMP	Impersonating or Impersonation
IMP OFC	Impersonating an Officer
IMPR ST LIC	Improper State License
INCORR	Incorrigible or Incorrigibility
IND	Indecent
IND COND	Indecent Conduct
IND EXP	Indecent Exposure
IND LIB (MIN CHILD)	Indecent Liberties (With Minor Child)
INF	Infamous
INF CR AGST NAT	Infamous Crime Against Nature
INFL	Influence

INJCT	Injunction
INM DH	Inmate Disorderly House
INN	Innocent. Plea of not guilty, found innocent by the jury.
INST	Instructed verdict, found innocent of charge. (FBI definition is Instrument)
INSUF FDS or INSF	Insufficient Funds
INT	Intent
IOC	Interception of Communications
INT CS IN CO FAC	Introducing a Controlled Substance into a County Facility
INTCRSE WITH CHILD	Intercourse With Child
INTERF	Interfering
INTIM	Intimidation or Intimidating
INTIM GOVT WIT	Intimidating Government Witness
INTOX	Intoxication or Intoxicated
INV	Investigation
INVET VAG	Inveterate Vagrancy
INVOL MANSL	Involuntary Manslaughter
IPGP	Illegal Possession of Government Property
IPPL	Illegal Possession Prohibited Liquor
IRA	Internal Revenue Act
IRC	Internal Revenue Code
IRL	Internal Revenue Law
IRLL	Internal Revenue Liquor Law
ISS	Involuntary Servitude and Slavery
ISS FRD INST	Issuing Fraudulent Instruments
IT	Interstate Theft
ITAR	Interstate Transportation in Aid of Racketeering
ITF	Interstate Transportation of Fireworks
ITGD	Interstate Transportation of Gambling Devices
ITLT	Interstate Transportation of Lottery Tickets
ITOM	Interstate Transportation of Obscene Matter
ITPMG	Interstate Transportation of Prison-Made Goods
ITSA	Interstate Transportation of Stolen Aircraft
ITSC	Interstate Transportation of Stolen Cattle
ITSMV	Interstate Transportation of Stolen Motor Vehicle
ITSP (CT or MT)	Interstate Transportation of Stolen Property (Commercialized Theft or Major Theft)

ITWI	Interstate Transmission of Wagering Information
ITWP	Interstate Transportation of Wagering Paraphernalia
IWC	Issue Worthless Check
IWFC	Interference With Flight Crew

- J -

J SATISF	Judgment Satisfied
JCCP	Plea of not guilty, found guilty by the jury and sentenced by the jury.
JCJG	Plea of not guilty, found guilty by the jury and sentenced by the judge.
JD	Juvenile Delinquency
JDA	Juvenile Delinquency Act
JGSA	Judgment Set Aside
JL B	Jail Breaking
JN CLOSED	Judicial Number Closed
JOY RID	Joy Riding
JVGR	Finding for defendant to stand trial as an adult. Case transferred to grand jury.
JVJV	Juvenile case returned to juvenile court.
JVTR	Defendant found to be juvenile by the judge, case transferred to juvenile court.

- K -

KCSP	Knowingly Concealing Stolen Property
KFO	Killing Federal Officer
KHIF	Keeping House of Ill Fame
KID	Kidnapping
KPO	Killing Police Officer
KRA	Kickback Racket Act
KRSP	Knowingly Receiving Stolen Property

- L -

L & R	Larceny and Receiving
L AFT TRUST	Larceny After Trust
L and L	Lewd and Lascivious
L FR IS	Larceny From Interstate Shipment
LARC (or L)	Larceny
LASCV	Lascivious

LEWD & DISSOL .... Lewd and Dissolute
LEWD & IND ACT .... Lewd and Indecent Act
LI-S/R/D/AL/SUS OP/NEV APPL .... License Suspended, Revoked, Denied;
                                            Applicant License Suspended, Never Applied
LIO .... Lesser Inclusive Offense
LIQ .... Liquor
LL .... Liquor Law
LMFR .... Larceny Merchandise From Retailer
LOIT .... Loitering
LOTT .... Lottery
LSA .... Leaving the Scene of an Accident
LV ACC .... Leaving the Scene of an Accident (FBI definition)

- m -

MAIN BAWDY H .... Maintaining Bawdy House
MAIN DH .... Maintaining Disorderly House
MAIN LIQ NUIS .... Maintaining Liquor Nuisance
MAL .... Malicious
MANSL .... Manslaughter
MAT WIT .... Material Witness
MF .... Mail Fraud
MIP .... Minor in Possession
MISAP BY PUB OFC .... Misappropriation by Public Officer
MISCOND .... Misconduct
MISD .... Misdemeanor Charge
MIST .... Mistrial
MKG FLS AFI .... Making False Affidavit
MOB ACTION .... Group Disruption
MOL .... Molesting
MUR .... Murder
MUTIL .... Mutilating
MVI .... Motor Vehicle Inspection
MVR .... Mandatory Release Violator
MVR .... Motor Vehicle Report

- n -

NACT	No Action
NADG	Non-Adjudication of Guilt (Agreed Plea)
NAFM	No Alabama Fuel Marker
NAJG	Non-Adjudication of Guilt (Open Plea)
NAOG	Deferred Probation
NARA	Narcotics Addict Rehabilitation Act
NARC	Narcotics
NAT A	Naturalization Act
NEG	Neglect
NFA	National Firearms Act
NFOG	No Finding of Guilt
NGRI	Not Guilty by Reason of Insanity
NMVTA	National Motor Vehicle Theft Act
NOL PRS	Nolle Pros, Nolle Prosequi, or Nolle Prossed
NON SUP	Nonsupport
NPCF BY MAGISTRATE	No probable cause found by Magistrate.
NRA (MD)	National Resource Authority (i.e. Fishing without a license, etc.)
NSP	National Stolen Property
NUIS	Nuisance
NWNI	Negotiating a Worthless Negotiable Instrument (bad check)

- o -

OAWI	Operating Auto While Intoxicated
OBS LIT	Obscene Literature
OBS PICT	Obscene Pictures
OBTS FORMAT	Offensive Base Tracking System (Florida computer system for law enforcement tracking of cases.)
OCC ROOM IMM PUR	Occupying Room for Immoral Purposes
OCI	Obstruction of Criminal Investigations
OCO	Obstruction of Court Orders
ODLA	Driver License Amended
ODLD	Driver License Dismissed
ODLG	Driver License Granted
OGFP	Obtaining Goods by False Pretense
OHIR	Operating House of Ill Repute
OMFP	Obtaining Money by False Pretense

OMV PRMT SUSP..Operating Motor Vehicle after Permit Suspended

OMV W/O (LIC PL or OC or PRMT) ....Operating Motor Vehicle Without (License Plates or Owner's Consent or Permit)

OMVWI (-D or –L)...Operating Motor Vehicle While Intoxicated (-Drugs or -Liquor)

OOJ..Obstruction of Justice

OP LOT & SL MACH.....................................Operating Lottery and Slot Machine

OP STILL..Operating Still

Open Lewdness...Lewd act observed by someone.

OPFP...Obtaining Property Under False Pretenses

OPIUM..Opium Resorts

ORD...Ordinance

OUI..Operating Under the Influence of Liquor or Drugs

OVUI (-D or –L)..Operating Vehicle Under Influence of (-Drugs or -Liquor)

OVUIL OR NARC ....Operating Vehicle Under Influence of Liquor or Narcotic

OVWD (-D or –L) ....Operating Vehicle While Drunk (-Drugs or -Liquor)

OWI..Operating While Intoxicated

- P -

P NC...Plead No Contest

P/W INT DEL COC..Possession with intent to deliver cocaine

PA ....Plea in Abeyance

PAND...Pandering

PANH...Panhandling

PASS BAD CHKS...Passing Bad Checks

PASS CTFT CURR ....Passing Counterfeit Currency

PASS FORG PO MO......................................Passing Forged Post Office Money Orders

PASS RAISED MO ....Passing Raised Money Orders

PASS WRTHLS CHKS...................................Passing Worthless Checks

Pawnbrokers Act..False reporting to a pawn broker

PBV...Parole Violator

PCT...Possession of Criminal Tools

PED ....Peddler or Peddling

PERJ..Perjury

PERV ....Pervert or Perverted

PERV PRAC...Perverted Practice

PFA ....Considered a Violation; Protection from Abuse

PGBC..Agreed Plea of Guilty Before the Court

PGBJ...Open Plea of Guilty Before a Jury

PGFR .... Agreed Plea of Guilty Before the Court. Felony reduced to a misdemeanor

PGJG .... Open Plea of Guilty Before the Court

PIC .... Possession of Implement of Crime

PIE .... Presence in Illegal Establishment

PIMP .... Pimping

PIST L .... Pistol Law

PJ or PJC .... Prayer for Judgment

PL .... Petty Larceny

POIS .... Poisoning

POLY .... Polygamy

POS/CON F-WN/LQ/MXBV UNAUTH PR ... Possession of a full container of wine, liquor or malt beverage (beer) by an unauthorized person

POSS .... Possession

POSS BURG TOOLS .... Possession of Burglary Tools

POSS CONTR SUB .... Possession Controlled Substance

POSS CP CS – LT 28G .... Criminal possession of a controlled substance less than (number of) grams

POSS DW .... Possession Dangerous Weapon

POSS SG .... Possession Stolen Goods

POSS STLN PROP .... Possession Stolen Property

POST L .... Postal Laws

PP .... Prepaid

PP .... Pickpocket (FBI Definition)

PRCS .... Probation Reduced and Case Set Aside

PRE-IND PROB .... Accelerated rehabilitation program. Defendant is placed on probation. Defendant must complete class before charges will be expunged from the record.

PRE/OBS EXT FIRE .... Preventing or Obstruction of Extinguishing Fire

PRES FLS CL .... Presenting False Claim

PROB .... Probation

PROC .... Procuring

PROC FEM FOR H OF IF .... Procuring Females For House of Ill Fame

PROC TO COMM ARSON .... Procuring Person to Commit Arson

PROF .... Profanity

PROST .... Prostitution

PROWL .... Prowling

PSC .... Public Safety Violation Code

PT... Petty Theft
PTI .... Pre-Trial Intervention
PUB INTOX .... Public Intoxication
PUB NUIS .... Public Nuisance
PUR/ATT F-WN/LQ/MXBV < 21 .... Purchase/Attempt to Purchase Fortified Wine/Liquor/Malt
                                                                             Liquor Beverage by Someone Under the Age of 21
PV .... Parole Violator
PWOC.. Passing Worthless Check

- q -

QUAR .... Quarantine

- r -

RA.. Registration Act
RAPE MNR .... Rape of Minor
RCA .... Red Cross Act
REC.. Receiving
REC & CONC... Receiving and Concealing
REC MON FR PROST .... Receiving Money From Prostitute
REC PO MO .... Receiving Post Office Money Orders
REAP .... Reckless Endangering Another Person
RECDG WGRS .... Recording Wagers
RECK DR .... Reckless Driving
REM OR CONC SPRTS............................. Removal or Concealment of Spirits Contrary to Law
REM IDENT ON GUN.............................. Removing Identification on Gun
RENT LEWD BKS.. Renting Lewd Books
RESIST ARR.. Resisting Arrest
RESIST OFC .... Resisting an Officer
REST ARR W/O VIOL .... Resisting Arrest Without Violence
REVK... Revoked
RICO.. Racketeer Influenced and Corrupt Organization
RIF US MAILS... Rifling U.S. Mails
RIOT .... Rioting
ROB (ARMED or UNARMED)................... Robbery (Armed or Unarmed)
RS OF W/O V .... Resisting Officer Without Violence
RSG.. Receiving Stolen Goods
RSP .... Receiving Stolen Property
RSPMV... Receiving Stolen Property – Motor Vehicle

RULE .... Probation Violation

RVRD .... Probation Revoked and Sentence Reduced

RVSP .... Non-Adjudicated Probation Revoked and
                                                       Sentenced to Straight Probation

- S -

SAB .... Sabotage

SAFECRK .... Safecracking

SALE IND LIT .... Sale of Indecent Literature

SALE LIQ .... Sale Liquor

SALE MTGD PROP .... Sale Mortgaged Property

SALE NARC .... Sale Narcotics

SALE SEC W/O REG .... Sale Securities Without Being Registered

SED .... Sedition

SEDCT .... Seduction

SEDD 1,500 .... Securing and Executing a Document of at Least $1,500 but
                                                       Less Than $20,000 by Deception or Fraud (Dallas County)

SELL SEC NO LIC .... Selling Securities, No License

SELL UNREG REVLVR .... Selling Unregistered Revolver

SES .... Suspend Entry Sentence

SEX A-V CH .... Sexual Assault of a Child, Anal and Vaginal

SFCAA .... State Firearms Control Assistance Act

SH .... Shooting

SHPB .... Shock Probation

SHPLFTG .... Shoplifting

SKA .... Switchblade Knife Act

SLAN .... Slander or Slanderous

SLIP .... Soliciting for Lewd and Immoral Purpose

SMUG .... Smuggling

SNL .... State Narcotic Law

SOD .... Sodomy

SOL .... Solicitation of Bribery (FBI Definition)

SOL .... Stricken of Leave

SOL COMM SOD .... Soliciting to Commit Sodomy

SOL FOR PROS .... Solicitation for Prostitution

SOL IMM PURP .... Soliciting for Immoral Purpose

SOL W/O LIC .... Soliciting Without License

SOLC .... Solicitation to Commit

SP .... Suspicious Person
SPEED .... Speeding
SSA .... Selective Service Act
ST POIS A .... State Poison Act
ST PROH .... State Prohibition
ST WAGE L .... State Wage Law
STAB .... Stabbing
STAB WITH INT KILL .... Stabbing With Intent to Kill
STAT RAPE .... Statutory Rape
STEAL FR COMN CARRIER .... Stealing from Common Carrier
STEAL SECR OR EMBZ MAIL .... Stealing, Secreting or Embezzling Mail Matter
STET .... Set Aside, Pending (non conviction)
STLN PROP... Stolen Property
STORE B .... Store Breaking
STSN... Running a Stop Sign
SUBV ACTIV... Subversive Activity
SUN L .... Sunday Law
SUP .... Support
SUS IMP SENT .... Suspended Imposition Sent. Non-Conviction.
SUSP... Suspicion
SW OVER $50.. Swindling Over $50
SW UNDER $50.. Swindling Under $50
SW W CHKS .... Swindle With Checks
SWIT LIC PL.. Switching License Plates
SWWC .... Swindle With Worthless Checks

- t -

T .... Theft
T BY BAIL .... Theft By Bailee
T BY DECEP.. Theft By Deception
T BY T .... Theft By Taking
T OVER $50 .... Theft Over $50
T UNDER $50 .... Theft Under $50
T/O 200 .... Theft Over $200
TA .... Tariff Act
TAMP .... Tampering
TAMP GOV REC .... Tampering with Government Records

TAWOP .... Taking Auto Without Owner's Permission
TBC.. Theft By Check
TBCI .... Plea of not guilty, found innocent by the judge.
TBCT .... Plea of not guilty, found guilty by the judge and
　　　　　　　　　　　　　　　　　　　　　　sentenced by the judge.
TBD .... Trial by Declaration
TDL... Texas Driver License
TFIS (-AH)... Theft from Interstate Shipment (-Armed Hijacking)
TGP .... Theft of Government Property
THEFT 750 R AND C .... Theft of $750 by Receiving And Concealing
THRT.. Threat (FBI Definition)
THRT.. Threat to Commit
THRT B OF P .... Threatened Breach of Peace
THRT TO EXT .... Threats to Extort
TOP .... Theft of Property
TR RIDER .... Train Rider
TRAF A .... Traffic Act
TRAF ORD... Traffic Ordinance
TRAF SIG... Traffic Signals (Running Signal Light)
TRAN.. Transfer to another County/District Court
TRANSP (LIQ or NARC)............................... Transporting (Liquor or Narcotics)
TRESP .... Trespassing
TRU .... Truancy
TWEA... Trading With the Enemy Act
TYPE OC.. Original Capias (Warrant information)

- U -

U & P .... Uttering and Publishing
U/U LIVESTOCK MV .... Unlawful Use of a Livestock Motor Vehicle
UBAL.. Unlawful Blood Alcohol Level
UCW .... Unlawful Carrying of a Weapon
UDAA... Unlawful Driving Away Auto
UDFC... Utter Distribute Forged Checks
UFA .... Uniform Firearms Act
UFAC.. Unlawful Flight to Avoid Custody or Confinement
UFAP .... Unlawful Flight to Avoid Prosecution
UFAT .... Unlawful Flight to Avoid Testimony
UIBC... Unlawful Issuance of a Bank Check

UISC .... Unreported Interstate Shipment of Cigarettes
UMTA... Using Mails To Defraud
UNA .... Uniform Narcotics Act
UNL ASM .... Unlawful Assembly
UNL DAA & ABNDN .... Unlawfully Driving Away and Abandoning Auto
UNL ENT.. Unlawful Entry
UNL MARR.. Unlawful Marriage
UNL POSS FIREARMS .... Unlawful Possession of Firearms
UNL POSS OR USE EXPLSV .... Unlawful Possession or Use of Explosives (bombs, etc.)
UNL SALE OF SEC .... Unlawful Sale of Securities
UNL USE W (OR UUW) .... Unlawful Use of Weapon
UNLIC CHAUF .... Unlicensed Chauffeur
UNREG STILL .... Unregistered Still
UPRF .... Unlawful Possession or Receipt of Firearms
UPUC .... Unauthorized Publication or Use of Communications
USCC .... U.S. Criminal Code or U.S. Criminal Court
USING MV W/O PRMS............................ Using Motor Vehicle Without Permission
USING PROF & AB LANG....................... Using Profane and Abusive Language
USTP... Unsatisfactory Termination of Probation
UTT... Uttering
UTT CHK .... Uttering Check
UTT FORG INST .... Uttering Forged Instrument
UTT FORG OBL .... Uttering Forged Obligation

- V -

VAG... Vagrancy
VAGA... Vagabond
VAM .... Veterans Administration Matters
VCSDDCA .... Violation Controlled Substance Drug Device & Cosmetic
VEH .... Vehicle
VEH NO LTS .... Vehicle No Lights
VGCSA .... Violation of Georgia's Controlled Substance Act
VIN .... Vehicle Identification Number
VIO CITY ORD...................................... Violating City Ordinance
VIO CSA... Violating Controlled Substance Act
VIO DAA... Violation Drug Abuse Act
VIO DDCA .... Violation Dangerous Drugs and Control Act

VIO DYER A	Violation Dyer Act
VIO FED INJ	Violation Federal Injunction
VIO HNA	Violation Harrison Narcotic Act
VIO IMMI L	Violation Immigration Law
VIO NMVTA	Violation National Motor Vehicle Theft Act
VIO OF HL	Violation of Health Laws
VIO OF LL	Violation of Liquor Law
VIO ST GAME & FISH L	Violating State Game and Fish Law
VIO ST LL	Violation State Liquor Law
VIO TRAF REG	Violation Traffic Regulation
VIO UFA	Violation Uniform Firearms Act
VIRL (-L)	Violation of Internal Revenue Laws (-Liquor)
VOL MANSL	Voluntary Manslaughter
VOL MUR	Voluntary Murder
VOP	Violation of Probation
VT	Vehicle Taking or Vehicle Theft

- W -

W/S	With Specifications
WAND	Wandering
WC	Worthless Check
WC-OBT PROB	Worthless Check to Obtain Property
WIND PEEP	Window Peeping
WOUND	Wounding
WPPDA	Welfare and Pension Plans Disclosure Act
WPT	Withdrawn Prior to Trial
WRONG LIC PL	Wrong License Plates
WRTD	Writ Denied
WRTG	Writ Granted
WRTHLS INST	Worthless Instrument
WSTA	White Slave Traffic Act

*Quick-***Find** *Index*

Adverse Action 105

Arrest Records, Use of... 108, 117, 121-122

Banking Industry Regulations 31-32

Bias Employment Practices.. 115

Biometric Systems.. 96

Business Justification... 117

Canada, Employees Entering 27

CM/ECF... 61, 314

Computerized County Courts 49

Computerized Federal Court Indexes...................................... 60, 314

Consumer Report, Definition of... 102

Consumer Reporting Agency... 85, 102, 112

Conviction Records, Use of 123-6

County Court Records 48, 51

Credit Headers 90

Criminal Justice Agencies 15

Criminal Record Quiz... 19-21

Criminal Record Vendor... 83-93

Database Records, Use of 87-89

Database Vendors.. 84, 87-89

Date of Birth, Asking For 97

Demographic Identifiers 97

Disposition 42-43

Diversion Programs 45

Docket Sheet 46, 49

Do-It-Yourself Search 77, 79, 82

Employers; Why they need to order criminal records................ 23, 27

Employment Purposes, Explained 103

Equal Employment Opportunity Commission (EEOC) 116, 353-374

Quick-**Find** *Index* <small>page 2</small>

Expunged Records.. 124, 133-312

Fair Credit Reporting Act.................................... 84,-6 Chapter 12/13

FBI Records 56, 62

Federal Aviation Regulations............................... 30-31

Federal Court Records.. 59, 313-336

Federal Fugitives.. 74

Federal Incarceration Records............................. 69-70

Federal Records Centers 315

Felony, Definition of 42

Fingerprints... 67, 96

First Offender Act 45

First Offense Records, Restricted Use of........................ 125

Freedom of Information Act 82

General Jurisdiction Courts 46, 48

Incarceration Records, State 71, 133-312

Interstate Dissemination Policies 58, 65

Interstate Identification System 63

Job Relatedness Issue.. 117

Juvenile Criminal Records................................... 41

Limited Jurisdiction Courts 46, 48

Local Searches.. 78

Mandated Regulations, Overview 32

Megan's Law 72-73

Military Criminal Records 74

Misdemeanor Records, Use of/Restrictions 100, 123

Misdemeanor, Definition of................................. 42, 100

National Crime Prevention and Privacy Compact 64

NCIC 62, 64

Negligent Hiring Doctrine 23

Quick-**Find** *Index*   page 3

Negligent Retention 23

Non-Biometric Identifiers 46, 96

Non-Criminal Justice Agencies 15

Non-Public Records 43

PACER 60-61, 314

Personal Identifiers on Criminal Records 34

Prayer for Judgment 45

Privacy 33-34, 103

Probation Records 71-72

Public Records from Databases 109

Record Retrievers 83-84

Release, Release Form 99, 105

Reporting Arrest Information, FCRA 108, 121-122

Reporting Conviction Information, FCRA 108

Sealed Records, Prohibited Use of 124

Sexual Offender Records 72, 134-312

Signed Release, State's Requiring 55, 133-312

State Central Repository 53

State Courts 47-50

State Court Administrators Contact Information 135-312

State Criminal Records, Sexual Predators, Incarcerations 133-312

State FCRA Laws 112

Statutory Authority, for State Record Release 56, 133-312

Unified Courts 54

U.S. District Courts 59-61, 313-336

U.S. Party/Case Index 314

Victimless Crime 37

Workplace Theft 26, 84